The Religion and Film Reader

The Religion and Film Reader brings together the key writings in this exciting and dynamic discipline. In over sixty essays, interviews and reviews from numerous directors, film critics and scholars, this eagerly anticipated anthology offers the most complete survey of this emerging field to date.

Ideal for students and researchers alike, *The Religion and Film Reader* is organized into the following thematic and chronological sections, each with an introduction by the editors:

- The Dawn of Cinema: Adherents and Detractors
- The Birth of Film Theory: Realism, Formalism, and Religious Vision
- Directors and Critics: Global Perspectives
  - African and Middle-Eastern Perspectives
  - Asian and Australasian Perspectives
  - European Perspectives
  - South and North American Perspectives
- Theological and biblical approaches to analyzing film
- Recent reflections on the relation between religion and film

Jolyon Mitchell is senior lecturer at New College, Edinburgh University. His previous publications include *Visually Speaking, Mediating Religion,* and *Media Violence and Christian Ethics.*

S. Brent Plate is Associate Professor of Religion and the Visual Arts at Texas Christian University. His recent publications include *Blasphemy: Art that Offends, Walter Benjamin, Religion and Aesthetics,* and *Representing Religion in World Cinema.*

The Religion and Film Reader

Edited by

Jolyon Mitchell and S. Brent Plate

 Routledge
Taylor & Francis Group

NEW YORK AND LONDON

First published 2007
by Routledge
270 Madison Ave, New York, NY 10016

Simultaneously published in the UK
by Routledge
2 Park Square, Milton Park, Abingdon, Oxon OX14 4RN

Routledge is an imprint of the Taylor & Francis Group, an informa business

Typeset in Joanna and Bell Gothic by
RefineCatch Limited, Bungay, Suffolk
Printed and bound in Great Britain by
TJ International Ltd, Padstow, Cornwall

British Library Cataloguing in Publication Data
A catalogue record for this book is available from the British Library

Library of Congress Cataloging in Publication Data
The religion and film reader / edited by Jolyon Mitchell and S. Brent Plate.—1st ed.
 p. cm.
 Includes bibliographical references and index.
 1. Motion pictures—Religious aspects. 2. Religion in motion pictures. I. Mitchell, Jolyon P.
II. Plate, S. Brent, 1966–
PN1995.5.F53 2007
791.43′682—dc22

                                        2007007857

ISBN10: 0–415–40494–5 (hbk)
ISBN10: 0–415–40495–9 (pbk)
ISBN13: 978–0–415–40494–5 (hbk)
ISBN13: 978–0–415–40495–2 (pbk)

Dedication

To

Sabina Elli and Camila Elli

Sebastian, Jasmine and Xanthe

Contents

Acknowledgements

First and foremost, we would like to thank Julene Knox for all her hard work on gathering permissions for well over sixty readings. She tracked down rights holders in all parts of the world and kept us constantly informed about whether a reading was likely to be available or not. We are grateful to the five anonymous readers of the original proposal, who each provided invaluable suggestions. Gemma Dunn, Geraldine Martin and Lesley Riddle at Routledge UK have continued to be extraordinarily helpful and prompt with all of our queries, making for a smoother process altogether.

Brent wishes to send out several thank yous. Thanks to the Baker-Nord Center for the Humanities at Case Western Reserve University for the Visiting Fellowship that allowed the time and space to work on this collection. Also, it was a great pleasure to work with my co-editor who keeps the humane in the study of the Humanities. Thanks also to: Megan Ammann for help in initial research stages; Tim Beal as a constant source of support; Simon Halliday who continues to prove his uncanny ability to watch any and all types of film and then discuss it cogently; David Nienhuis for almost two decades of film chat over pints and phonelines; and Tel Mac's intellectual foundations. Final and most important thanks to Brent's holy trinity: Edna Melisa, Sabina Elli, and Camila Elli. They continue to put up with his incessant banging on the computer keyboard, wishing it was something more soothing like a piano keyboard.

Jolyon wishes to thank his co-editor for traveling to Edinburgh to discuss the project, and to Elizabeth Smith, Dwight Friesen, and Jenni Green for their careful and enthusiastic help at various stages of this lengthy project. I am also grateful for conversations about many different films and suggestions, both direct and indirect, from a good number of colleagues and friends, including: Nick Adams, Michael Banner, Catharine Beck, Judith Buchanan, Eric Christianson, Mark Cousins, Ian Christie, Chris Deacy, Peter Francis, Tim Jenkins, Rob John-ston, Elizabeth Koepping, Anna King, Clive Marsh, John McDowell, Jill Northcott, Michael Northcott, Dorota Ostrowska, John Orr, Marcella Althaus-Reid, Joshua Rey, Rod Taylor, William Telford, and Melanie Wright. I am indebted to col-leagues at New College, Edinburgh University for the gift of research leave, which provided some of the necessary space not only to go in search of many of these readings, but also to discover several unexpected gems. I have also very much valued the suggestions from undergraduates and postgraduates who have partici-pated in my Film, Religion and Ethics courses at Edinburgh University. As we were completing this book my father, Peter Mitchell, had to go into hospital, but he remained interested in and encouraging about this reader. It is a delight to see him now back to lecturing and supervising even after his 79th birthday. Last, but by no means least, I would like to say a big thank you to Sebastian, Jasmine, and Xanthe for creating so much laughter en route and to Clare for generously help-ing create the environment in which it was possible to finish this project.

Both the editors and publishers would like to acknowledge the following:

1. Herbert Jump, from "The Religious Possibilities of the Motion Picture" (1910).
2. G. Shundiraj Phalke, from "The Problem of Capital Formation in the Indian Cinema" (1917) in Continuum 2/1 (1988–89) pp. 54–52 (Taylor & Francis Ltd., http://www.tandf.co.uk/journals), reprinted by permission of the publisher.
3. Rev. Dr. Percy Stickney Grant, from "If Christ Went to the Movies" (1920) originally published in Photoplay Magazine. Source: Terry Lindvall The Silents of the Gods, The Scarecrow Press, Inc.
4. R.G. Burnett and E.D. Martell, from The Devil's Camera (1920). Reproduced by permission of The Epworth Press/MPH.
5. Pope Pius XI, from Vigilanti cura (1936). Reproduced by permission of Libreria Editrice Vaticana.
6. Jean Epstein, from "On Certain Characteristics of Photogénie" (1924) from Abel, Richard, French Film Theory and Criticism. Reprinted by permission of Princeton University Press.
7. Antonin Artaud, from "Sorcery and Cinema" (1927) from The shadow and its Shadow, ed. Paul Hammond (City Lights, 2000), pp. 103–105 © Editions Gallimard, Paris, 1978.
8. André Bazin, from "Le Journal d'un Curé" (1951).
9. Stan Brakhage, from "Metaphors on Vision" (1963) from Film Culture no. 30 (1963). Reproduced by kind permission of Marilyn Brakhage.
10. Amos Gitai, from "In a Harsh Light" (2000) from Sight & Sound 10(8) August 2000. Reproduced with permission.
11. Abbas Kiarostami, from "In Dialogue with Kiarostami" interview by Ali Akbar

Mahdi (1998) *The Iranian* 25 August 1998, available from http://www.iranian.com/Arts/Aug98/Kiarostami. Reproduced with permission.

12. Mohsen Makhmalbaf, "Once Upon a Filmmaker: Conversation with Mohsen Makhmalbaf" from *Close Up: Iranian Cinema Past, Present, and Future*, by Hamid Dabashi (London: Verso, 2001). Reproduced with permission.

13. Birgit Meyer, from "Religious Remediations. Pentecostal Views in Ghanaian Video-movies", from *Postscripts* (2005, 2/3, special issue 'Mediating Film and Religion' guest-edited by Stephen Hughes and Birgit Meyer), Equinox Publishing Ltd. © Equinox Publishing Ltd 2005. Reproduced with permission.

14. Jolyon Mitchell, from "Towards an Understanding of the Popularity of West African Video Film" (2004) from © *Belief in Media*, eds. Peter Horsfield, Mary E. Hess, and Adan M. Medrano, 2004, Ashgate. Reproduced with permission.

15. Elia Suleiman, from "Notes from the Palestinian Diaspora: An Interview with Elia Suleiman" from *Cineaste* (Summer 2003), by Richard Porton. Copyright 2003 by Cineaste Publishers Inc. Reproduced with permission of Cineaste Publishers Inc. in the format Other Book via Copyright Clearance Center.

16. Ousmane Sembene, "The Power of Female Solidarity: An interview with Ousmane Sembene" from *Cineaste* Vol. 30 No. 1 (2004) by Sembene, Ousmane. Copyright 2004 by Cineaste Publishers Inc. Reproduced with permission of Cineaste Publishers Inc. in the format Other Book via Copyright Clearance Center.

17. Cheick Oumar Sissoko, from "I Make Films about the Big Problems of Our Continent: An Interview with Cheick Oumar Sissoko" from *Cineaste* Vol. 25 Issue 2 (March 2000) by Ray Privet. Copyright 2000 by Cineaste Publishers Inc. Reproduced with permission of Cineaste Publishers Inc. in the format Other Book via Copyright Clearance Center.

18. From *Filming the Gods: Religion and Indian Cinema* by Rachel Dwyer, © 2006 by Rachel Dwyer, Routledge. Reproduced by permission of the author and Taylor & Francis Books UK.

19. Geeta Kapur, from "Revelation and Doubt in *Sant Tukaram* and *Devi*" (2000) from *When Was Modernism?* (New Delhi: Tulika Books). Reproduced with permission.

20. Im Kwon-Taek, from "An interview with Im Kwon-Taek" reprinted from David E. James and Kyung Hyun Kim's *Im Kwon-Taek: The Making of Korean National Cinema*, 2002, pp. 256–60, with permission of Wayne State University Press.

21. William R. LaFleur, from "Suicide off the Edge of Explicability: Awe in Ozu and Kore'eda" from *Film History* 14.2 (2002): pp. 159–164. Reproduced by permission of Indiana University Press.

22. Philip Lutgendorf, "*Jai Santoshi Maa* Revisited: On Seeing a Hindu 'Mythological' Film" (2003) from *Representing Religion in World Cinema*, ed. S. Brent Plate (New York: Palgrave, 2003). Reproduced by permission of the publisher.

23. Mira Nair, from "I Want my Films to Explode with Life" from *Cineaste* 30/1 (2004) by Mira Nair. Copyright 2004 by Cineaste Publishers Inc. Reproduced with permission of Cineaste Publishers Inc. in the format Other Book via Copyright Clearance Center.

24. Paul Schrader, from *Transcendental Style on Film* (1972).
25. Jolyon Baraka Thomas, "*Shûkyô Asobi* and Miyazaki Hayao's *Anime*", *Nova Religio*, Vol. 10, No. 3: 73–95. © 2007, The Regents of the University of California. Used by permission. All rights reserved.
26. Patrick McGilligan, "Under Weir and Theroux: An Interview with Peter Weir," *Film Comment* 22/6 (1986): 23–32. © 1986 by Patrick McGilligan. All rights reserved. Reproduced with permission.
27. Lloyd Baugh, from "The Masterpiece: *The Gospel According to St Matthew*" (1997) in *Imaging the Divine* by Lloyd Baugh, Sheed and Ward an imprint of Rowman and Littlefield Publishers. © 1997 by Lloyd Baugh. Reproduced with permission.
28. Ingmar Bergman, from the Introduction to *The Seventh Seal* (1968). Reprinted with permission from *Four Screenplays of Ingmar Bergman*. Translated from the Swedish by Lars Malmstrom and David Kushner. Copyright © 1960 by Ingmar Bergman. Translation Copyright © 1960, and renewed © 1988, by Simon & Schuster, Inc. Film produced in 1957.
29. Costa-Gavras, from "Filming the Story of a Spy for God: An Interview with Costa-Gavras" from *Cineaste* Vol. 28 Issue 2 (Spring 2003) by Gary Crowdus and Dan Georgakas. Copyright 2003 by Cineaste Publishers Inc. Reproduced with permission of Cineaste Publishers Inc. in the format Other Book via Copyright Clearance Center.
30. Jean-Luc Godard, from "Godard in his Fifth Period": an interview by Katherine Dieckmann. Originally published in *Jean-Luc Godard's Hail Mary: Women and the Sacred in Film* by Maryel Locke and Charles Warren © 1993 by the Board of Trustees, Southern Illinois University, reprinted by permission of the author and publisher.
31. Krzysztof Kieslowski, from the Introduction to *Decalogue: The Ten Commandments*, translated by Phil Cavendish and Susanna Bluh. Faber & Faber Ltd. 1991. Reproduced by permission of the publisher.
32. Derek Malcolm, on *Days of Wrath* from *Derek Malcolm's Personal Best: A Century of Films*, I.B. Tauris & Co Ltd. © by Derek Malcolm 2000. Reproduced by permission of the publisher.
33. Andrey Tarkovsky, from *Sculpting in Time* (1989).
34. Lars von Trier, from *Trier on von Trier*, ed. Stig Björkman. Faber & Faber Ltd. 2003. Reproduced by permission of the publisher.
35. Woody Allen, from *Woody Allen on Woody Allen*, ed. Stig Björkman. Faber & Faber Ltd. 1994. Reproduced by permission of the publisher.
36. Guillermo Arriaga, from "Basic: An interview with 21 *Grams* screenwriter Guillermo Arriaga" by Warren Curry 11/19/03 available from http://www.cinemaspeak.com/Interviews/gaint.html. All rights reserved. Reproduced by kind permission of Warren Curry.
37. "David Cronenberg", from *Inner Views: Filmmakers in Conversation*, by David Breskin, Da Capo Press 1997. © 1992, 1997 by David Breskin. Reproduced by kind permission of David Breskin.

38. Julie Dash, "Dialogue between bell hooks and Julie Dash" (1992) from *Daughters of the Dust: The Making of an African American Woman's Film*, The New Press, 1992. Reproduced by permission of the author and publisher.

39. "Spike Lee", from from *Inner views: Filmmakers in conversation*, by David Breskin, Da Capo Press 1997. © 1992, 1997 by David Breskin. Reproduced by kind permission of David Breskin.

40. George Lucas, from "Of Myth and Men" (1999).

41. Martin Scorsese, from *Scandalizing Jesus?: Kazantzakis's The Last Temptation of Christ Fifty Years on* by Darren J. Middleton, The Continuum International Publishing Group, 2005. Reproduced with permission.

42. Antonio Sison, from *Screening Schillebeeckx*, Palgrave Macmillan 2006. Reproduced by permission of the publisher.

43. Walter Salles, from "Sentimental Journey as National Allegory: An Interview with Walter Salles," from *Cineaste* Vol. 24 Issue 1 (Winter 1998) by Anthony Kaufman. Copyright 1998 by Cineaste Publishers Inc. Reproduced with permission of Cineaste Publishers Inc. in the format Other Book via Copyright Clearance Center.

44. From "Steven's Choice", Spielberg, Steven, interviewed by Richardson, John H. "Steven's Choice." *Steven Spielberg: Interviews*. Edited by Lester D. Friedman and Brent Notbohm. Jackson: University Press of Mississippi, 2000. Reproduced by kind permission of the author.

45. From *Mouse Morality: The Rhetoric of Disney Animated Film* by Annalee R. Ward, Copyright © 2002. By permission of the University of Texas Press.

46. Judith Weisenfeld, from "Projecting Blackness: African-American Religion in the Hollywood Imagination" from eds. Henry Goldschmidt and Elizabeth McAlister *Race, Nation, and Religion in the Americas*, Copyright © 2004 by Oxford University Press, Inc. Reproduced by permission of the author and publisher.

47. Roy Anker, from *Catching Light: Looking for God in the Movies* © 2004 Wm. B. Eerdmans Publishing Company, Grand Rapids, Michigan. Reprinted by permission of the publisher; all rights reserved.

48. Christopher Deacy, from *Faith in Film*, Ashgate 2005. © Christopher Deacy 2005. Reproduced by permission of the publisher.

49. Robert Johnston, from *Reel Spirituality: Theology and Film in Dialogue*, Baker Academic, a division of Baker Publishing Group 2000. © 2000 by Robert K. Johnston. Reproduced by permission of the publisher.

50. Clive Marsh, from *Cinema and Sentiment* (2004).

51. John R. May, from *New Image of Religious Film*, Sheed & Ward, an imprint of Rowman and Littlefield Publishers, Inc. 1997. © 1997 by John R. May. Reproduced by permission of the publisher.

52. Gerard Loughlin, from *Alien Sex: The Body and Desire in Cinema and Theology* pp. 50–53, 57, Blackwell Publishing 2004. © 2004 by Gerald Loughlin. Reproduced by permission of the author and publisher.

53. Jolyon Mitchell and S. Brent Plate, 'Viewing and Writing on the *Passion of the Christ*' based on Jolyon Mitchell "Film and Theology" in *The Modern Theologians*,

third edition, eds. David Ford and Rachel Muers, Blackwell Publishing, 2005, pp. 736–59. Reproduced by permission of the publisher.

54. Theresa Sanders, from *Celluloid Saints: Images of Sanctity in Film*, Mercer University Press, 2002. © 2002 Mercer University Press. Reproduced by permission of the publisher.

55. Eric Christianson, from *Cinéma Divinité: Religion, Theology and the Bible in Film*, eds. Eric Christianson, Peter Francis, and William R. Telford, SCM-Canterbury Press, 2005. © Eric Christianson, Peter Francis, and William R. Telford 2005. Reproduced by permission of the publisher.

56. From *St Paul goes to the Movies: The Apostle's Dialogue with American Culture* © 1993 Robert Jewett. Used by permission of Westminster Knox Press.

57. Cheryl Exum, from *Plotted, Shot, and Painted: Cultural Representations of Biblical Women*, JSOTSUP, 215: Sheffield: Sheffield Academic Press (1996), 23–29, 232–234

58. Larry J. Kreitzer, from *The New Testament in Fiction and Film: On Reversing the Hermeneutical Flow*, JSOT Press (1993), 16–19.

59. From *Scripture on the Silver Screen*. © 2003 Adele Reinhartz. Used by permission of Westminster John Knox Press.

60. Erin Runions, from *How Hysterical: Identification and Resistance in the Bible and Film* (2003), Palgrave Macmillan. Reproduced by permission of the author and publisher.

61. Michael Bird, from "Film as Hierophany" originally appeared in a different form in *Religion and Film*, edited by John R. May and Michael Bird. Copyright 1982 by the University of Tennessee Press. Reprinted with permission.

62. Francisca Cho, from "Imagining Otherness and Imagining Nothing in Buddhist Film", in eds. Brent Plate and David Jasper *Imag(in)ing Otherness*, Copyright © 1999 by The American Academy of Religion. Reproduced by permission of the author and Oxford University Press.

63. Nathaniel Dorsky, from "Devotional Cinema", published by Tuumba Press, Berkeley, CA. (2003). © Nathaniel Dorsky. Reproduced by permission of the author.

64. John C. Lyden, from *Film as Religion: Myths, Morals and Rituals* © 2003 by New York University Press. All rights reserved. Reproduced by permission of the author and publisher.

65. Joel Martin, from "Introduction" to *Screening the Sacred: Religion, Myth, and Ideology in Popular American Film*, Joel W. Martin and Conrad Ostwalt, eds. © 1995 by Westview Press, Inc. Reproduced with permission of the publisher.

66. S. Brent Plate, from "Footprints of Film" in *Faith in America*, volume three. Copyright © 2006 by Charles H. Lippy. Reproduced with permission of Greenwood Publishing Group, Inc. Westport, CT.

67. Melanie Wright, from *Religion and Film: An Introduction* (2007), I.B. Tauris & Co Ltd. © by Melanie J. Wright 2007. Reproduced by permission of the publisher.

At this time there are several extensive bibliographies on religion and film in existence. We are grateful to a number of scholars for their help with this bibliography, including Dwight Friesen, Gordon Matties (see http://

www.cmu.ca/library/faithfilm.html), and Steve Nolan (see his annotated bibliography on 'Film and Religion' in *Mediating Religion*) who by their work have further enriched the breadth of our reading and subsequent bibliography.

GENERAL INTRODUCTION

T H E   S E T T I N G for cinema's creation myth is Paris's Grand Café in December, 1895. An expectant audience had gathered to see the Lumière brothers' new invention, the *cinématographe*, the latest in a string of visual technologies that emerged through the nineteenth century: from the camera lucida to the stereoscope, from the daguerreotype to photographic film. Each of these inventions offered fascinating possibilities for seeing the world in new ways. The viewers on that Parisian winter night were apparently not disappointed with the unveiling of the latest high-tech gadget. The films were all silent, single-reel, lasting less than a minute, portraying everyday events of modern urban life such as workers leaving a factory, the demolition of a wall, and, most famously, a train arriving at a station. Despite the events being seemingly mundane, the experience was nonetheless profound, prompting the early filmmaker George Méliès to respond: "We were openmouthed, dumbfounded, astonished beyond words in the face of this spectacle."[1] Within the next year, the Lumières had taken their technology to Egypt, India, Japan, and Australia, while at the same time Thomas Edison took his similar invention, the Vitascope, around the United States. Over the following few decades, cinema would begin a subtle and not-so-subtle transformation of the world.

Film theorist André Bazin suggests that "The cinema has always been interested in God,"[2] and a history of filmmaking proves Bazin's assertion correct. The first decade of cinema saw at least a half dozen filmed restagings of the life of Jesus Christ, including those made by Edison and Louis Lumière. Versions of "The Passion of Christ" played in various cinematic venues throughout Europe from the beginnings of cinema until the 1920s, often produced from a pious standpoint. Meanwhile, the proclaimed "father of Indian cinema," D.G. Phalke, relates in a following excerpt how he was inspired to make his own films of Hindu deities in the 1910s after initially watching a film about Jesus in an Indian theatre. Films appropriated religious subject matter from the start, and religious groups used films as promotional tools as soon as they could find the means to do so.

Not only has cinema been intertwined with religion from its conception, but this intertwining has become a global phenomenon. In Ghana, theater spaces have been refurbished in order to project the latest Pentecostal-produced "video-films." Across North America, devout Christians watch Mel Gibson's *The Passion of the Christ* on DVD in their own living rooms during Lent. Japan's popular culture produces *anime* films filled with references to Shinto and Buddhist ghosts and spirits. In South India, villagers gather in front of an outdoor screen to watch the life of Jesus in the Telugu production, *Karunamayudu*, now seen by over 100 million viewers. Meanwhile, in northern India, cinema-goers attend sold-out Hindu mythologicals in New Delhi theaters. These are but a few examples, with many more to follow throughout this reader, of the ways the religiosity of billions of people around the world has been reflected and even shaped by film production.

In short, what we attempt to demonstrate through this volume is that the relation between film and religion has deep historical and broad global dimensions. In the following we provide readings from around the world, and from the last one hundred years, that show the myriad ways religion and film are tied to each other and have come to be reliant on each other. "Religion and Film" as an interdisciplinary, academic enterprise may be a thought of as a new category of scholarly enquiry, but the actual interrelation is very old.

In preparing this reader, we have sought to highlight readings that deepen and broaden the religion–film relation as it is often understood in the current academic climate, both in religious studies and film studies. The critical study of religion and film is certainly coming of age, as evidenced by a number of developments over the last decade or two. These include: the tremendous upsurge of publications in the field; the establishment of a program unit on film and religion within the American Academy of Religion; the launch of the online *Journal of Religion and Film*; a growing number of undergraduate and postgraduate courses devoted to the study; and an increasing number of students writing theses and dissertations on related topics. Our reader comes along at a critical time in the field's maturation process. Our goal here is to provide a volume that charts the field and its history, shows the diversity of ways the relation between religion and film can be understood, points to transactions in the past, and explores some of the new interactions between the two arenas.

In wanting to create a globally oriented reader in religion and film, we have constantly come up against the problem of what exactly "religion" and "film" might mean in various contexts. How, for example, do we find readings in religion and film from a West African Ewe context when there is no word for "religion"? Or when the famed Japanese film director Akira Kurosawa creates a film that includes many elements of what an Anglo-American academic might call "religion" yet he does not have a religious interest himself, can we still call it "religious"? Or when a self-professed atheist like David Lynch creates a film that pretends to ignore religion and yet deals directly with "ultimate significance," as Paul Tillich phrased the category of the religious, how do we consider it?

Alternatively, we can question whether "film" is something distinct from religion, or whether it is simply a by-product of it, as seems to be the case in many instances. If, for example, Mormon production companies create films for proselytizing purposes, is it really a "film" in the cultural, artistic sense? Or is it simply an extension and tool of religion? Is film a cultural category that at time competes with religion? When is it synonymous with religion?

Of course, answers to such questions must be taken into account on a case-by-case basis. What we provide here are some critical readings that display the broad variety of ways the religion and film relation can be understood. Some of the readings see the relation as religion *in* film, exploring the ways religious symbols, themes, or figures are portrayed through the narratives, sounds, and images on screen. Other readings might be said to see the relation in terms of film *as* religion, in which film and religion serve analogous functions in their ritualizing, mythologizing activities, particularly in the cinematic viewing experience. Still others retain a more broad view of religion *and* film, maintaining a distinction between them, though gauging their overlaps and crossings on screen and in everyday life. Sometimes religion and film are inseparable, sometimes not, and sometimes their connections can only be made by outside observers.

Rationale for the reader

We emphasize that this is a "reader" and not a "greatest hits," nor an exhaustive encyclopedia of the religion–film relation. We have tried to broaden the categories and the multiple ways in which the relation takes place, but there are limits. Many selections were left out, usually because they repeated ideas already expressed, or because they crowded out other selections for the broad range of subjects we have tried to cover. We provide what we believe are strong, clear writings on topics in religion and film, but we also want to expand the dialogue to look at historical and global dimensions, including discussions of a number of other important and overlooked filmmakers and films from around the world.

The readings here are arranged according to a particular logic into five main parts, while several of these extracts could equally easily have served in another part. A general outline is as follows, with more in-depth introductions appearing at the beginning of each part.

The volume begins historically, with parts 1 and 2 presenting documents ranging from 1910 to 1965, thus providing some historical grounding for understanding the relation of religion and film. The readings in part 1 indicate how the new medium of film challenged older religious structures and how some religious groups *adapted* to it and others simply *reacted*. The extracts in part 2, while relatively brief, indicate some of the ways early to mid-century theorists and filmmakers saw the religious functions of film, with the debate between realism and formalism providing the setting. At heart was a formal question as to whether film should show the world-as-it-is, albeit with a different lens, or whether filmmakers might offer alternative glimpses of other worlds, even when tending toward the fantastic. Thus, alongside the historical dimension, the first two parts challenge us to think through the specificities of the *medium* of film, and of the formal properties that it brings in ways utterly distinct from theater, literature, photography, and other arts.

In part 3, the largest of the volume, we offer writings from filmmakers and critics from all around the globe. Here we have worked to push beyond the Christian theological and Euro-American approaches that have prompted much of the recent scholarship on film from a religious studies perspective. Included are excerpts from interviews with filmmakers from Africa, the Middle East, Asia, the Americas, and Europe, alongside critical writings on world cinemas. Again, we have tried to be inclusive but not exhaustive, and so there are noticeable gaps. In part this is due to the availability of works in English, or due to the fact that many nations around the world do not have a film industry. The nation of Chad, for example, has only ever produced three or four films in its history, while dozens of films are produced in Egypt every year. In the end we believe we have been able to present the most diverse set of readings on religion and world cinema ever published as a set, and we hope they will spur English-speaking scholars to take notice of the amazing productions beyond Europe and North America.

In parts 4 and 5 we provide a range of scholarly publications regarding the relation of religion and film from the past two decades. These readings represent the emergent interdisciplinary field of "religion and film." With one exception, all the writings in these final parts are by scholars of theology, biblical studies, or religious studies.

Part 4 includes readings from Christian theological and biblical studies perspectives. We have given a large amount of space to these chiefly because this is where a majority of the current English-language writings have focused. Again we were spoilt for choice. Films have been and are being put to use by theologians and biblical scholars in a myriad of ways. Books on Jesus or Christ figures in film continue to proliferate, as do intertextual works between the (Christian) bible and film; meanwhile, there are only a handful of scholarly works anywhere that address Buddhism or Islam and film. Here we have chosen what we judge to be a representative selection of works addressing the ways Christian theological ideas and biblical references appear in films, and the ways in which religious studies scholars are using cinema to rethink, reimagine, and reinvigorate the study of religion.

In the final part of this reader we provide a handful of recent, broad theoretical approaches to the relation between religion and film. While part 2 offered some early musings on how film becomes religious and how film portrays religion, part 5 works as something of a bookend, returning to newer theories on how religion is screened, and/or how the screen becomes the site for religious doctrine, practice, and experience. Excerpts here range from methodological chartings for analyzing the religion–film relation to analyses of the film viewing event as a form of religious experience itself, thus moving beyond the screen to examine the ways that film can reconfigure everyday life and religious practice.

As stated above, our aim in this volume has been to historicize and globalize the scholarly approaches to religion and film. Through each of the five parts of this volume we have attempted to highlight, among other things: first, the medium of film, and its distinctive representational abilities, as well as its utilitarian function in the promotion of religion; second, film's ability to respond to specific religious interests around the world, it is now a universally-accessible technology that yet lends itself to local needs and concerns; third, the ways films provide sites for theological discussion, biblical interpretation, and even devotion, often in creative and unexpected fashions; and fourth, the rich seam of insight brought to understanding many films from a religious studies perspective, while also exploring religious practices, beliefs, and communities through the lens of visual media. We ourselves have been challenged to comprehend just how vast is the relation between the two modes of experience, how universal and yet how local are the shared experiences. We hope we have offered some stepping stones to students and scholars seeking to analyze further this fascinating relation.

Notes

1   George Méliès quoted in Emmanuelle Toulet, *Birth of the Motion Picture* (New York: Harry Abrams, 1995), 15. The "myth" of the origin of cinema certainly belongs to the Lumières, though the German Max Skladanowsky and the American Thomas Edison were simultaneously projecting film with similar technologies.

2   André Bazin, *Bazin at Work: Major Essays & Reviews from the Forties & Fifties*, edited by Bert Cardullo and translated by Cardullo and Alain Piette (New York: Routledge, 1997), 61.

The Dawn of Cinema: Advocates and Detractors

INTRODUCTION

THE HISTORY OF THE RELIGION–FILM relation is one of reluctance, dis-ease, and controversy, but also delight, expectancy, and euphoria. Cinema can be a shock to the central nerve of religious systems. Sometimes this shock is believed to be the means to revival, sometimes it is seen as a lethal charge. To understand the depths of the relationship between religion and film in the present day, it is valuable to start with the origins of cinema itself, and with the ways the new technology was sometimes believed to strengthen, and oftentimes threaten, the experiences, beliefs, and morality of religious groups. To that end, this first part begins with readings from the first few decades of film, displaying the perceived compatibilities and incompatibilities between cinema and religion.

Within the first 15 years after the invention of film, just as early feature-length films were lighting up screens across the globe, censorship boards and watchdog groups were established in many nations, often springing from the moral concerns of religious authorities who disliked what they saw as indecent subject matter displayed on screen: usually scenes of violent crime and inappropriate romantic engagements.

In 1904, Sheyk Fazlollah Nuri attended a cinema in Tehran and was so upset that he had the theater shut down, though it is not clear what he saw there.[1] In Spain, many Roman Catholic clergy and intelligentsia were initially against the cinema; the writer Ramon Rucabado, for one, published a diatribe against the cinema in 1908 and then spent the rest of his life crusading against it. By 1909 in Italy, a review commission was established and created a prototype of the first "ratings system."[2] Later in the twentieth century, many ad hoc Christian groups in the United States reacted to the "menace" of the movies. People like the evangelist John Rice, in his 1938 *What is Wrong with the Movies*, pleads with his readers, "I warn you that continuing to see the movies may harden your heart until you will be enamored of sin."[3] In 1942, Dan Gilbert, Chairman of the Christian Newspaper Men's Committee to Investigate the Motion Picture Industry, said: "Hollywood is the nearest thing to 'hell on earth' which Satan has been able thus far to establish in this world. And the influence of Hollywood is undermining the Christian culture and civilization which our fathers built in this land."[4]

Even the most critical voices found some value in aspects of cinema, while the most vociferous advocates regularly sounded notes of caution about using moving pictures for religious purposes. In other words, a simple dichotomy between "adherents" and "detractors" may be a useful way of categorizing these early responses to moving pictures, but a careful reading of the kinds of texts we provide here demonstrate how criticism and celebration were not always mutually exclusive. From its earliest days film was used for many religious purposes, including as an aid to teaching, a memorable way of presenting familiar stories, a tool for proselytism, a focal point for moral censure, a catalyst for expressing pastoral concerns, and a way simply of attracting a crowd. Early filmmakers also used religion for their own ends, including, for example, retelling biblical stories cinematically to increase sales at the box office, to promote their own beliefs, and, at a time when some saw film as a sordid form of entertainment, to underline the value and respectability of their craft. The result of these multiple uses of film was that institutional religion and industrial cinema sometimes became allies, sometimes enemies, and at other times competitors.

In this first part we include four readings by religious authorities and one by a filmmaker from the early twentieth century, each commenting on the challenges and promises that the young medium of film posed to religion. Some see great possibilities for film to positively affect devotion and education. Others are more skeptical. All suggest that film cannot be shown and viewed without restriction, and there are several suggestions for censoring mechanisms to be put in place.

The Reverend Herbert Jump was a forward thinking Christian minister whose 1910 article, "The Religious Possibilities of the Motion Picture," makes a strong early argument for the use of film in Christian religious settings. Jump argues his case by means of an analogy to Jesus' parable of the Good Samaritan, a story that has a moral message even as it is entertaining and gets its message across by discussing a crime. According to Jump, films, like Jesus' parables, do what sermons oftentimes do not: engage the crowd by reference to contemporary life. Jump even goes so far as to propose "a Sunday evening motion picture service" for churches, a practice that is increasingly popular in the early twenty-first century.

The second reading comes from D.G. Phalke, the man who is normally credited with starting India's massive cinema industry (over 800 films a year are currently produced in India, several times more than Hollywood produces). In this 1917 article, Phalke describes his early obsessions with watching films in the cinemas around Bombay, and how these visions sparked an interest in creating his own films based on the Hindu mythological tradition. Significantly, Phalke's filmmaking was firmly in line with the Indian *Swadeshi* (literally, "indigenous") movement, which sought political and economic independence from Britain. The filming of Indian myths by an Indian filmmaker was a strong reaction to Western cinema, and perhaps colonialism in general. There is some debate about which was the first ever Indian feature film. Some scholars suggest that Shri Ramchandra Gopal's *Pundalik* (1912) was the earliest, but that honor is more often bestowed upon Phalke's *Raja Harischandra* (1913), which is based on a story from the *Ramayana* about the eponymous ancient king. This may be because Phalke's *Raja Harischandra* was also processed in India and was twice the length of *Pundalik*.

Another Protestant Minister, Dr. Percy Stickney Grant, contributed an article to a 1920 edition of the film magazine *Photoplay*, from which we take the third reading. Grant begins by asking a revised version of the modern Christian question: "What would Jesus do?" The answer is that Jesus would approve of the movies. Like Jump, Grant argued for motion pictures based on analogies to the teachings of Jesus Christ who, Grant suggests, was all for human happiness and entertainment after a hard day's work. Grant too realizes the lurking dangers in film, whose producers may be in it just for the money and have little regard for morality, but he believes that any true immorality on screen can be overcome by progressive activism based in the church.

The fourth reading is taken from the book *The Devil's Camera: Menace of a Film-Ridden World*, published in London in 1932. As the title indicates, the authors, R.G. Burnett and E.D. Martell, through most of their book argue strongly against the cinema, asserting that the "devil is in full, spiritual control of modern film production." For them "film poison" is doing "unimaginable harm," feeding the worst passions and seducing the "imaginations of the peoples of the world." In a book which reflects anti-semitic prejudices, they claim that the cinema "grossly" misrepresents many different aspects of life. Their polemic is qualified, however, in contrast to the melo-dramatic section reproduced here, as in their final chapter they praise film technology as a "marvelous instrument," which has the potential to educate, to entertain, and even build up the churches. Reading between the lines of this and similar early accounts of film it is possible to detect feelings both of anxi-ety about the perceived power of this new medium and disappointment that the authors are unable themselves to control film production and viewing.

A Papal Encyclical from 1936 concludes the first part (reading 5). As cinema grew in social power and popularity, particularly in the United States, various regulatory groups began to rise up in order to identify and combat immoral depictions on screen. In *Vigilanti Cura* (literally, "with a vigilant eye") Pope Pius XI responds to new challenges from the cinema and praises the newly arisen "Legion of Decency" begun by Roman Catholic bishops in the United States in the 1930s.[5] The encyclical attempts to be balanced by noting how motion pictures can promote good or equally insinu-ate evil, but clearly falls on the side of caution, arguing strongly for regula-tions begun by the Legion of Decency. As with the Reverend Grant, the Encyclical acknowledges the need for "recreation" for those "who labor under the fatiguing conditions of modern industry," but there is an implicit argument that such recreation makes the viewer "relaxed," and therefore susceptible to the seductive music and images portrayed on screen. Thus, the need for vigilance and, if necessary, avoidance of suspect films on the part of filmgoers everywhere.

Notes

1   See Hamid Naficy, "Islaming Film Culture in Iran," in Richard Tapper, ed., *The New Iranian Cinema: Politics, Representation, and Identity*. London: I.B.Tauris, 2002, 27.

2   For more on early cinema and the religious precautions, see the chapters in Roland Cosandey, André Gaudreault, Tom Gunning, eds. *Une Invention du Diable? Cinéma des premiers temps et religion*. Sainte-Foy: Les Presses de L'Université Laval; Lausanne: Éditions Payot Lausanne, 1992; and also Terry Lindvall, *The Silents of God*. Lanham, MD: Scarecrow Press, 2001.

3   John R. Rice, *What is Wrong with the Movies?* Murfreesboro, TN: Sword of the Lord Publishers, 1938, 111–112. Similarly, see A.W. Tozer, *The Menace of the Religious Movie*. Harrisburg, PA: Christian Publications, 1950–59?.

4   Dan Gilbert, LL.D., *Hell Over Hollywood: The Truth About the Movies!* Grand Rapids, MI: Zondervan Press, 1942.

5   This Encyclical updates the 1929, *Divini Illius Magistri*, and precedes the 1957 *Miranda Prorsus*, both of which are worth reading in relation to the history of film and religion. See also, Frank Walsh, *Sin and Censorship: The Catholic Church and the Motion Picture Industry*. New Haven, CT: Yale University Press, 1996; and Gregory Black's works, *Hollywood Censored*. Cambridge: Cambridge University Press, 1994 and *The Catholic Crusade Against the Movies, 1940–1975* (Cambridge: Cambridge University Press, 1998).

Chapter 1

Herbert A. Jump

THE RELIGIOUS POSSIBILITIES OF THE MOTION PICTURE

A statement

IN APRIL 1910, the minister of the South Church, New Britain, Conn., in a session of the Men's Civic Class, expressed a hope that some time a moving picture equipment might be owned and used by the Church. In a city of 15,000 wage-careers, many of them of foreign birth, he felt that the motion picture could be made a most serviceable adjunct to religious education.

Two months later, ex-Mayor George M. Landers, at the invitation of Mr. Jump, generously consented to endow a moving picture service in the South Church for thirty Sunday evenings purchasing all necessary apparatus and meeting the expense of operating it. The announcement of his gift excited considerable newspaper notice and editorial comment throughout the East as being a decided innovation in church methods. Meanwhile the question of introducing the service was taken under consideration by the Standing Committee of the church.

Mr. Jump spent considerable time during the summer making a study of motion pictures, visiting the manufacturers, studios, sitting with the Censorship Board, consulting with exhibitors and managers of exchanges and social workers, and preparing his series of services for the winter of 1910–1911.

In October, it was decided by the Standing Committee of the church that circumstances made it unwise for the South Church to conduct a motion picture service this year, so the plan was abandoned.

The interest aroused by the proposal, however, and the correspondence stirred up by it, seem to justify the publishing of some memoranda setting forth the considerations which led to the original suggestion. Evidently many religious and quasireligious organizations and also many thoughtful individuals will welcome information on this topic of the times, the motion picture. Accordingly, this pamphlet covers more than is demanded by its title, and it is also equipped with an appendix containing a few facts that may be of service to the inquiring social worker.

In conclusion, it is appropriate to quote the words with which one of the most refined and far-sighted of the film manufacturers greeted Mr. Jump: "The interests which you represent," he said, "are the interests which we wish to satisfy."

> Jesus said, "A certain man was going down from Jerusalem to Jericho, and he fell among robbers which both stripped him and beat him and departed, leaving him half dead. And by chance a certain priest was going down that way; and when he saw him, he passed by on the other side. And in like manner a Levite also, when he came to the place and saw him, passed by on the other side. But a certain Samaritan as he journeyed came where he was; and when he saw him he was moved with compassion, and came to him, and bound up his wounds pouring on them oil and wine; and he set him on his own beast and brought him to an inn and took care of him. And on the morrow he took out two pence and gave them to the host and said, 'Take care of him; and whatsoever thou spendest more, I when I come back again will repay thee.' Which of these three, thinkest thou, proved neighbor unto him that fell among the robbers?" And the lawyer said, "He that showed mercy on him." And Jesus said unto him, "Go, and do thou likewise."
>
> Luke 10:30–37

The religious possibilities of the motion picture

When Jesus desired to set forth the essential meaning of Christianity in a universal language that should speak to men of every age and all races, he chose a dramatic story. He told the parable of the Good Samaritan, and therein gave an example of ideal preaching which many preachers of the present day, alas! seem to have completely overlooked.

Note some of the details of that sermon-story. It was not taken from the Bible – the Old Testament used as a Bible by Jesus' auditors – but from contemporary experience. It was the sort of thing that might have happened any day and to any one in his audience. Secondly, it was an exciting story. Robber-tales always thrill the emotions, and much more in the ancient world perhaps than today, because then the risk and the likelihood of such deeds of violence were immeasurably greater than now. Thirdly, this narrative-sermon frankly introduces morally negative elements and leaves them negative to the end of the chapter. Was it not dangerous to the church establishment of that day to have its priest and Levite pictured as failing so utterly in the grace of compassion, held up to ridicule as hypocrites and poseurs? And as for the robbers themselves, not only did the story give a most realistic description of precisely how they perpetrated the cowardly crime of violence, but it leaves them victorious in their wickedness, scurrying off with their booty, unrepentant of their sins, probably chuckling at the folly of the traveler for venturing upon the notorious Jerusalem-Jericho road without a caravan to protect him from the highwaymen. And yet, despite these three dubious characteristics of not being Scriptural to the people who heard it, of being exciting, and of having realistic and morally negative features in it, who dare assert that the story of the Good Samaritan has wrought harm in the world? Rather, has it not earned for itself recognition as being the central parable of all the Master's teachings? Has it not exhibited in complete and convincing fashion the very heart of the Gospel? Has it not urged more men into lives of ministry and helpfulness than any piece of literature of equal length which the race has ever known?

Prejudice against motion pictures

We have delayed thus on the story of the Good Samaritan in order to disarm if possible that mood of antagonism with which some of you approach the general subject of motion pictures. You "know that they are bad," because they are exhibited in a theater that charges only five or ten cents admission. You have never seen many of them, perhaps not any of them; but from various sources, you hardly remember when, the suspicion has been bred in your mind that the motion picture is evil and evil altogether. To assert therefore that there are any "religious possibilities" in the motion picture strikes you as the acme of absurdity. It is as though one were to announce a sermon on "The Spiritual Value of the Clog Dance." You have heard that motion picture stories are likely to represent crime, that they are exciting, and that scarcely a phase of modern experience has been overlooked by the manufacturer as he scoured the universe to find novel subjects for his motion picture films.

And now we come to the point: the objections which you and others thus make against the religious use of motion pictures can all of them be urged with equal force against the use of the most convincing parable which the Christ ever uttered. The films that have value for religious education today are those which portray truth as the Good Samaritan portrays it – in a dramatic story, of contemporary experience, exciting in character and thus interesting even to the morally sluggish, picturing negative elements such as crime, accident, ignorance, sin, and thus commending itself as true to life, but in the end showing the defeat and expulsion of these negative elements by positive qualities, virtuous souls, God-like traits. The only thing needed to make the parable of the Good Samaritan a conspicuously successful motion picture film is a new title. Call it "The Adventure of the Jerusalem Merchant," and it would appeal perfectly to the habitué of the dime theater, and he would catch the noble moral of it far more swiftly, perhaps, than do many of the more well-to-do Christians, who hear it rather than see it, when it is droned forth from the pulpit by the preacher of a Sunday morning as the New Testament lesson.

How to make sermons interesting

The visible drama shown in the right sort of motion picture, accordingly, has religious possibilities just as the spoken dramatic story or parable has them. Both help to make the Gospel vivid. Indeed, one may venture the statement that the modern motion picture offers the most colossal opportunity for making a fresh moral and religious appeal to the non-churched portions of the community that has risen in the history of recent Christianity. Why is it that people do not come to church? Many of them will say frankly, "Your church is not interesting; your service of worship is adapted only to the taste of those who have been trained up to it; I cannot understand your music and cannot keep awake through your sermons; the interest of the clergymen seems to be far more with Jehoikim and Ancient Babylon than with the living men and the living issues of today. In a word the church is dull, therefore I stay away."

How far these criticisms are warranted need not occupy us here. Suffice to say we shall meet these criticisms in part if we try to present Christian truth in forms of present-day life, illustrating its issues from modern America more than from Ancient Samaria. We also need to put Christian truth into pictorial and story form so that it will appeal to the imagination. The great popular preachers, Beecher, Moody, Spurgeon and Gipsy Smith, all were masters in the use of word pictures. The moving picture machine enables the church to make the same form of appeal with visible and animated pictures. The pulpit orators and evangelists use "moving pictures" in one sense of the term, pictures that move the heart by their thrilling quality; but the picture that literally is moving, that portrays dramatic sequence and life-like action, possesses tenfold more vividness and becomes therefore a more convincing medium of education. The common people love stories and buy the cheap magazines to an amazing degree; these persons would love the motion picture church service which gave them religious truths through acted stories.

We men and women who have ever shown interest in pictures, hanging them on the walls of our homes, seeking them in illustrated books and now in picture-postcards, should turn naturally to the motion picture sermon which puts the gospel in a pictorial form. Some of you who attend church love the doctrinal phraseology of St. Paul. There is many a hardheaded American working man, however, who confesses freely that to him St. Paul is only a prosy old theologian. Paul, however, was not a prosy theologian to the men of his day. Why not? Because his illustrations for the gospel were taken from the life of his contemporaries – the racing habits of his day, for example, and the boxing matches. We ministers of today may not quite dare follow Paul in illustrating spiritual truth from the trotting park or a recent famous prize fight in a western city, but we have a right to use stories taken from life in the shop and factory and on the street as illustrations of the gospel to the men of today. Because the motion picture carefully selected will tell to the eye moral truths with vigor of illustration and an eloquence of impression which the most enthusiastic orator cannot command, it has a proper place in the equipment of any church which is trying to reach the masses.

[. . .]

The moving picture as an invention

A good argument could be made in the support of the proposition that the motion picture, in some respects, is the most wonderful invention which has come into existence since the invention of printing in the fifteenth century. One day by accident Gutenberg discovered the art of using movable type. By help of this new art of printing, books which before had been only the luxury of the rich now became the possession of the many. Strikingly enough, the earliest use of the printed page was the religious use, for the first printed book was the Bible. The invention of the moving picture machine has resulted in the same popularizing of a privilege which previously had been confined to a few. As printing made literature universal, so the cinematograph is rapidly making the drama universal. Who knows but what this new invention may also serve religion as soon as religion is willing to accept its assistance? The typical motion picture film today is a short acted story put on the stage by high grade actors, working out the plot contributed in some cases by such literary experts as Shakespeare, Victor Hugo, Goethe, Dickens. The moving picture began as photographs of scenery, later it employed living people, then pictures of living people doing interesting things, and thus came about the "picture play" which is a little story of real life acted in front of the camera and distributed throughout the country on a celluloid film.

What Mr. Edison says

No one has ever charged Thomas Edison with being a cheap panderer to the vicious tastes of a debased society. Rather he has been always a friend and uplifter of the race, and it is by Mr. Edison that such words as these are written:

> Moving pictures bring to everyone an absolutely clear idea of foreign peoples through their customs and through scenes of the world and through the industries and pursuits of man. They have a tremendous educational effect. This is true even of the seemingly purely amusement moving pictures. Little cross-sections of life are shown, staged and acted better than are the cheap shows given at considerably higher prices. The motion picture is an important factor in the world's intellectual development. It will have a great uplifting effect on the morality of mankind. It will wipe out various prejudices which are often ignorance. It will create a feeling of sympathy and a desire to uplift the downtrodden peoples of the earth. It will give new ideals to be followed. For these reasons I believe that moving pictures present the right means in the hands of broad-minded, intellectual and informed workers for the world's good, for the innocent amusement, efficient instruction and the moral advance of the great masses of people.

What an editor of The Congregationalist says

The Congregationalist contained two illuminating articles on motion pictures in its issues of July 9 and 16, 1910. From this writer we quote the following sentences:

> Within almost a single round of seasons the picture show has become an immense enterprise, a world-wide amusement, a universal influence. When you hear that in France during the eviction

of the ecclesiastics the films played such an important part that they nearly created a rebellion; that Sweden has endowed a moving picture theater for presenting historical scenes; that a foreign manufacturer made an offer of $200,000 for the privilege of taking the Oberammergau Passion Play, which offer was refused – you begin to get an idea of the magnitude of the subject. Not only this, but the moving picture is rapidly taking its place beside commerce and foreign missions in making for a world brotherhood. Read this from a staff writer of the Survey:

"On an island two thousand miles out in the Pacific Ocean the exiled lepers of Molokai gather daily before the flickering wonders of a screen that shows them the world of life and freedom. Seated in the luxurious saloon of an ocean liner a group of travelers study life-like pictures of the countries for which they are bound. In Iceland excited Eskimos applaud the heroism of a cowboy who rescues a maiden from the redskins. Halfway around the world in Northern Russia tearful peasants sorrow over the pictured flight of a forlorn French lover. The newspaper correspondents with the battleship fleet tell us that in every corner of the globe they found the dimly lighted rooms where living tragedy and comedy flash across the screen."

Facts like the foregoing explain why a religious journal like The Congregationalist sees a reason for examining such a feature of our modern life. Not only because the moving picture has become so widespread an influence is it of interest to us; but also because its possibilities have only begun to be uncovered, and in this undeveloped and unknown future educational and religious agencies seem destined to have a great share. While no one can be blind to the fact of its great possibilities for evil, the moving picture has neither done so much harm nor deserved such imprecations as have been put upon it by well-meaning but uninformed Christian people.

[. . .]

The National Board of Censorship

In 1909 the People's Institute of New York, under the leadership of Prof. Charles Sprague Smith, and several of the more progressive firms of film manufacturers decided that it would be conducive both to the public morals and good business to have the motion picture output of the country censored by a disinterested body of intelligent critics. Accordingly in March of that year the Board was formed with such men on its advisory committee as Lyman Abbott, Andrew Carnegie, Robert De Forest, Samuel Gompers, Jacob Riis, Anson Phelps Stokes and Rabbi Wise. The general committee of supervision is headed by Professor George W. Knox of Union Seminary, and it has representatives from the Charity Organization Society, the City Vigilance League, the International Committee, YMCA, the New York City Federation of Women's Clubs and other philanthropic organizations. This committee uses two secretaries and arranges for the inspection of new films by a group of critics, who shall approve or disapprove them. The Censorship attempts on its part not to place unreasonable and Puritanic handicaps upon the manufacturers, while manufacturers agree not to release any film until it has the sanction of this Board. During the eighteen months since the Board was organized its services have been accepted by an ever increasing proportion of the manufacturers until now it can be reported (I quote a letter from the Censorship Board under date of November 23, 1910) that the Board "passes upon every new film produced or imported into the United States."

This frank, willing and complete submission of an amusement industry to intelligent supervision in behalf of public morals is something absolutely new in human society, and the fact should have the attention which it deserves. After a few months to allow for the recall of films put out by firms that only lately accepted the Censorship, it will be true that in not a single one of the 10,000 M. P. [Moving Picture] theaters in the country can a film be seen by man, woman or child but has been passed upon by a committee of criticism whose sole reason for being was a desire to uplift the standard of the picture drama. In view of this fact it surely behooves social reformers and zealous charity workers and well-meaning clergymen to secure first-hand evidence before they let themselves accept and repeat the careless and often unjust criticism passed upon the picture drama. Meanwhile the Board welcomes suggestions as to its work, and will attend to any criticisms on the motion pictures shown in any part of the country if only definite information is furnished of the title of the film, the manufacturer, the date and place where it was seen.

Of course the work of this Board has imperfections, which it admits frankly: and even if its work were leisurely and perfectly done, it would fail to satisfy all interested parties.

[. . .]

The motion picture as a religious tool

First, it can help the church merely as an entertainment device. The spiritual value of the church sociable has long been admitted; the indirect possibilities of religion in the oyster stew and bean supper are commonly conceded. Let the church that wishes to minister to the masses do what a few Roman Catholic churches are doing, what Rev. Charles Stelzle of New York is doing in his new Labor Temple – provide free picture shows as it provides free concerts and organ recitals.

Secondly, the motion picture can help in giving religious instruction in the Sunday school. Pictures of travel through Palestine, of biblical scenes, of events in the history of the church are available and ought to be used extensively. In one of our public schools lately the story-hour had to do with Ulysses' adventures as recorded in the Odyssey. Imagine the teacher's surprise when she learned that her best-informed pupil had obtained his knowledge of the Greek hero through a moving picture film. As with classical heroes, so it is with religious heroes. Joseph and Esther and Moses and Paul and Jesus are better known to the theater-goers today than they ever were before, thanks to Mr. Edison's invention. Ere long we shall give our Sunday School scholars the same advantages in vivid biblical instruction that are now offered to the patron of the nearest "Pastime" or "Bijou."

Graphic missionary education

Thirdly, the motion picture film can do more for foreign and home missions than any agency yet utilized by our assiduous and ingenious missionary secretaries. The reason for the skeptic's opposition to missions is usually to be found in his ignorance of how mission work is done and of what social conditions it aims to transform. Films dealing with travel and ethnology are very numerous – they enlighten the latter half of this ignorance; and after the critic has looked at films picturing the operations of medical and industrial missions in distant lands, he is a sluggish egoist indeed if he doesn't entertain a more tolerant mood toward the "skirmish line of the Kingdom of God."

Fourthly, the church needs to be an agent of broad civilization in its community; one aspect of its religious ministry should be the social education of the needy. All the philanthropies, the united charities, the district nurse, the hospital, the day nursery, the YMCA and YWCA; all the up-lift campaigns against tuberculosis and crowded tenements and in behalf of playgrounds, public baths, and neighborhood centers; all lines of civic education in American history, political institutions, municipal betterment – all these aspects of the community's higher life need to be brought home to the public conscience and consciousness. The church should assist in this process of social illumination, and it can use no more potent aid in doing this work than the motion picture. Especially should cities where there are large alien populations, have the advantage of such dramatic instruction on the lantern screen as needs no interpreter. A picture is a sort of a graphic esperanto, a universal language; and social and domestic and personal hygiene may well be taught through its aid.

The motion picture sermon

Fifthly, the crowning possibility of the motion picture, though, is its usefulness to the preacher as he proclaims moral truth. It will provide the element of illustration for his discourse far better than it can be provided by the spoken word. It will make his gospel vivid pictorial, dramatic, and above all, interesting. The motion picture preacher will have crowded congregations, not because he is sensational but because he is appealing to human nature more successfully than his fellow-clergymen, because he is adapting his message to the psychology of his hearers, because he is employing a better pedagogical method.

Why do not men, especially the common people, want to go to church more than they do? Is it not in part because they feel that the preaching of today, at many points, fails to fit their natures and meet their needs? We ministers use too often a technical jargon which the outsider characterizes only as a pitter patter of dreary nonsense and a hodge-podge of unintelligible stupidity. They say of us what the little girl said of her pastor, "he talks to himself out of a piece of paper." If ministers as a whole were to return to Jesus' method of sermonizing, and with story and dramatic pictures drawn from contemporary experience were to illustrate a few simple ethical and spiritual realities, would not the constituency of the church become larger and more loyal?

To go one step further, if preachers gave their illustrations of spiritual truth to their hearers, not through the art of elocution to be listened to, but through the vastly higher art of pictorial drama to be seen, would not their persuasiveness be mightily enhanced? Applying these suggestions, a Sunday evening motion picture service could be arranged as follows, and it would go far toward solving the "second service problem" in many a community.

A motion picture service of worship

Let the hymns and prayers be as usual. Let the Scripture lesson be illustrated with a film exhibiting the very incident narrated by the Bible. Let the sermon be on a practical topic like temperance, honesty, loyalty, prayer, the purity of the home pluck or self-sacrifice, and let the sermon be illuminated by two "motion picture parables" from present-day life.

The three films will use up about an hour, the entire service being put into an hour and a quarter. The preacher can combine his Bible reading on sermon with the motion picture, or the picture can be run off silently or to an organ accompaniment, while the words before and after the picture help to drive home the message. One man may find it easier to follow the example of the stereopticon lecture where the pictures are interpreted by speech, another man may follow the example of the moving picture entertainment where the pictures speak for themselves. In many places a licensed operator from a local M. P. theater which is not open on Sunday can be obtained to manage the lantern.

[. . .]

The lesson of history

The motion picture is as yet a novelty in religious work. Hence it will be opposed by some. But if there are conscientious scruples against adopting the motion picture as one of the church tools, at least we may comfort ourselves with our reading of church history. The disfavor which is not meted out to the motion picture was aimed at the stereopticon a decade ago, at quartet singing several decades earlier, at the pipe organ before that, and still earlier at the Holy Bible printed in the vernacular; and yet, in God's own time every one of these religious agencies commended itself to the approval of Christian people. So it will be in this case. Meanwhile borrowing and rearranging words from a great American pioneer, let us of the church say that "with malice toward none, with charity towards all, with firmness in the right as God gives us to see the right, let us finish the work we are in, highly resolved that religion, under God, shall have a new birth of freedom; and that the church of Christ, the Son of Man, shall become a church of the people, by the people, for the people, never to perish from the earth."

Chapter 2

D.G. Phalke

THE PROBLEM OF CAPITAL
FORMATION IN THE INDIAN CINEMA

IN 1910, I happened to see the film *The Life of Christ* in the America-India Picture Palace in Bombay. I must have seen films on many occasions before this, along with my friends or family, but that day, that Saturday in Christmas, marked the beginning of a revolutionary change in my life. That day also marked the foundation in India of an industry which occupies the fifth place in the myriads of big and small professions that exist. And, all this could have happened at the hands of a poor Brahmin! I experienced a strange indescribable feeling while I was unconsciously clapping hands at the sight of the noble incidents in Christ's life. While the life of Christ was rolling fast before my physical eyes I was mentally visualising the Gods, Shri Krishna, Shri Ramchandra, then Gokul and Ayodhya. I was gripped by a strange spell. I bought another ticket and saw the film again. This time I felt my imagination taking shape on the screen. Could this really happen? Could we the sons of India, ever be able to see the Indian images on the screen? The whole night passed in this mental agony.

For two consecutive months I was never at ease unless I saw each and every film shown in every cinema house in Bombay. During this period, I was constantly preoccupied with the analysis of every film which I saw and in considering whether I could make them here. There was no doubt whatsoever about the utility of the profession and its importance as an industry. But how was one to realise all this? Fortunately, this did not appear to me as a problem at all, and I felt confident that, God willing, I will definitely succeed. I also came to realise that I had also acquired knowledge of fundamental crafts like drawing, painting, architecture, photography, theatre and magic, which are necessary for filmmaking. I had even won gold and silver medals for excellence of skill in these crafts. It was this preliminary training in these crafts which could make my film work success and acceptable to all. But how was I going to realise it all?

In spite of my enthusiasm and confidence in my success, I knew very well that nobody would dare to give me the capital unless I had something tangible in hand to attract them. So I liquidated whatever possessions I had and directed all my efforts toward this end. Thus I soared in the boundless skies without caring where I would land.

This was the period of the Swadeshi movement and there was profuse talking and lecturing on the subject. For me, personally, it led to the resignation of my comfortable government job and taking to an independent profession. I took this opportunity to explain my ideas about cinema to my friends and to the leaders of the Swadeshi movement. Even people who were familiar with me for over 15 years considered my ideas impracticable. And thus I became a laughing stock for them.

[. . .]

I left Bombay for England on 1st February, 1912. This was my second trip abroad. This made me more sure of my work because my own ideas of filmmaking and the actual details of the process of filmmaking tallied completely. I purchased some equipment and was able to see a famous studio with great difficulty . . . Within a month or so on my return from abroad I made some 100–200 feet long films for the satisfaction of my friend. Those films were produced with the help of my wife and children only. However, I badly required further money for employing paid actors. A money lender gave me the required money against proper security when he was convinced of my success after seeing those films on the screen. I advertised and brought together my disciples and other employees. I trained them well and brought *Raja Harischandra* on the screen only within six months. I got amazing returns only on one print of this film. There was demand for a dozen prints of the film. But I feared that this income on one film might be short lived, like the Swadeshi movement, and it would not be proper to judge the income on a permanent basis. With these thoughts, I made the second film *Mohini Bhasmasur*. I suspended the work for three or four monsoon months and shifted my studio from Bombay to Nasik on the 3rd October 1913. This place was convenient from many points of view. There I made *Mohini Bhasmasur*. Fortunately, this also brought me fortune like the first film. This encouraged me further and I brought my third film *Savitri Satyavan* before the world. This film added to the success and the income of the first two films.

Chapter 3

Percy Stickney Grant

IF CHRIST WENT TO THE MOVIES

IF **CHRIST** went to the "movies" – He would approve.

Christ said "Come unto me all ye that labor and are heavy laden and I will give you rest."

Could the Divine Master who lightens our heavy burdens and refreshes our weary minds give any but entire approval to an agency like moving pictures that makes for the happiness of His people?

If you were to ask me what Jesus would say at the sight of fourteen thousand churches in America, most of which were built in honor of His name but which are closed except for a few hours every week, I would reply that He would cry out, "Open the doors of these churches and let my people enter; let my churches be put to the uses that pertain to the happiness, best interests and development of my people!"

Christ approves of anything that makes for the happiness of mankind; anything that lifts the minds of His people to a higher plane; to anything that refreshes and interests them after a day's hard grind.

Our churches are most excellent auditoriums. The majority of them are furnished with good organs, and skilled organists are engaged. These churches are a natural meeting place for establishing advantageous gatherings of people who are concerned with the betterment of their positions, educationally, politically and in the terms of human culture. Motion pictures combine amusement, entertainment and education. Pictorial education is of extreme value. It establishes a quickening of the imagination. These pictures put us in contact with new scenes, give us new ideas, make us better acquainted with new personalities and belong in God's church as well as in the theatre.

My friend Cleveland Moffet, a brilliant-minded author, suggested some years ago that the New York churches provide free moving picture entertainment. Money was subscribed to carry out this plan, several picture producers became philanthropically interested and evenings were devoted to delightful programs in many churches, the pictures being carefully selected.

There is yet a wide difference of opinion as to the use of churches for anything other than religious services. Many believe that only solemn services should be conducted in our churches which they hold to be hallowed by years of sacred use. This closes to the public more than three billion dollars worth of taxable property, save for three or four hours every week.

Coming from a rector of an Episcopal church this may seem somewhat startling, but there is in that church a broad comprehensiveness which, even here in New York, contains two such extremes as the Church of St. Mary the Virgin and Dr. Heber Newton's church. I am called broad-minded or a "Broad churchman," I take a stand for anything that makes for human happiness and the betterment of mankind.

Even in the matter of news, which we all ought to have in as complete and comprehensive a form as possible, the movies can give the big essentials, unencumbered by the mass of reading matter and advertisements on which the commercial success of the press depends. The movies present no such dreadful looking abortions as are exploited in the newspapers on their cartoon pages. I will not call the cartoons by name, but in the movies one sees no such disgusting, unnatural distortions of human form and human nature.

I believe that there is a difficult line between admiration for the human form and pruriency. A certain magazine of physical culture in its effort to show the public high ideals of physical strength and perfection has encountered this difficulty. I believe that just as the picture of Ebert and Noske recently published in the pictorial section of a great newspaper, almost naked, in bathing dress, disgusts the observer with the uncovered forms and unathletic masculine flesh and bones, and has made this picture serviceable to the enemies of the German republic, so, on the other hand, the representation to the eye of beautiful human beings can encourage more ideal care and development of the body as well as giving legitimate pleasure. A pathetic side of human nature presents itself in the "bald head row" in our theatres. There is no suggestion of salacity or pruriency in the beautiful pictures of types like Annette Kellermann. They present the glory and beauty of physical perfection, the strongly developed human body battling against the waves or exhibited among beautiful natural surroundings. There is no trace of sex emotion here. The movies of today are our cleanest form of amusement. They are well censored; morality and right prevail.

There are thousands of people who come to New York for a good time. Perhaps they select a Broadway theatre performance, a popular show. There is a snappy plot, catchy music and beautiful girls, but it is no part of culture, there is no uplift, no better ideals fill the mind. Georg Brandes said of William August Slaegel, the translator of Shakespeare, that he made Shakespeare part of German Culture. The Germans embraced Shakespeare to a far greater extent than Shakespeare's own fellow-countrymen. Not the theatre but the dramatic art occupies an important place in our development. The movies are in that class. Nothing sticks in the memory like visible images. I remember as a boy I had to practice my piano lessons over and over, playing the same piece of music again and again. Now, I am told great soloists visualize their notes. When they sing or play they are reading from the mind – modern psychology stresses this point.

In a Boston church which I used to frequent as a boy there was a most eloquent preacher, the Rev. Wayland Hoyt. He employed the old fashioned oratorical method of word-painting. I freely confess that the only sermon I remember was a description by Dr. Hoyt of his visit to Salisbury cathedral. Pen and word pictures are going out. The movies are supplanting them. Pictures are the supreme thing that the mind can see. Education by means of visual impressions is of the first importance.

There is much that bears closely upon religion and social uplift in the Freudian psychoanalytic psychology. Most people spend much time in fantasy, day-dreaming, wool-gathering. The coward paints himself in heroic scenes, the shop girl pictures herself in a beautiful dress seated in the parterre of the opera. This is the stuff that "dreams are made of." Ideas fall into the mind not regulated by will or checked up by reality. People not only sit in dreams, but act in dreams.

Our motion pictures are of the sort that the individual craves. First and foremost they possess whatever reality is to be had in story, drama, or educational films. The movies clear out the cobwebs of the mind, putting in carefully prepared facts. They are a tonic, a regulator, a clarifier of the inner life, of the imagination. We must think of the movies as that wonderful clean sweep that is clearing out the unhealthful fantasies of the brain.

There is the problem of our adolescents. If our boys and girls do not stay at home, what place have they where they may seek amusement? The street and the dance halls. What happens if they stay at home? I should rather have boys and girls go to the movies than to sit at home twirling their thumbs in a corner, imagining discordant, unruly, abnormal thoughts and brooding over budding and badly understood sex ideas. The movies furnish a clarification of youthful homebrewed fancies.

A friend of mine says that there is no theatrical production which is worth more than fifty cents to see. Prices of a dollar or more make movies a recreation for the well-to-do. These advanced prices of admission destroy democracy. All people have a yearning for something fine. Big theatrical people, the state and the church must meet this need. What we have go to do today is to present clean, fine, interesting performances for people of small means, people who need to have their burdens lightened.

Christ taught his followers by "Pictures." Parables, we call them. He used that marvelous pictorial element which is part and parcel of human life. What is the parable of the Prodigal Son but a series of pictures divinely presented? We must think of Christ as an ideal personality having vital, ethical ideas bearing on our life today, not as the vicarious offering perpetuated in the sacraments of the church. Christ lived and walked among the men of his day. He shared in the life of the common people. He ate at the Pharisee's house. He took part in the marriage celebration at Cana of Galilee. He labored and taught among the people. Were the Lord to descend upon the earth today can we doubt His approval of this form of education when we consider His own method of pictorial teaching?

If Christ went to the movies would he not say, "Let my people enjoy this thing. Let my Church employ it. Blessed be that which uplifts, restores, and refreshes the weary souls of men."

Over 2,000 churches in the United States now utilize the motion pictures.

Broad-minded clergymen everywhere recognize that a force that can build and operate 14,000 theatres, and attract a daily attendance of 12,500,000 should be an ally in the work of carrying religion to the people.

Every great denomination is considering ways and means of applying the influence of the screen to religion. The Methodist church committed itself quite avowedly to a motion picture program at its centennial celebration at Columbus, Ohio, last Summer.

The motion pictures were criticized, despised, and buffeted by clergymen generally five years ago. The attitude of the church has changed with the gradual but certain improvement in the standards of entertainment and decency.

The church was absolutely right in its first position. It is right today. But there is still much to be done, for there are still producers who believe that questionable pictures are sure-fire successes. And the church can by encouraging exhibitors who believe in clean pictures, and discouraging the others, make itself felt.

The Better Photoplay League of America, which was sponsored by this publication, has shown the way. An organized majority is helpless. Photoplay carried on the work of organizing the patrons of motion pictures against exhibitors who showed salacious pictures, and the results were felt immediately in the box office, the most vulnerable part of the exhibitors' and producers' anatomy.

If picture conditions are not right in your town, organize your community and your exhibitor will listen attentively. If he does not, hit him in the box-office. He will hear you then.

The Editor

Chapter 4

R.G. Burnett and E.D. Martell

THE DEVIL'S CAMERA

A SCHOOLBOY AND a schoolgirl sat huddled together in the darkened, stuffy, erotic atmosphere of a London super-cinema. The film they were watching was one of the sensationally realistic productions that have dominated the screen since the 'talkies' revolutionized this most popular of all entertainments. Hundreds of thousands of pounds had been squandered on it. 'Stars' earning, or reputed to be earning, fabulous salaries, were featured in it. Amazing patience and ingenuity had been lavished upon its smallest details. And now a crowded audience was revelling in its hair-raising escapades.

Handsome, well set-up, full of promise were the boy and the girl. It would have been difficult to pick out a finer pair in the whole of London, judged by appearances. But they were 'film fans', steeped in the artificial sentimentality of the modern screen, familiar with the whole sordid concoction of adultery, deception and murder.

True to the code of the 'talkies', they had come together in defiance of their parents' strict prohibition. The film having run its appointed race in the project-ing apparatus, they left the gigantic picturedome. They walked across the broadway, through a park, to a district where houses were being rushed up in a feverish attempt to reap the harvest provided by the latest underground railway extension; and as they walked in silence the lad fingered in his pocket a clasp knife he had recently acquired.

They came to one of a number of almost completed, empty houses;

paused; looked about to make sure they were not observed; and went boldly in at the front door and up the stairs. . . .

It was past midnight when the police were called to that house. They mounted the stairs by the light of electric torches. Little search was needed to reveal the object of this nocturnal visit; in an unfinished bedroom, lying on the floor-boards in one corner, lay the girl's body. There was a deep wound in her breast. Her clothes were saturated with blood. Besides her lay the clasp knife which had brutally ended her fragrant young life.

The lad was put on trial for his life; but he ought not to have stood alone in the dock. What of those who, for the lowest of all human ends, had exploited his immature imagination with their screen crimes? If he had been a few years older, the cinema would have brought him to the gallows. Fortunately British justice takes youth into account and he was sent for a prolonged term of Borstal treatment, where it is to be hoped effective measures can be taken to undo the harm done by the films. They can never wipe from his mind the memory of that dreadful experience in the uninhabited house. A girl's terror-stricken face will haunt him as long as he lives.

This is no exaggeration, only the slightly disguised but otherwise authentic story of a recent occurrence. It is merely a degree more appalling than hundreds of stories that magistrates can tell of juvenile crime directly inspired by the films. No wonder a famous critic of the screen has described it as 'the greatest crime-producing agency of this generation'.

This book is not an indiscriminate and irresponsible attack on cinematography as such. We object not to the film camera but to the prostitution of it by sex-mad and cynical financiers. That it can be, and sometimes is, used not only for clean entertainment but also for high educational purposes we fully and gladly admit.

There have been many splendid films; our point is that they are, nevertheless, few in number compared with the vast output. For every production of the moral tone and superlative merit of King of Kings, Ben Hur, or Disraeli, there have been scores of sinister exploitations of vice and crime and blasphemy. And even when films of such high accomplishment are shown, more often than not the programme is spoiled by filth and evil suggestion in other pictures.

A few of the 'stars' have stood out commendably against the evil which corrupts good morals, but these upholders of a great tradition are in a small minority. Most of the actors and actresses seem ready to go to any length in nakedness and decadence to earn the salaries doled out to them by the little group of mainly Jewish promoters who control the greater part of what is now one of the most skilfully organized industries in the world.

The news gazettes in which the outstanding events of the week are chronicled pictorially achieve a high standard of usefulness and recreation. Travel pictures such as *With Byrd to the South Pole* and *Avalanche*, in which much money and courage are devoted to educating the cinema-going public, reveal the industry at its best. All honour to those who promote such films. We do not wish to belittle in the slightest degree what is being done by such people to make the best practical use of a mechanical device which ought to be a source of genuine amusement and widening of outlook to the masses of the people. But when all the possible bouquets have been handed out to those who deserve them the cinema is still revealed as at present a dread menace to civilization. Unless it is cleaned up within this generation it will undermine every existing agency for decency and public order. The parsons may as well shut up their churches and the schoolmasters their schools; for idealism and morality and learning will be discredited and all forms of beauty will be dragged into the mud.

Dr. W. Sheafe Chase, rector of Christ Church, Brooklyn, U.S.A., has said:

> 'The motion picture industry is the greatest enemy of civilization, greater even than the liquor traffic. For a generation it has been the universal school of crime in all nations, creating the international ill-will of foreign peoples against the United States and seriously interfering with our commerce abroad.'

Mr. G. A. Atkinson, one of the leading English critics, writing of crime and sex films in *The Methodist Times*, recently declared:

> 'Crimeless and sexless films have never had a proper trial since the arrival of the "talkies". Hollywood knows what excites morbid interest in the public. It has it analysed and studied by trained psychologists, who conduct elaborate experiments on young people with a view to ascertaining their pulse, salivary and glandular reactions while they are watching a drama of erotic emotion. There is nothing haphazard about it. What you see on the screen is the rigid application of the factory principle in the commercialization of sex.'

Nothing is sacred. There is no reticence. The basest passions are exhibited in their morbid brutality to a degree that would have been unthinkable a few years ago. Decent people dare not contemplate this disgusting revolution without wishing to strike a blow against it. Our very civilisation is at stake. The cinema, as at present debased, is the Hun of the modern world.

Chapter 5

Pope Pius XI

ENCYCLICAL LETTER
VIGILANTI CURA

TO OUR VENERABLE BRETHREN,
THE ARCHBISHOPS AND BISHOPS
OF THE UNITED STATES OF AMERICA,
AND TO OTHER ORDINARIES ENJOYING PEACE AND COMMUNION WITH
THE APOSTOLIC SEE

On Motion Pictures

POPE PIUS XI
VENERABLE BRETHREN
GREETINGS AND APOSTOLIC BENEDICTION

IN FOLLOWING with vigilant eye, as Our pastoral office requires, the beneficent works of Our Brethren in the Episcopate and of the faithful, it has been highly pleasing to us to learn of the fruits already gathered and of the progress which continues to be made by that prudent initiative launched more than two years ago as a holy crusade against the abuses of motion pictures, and which was in a special manner entrusted to "The Legion of Decency."

It is an excellent experiment, that now offers Us a most welcome opportunity, manifesting more fully Our thought in regard to a matter which touches intimately the moral and religious life of the entire Christian People.

Gratitude expressed to hierarchy of U. S.

First of all, We express Our gratitude to the Hierarchy in the United States of America, to the faithful who cooperated with them, for the important results already achieved, under their direction and guidance, by the "Legion of Decency." And Our gratitude is all the livelier for the fact that We were deeply anguished to note with each passing day the lamentable progress, *magni passus extra viam*, of the motion picture art and industry in the portrayal of sin and vice.

Part I

As often as the occasion has presented itself, We have considered it the duty of Our high office to direct to this condition the attention not only of the Episcopate and clergy, but also of all men who are right-minded and solicitous for the public weal.

In Our Encyclical *Divini Illius Magistri*, We had already deplored that "potent instrumentalities of publicity (such as motion pictures), which might be of great advantage to learning and education, were they properly directed by healthy principles, often unfortunately serve as an incentive to evil and passion and are subordinated to sordid gain."

In August of 1934, addressing Ourselves to a delegation of the International Federation of the Motion Picture Press, We pointed out the very great import-ance which the motion picture has acquired in our days, and its vast influence alike in promotion of good and insinuation of evil. We called to mind that it is necessary to apply to the cinema a supreme rule which must direct and regulate even the highest art in order that it may not find itself in continual conflict with Christian morality, or even simply with human morality based upon natural law. The essential purpose of art, its *raison d'etre*, is to assist in the perfecting of the moral personality, which is man. For this reason it must itself be moral.

And We concluded, amid the manifest approval of that elect body – a memory still dear to Us – by recommending to them the necessity of making the motion picture "moral, an influence for good morals, an educator."

And even as recently as April of this year, when We had the happiness to receive in audience a group of delegates of the International Congress of the Motion Picture Press held in Rome, We again drew attention to the gravity of the problem, and warmly exhorted all men of good will, in the name not only of religion but also of the true moral and civil welfare of the people, to use every means in their power, such as the press, to make of the cinema a valuable auxiliary of instruction and education rather than of destruction and ruin of the soul.

The subject, however, is of such paramount importance in itself, and because of the present condition of society, that We deem it necessary to return to it again, not alone for the purpose of making particular recommendations as on past occasions, but rather with a universal outlook, which while embracing the needs of your own dioceses, Venerable Brethren, takes into consideration those of the entire Catholic world.

It is, in fact, urgently necessary to make provision that in this field also, progress of art, science and human technique in the industry, since they are all true gifts of God, may be ordained to His glory and to the salvation of souls, and may be made to serve in a practical way to promote the extension of the Kingdom of God upon earth. Thus, the Church bids us pray that we may all profit by them in such manner as not to lose the eternal good: *sic transeamus per bona temporalia ut non amittamus aeterna.*

Legion of decency is warmly praised

Now, then, it is a certainty which can readily be verified that the more marvelous is the progress of the motion picture art and industry, the more pernicious and deadly has it shown itself to morality, religion and even to the very decencies of human society.

The directors of the industry in the United States recognized this fact themselves, when they confessed that the responsibility before the people and the world was their very own. In the agreement entered into by common accord in March, 1930, solemnly sealed, signed and published in the press, they formally pledged themselves to safeguard in the future the moral welfare of patrons of the motion picture.

It is promised in this agreement that no film which lowers the moral standard of spectators, which casts discredit on natural or human laws, or arouses sympathy for their violation, will be produced.

Nevertheless, in spite of this wise and spontaneously taken decision, those responsible showed themselves incapable of carrying it into effect. It appeared operators were not disposed to stand by principles to which they obligated themselves. Since, therefore, the above-mentioned undertakings proved they have but slight effect, since the parade of vice and crime continued on the screen, the road seemed almost closed to those who sought honest diversion in the motion picture.

In this crisis, you, Venerable Brethren, were among the first to study the means of safeguarding the souls entrusted to your care. You launched the "Legion of Decency" as a crusade for public morality designed to revitalize the ideals of natural and Christian rectitude. Far from you was the thought of doing damage to the motion picture industry; rather, indeed, did you arm it beforehand against the ruin which menaces every form of recreation which in the guise of art degenerates into corruption.

Your leadership calls forth the prompt and devoted loyalty of your faithful people. Millions of American Catholics signed the pledge of the "Legion of Decency" binding themselves not to attend any motion picture which was offensive to Catholic moral principles or to the proper standards of living. We thus were able to proclaim joyfully that few problems of these latter times have so closely united the Bishops and the people as the one resolved by cooperation in this holy crusade. Not only Catholics, but also high-minded Protestants and Jews and many others accepted your lead and joined their efforts with yours in restoring wise standards, both artistic and moral, to the motion picture.

[. . .]

Part II

Recreation in its manifold variety has become a necessity of people who labor under the fatiguing conditions of modern industry. But it must be worthy of the rational nature of man and therefore must be morally healthy. It must be elevated to the rank of a positive factor for good, and must seek to arouse a noble sentiment. A people who, in time of repose, give themselves to diversions which violate decency, honor or morality; to recreations which, especially to the young, constitute occasions for sin, are in grave danger of losing their greatest, even their national power.

It admits of no discussion that the motion picture has achieved in these last years a position of universal importance among modern means of diversion.

There is no need to point out the fact that millions of people go to motion pictures every day; that motion picture theaters are being opened in ever-increasing numbers in civilized and semi-civilized countries; that the motion picture has become the most popular form of diversion which is offered for the leisure moments, not only of the rich, but of all classes of society.

At the same time there exists today no means of influencing the masses more potent than the cinema. The reason for this is to be sought for in the very nature of the pictures projected upon the screens, in the popularity of the motion picture plays and in the circumstances which accompany them.

Peculiar power of motion picture

The power of the motion picture consists in this: that it speaks by means of vivid and concrete imagery, which the mind takes in with enjoyment and without fatigue.

Even the crudest and most primitive minds, which have neither the capacity nor the desire to make the efforts necessary for abstraction or deductive reasoning, are captivated by the cinema. In place of the efforts which reading or listening demand, there is the continued pleasure of a succession of concrete and, so to speak, living pictures.

This power is still greater in the talking picture, for the reason that the interpretation becomes even easier and the charm of music is added to the action and drama. The dances and variety acts which sometimes are introduced between films serve to increase the stimulation of the pageant.

Since, then, the cinema is in reality an object lesson which, for good or for evil, teaches the majority of men more effectively than abstract reasoning, it must be elevated to conformity with the aims of the Christian conscience and saved from depraving or demoralizing effects.

Bad films occasion sin and create prejudices

Everyone knows what damage is done to the soul by bad motion pictures. They are occasions of sin; they seduce young people along the ways of evil by glorifying the passions; they show life under a false light; they cloud ideals; they destroy pure love, respect for marriage and affection for the family. They are capable also of creating prejudices among individuals, misunderstandings among nations, among social classes, and among entire races.

On the other hand, good motion pictures are capable of exercising a profoundly moral influence upon those who see them. In addition to affording recreation, they are able to arouse noble ideals of life, to communicate valuable conceptions, to impart better knowledge of the history and beauties of the fatherland and other countries, to present truth and virtue under attractive forms, to create at least the flavor of understanding among nations, social classes and races, to champion the cause of justice, to give new life to the claims of virtue, to contribute positively to the genesis of a just social order in the world.

These considerations take on greater seriousness from the fact that the cinema speaks not to individuals but to multitudes, and does so in circumstances, time, place and surroundings which are the most apt to arouse unusual enthusiasm for good as well as for bad and to conduce to that collective exultation which, as experience teaches us, may assume the most morbid form.

A motion picture is viewed by people who are seated in a dark theater, and whose faculties, mental, physical and often spiritual, are relaxed. One does not need to go far in search of these theaters: they are close to home, to church, to school, and they thus bring the cinema to the very center of popular life.

Theaters bring cinema to center of popular life

Moreover, the acting out of the plot is done by men and women selected for their art, for all those natural gifts, the employment of those expedients, which can become, for youth particularly, the instruments of seduction. Further, the motion picture has enlisted in its service luxurious appointments, pleasing music, the vigor of realism and every form of whim and fancy. For this very reason it attracts and fascinates particularly the young, adolescent, or even the child. Thus, at the very age when moral sense is being formed, when notions and sentiments of justice and rectitude, of duty, obligations, and ideals of life are being developed, the motion picture, with its direct propaganda, assumes a position of commanding influence.

It is unfortunate that in the present state of affairs this influence is frequently exerted for evil. So much so that when one thinks of the havoc wrought in the souls of youth and childhood, of the loss of innocence so often suffered in motion picture theaters, there comes to mind the terrible condemnation pronounced by Our Lord upon the corrupters of little ones: "But he that shall scandalize one of these little ones that believe in Me, it were better for him that a millstone should be hanged about his neck, and that he should be drowned in the depth of the sea."

[. . .]

Part III

The problem of the production of moral films would be solved radically if it were possible for us to have the production wholly inspired by the principles of Christian morality. We can never sufficiently praise all those who have dedicated themselves, or who are to dedicate themselves, to the noble cause of raising the standard of the motion picture to meet the needs of education and the requirements of Christian conscience.

For this purpose they must make full use of the technical ability of experts, and not permit the waste of effort and money by the employment of amateurs.

But since We know how difficult it is to organize such an industry, especially because of considerations of a financial nature, and since on the other hand it is necessary to influence the production of all films so they may contain nothing harmful from the religious, moral or social viewpoint, pastors of souls must exercise their vigilance over films wherever they may be produced or offered to Christian peoples.

As to the motion picture industry itself, We exhort Bishops of all countries, but in particular you, Venerable Brethren, to address your appeal to those Catholics who hold important positions in this industry. Let them take serious thought of their duties and the responsibility which they have as children of the Church to use their influence and authority for the promotion of the principles of sound morality in the films which they produce or aid in producing.

The number of Catholics who are executives, directors, authors or actors is not inconsiderable, and it is unfortunate their influence has not always been in accordance with their Faith and their ideals. You will do well, Venerable Brethren, to pledge them to bring their profession into harmony with their conscience as respectable men and followers of Jesus Christ.

In this, as in every other field, the apostolate of pastors of souls will surely find the best collaborators in those who fight in the ranks of Catholic Action, and in this letter We cannot refrain from addressing to them a warm appeal that they give this cause their full contribution and their unwearying and unfailing activity.

From time to time Bishops will do well to recall to the motion picture industry that amid the cares of their pastoral ministry they, as Bishops, are under obligation to interest themselves in every form of decent and healthy recreation because they are responsible before God for the moral welfare of their people, even during their leisure.

Must proclaim danger to nation's moral fibre

Their sacred calling constrains them to proclaim clearly and openly that unhealthy and impure entertainment destroys the moral fibre of the nation. They will likewise remind the motion picture industry that the demands they make regard not only Catholics, but all who patronize the cinema.

In particular, you, Venerable Brethren of the United States, will be able to insist with justice that the industry in your country has recognized and accepted its responsibility before society.

The Bishops of the whole world will take care to make clear to leaders of the motion picture industry that the force of such a power of universality as the cinema can be directed with great utility to the highest ends of individual and social improvement. Why, indeed, should there be a question of merely avoiding evil? Why should the motion picture simply be a means of diversion and light relaxation to occupy an idle hour? With its magnificent power, it can and must be a light and a positive guide to what is good.

And now, in view of the gravity of the subject, we consider it timely to come down to certain practical indications.

[. . .]

Will accomplish great work for morality of their people

If the Bishops of the world assume their share in the exercise of this painstaking vigilance over the motion picture – and of this We, who know their pastoral zeal, have no doubt – they will certainly accomplish a great work for the protection of the morality of their people during their moments of leisure and recreation.

They will win the approbation and approval of all right-thinking men, Catholic and non-Catholic, and they will help assure that this great international force – the motion picture – shall be directed toward the noble end of promoting the highest ideals and the truest standard of life.

That these desires which spring up in Our paternal heart may be realized, We implore the help of the grace of God; and in pledge thereof, We impart to you, Venerable Brethren, and to the clergy and the people entrusted to you, Our affectionate and Apostolic Benediction.

Given at Rome, at St. Peter's, the twenty-ninth day of June, the Feast of Saints Peter and Paul, in the year of Our Lord 1936, the fifteenth of Our Pontificate.

PIUS XI, POPE.

PART 2

The Birth of Film Theory: Realism, Formalism, and Religious Vision

INTRODUCTION

I N 1896, in a scene lasting less than 20 seconds, Thomas Edison filmed a man and a woman kissing. The pair were clothed up to the neck and by contemporary standards there was nothing passionate about the physicality of the kiss. Nonetheless, the scene, the first ever cinema kiss, was enough to cause some consternation in journalists' opinion pieces and preachers' sermons of the time. "The Kiss" was actually a restaged scene from a New York musical called *The Widow Jones*, but the film's controversy had much to do with the close-up, projected, and tightly framed quality of the kiss itself. As the painter John Sloan commented soon after: "When only life-size it was pronounced beastly. But that was nothing to the present sight. Magnified to Gargantuan proportions and repeated three times over it is absolutely disgusting. . . . Such things call for police interference."[1]

The readings in part 1 began to demonstrate how some religious leaders in the early days of cinema were concerned with the influence of film on the moral fiber of society, especially when it portrayed scenes of criminal activity and erotic behaviors. But crime and sex (even just kissing) occurred off-screen as well as on, and observers began to realize that there was something uniquely powerful about the very nature of film that challenged again the boundaries between "art" and "real life" in ways that literature, theatre, and photography had done in the past.

In the second part of this volume we therefore provide extracts which focus more on such observations and on the *medium* of film itself. Several authors explore the ways in which the specificities of the film form can stand at the root of the relation between religion and film: larger-than-life images, providing a view of reality that can be endlessly manipulated through cinematography, editing, lighting, and sound. Film offers a glimpse of another world, or even of the "real world" in more stunning detail than that possible without the aid of technology.

The difference implied here, between imaginatively portraying *other* worlds or in showing *this* world in a new way, has been at the heart of film theory and filmmaking from the earliest days of cinema and is often couched in language of *formalism* and *realism*, respectively. The very first films, such as those by the Lumières and Edison, were created in the realistic vein, simply showing trains arriving at stations or people kissing, and thus seeming to mirror reality directly. Soon after, filmmakers like George Méliès realized how simple tricks could be enacted through editing and special effects, and fantastic cinema was born, allowing imaginary, alternative worlds to come into view.[2]

Such renewed perceptions, by way of analogy, are very often what religions attempt through their myths, rituals, texts, and symbols. Religious structures operate in both formalist and realist modes: sometimes showing the viewer other worlds (heavens and hells, or apocalyptic scenarios) and other times revealing the true depths of this actual world that we inhabit, displaying connections, possibilities, and temptations in ways often difficult to see through unaided human perception. Religion, in either mode, is a lens through which the world can be described, redescribed and then comprehended in a deeper manner.

Beginning with the potentials of cinema to either mirror or reveal the world, the readings in this second part invite imaginative, critical ways to re-examine the history of the religion–film relation. The readings provided here are early articulations of how religion and film might intersect. In this section the excerpts run from the beginnings of film theory in the 1920s through to the 1960s, while the final section of this reader provides more contemporary approaches to the relation. We have arranged the readings here as they originally appeared chronologically, and it is important to bear in mind that the first two readings were written before the implications of sound were fully understood for film.

The first reading is from 1924, by the French filmmaker and theorist, Jean Epstein (reading 6). Epstein was actively producing experimental and documentary films, alongside theoretical musings on film, from the 1920s to the 1940s. Along with fellow film theorists such as Louis Delluc, he promoted the idea of *photogénie*, which refers to the ways in which the technological medium of film enhances and actively re-creates the world in new styles. This concept has an intriguing mystical dimension to it: film contains an animating quality, magically bringing things to life. He even claims "that the cinema is polytheistic and theogonic," and it is through film that we can come to understand how the sacred operates.

A reading from theorist and playwright Antonin Artaud follows in this magical vein. His 1928 excerpt develops an intriguing sacred potential of the cinema (reading 7). Even though he was quite critical of Christianity, Artaud, like Epstein and others at the time, saw in moving pictures a possibility to re-enchant an industrial world that had lost its magic through a cataclysmic World War and the drudgery of modern working life in "which an exhausted language loses its power as a symbol." The film and the filmmaker, from his perspective, can function as a kind of shaman, or holy person, calling out the supernatural from the midst of the natural.

Moving away from the formalist-magical enthusiasm for cinema, the reading by theorist André Bazin focuses on the work of one of the greatest directors of religious film of all time, Robert Bresson, and specifically his film, *Diary of a Country Priest* (*Journal d'un cure de campagne*) (reading 8). Bresson's style was one of marked restraint, like Carl Theodor Dreyer's before him. Bazin's 1951 article champions the ways in which transcendence can come through utterly physical means, as it does in Bresson's films. Indeed, even the interpretations of this film which focus on the country priest as a Christ-like figure overlook Bresson's belief that every human life, however apparently insignificant, has meaning. Bazin saw the world as infused with God's creation, and over-reliance upon lighting tricks, editing, and cinematography distract from that reality. Film must take a passive, objective role in its revealing of the world.

Later in this volume we will encounter the work of filmmakers such as Pasolini, Ozu and Kore-eda, and the critical work of Paul Schrader, who all represent the continuation of realism and its relations to religion. Meanwhile, the final reading (9) in this part is by the filmmaker, Stan Brakhage, whose 1963 avant-garde manifesto encourages readers to continue thinking through the formalist-realist approaches to film, and their implications for understanding the religious dimensions of film. Brakhage believed that through careful attention to the spectacle of the world, and aided by filmic technologies, we might gain "an increased ability to see." Modern society has rendered its symbols useless, and so rather than seeking out new symbols, our eyes need to be re-trained. Cinema offers just such a re-training as his mystical-mythical ideas suggest.

Notes

1   John Sloan quoted in Michéle C. Cone, "Naughty Films, Prissy Art," in *Artnet* online at: http://www.artnet.com/magazineus/reviews/cone/cone10-24-06.asp (accessed 1 December 2006).

Edison's short film has been preserved and is widely accessible on the Internet. It offers a telling insight into the changing visual mores over the past 100 years. For interesting analyses of the film and its effects, see Linda Williams, "Of Kisses and Ellipses: The Long Adolescence of American Movies," *Critical Inquiry* 32.2 (2006), 288–340; and Charles Musser, "The May Irwin Kiss: Performance and the Beginnings of Cinema," in *Visual Delights II*, ed. Vanessa Toulmin and Simon Popple. London: John Libbey, 2005, 96–115.

2   Tom Gunning's article, "The Cinema of Attractions: Early Film, Its Spectator, and the Avant-Garde," in *Early Cinema*, ed. Thomas Elsaesser. London: BFI, 1990, 56–62, is absolutely essential to the theoretical dimensions of part two here.

Chapter 6

Jean Epstein

ON CERTAIN CHARACTERISTICS OF *PHOTOGÉNIE**

THE CINEMA seems to me like two Siamese twins joined together at the stomach, in other words by the base necessities of life, but sundered at the heart, or by the higher necessities of emotion. The first of these brothers is the art of cinema, the second is the film industry. A surgeon is called for, capable of separating these two fraternal foes without killing them, or a psychologist able to resolve the incompatibilities between these two hearts.

I shall venture to speak to you only of the art of cinema. The art of cinema has been called "*photogénie*" by Louis Delluc. The word is apt, and should be preserved. What is *photogénie*? I would describe as photogenic any aspect of things, beings, or souls whose moral character is enhanced by filmic reproduction. And any aspect not enhanced by filmic reproduction is not photogenic, plays no part in the art of cinema.

For every art builds its forbidden city, its own exclusive domain, autonomous, specific, and hostile to anything that does not belong. Astonishing to

* Translated by Tom Milne in *Afterimage* 10 (Autumn 1981), 20–23. Reprinted by permission. Epstein delivered versions of this essay at the Salon d'Automne in November 1923, to the Paris-Nancy Group at Nancy on 1 December 1923, at the Pathé-Palace in Montpelier on 7 January 1924, and to the Philosophical and Scientific Studies Group at the Sorbonne on 15 June 1924. The original French text first appeared as "De quelques conditions de la photogénie" in *Cinéa-Ciné-pour-tous* 19 (15 August 1924), 6–8.

relate, literature must first and foremost be literary; the theater, theatrical; painting, pictorial; and the cinema, cinematic. Painting today is freeing itself from many of its representational and narrative concerns. Historical and anecdotal canvases, pictures which narrate rather than paint, are rarely seen nowadays outside the furnishing departments of the big stores – where, I must confess, they sell very well. But what one might call the high art of painting seeks to be no more than painting, in other words color taking on life. And any literature worthy of the name turns its back on those twists and turns of plot which lead to the detective's discovery of the lost treasure. Literature seeks only to be literary, which is seen as a justification for taking it to task by people alarmed at the idea that it might resemble neither a charade nor a game of cards and be put to better use than killing time, which there is no point in killing since it returns, hanging equally heavy, with each new dawn.

Similarly, the cinema should avoid dealings, which can only be unfortunate, with historical, educational, novelistic, moral or immoral, geographical or documentary subjects. The cinema must seek to become, gradually and in the end uniquely, cinematic; to employ, in other words, only photogenic elements. *Photogénie* is the purest expression of cinema.

What aspects of the world are photogenic, then, these aspects to which the cinema must limit itself? I fear the only response I have to offer to so important a question is a premature one. We must not forget that where the theater trails some tens of centuries of existence behind it, the cinema is a mere twenty-five years old. It is a new enigma. Is it an art? Or less than that? A pictorial language, like the hieroglyphs of ancient Egypt, whose secrets we have scarcely penetrated yet, about which we do not know all that we do not know? Or an unexpected extension to our sense of sight, a sort of telepathy of the eye? Or a challenge to the logic of the universe, since the mechanism of cinema constructs movement by multiplying successive stoppages of celluloid exposed to a ray of light, thus creating mobility through immobility, decisively demonstrating how right was the false reasoning of Zeno of Elea?

Do we know what radio will be like in ten years time? An eighth art, no doubt, as much at odds with music as cinema currently is with the theater. We are just as much in the dark as to what cinema will be like in ten years time.

At present, we have discovered the cinematic property of things, a new and exciting sort of potential: *photogénie*. We are beginning to recognize certain circumstances in which this *photogénie* appears. I suggest a preliminary specification in determining these photogenic aspects. A moment ago I described as photogenic any aspect whose moral character is enhanced by filmic reproduction. I now specify: only mobile aspects of the world, of things and souls, may see their moral value increased by filmic reproduction.

This mobility should be understood only in the widest sense, implying all directions perceptible to the mind. By general agreement it is said that the dimensions deriving from our sense of direction are three in number: the three spatial dimensions. I have never really understood why the notion of a fourth dimension has been enveloped in such mystery. It very obviously exists; it is time. The mind travels in time, just as it does in space. But whereas in space we imagine three directions at right angles to each other, in time we can conceive only one: the past-future vector. We can conceive a space-time system in which the past-future direction also passes through the point of intersection of the three acknowledged spatial directions, at the precise moment when it is between past and future: the present, a point in time, an instant without duration, as points in geometrical space are without dimension. Photogenic mobility is a mobility in this space-time system, a mobility in both space and time. We can therefore say that the photogenic aspect of an object is a consequence of its variations in space-time.

This definition, an important one, is not simply a mental intuition. A number of films have already offered concrete examples. First, certain American films, demonstrating an unconscious and highly precocious feeling for cinema, sketched the spatiotemporal cinegrams in rough outline. Later Griffith, that giant of the primitive cinema, gave classical expression to these jostling, intersecting denouements that describe arabesques virtually simultaneously in space and time. More consciously and more lucidly, Gance – today our master, one and all – then composed his astonishing vision of trains swept along on the rails of the drama. We must be clear why these racing wheels in La Roue comprise the most classic sentences yet written in the language of cinema. It is because in these images the most clearly defined role is played by variations, if not simultaneous at least approximately so, in the spatiotemporal dimensions.

For in the end it all comes down to a question of perspective, a question of design. Perspective in drawing is a three-dimensional perspective, and when a pupil executes a drawing which takes no account of the third dimension, the effect of depth or relief in objects, it is said that he has done a bad drawing, that he cannot draw. To the elements of perspective employed in drawing, the cinema adds a new perspective in time. In addition to relief in space the cinema offers relief in time. Astonishing abridgments in this temporal perspective are permitted by the cinema – notably in those amazing glimpses into the life of plants and crystals – but these have never yet been used to dramatic purpose. If, as I said earlier, a drawing which ignores the third spatial dimension in its perspective is a bad drawing, I must now add that cinema composed without taking the temporal perspective into account is not cinematic.

Moreover, cinema is a language, and like all languages it is animistic; it attributes, in other words, a semblance of life to the objects it defines. The more primitive a language, the more marked this animistic tendency. There is no need to stress the extent to which the language of cinema remains primitive in its terms and ideas; so it is hardly surprising that it should endow the objects it is called upon to depict with such intense life. The almost godlike importance assumed in close-ups by parts of the human body, or by the most frigid elements in nature, has often been noted. Through the cinema, a revolver in a drawer, a broken bottle on the ground, an eye isolated by an iris, are elevated to the status of characters in the drama. Being dramatic, they seem alive, as though involved in the evolution of an emotion.

I would even go so far as to say that the cinema is polytheistic and theogonic. Those lives it creates, by summoning objects out of the shadows of indifference into the light of dramatic concern, have little in common with human life. These lives are like the life in charms and amulets, the ominous, tabooed objects of certain primitive religions. If we wish to understand how an animal, a plant, or a stone can inspire respect, fear, or horror, those three most sacred sentiments, I think we must watch them on the screen, living their mysterious, silent lives, alien to the human sensibility.

To things and beings in their most frigid semblance, the cinema thus grants the greatest gift unto death: life. And it confers this life in its highest guise: personality.

Personality goes beyond intelligence. Personality is the spirit visible in things and people, their heredity made evident, their past become unforgettable, their future already present. Every aspect of the world, elected to life by the cinema, is so elected only on condition that it has a personality of its own. This is the second specification which we can now add to the rules of photogénie. I therefore suggest that we say: only mobile and personal aspects of things, beings, and souls may be photogenic; that is, acquire a higher moral value through filmic reproduction.

An eye in close-up is no longer the eye, it is AN eye: in other words, the mimetic decor in which the look suddenly appears as a character ... I was greatly interested by a competition recently organized by one of the film magazines. The point was to identify some forty more or less famous screen actors whose portraits reproduced in the magazine had been cropped to leave only their eyes. So what one had to do was to recognize the personality in each of forty looks. Here we have a curious unconscious attempt to get spectators into the habit of seeking and recognizing the distinctive personality of the eye segment.

And a close-up of a revolver is no longer a revolver, it is the revolver-character, in other words the impulse toward or remorse for crime, failure, suicide. It is as dark as the temptations of the night, bright as the gleam of gold lusted after, taciturn as passion, squat, brutal, heavy, cold, wary, menacing. It has a temperament, habits, memories, a will, a soul.

Mechanically speaking, the lens alone can sometimes succeed in revealing the inner nature of things in this way. This is how, by chance in the first instance, the photogénie of character was discovered. But the proper sensibility, by which I mean a personal one, can direct the lens towards increasingly valuable discoveries. This is the role of an author of film, commonly called a film director. Of course a landscape filmed by one of the forty or four hundred directors devoid of personality whom God sent to plague the cinema as He once sent the locusts into Egypt looks exactly like this same landscape filmed by any other of these locust filmmakers. But this landscape or this fragment of drama staged by someone like Gance will look nothing like what would be seen through the eyes and heart of a Griffith or a L'Herbier. And so the personality, the soul, the poetry of certain men invaded the cinema.

I remember still *La Roue*. As Sisif died, we all saw his unhappy soul leave him and slip away over the snows, a shadow borne away in angels' flight.

Now we are approaching the promised land, a place of great wonders. Here matter is molded and set into relief by personality; all nature, all things appear as a man has dreamed them; the world is created as you think it is; pleasant if you think it so, harsh if you believe it so. Time hurries on or retreats, or stops and waits for you. A new reality is revealed, a reality for a special occasion, which is untrue to everyday reality just as everyday reality is untrue to the heightened awareness of poetry. The face of the world may seem changed since we, the fifteen hundred million who inhabit it, can see through eyes equally intoxicated by alcohol, love, joy, and woe, through lenses of all tempers, hate and tenderness; since we can see the clear thread of thoughts and dreams, what might or should have been, what was, what never was or could have been, feelings in their secret guise, the startling face of love and beauty, in a word, the soul. "So poetry is thus true, and exists as truly as the eye."

Here poetry, which one might have thought but verbal artifice, a figure of style, a play of antithesis and metaphor – in short, something next to nothing – achieves a dazzling incarnation. "So poetry is thus true, and exists as truly as the eye."

The cinema is poetry's most powerful medium, the truest medium for the untrue, the unreal, the "surreal" as Apollinaire would have said.

This is why some of us have entrusted to it our highest hopes.

Chapter 7

Antonin Artaud

SORCERY AND CINEMA

WE HEAR IT endlessly repeated that the cinema is in its infancy and that we're only witnessing its first stammerings. I confess to not understanding this way of seeing things. The cinema arrives at an already advanced stage of development within human thought and it benefits from this development. It is, to be sure, a means of expression that, materially speaking, is not yet completely perfected. We may imagine a certain number of advances capable of giving the camera, for instance, a stability and mobility it does not possess. One day soon we will probably have cinema in three dimensions, even cinema in color. Yet these are secondary resources that cannot add much to what is the bedrock of the cinema itself and which makes a language out of it, as music, painting, and poetry are a language. In cinema I've always been aware of a virtue proper to the secret movement of images, to their matter. There's a whole element of contingency and mystery in cinema that isn't found in the other arts. Indeed, any image, even the slightest and most banal, is transfigured on the screen. The smallest detail and the most insignificant object take on the meaning and the life that pertains to each of them. And this, in addition to the value of the meaning of the images themselves, in addition to the thought they express, the symbol they constitute. Due to the fact that it isolates objects, it endows them with a second life, one that tends to become ever more independent and to detach itself from the habitual meaning these objects have. Foliage, a bottle, a hand, etc., live a quasi-animal life which asks only to be utilized. There are also the distortions of the camera itself, the unexpected use it makes of the things it is asked to film. At the moment the image disappears, a detail which it was thought wouldn't particularly stand out takes leave of the expression chosen for it. Then there's the physical intoxication of sorts that the rotation of the images communicates directly to the brain. The spirit is moved, whatever the representation. The kind of virtual power images have goes rummaging in the depths of the mind for hitherto unused possibilities. In essence, the cinema reveals a whole occult life, one with which it puts us directly in contact. But we have to know how to divine this occult life. There are better ways of divining the secrets that stir in the depths of our consciousness than the simple play of superimpositions. Considered as such, in an abstract way, cinema in its raw state [le cinéma brut] emits something of the atmosphere of trance conducive to certain revelations. To use it to tell stories, a superficial series of deeds, is to deprive it of the finest of its resources, to disavow its most profound purpose. That's why the cinema seems to me to be made, above all else, to express things of the mind; the inner life of consciousness, not so much through the play of images as through something more imponderable that restores them to us with their matter intact, without intermediate forms, without representations. The cinema arrives at a turning point in human thought, at the precise moment in which an exhausted language loses its power as a symbol, in which the mind is sick and tired of the play of representations. For us clear thinking is not enough. It defines a world exhausted to the point of collapse. What is clear is what is instantly accessible, but the instantly accessible is what serves life as an outer shell. We begin to perceive that this over-fair life, which has foregone all its symbols, is not life in its entirety. And it's a wonderful time, right now, for sorcerers and saints, more wonderful than ever before. A whole insensate substance takes on form, strives to reach the light. The cinema brings us closer to this substance. If the cinema isn't made to express dreams or everything that in waking life has something in common with dreams, then it has no point. Nothing differentiates it from theater. Yet the cinema, a direct and rapid-fire language, has no need of a certain slow and ponderous logic in order to subsist and prosper. Cinema will bear a greater and greater resemblance to the fantastic, that fantastic of which it is increasingly observed that it is really the real in its entirety; otherwise, it doesn't exist. Or cinema will ultimately come to the same end as painting, as poetry. What is certain is that most forms of representation have had their day. It's been a long time since good painting serves for anything other than to reproduce the abstract. It's not just a question of choice, therefore. There won't be a cinema that represents life, on the one hand, and another cinema that represents the functioning of thought, on the other. Because life, what we call life, will become increasingly inseparable from mind. A certain profound domain tends to blossom on the surface. More than any other art the cinema is capable of expressing the representations of this domain, because stupid order and habitual clarity are its enemies.

The Seashell and the Clergyman belongs to this research into a subtle order,[1] into a hidden life I have wished to make plausible, as plausible and real as the other life.

In order to understand this film it will be enough to look deep within ourselves. To submit to the kind of plastic, objective examination that's attentive to an inner *self* that's hitherto been the exclusive domain of the "Illuminati."

Notes

1   Editors: *The Seashell and the Clergyman* (1928, *La Coquille et le clergyman*) is sometimes described as the "first surrealist film." It was written by Antonin Artaud and directed by Germaine Dulac. The film was banned by the British Board of Film Censors in 1929. Lasting for over 30 minutes, this silent film depicts a clergyman's bizarre, obsessive and at times lustful visions. The British censors memorably declared at the time that: "This film is so obscure as to have no apparent meaning. If there is a meaning, it is doubtless objectionable." Some accounts suggest that Artaud was far from happy with the way that the director Dulac had interpreted his original script.

Chapter 8

André Bazin

LE JOURNAL D'UN CURÉ DE CAMPAGNE AND THE STYLISTICS OF ROBERT BRESSON

IF *The Diary of a Country Priest* impresses us as a masterpiece, and this with an almost physical impact, if it moves the critic and the uncritical alike, it is primarily because of its power to stir the emotions, rather than the intelligence, at their highest level of sensitivity. The temporary eclipse of *Les Dames du Bois de Boulogne* was for precisely the opposite reason. This film could not stir us unless we had, if not exactly analyzed, at least tested its intellectual structure and, so to speak, understood the rules of the game.

While the instantaneous success of *Le Journal* is undeniable, the aesthetic principles on which it is based are nevertheless the most paradoxical, maybe even the most complex, ever manifest in a sound film. Hence the refrain of those critics, ill-equipped to understand it. "Paradoxical," they say, "incredible – an unprecedented success that can never be repeated." Thus they renounce any attempt at explanation and take refuge in the perfect alibi of a stroke of genius. On the other hand, among those whose aesthetic preferences are of a kind with Bresson's and whom one would have unhesitatingly thought to be his allies, there is a deep sense of disappointment in proportion as they expected greater acts of daring from him.

Naturally Bresson, like Dreyer, is only concerned with the countenance as flesh, which, when not involved in playing a role, is a man's true imprint, the most visible mark of his soul. It is then that the countenance takes on the dignity of a sign. He would have us be concerned here not with the psychology but with the physiology of existence. Hence the hieratic tempo of the acting, the slow ambiguous gestures, the obstinate recurrence of certain behavioral patterns, the unforgettable dream-like slow motion. Nothing purely accidental could happen to these people – confirmed as each is in his own way of life, essentially concerned either against the influence of grace, to continue so, or, responding to grace, to throw off the deadly Nessus-mantle of the old Adam.

There is no development of character. Their inner conflicts, the various phases of their struggle as they wrestle with the Angel of the Lord, are never outwardly revealed. What we see is rather a concentration of suffering, the recurrent spasms of childbirth or of a snake sloughing off its skin. We can truly say that Bresson strips his characters bare.

Eschewing psychological analysis, the film in consequence lies outside the usual dramatic categories. The succession of events is not constructed according to the usual laws of dramaturgy under which the passions work towards a soul-satisfying climax. Events do indeed follow one another according to a necessary order, yet within a framework of accidental happenings. Free acts and coincidences are interwoven. Each moment in the film, each set-up, has its own due measure, alike, of freedom and of necessity. They all move in the same direction, but separately like iron filings drawn to the overall surface of a magnet. If the word tragedy comes to one's pen, it is in an opposite sense since we can only be dealing here with a tragedy freely willed. The transcendence of the Bernanos-Bresson universe is not the transcendence of destiny as the ancients understood it, nor yet the transcendence of Racinian passion, but the transcendence of grace which is something each of us is free to refuse.

If nevertheless, the concatenation of events and the causal efficiency of the characters involved appear to operate just as rigidly as in a traditional dramatic structure, it is because they are responding to an order, of prophecy (or perhaps one should say of Kierkegaardian "repetition") that is as different from fatality as causality is from analogy.

The pattern of the film's unfolding is not that of tragedy in the usual sense, rather in the sense of the medieval Passion Play, or better still, of the Way of the Cross, each sequence being a station along that road. We are given the key to this by the dialogue in the hut between the two curés, when the one from Ambricourt reveals that he is spiritually attracted to the Mount of Olives. "Is it not enough that Our Lord should have granted me the grace of letting me know today, through the words of my old teacher, that nothing, throughout all eternity, can remove me from the place chosen by me from all eternity, that I was the prisoner of His Sacred Passion?"

Death is not the preordained end of our final agony, only its conclusion and a deliverance. Henceforth we shall know to what divine ordinance, to what spiritual rhythm the sufferings and actions of the curé respond. They are the outward representation of his agony. At which point we should indicate the analogies with Christ that abound towards the end of the film, or they may very well go unnoticed. For example, the two fainting fits during the night; the fall in the mud; the vomitings of wine and blood – a remarkable synthesis of powerful comparisons with the falls of Jesus, the Blood of the Passion, the sponge with vinegar on it, and the defiling spittle. These are not all. For the veil of Veronica we have the cloth of Seraphita; then finally the death in the attic – a Golgotha with even a good and a bad thief.

Now let us immediately put aside these comparisons, the very enumeration of which is necessarily deceptive. Their aesthetic weight derives from their theological value, but both defy explanation. Bresson like Bernanos avoids any sort of symbolic allusion and so none of the situations, despite their obvious parallel to the Gospel, is created precisely because of that parallel. Each carries its own biographical and individual meaning. Its Christlike resemblance comes second, through being projected onto the higher plane of analogy. In no sense is it true to say that the life of the curé of Ambricourt is an imitation of its divine model, rather it is a repetition and a picturing forth of that life. Each bears his own cross and each cross is different, but all are the Cross of the Passion. The sweat on the brow of the curé is a bloody sweat.

So, probably for the first time, the cinema gives us a film in which the only genuine incidents, the only perceptible movements are those of the life of the spirit. Not only that, it also offers us a new dramatic form, that is specifically religious – or better still, specifically theological; a phenomenology of salvation and grace.

Chapter 9

Stan Brakhage

METAPHORS ON VISION

IMAGINE AN EYE unruled by man-made laws of perspective, an eye unprejudiced by compositional logic, an eye which does not respond to the name of everything but which must know each object encountered in life through an adventure of perception. How many colors are there in a field of grass to the crawling baby unaware of "Green?" How many rainbows can light create for the untutored eye? How aware of variations in heat waves can that eye be? Imagine a world alive with incomprehensible objects and shimmering with an endless variety of movement and innumerable gradations of color. Imagine a world before the "beginning was the word."

To see is to retain — to behold. Elimination of all fear is in sight — which must be aimed for. Once vision may have been given — that which seems inherent in the infant's eye, an eye which reflects the loss of innocence more eloquently than any other human feature, an eye which soon learns to classify sights, an eye which mirrors the movement of the individual toward death by its increasing inability to see.

But one can never go back, not even in imagination. After the loss of innocence, only the ultimate of knowledge can balance the wobbling pivot. Yet I suggest that there is a pursuit of knowledge foreign to language and founded upon visual communication, demanding a development of the optical mind, and dependent upon perception in the original and deepest sense of the word.

Suppose the vision of the saint and the artist to be an increased ability to see – vision. Allow so-called hallucination to enter the realm of perception, allowing that mankind always finds derogatory terminology for that which doesn't appear to be readily usable, accept dream visions, day-dreams or night-dreams, as you would so-called real scenes, even allowing that the abstractions which move so dynamically when closed eyelids are pressed are actually perceived. Become aware of the fact that you are not only influenced by the visual phenomenon which you are focused upon and attempt to sound the depths of all visual influence. There is no need for the mind's eye to be deadened after infancy, yet in these times the development of visual understanding is almost universally forsaken.

This is an age which has no symbol for death other than the skull and bones of one stage of decomposition . . . and it is an age which lives in fear of total annihilation. It is a time haunted by sexual sterility yet almost universally incapable of perceiving the phallic nature of every destructive manifestation of itself. It is an age which artificially seeks to project itself materialistically into abstract space and to fulfill itself mechanically because it has blinded itself to almost all external reality within eyesight and to the organic awareness of even the physical movement properties of its own perceptibility. The earliest cave paintings discovered demonstrate that primitive man had a greater understanding than we do that the object of fear must be objectified. The entire history of erotic magic is one of possession of fear thru the beholding of it. The ultimate searching visualization has been directed toward God out of the deepest possible human understanding that there can be no ultimate love where there is fear. Yet in this contemporary time how many of us even struggle to deeply perceive our own children?

The artist has carried the tradition of vision and visualization down through the ages. In the present time a very few have continued the process of visual perception in its deepest sense and transformed their inspirations into cinematic experiences. They create a new language made possible by the moving picture image. They create where fear before them has created the greatest necessity. They are essentially preoccupied by and deal imagistically with – birth, sex, death, and the search for God.

Camera eye

Oh transparent hallucination, superimposition of image on image, mirage of movement, heroine of a thousand and one nights (Scheherazade must surely be the muse of this art), you obstruct the light, muddie the pure white beaded screen (it perspires) with your shuffling patterns. Only the spectators (the unbelievers who attend the carpeted temples where coffee and paintings are served) think your spirit is in the illuminated occasion (mistaking your sweaty, flaring, rectangular body for more than it is). The devout, who break popcorn together in your humblest double-feature services, know that you are still being born, search for your spirit in their dreams, and dare only dream when in contact with your electrical reflection. Unknowingly, as innocent, they await the priests of this new religion, those who can stir cinematic entrails divinely. They await the prophets who can cast (with the precision of Confucian sticks) the characters of this new order across filmic mud. Being innocent, they do not consciously know that this church too is corrupt; but they react with counter hallucinations, believing in the stars, and cast themselves among these Los Angelic orders. Of themselves, they will never recognize what they are awaiting. Their footsteps, the dumb drum which destroys cinema. They are having the dream piped into their homes, the destruction of the romance thru marriage, etc.

So the money vendors have been at it again. To the catacombs then, or rather plant this seed deeper in the undergrounds beyond false nourishing of sewage waters. Let it draw nourishment from hidden uprising springs chan-neled by gods. Let there be no cavernous congregation but only the network of individual channels, that narrowed vision which splits beams beyond rainbow and into the unknown dimensions. (To those who think this is waxing poetic, squint, give the visual objects at hand their freedom, and allow the distant to come to you; and when mountains are moving, you will find no fat in this prose.) Forget ideology, for film unborn as it is has no language and speaks like an aborigine – monotonous rhetoric. Abandon aesthetics – the moving picture image without religious foundations, let alone the cathedral, the art form, starts its search for God with only the danger of accepting an architectural inherit-ance from the categorized "seven," other arts its sins, and closing its circle, stylistic circle, therefore zero. Negate technique, for film, like America, has not been discovered yet, and mechanization, in the deepest possible sense of the word, traps both beyond measuring even chances – chances are these twined searches may someday orbit about the same central negation. Let film be. It is something. . . becoming. (The above being for creator and spectator alike in searching, an ideal of anarchic religion where all are priests both giving and receiving, or rather witch doctors, or better witches, or . . . O, for the unnamable.)

And here, somewhere, we have an eye (I'll speak for myself) capable of any imagining (the only reality). And there (right there) we have the camera eye (the limitation the original liar); yet lyre sings to the mind so immediately (the exalted selectivity one wants to forget) that its strings can so easily make puppetry of human motivation (for form as finality) dependent upon attuna-tion, what it's turned to (ultimately death) or turned from (birth) or the way to get out of it (transformation). I'm not just speaking of that bird on fire (not thinking of circles) or of Spengler (spirals neither) or of any known progression (nor straight lines) logical formation (charted levels) or ideological formation (mapped for scenic points of interest); but I am speaking for possibilities (myself), infinite possibilities (preferring chaos).

And here, somewhere, we have an eye capable of any imagining. And then we have the camera eye, its lenses grounded to achieve nineteenth-century Western compositional perspective (as best exemplified by the nineteenth-century architectural conglomeration of details of the "classic" ruin) in bending the light and limiting the frame of the image just so, its standard camera and projector speed for recording movement geared to the feeling of the ideal slow Viennese waltz, and even its tripod head, being the neck it swings on, balled with bearings to permit it that Les Sylphides motion (ideal to the contemplative romantic) and virtually restricted to horizontal and vertical movements (pillars and horizon lines), a diagonal requiring a major adjustment, its lenses coated or provided with filters, its light meters balanced, and its color film manufactured, to produce that picture post card effect (salon painting) exemplified by those oh so blue skies and peachy skins.

By deliberately spitting on the lens or wrecking its focal intention, one can achieve the early stages of impressionism. One can make this prima donna heavy in performance of image movement by speeding up the motor, or one can break up movement, in a way that approaches a more direct inspiration of contemporary human eye perceptibility of movement, by slowing the motion while recording the image. One may hand hold the camera and inherit worlds of space. One may over- or under-expose the film. One may use the filters of the world, fog, downpours, unbalanced lights, neons with neurotic color temperatures, glass which was never designed for a camera, or even glass which was but which can be used against specifications, or one may photograph an hour after sunrise or an hour before sunset, those marvelous taboo hours when the film labs will guarantee nothing, or one may go into the night with a specified daylight film or vice versa. One may become the supreme trickster, with hatfuls of all the rabbits listed above breeding madly. One may, out of incredible courage, become Méliès, that marvelous man who gave even the "art of the film" its beginning in magic. Yet Méliès was not witch, witch doctor, priest, or even sorcerer. He was a nineteenth-century stage magician. His films *are* rabbits.

What about the hat? the camera? or if you will, the stage, the page, the ink, the hieroglyphic itself, the pigment shaping that original drawing, the musical and/or all other instruments for copula-and-then-procreation? Kurt Sachs talks sex (which fits the hat neatly) in originating musical instruments, and Freud's revitalization of symbol charges all contemporary content in art. Yet possession thru visualization speaks for fear-of-death as motivating force – the tomb art of the Egyptian, etc. And then there's "In the beginning," "Once upon a time," or the very concept of a work of art being a "Creation." Religious motivation only reaches us thru the anthropologist these days – viz., Frazer on a golden bough. And so it goes – ring around the rosary, beating about the bush, describing. One thread runs clean thru the entire fabric of expression – the trick-and-effect. And between those two words, somewhere, magic . . . the brush of angel wings, even rabbits leaping heavenwards and, given some direction, language corresponding. Dante looks upon the face of God and Rilke is heard among the angelic orders. Still the Night Watch was tricked by Rembrandt and Pollack was out to produce an effect. The original word was a trick, and so were all the rules of the game that followed in its wake. Whether the instrument be musical or otherwise, it's still a hat with more rabbits yet inside the head wearing it – i.e., thought's trick, etc. Even the Brains for whom thought's the world, and the word and visi-or-audibility of it, eventually end with a ferris wheel of a solar system in the middle of the amusement park of the universe. They know it without experiencing it, screw it lovelessly, find "trick" or "effect" derogatory terminology, too close for comfort, are utterly unable to comprehend "magic." We are either experiencing (copulating) or conceiving (procreating) or very rarely both are balancing in that moment of living, loving, and creating, giving and receiving, which is so close to the imagined divine as to be more unmentionable than "magic."

[. . .]

What reflects from the screen is shadow play. Look, there's no real rabbit. Those ears are index fingers and the nose a knuckle interfering with the light. If the eye were more perceptive it would see the sleight of 24 individual pictures and an equal number of utter blacknesses every second of the show. What incredible films might ultimately be made for such an eye. But the machine has already been fashioned to outwit even that perceptibility, a projector which flashes advertisement at subliminal speed to up the sale of popcorn. Oh, slow-eyed spectator, this machine is grinding you out of existence. Its electrical storms are manufactured by pure white frames interrupting the flow of the photographed images, its real tensions are a dynamic interplay of two-dimensional shapes and lines, the horizon line and background shapes battering the form of the horseback rider as the camera moves with it, the curves of the tunnel exploding away from the pursued, camera following, and tunnel perspective converging on the pursuer, camera preceding, the dream of the close-up kiss being due to the linear purity of facial features after cluttersome background, the entire film's soothing syrup being the depressant of imagistic repetition, a feeling akin to counting sheep to sleep. Believe in it blindly, and it will fool you – mind wise, instead of sequins on cheesecloth or max-manu-factured make-up, you'll see stars. Believe in it eye-wise, and the very comet of its overhead throw from projector to screen will intrigue you so deeply that its fingering play will move integrally with what's reflected, a comet-tail integrity which would lead back finally to the film's creator. I am meaning, simply, that the rhythms of change in the beam of illumination which now goes entirely over the heads of the audience would, in the work of art, contain in itself some quality of a spiritual experience. As is, and at best, that hand spreading its touch toward the screen taps a neurotic chaos comparable to the doodles it produces for reflection. The "absolute realism" of the motion picture image is a twentieth-century, essentially Western, illusion.

Global Perspectives: Filmmakers and Critics

INTRODUCTION

T HE RELATION OF RELIGION AND film is as old
as cinema itself, as the first two parts of this reader have demonstrated.
The religion–film relation is also global, taking place in small villages in East
Africa and metropolises in East Asia, at international film festivals, and in
the living rooms of families across the world.

To help chart this worldwide phenomenon, part 3, the largest of the
reader, provides readings from filmmakers and critics living and working
around the world. We have chosen excerpts from filmmakers (mainly directors) commenting on the role of religion in their lives, and in their films.
Sometimes religion is a key subject of a film, sometimes the issues raised in a
film trigger religious responses not intended by the filmmaker, and sometimes
religion is directly critiqued. We have included comments by filmmakers who
are confessionally religious, some who grew up in religious environments but
moved away from their family faith, and others who are outright hostile
to religion. Our desire is to investigate the religion–film relation from as
many perspectives as possible, and sometimes it is those outside established
religious institutions who can provide rich insights into religious life. We also
include a number of critical readings by scholars or film critics writing
about specific films, filmmakers, or regional cinemas. Our intention here is
not simply to highlight the voices of filmmakers, but also to show the truly
international dimensions of the impact of religion on film, and sometimes
scholars can offer the best insights.

Few directors or screenwriters have studied religion or theology in depth and comparatively few consciously attempt to articulate religious and theological themes through their work. Their intention is rarely, if ever, explicitly religious or theological. A large number of directors tend to express sacred, religious or theological themes without formally naming them as such. The theme emerges from the narrative because it is expressive of primal fears, aspirations, and predispositions, not because it has been consciously planted there. By attending to specific scenes, films, or directorial statements it is possible, however, to discern how even directors can express themselves like creative religious educators or theologians, despite their opposition to specific religious beliefs or practices. Directors can be seen as visual storytellers grappling with religious and theological issues in new and original ways. Their craft is neither primarily text-based nor rooted in logical arguments, but rather partly dependent upon the skilful juxtaposition of images, sounds, and dialogue to create a narrative. "I've turned from an image maker into a storyteller," German director Wim Wenders claims, "only a story can give meaning and a moral to an image."[1]

Narratives resonate with other stories, and are often given meaning by some viewers that the filmmakers or *auteurs* did not originally intend. So, for example, the story of the science fiction blockbuster *E.T.* (1982) was sometimes compared to the story of Christ: an extra terrestrial comes down from the heavens, collects a band of followers, is persecuted by the authorities, dies, and then come backs to life. This was clearly not the aim of *E.T.*'s director Steven Spielberg, who insisted that he had not intended *E.T.* to be a "spiritual parable"; but, he "admitted that the only time Melissa (one of the scriptwriters) and I sort of looked at each other and said, 'Gee, are we getting into a possibly sticky area here?' was when E.T. is revealed to the boys on the bicycles and he's wearing a white hospital robe and his 'immaculate heart' is glowing. We looked at each other at that point and said, 'This might trigger a lot of speculation.' We already knew that his coming back to life was a form of resurrection. But I'm a nice Jewish boy from Phoenix, Arizona. If I ever went to my mother and said, 'Mom, I've made this movie that's a Christian parable, what do you think she'd say?' She has a kosher restaurant on Pico and Doheny in Los Angeles."[2] As is so often the case with contemporary films the end product is the result of many different sets of hands. In the words of another biographer: "The antecedents of *E.T.* are about the most convoluted of any Spielberg film. It grew out of three scripts, four writers, six titles and two special effects wizards, every bit as much as out of the Spielbergian soul."[3] Such creative interactions and communities are behind many cinematic projects.

Directors work not in a closed study or quiet library, but amongst a large group of industry professionals. By concentrating extensively, though not exclusively, upon the director's perspective we are not suggesting that the role of other members of the team, such as the screenwriter, producer, director of photography, film editor, composer, casting director, or actor can be ignored. To focus upon the director's reflections, writings, and background, is not to ignore the inherently communal and collaborative nature of their profession, nor the economic constraints or social pressures faced by filmmakers, but it is one valuable approach to reflecting critically upon the religious significance of film production and content.

Many of the filmmakers in this section skillfully bring together diverse religious or cultural traditions in their films. For example, consider the puppet scene in *The Year of Living Dangerously* (1982). Australian journalist, Guy Hamilton (played by a youthful Mel Gibson) is introduced by his local guide Billy Kwan (played in an oscar-winning performance by Linda Hunt) to the craft of *wayang Alit*, Javanese shadow theater. As in many Peter Weir films two distinct cultures are brought together through the narrative. The Western journalist Guy is told: "to understand Java, you'll have to understand the *wayang*," and he is encouraged to look not at the puppets but at the shadows. While this scene is reminiscent of Plato's well-known story described in *The Republic* of chained prisoners in a cave who watch shadows on the wall in front of them,[4] the film itself goes some distance beyond the Western philosophical tradition, bringing a more so-called "Eastern" perspective into the cinematic conversation. Guy is told by Billy that: "the unseen is all around us, particularly here, in Java." How filmmakers from around the globe try to make the unseen seen is a topic worth careful consideration, so too is the way in which they cross religious divides and cinematic continents.

The four subheadings into which the readings are grouped here are, of course, somewhat artificial. We do not intend to impose a homogeneous ordering on these vast regions, and we are well aware of the many strong and distinct national and regional cinemas around the world. The alphabetical ordering here is chiefly for indexical reasons. Each of the four sub-sections will be introduced separately.

Perhaps the two most glaring omissions, though there are others, are from Chinese filmmakers, and comments from women filmmakers. There are reasons for this. Leaders throughout the modern Republic of China worked to eradicate religion and "superstition" from cultural productions. Concerned as they were not to appear backward to the rest of the world, governmental ideologies made it difficult to finance films with explicit religion in them. Meanwhile, intellectuals and artists, even when critical of the government, have often internalized such concerns and created works that ignore the deep impact of traditional religious structures on Chinese society. There are significant qualifications to these observations about the apparent absence of religion in Chinese cinema. In particular, recurring representations of the martial arts fighter who develops superhuman combat skills and fighting techniques through spiritual exercises. Some scholars have even suggested that such cinematic depictions of the mysterious Buddhist fighter are used to subvert Confucian and Daoist values.[5]

The lack of women filmmakers also has deep-set social, political, and religious roots. Even societies like those of Western Europe and North America that boast good gender equity have yet to promote more women filmmakers. With over two hundred films produced every year in the United States, it is staggering how few are made by women directors as we move well into cinema's second century. Recall that 2004 was the first year a woman, Sofia Coppola, was ever nominated for an Academy Award for Best Director (she won for best screenplay, not for director).[6]

Finally, it must be noted again that we in no way imagine this reader to be comprehensive. There are many good filmmakers who deal with religious issues on a regular basis, but that does not necessarily mean there is thoughtful verbal discussion to be found about these religious topics. Since we are creating a "reader," we are bound by the printed materials already available. Nevertheless, a further aim is to highlight the *lacunae* in the scholarship, and encourage others to pursue original research that develops the field in new directions.

Notes

1   Geoffrey Nowell-Smith (ed.) *The Oxford History of World Cinema*. Oxford: Oxford University Press, 1996, 625.

2   Joseph McBride, *Steven Spielberg: A Biography*. New York: Faber and Faber, 1997, 336.

3   Tony Crawley, *The Steven Spielberg Story*. London: Zomba Books, 1983, 107.

4   For an extended discussion of this story in relation to cinema see Gerard Loughlin's *Alien Sex: The Body and Desire in Cinema and Theology*. Oxford: Blackwell, 2004, 41–48, and for an excerpt from a later part of this discussion see reading 52 of this volume.

5   For more on Chinese cinema see: http://www.llc.ed.ac.uk/cinema_china/ lectures.html and in particular Joachim Gentz, "Non-action in Action: Martial Arts Landscape and Religious Concepts in Chinese film.".

6   Interesting to note, there were many prominent women filmmakers in the

1910s and 1920s in the United States, Alice Guy-Blaché and Lois Weber most prominently, but that trend disappeared by the 1930s as the major production companies took control of the industry. Worth seeing is the Kino Video collection *First Ladies: Early Women Filmmakers*. Significant here is the fact that while there were so many films made by women in early cinema, most of them were not preserved and their work is now lost to us.

PART 3.A

African and Middle-Eastern Perspectives

INTRODUCTION

IN THE PAST AFRICA HAS been seen, in the words of the author of *Black African Cinema* (1995) Nwachukwu Ukadike, as "a cinematographic desert, a filmic cul-de-sac." The current reality, as Ukadike and other African film-scholars and filmmakers have demonstrated, is far from the case. It is valuable to reflect on how film has traveled beyond its comparatively arid beginnings on a continent with over fifty nation states. Colonial Africa saw few films produced by Africans, while the making of films by locals in the French colonies was formally prohibited. In the early days of cinema, film was first primarily made and used by outsiders in Africa. As a natural successor to magic lantern slide shows, the "bioscope," as it was known in some countries, became an educative or evangelistic tool often used by foreign missionaries. Both mobile and more permanent outdoor cinemas became sites of popular entertainment. At the same time several colonial powers, observing how the cinema was being used as a tool for propaganda in Communist Russia, invested in making films for different parts of Africa. In East Africa, the Bantu Educational Kinema Experiment (BEKE) supported by the International Missionary Council, the Carnegie Trust, and the British Colonial office, was set up in 1936. In over three years it produced thirty-five 16 mm black and white films covering topics such as infant malaria, boy Scouts, and soil erosion. In 1936 and 1937 it toured around East Africa showing these films to over 100,000 people. In 1939 the Colonial Film Unit was established to persuade African viewers of the value of the Second World War. These Colonial Film Units have been criticized by several African film scholars for their idealizing of the West and their caricaturing and stereotyping of African culture and traditional religions.

It was not until the 1960s that films were produced in numbers by Africans in sub-Saharan Africa. Since the establishment in 1969 of an All African film festival, FESPACO, in Burkino Faso there has been a steady growth of cinema emerging from Africa, in particularly from Francophone countries such as Niger, Cameroon, and Mali, as well as Algeria, Morocco, and Tunisia. This movement is sometimes called the "decolonization of the gaze", which has included questioning of incoming religions to Africa. The Senegalese filmmaker, Sembene Ousmane (1923–), is often described as the father of African cinema. His film *Ceddo* (*The People*, 1977), said by many to be his masterpiece, is set at an unspecified time in the past in a Wolof-speaking village. Through a simple narrative it depicts a traditional culture attempting to resist the missionary efforts of Islam, and to a lesser extent Christianity, along with the evils of the slave-trade and the related forces of colonization. In many other films, such as *Xala* (1975), Ousmane has developed a unique style, an "anti-naturalistic acting style" in which the performers "deliver their lines slowly and clearly, reciting them rather than embodying them, almost as if they are taking part in a ritual."[1] The reading that we offer here (reading 16) reveals Ousmane's distinctive view of "the power of female solidarity" in relation to his film *Mooladé* (2004), which takes as its subject matter the practice of female circumcision. In this film, where politics, individual human rights, and religious traditions clash, we find firm attention to the local and global, where communal solidarity rises up to question traditions. Yet, significantly, this is not simply a common Western view in which the individual challenges historical authority structures and comes out triumphant; here, change is rooted in a social community.

Like Ousmane, the Malian filmmaker Cheick Oumar Sissoko (1945–) locates global, historical religious belief and struggle in local environments. This may be best seen in *La Genèse* (*Genesis*, 1999), which retells the story of Jacob, Esau, and Hamor, from the Hebrew Bible, setting the story in a vast, rocky African desert. The reading (17) reveals how Sissoko attempts cinematically to offer insights into some of the major difficulties facing the African continent. Fraternal struggles become international battles, as the story allegorically becomes both local and current, meanwhile maintaining its links to the global and historical; as Sissoko suggests in the reading, "Genesis belongs to all humanity."

In spite of the work of directors such as Sissoko and Sembene, there are several African countries which are still to produce their first full-length feature film.

In most cinemas or video shops in Africa, films from Hollywood or Bollywood continue to dominate the screens and shelves. The main exception to this is found in Nigeria and Ghana, where locally produced video films have taken the place of cinematic imports. As this is an extraordinary phenomenon we provide two readings from different viewpoints. First, Birgit Meyer, an anthropologist with extensive experience researching this subject in West Africa, reflects on how these films can be understood as "remediations" with a special relation to Pentecostal Christianity. Religion plays a highly significant role in these films, reflecting local beliefs and practices (reading 13). Second, Jolyon Mitchell then investigates the popularity of this phenomenon from a number of different perspectives (reading 14).

In the same way that West Africa has recently experienced a renaissance in local filmmaking so too have "Middle Eastern" countries, like Iran for instance. We have therefore provided several approaches to current cinema in Iran, as well as Israel and Palestine. The most recent origins of the flourishing of Iranian film are to be found in the early 1970s with the appearance of what was described as "New Iranian Cinema." While the 1978–79 Revolution saw the burning or closing of many cinemas around Iran, far from undermining the new wave of Iranian filmmaking, aspects of the Revolution appear to have contributed toward an environment in which the new cinematic movement could thrive. With the rejection of many Western films and themes, as well as poor quality dubbed "Farsi Films," filmmakers returned to their own cultural roots, drawing upon the rich Persian traditions of poetry, passion plays (rowzeh and tazieh), architecture, music, and storytelling.

There is a poetic quality which regularly focuses on the minutiae and the mundane, the everyday practices of daily life. The mosque remains a shimmering presence in the background while teenagers play in the street. Children search for lost shoes (Majid Majidi, *Children of Heaven*, 1997) or for mislaid money intended to buy a large goldfish (Jafar Panahi, *The White Balloon*, 1995). Siblings argue. Parents chide their offspring. Wives assert their independence within the constraints of violent marriage and a patriarchal society (Tahmineh Milani, *Two Women*, 1999). Women confront domestic violence or simply acquiesce to living in a masculine world (Jafar Panahi, *The Circle*, 2000).

Many of these films are located in everyday settings. A good number of recent Iranian films concentrate upon the difficulties faced by a central protagonist trying to cope with urban or village life in a rapidly changing world or simply trying to survive in the midst of difficult circumstances. In

Majid Majidi's film *The Willow Tree* (2005) a middle-aged blind man struggles after recovering his sight. Of course, some Iranian filmmakers concentrate upon idiosyncratic tales. For example, another movie is based on the true story of a man who is put on trial for impersonating a favorite film director (Abbas Kiarostami, *Close Up*, 1990). Through revealing shots of the director or camera Kiarostami often reminds viewers that they are watching a film, thereby shattering the suspension of disbelief. Kiarostami's attitude towards happiness, sadness, and Islamic culture is revealed in the reading taken from *The Iranian* (1998) and offered here (reading 11). This is part of a public conversation between the curator of the media center at Ohio State University, Bill Horrigan, and Abbas Kiarostami, where they are discussing his film *Taste of a Cherry* (1997), which highlights that even in the midst of despair life can be beautiful.

Apart from discussions about the work of Kiarostami, studies of this new wave of Iranian cinema have tended to highlight the work of directors such as Majid Majidi, Mohsen Makhmalbaf, and his daughter Samira Makhmalbaf. We provide a reading taken from a short conversation with Mohsen Makhmalbaf, the director of films such as *From Evil to God* (1984), *Once Upon a Time Cinema* (1992), and *Kandehar* (2001) (reading 12). This reflects his own vision for "art," in distinction from "religion" and "politics," though Makhmalbaf's films undoubtedly touch on all three. He describes his own movement from wanting to save others, then his country, and ultimately himself. As with many directors in Iran, the goal is to produce understated cinematic tales which highlight, subvert, and criticize social injustices. There is little religious preaching or moralizing to be found here. Rather, it is often a neo-realistic, slowed down form of cinema, where stories matter and characters develop.

There are similarities between Iranian and Arab cinema, though the distinct political situation in Palestinian and Israeli contexts inevitably shapes the cinematic narratives. For example, consider the work of Elia Suleiman, a noted, albeit young, "third cinema" director, who introduces the political realities of Israel and Palestine through everyday images of life on the streets (reading 15). Sometimes, however, these are fantastical images, as when "Santa Claus" appears in Nazareth, having been stabbed by local youths, as in *Divine Intervention*: Suleiman says, "Nazareth is the best place to stab Santa." In the midst of such humorous, cynical takes on mythological belief structures, Suleiman nonetheless approaches the importance of silence in the confrontation with deep-seated political-religious issues, not unlike that of Dreyer, Von Trier, and Bergman, in the European traditions.

From a Jewish perspective it is valuable to see Amos Gitai's (1950–) films in light of the Israel–Palestine conflict. Gitai, who has had experiences as an Israeli soldier in the 1973 Yom Kippur war and as an architectural student in the United States, explores the conflict between ancient religious traditions and modern life, and the oftentimes difficult work of maneuvering between the two. In films such as *Kadosh* (1999) and others, he explores the conflict of traditions, attempting to find a way forward into a global, interreligious age (reading 10).

Note

1   Jared Rapfogel, "The Power of Female Solidarity: An Interview with Ousmane Sembene," *Cineaste* 20 (Winter 2004), 20.

Chapter 10

Amos Gitai, with Nick James

IN A HARSH LIGHT

Nick James: Which particular community does *Kadosh* focus on?

Amos Gitai: All the exteriors were shot in the quarter of Mea Shearim, which is the orthodox section of Jerusalem. Theologically, since in Judaism you don't have a human representative of God on earth and there is no centralised authority, it's a rather anarchic structure. So you have a lot of people who claim to be the real representative. There's a very large spectrum from secular Israelis to semi-religious and national-religious – the last are quite territorial. The community that *Kadosh* is describing is a synthesis of different traits.

Nick James: How familiar were you with these people before you had the idea for the film?

Amos Gitai: I did a lot of research but Mea Shearim itself is a very powerful gesture. When we walk around Paris or Rome it takes time to recompose for ourselves how the streets might have looked in another century. Here you walk into history and it's intact. There are posters that say, "Tourists are not welcome here."

Nick James: And it's nothing like a theme-park experience?

Amos Gitai: Not at all. It's a living community, maybe a gesture these people made to preserve an image of the communities of Eastern Europe that don't exist any more. You really have a sense of what these 16th- or 17th-century communities looked like: the habits, rituals and everything.

Nick James: Was there anything about their lifestyle that appealed to you?

Amos Gitai: The fact that they don't want to be integrated as another landmark of the city. Also I had a curiosity about the text, the Talmud. It's a complete script that regulates all the actions of human beings around the clock.

Nick James: You exclude the depiction of work from the film.

Amos Gitai: Most of the orthodox don't work. A big part of the community is studying the Torah and the Talmud and if there's work it's done by the women, like in the shop in the film. One of the issues with any film that has the potential for melodrama is how to avoid the exoticisation of what you're looking at. How did you deal with that?

It took a very long period of study with the actors. I don't like actors to act mechanically, I don't like them to arrive a few days before the shoot, learn their lines and just do it. I see the scenario as more organic and I like to modify it by questioning.

One of the problems with contemporary architecture is that it's planned in the architect's office and then strictly executed. So when we come to a hillside we erase it because it wasn't planned for. And sometimes the hazard, the coincidence of the hillside would create a much better building. One of the reasons I left architecture for cinema is that the cinema preserves an artisan quality and the process allows us not to be hermetic, so we can write the script, the plan, but when we get to the site it's composed of people, actors, sets and so on. We should apply a continual process of adaptation until we get the best from what we have.

So when I cast a film I look to the inner identity of the actors for what they can bring me from their heritage and thoughts. Meital Barda, who plays the elder sister, is from a religious family and some of her memories are included. Yoram Hattab, who plays Meir, came in one day with a laptop computer and a complete CD-Rom of the Talmud, and we found certain decrees which we integrated. What fascinates me about this process is that it's a continuous act. There was a rabbi with whom I discussed matters, and when he came to see the couple's bedroom he said, "No. You've put the bookshelf next to the bed. That's not possible."

Nick James: How much was he allowed to know about what you were doing?

Amos Gitai: He didn't want to read the script because he wanted to keep it ambiguous. Even finding him was a process. I was looking for a working-class rabbi. I asked someone who was fixing the heating system in my apartment in Tel Aviv about his rabbi and he said, "No. He's not good. He just came out of jail." Then a carpenter said, "I have a rabbi, but he's from Tripoli," and this was the guy. He had a very concrete attitude. The actors did evening prayers every day for three months because I wanted them to be in command of the nuances, the details, the choreography of the gestures.

Nick James: Are there many women in Rivka's situation?

Amos Gitai: There are some. Women in this society are restricted to the role of reproduction. They don't study the Bible – which by the way is a common thing to all the three monotheistic religions, where women accept more modern attitudes but are denied authority in the religious circle.

Nick James: And there's no sex education at all?

Amos Gitai: Not in the way we mean it. Maybe to soften my answer I should say that perhaps during the ritual bathing they receive some instruction.

Nick James: What about the orthodox attitude to male infertility? Is there a blanket refusal to believe it exists, or is it just never spoken about?

Amos Gitai: I'm not sure it's even a refusal. I spoke to some doctors who are active in the orthodox community and they told me they cannot perform sperm tests because masturbation is forbidden.

Nick James: But they've found another way of doing it?

Amos Gitai: They are trying to find another way of doing it but it's not an easy operation. In a very patriarchal relationship you tend to blame the woman initially, even if eventually you know it's the man.

Nick James: You co-wrote *Kadosh*. How did the organic process work in screenwriting?

Amos Gitai: It was the idea of the French producer Michel Propper, who also worked on Peter Brook's *The Mahabharata*. He introduced me to Eliette Abecassis, an observant Jewish writer in France. Eliette was sometimes caught in the contradiction between being observant and being a woman.

Nick James: Does one of you do a draft and then the other?

Amos Gitai: Eliette wrote a very strong treatment of 40 pages, the skeleton of the narrative. Then she wrote some of the more powerful scenes which remain in the film – mainly the relations between the sisters. Then came my work with the actors, and recomposing the structure of the script, which happened sometimes during the shoot or later.

Nick James: You rigorously avoid anything that tends towards a representation of the transcendental.

Amos Gitai: Judaism is composed of a very hermetic script which defines every intimate gesture of every hour of the day. Individual and collective prayers punctuate this schedule. But formal requests are minimal – if you look for instructions as to how to build a synagogue you won't find them. Some synagogues are on the second floor of an existing building – they're not even a structure apart.

Nick James: Is that an expression of a particular kind of faith or of the circumstances of Judaism through the centuries?

Amos Gitai: It's both the nomadic nature of the religion and the fact that perhaps the greatest traumas in collective memory are connected to the destruction of a temple – by the Romans, or by the Syrians, or by the Babylonians. It's always associated with the loss of sovereignty, and this loss is likewise associated with persecution and suffering. Hebrew is a strange mixture of the physical and the metaphysical. Take, for instance, the King James Bible. The translators had a problem because most of the terms in Hebrew are dualistic – there's the same word for sky and heaven, for instance. The King James translation always privileged the metaphysical, so you lose the concrete nature of the text. I like the resonance between this archaic language and the problem of adopting it into a modern state, a language of taxis and discotheques. In a film like *Kadosh* there are different layers of language that aren't always apparent to the foreign spectator.

Nick James: You've said you like a shot to continue until everything that's there can be read and only then do you cut. That's a very low-budget way of making films, yet you had the luxury of three months of preparation.

Amos Gitai: Budgets are really about choices. I like a budget that's not too high so I can retain the liberty to do things financiers don't want if they invest large amounts. But one must make the right decisions about where to spend the money. Take the director of photography: I showed him the sets, which are not enormous, and I wanted to keep their dense quality, and he said, "If you want that I need a Panavision camera, because they have short lenses so you can keep the small spaces and not glue the actors to the walls." So he gets the Panavision camera but I have to make economies elsewhere.

Nick James: What about the look of the film?

Amos Gitai: As an ex-architect I like the anarchistic and decentralised composition of space in the synagogue. When you walk in, it doesn't use elements of shrines or temples that impose the existence of God on you. It's composed in an anecdotal manner: you see plastic cups, a faucet for water, a used couch, maybe somebody sleeping there. This kind of composite space is very inviting.

Renato Berta, the director of photography, and I leaned a lot on natural lighting. We used the violence of the natural light in the Middle East. Sometimes in Tel Aviv you see old ladies covering their faces with newspapers. For people who grew up in Eastern Europe this hostile bombardment of light can be more threatening than the political situation or the possibility of war. Jerusalem is situated exactly on the cusp between typical Mediterranean hills and the cliffs of the desert which are absolutely dry. One kilometre makes this transition. Go west and you see olive trees, the classical Mediterranean; go east and it's cliffs and the dramatic landscape of the desert. This meeting point makes the light of Jerusalem extremely powerful in a magical way and we wanted to keep this context.

Chapter 11

Abbas Kiarostami, with Bill Horrigan

IN DIALOGUE WITH KIAROSTAMI

Horrigan: *Taste of Cherry* is your most recent film and we will talk a little bit about that. Maybe we should begin with the amazing spectacle when the film won the award at the Cannes festival. There was the issue of the uncertainty about the film getting shown. What was that all about?

Kiarostami: When I was at the Cannes festival and was awarded the prize, Catherine Deneuve came forward to give it to me. As a tradition in that ceremony, she hugged and kissed me. As you can imagine, such a demonstration of affection in public would have been an absolute disaster in Iran! Immediately after that event, I called my son in Tehran. He told me that I should not come back for a while because things did not look good after that disastrous kiss. So, I stayed for a week and when I went back I had to avoid the welcoming audience and go out of the back door. One of the fortunate things, though, was that this event coincided with the elections of President Khatami and so the political atmosphere was changing in Iran. As a result, it didn't take on the kind of significance that it could have without the political and social changes at the time. Nevertheless the film has not been shown in Iran yet, but it will be soon!

Horrigan: Is that primarily because it is about suicide?

Kiarostami: Partially so. It is partially due to the subject of the film, which is suicide. This could have been an issue but fortunately it did not become as problematic as it could have been since all religions view it as a taboo, a sinful act. The movie should be viewed, as I have been talking about it in many hours in the past few months, as a way of discovering taboos and dealing with them.

Why are they there? The opportunity to talk about these taboos, explore what they are and why they exist, has given me a new outlook. It is the role of the art to discover, question, and expose these taboos for what they are and what they are worth – what we are told as a child not to do and what we consequently do not do as an adult.

[. . .]

Mahdi: It is often said that there is a negative tone to the Iranian culture emphasizing the negative aspects of life like death and fatalism. But this clip [from *Taste of Cherry*] despite its apparent subject of death displays a positive way of thinking about life. Mr. Badie seems to be as much concerned about the way he is going to die than whether he could die. This represents a lot more positive thinking than we can expect from a man ready to die. To what extent is this way of thinking becoming widespread in Iran? Are we seeing a change?

Kiarostami: What you are referring to is basically the Islamic culture. The Iranian culture does not have that kind of emphasis. This negative emphasis has a permanent place in the Islamic culture where the crying and grief, in which Muslim people have been historically engaged, are very significant. These elements have carried the religion through time and are part of what keeps Islam alive.

It should be said that this positive way of looking at things is not necessarily related to culture – I see this as an intrinsic issue in one's individual outlook. Happiness and sadness are intricately tied. Beneath any layer of despair, there is hope and a reach out for happiness. At the same time, beneath any kind of happiness there is a layer of anxiety and despair. So I see this as a cycle of life, happiness and despair go with one another and not as separate. This man could not have enjoyed that fruit so much if it wasn't for the despair connected with the experience. As you saw in the film clip, the man had indicated that in the depths of darkness he saw the light at the end of the tunnel. So thus, he came to discover that life is beautiful when he was so desperate and exhausted of options. This is not connected to culture, this is a universal phenomenon. Realities generate their own opposite and this must be viewed in a dialectical way. At the depth of sadness one seeks for happiness and at the height of happiness one has to court the reality of sadness.

[. . .]

Question: I have two questions. The ending of this movie, *Taste of Cherry* had me very baffled. Even in your other films, which I love, there are parts that I do not understand. But this part in particular bothered me because I didn't understand it. What is supposed to happen? Your ending leaves us in a blank. Why do you have a scene in which Mr. Badie is smoking a cigarette after he committed suicide? That is my first question. My second question is related to politics. Obviously a lot of films have been made about Iran that have become the great films of the nineties just like Chinese movies were the greats of the eighties. It seems to me like a lot of great art is coming out of oppressive cultures or regimes so that while the Westerners can praise their art they condemn their cultures. How much of this factor influences your work and would you be the same person, would your films be the same, if you were making films in the West?

Kiarostami: I start with the second part of your question. I like to use the phrase restrictive to describe the conditions I work under rather than oppressive and I understand that oppressive means many different things under different contexts but for us as artists and filmmakers what we are dealing with are the realities of restrictions and I like to approach it from that angle. I look at these restrictions not in the context of the film alone but in the broader context of life. For me these restrictions exist everywhere and have always been there. Life in the East has never been without them. We have to always live within certain boundaries. Life is the combination and movement between restriction and freedom – the field of action is limited, the field of power is limited, when we were kids we were always told what we could do and what we couldn't and how far we could go in doing things we could.

The best example I can give for this concept is when our teachers told us to do a composition for the class. When he gave us a topic, we would write about that topic and come up with something worthwhile. But when he did not specify the topic and left us free to choose our own, we usually couldn't come up with something worth writing about. We needed to be told what the boundaries and restrictions were. This has been the nature of our society and has been replicated in the realities of our film industry. For instance, during the first four years of the Iranian revolution, there was a great deal of chaos in the film industry because not many rules were set yet. Interestingly enough, most of the Iranian movie-makers didn't produce much during this time though a great deal could have been done. No one used the opportunity because everyone was waiting to find out what the restrictions were!

Most of the time we seek an excuse for running away from the responsibility. Restrictions give us this kind of excuse. Therefore, unfortunately, we seek energy from these boundaries set for us. I don't want to imply that these limitations are good and should be there, but we have been brought up with these and it is in our mentality. This is not limited to my profession – it's in every profession, creativity is a necessity and limitation makes people more creative. I have a friend who is an architect. He tells me that he is at his best professionally when he designs structures for odd lots because these lands do not fit into the normal patten and he has to work within a great deal of limitations. So, he must be creative and he enjoys this. It is these restrictions that provide an opportunity for people to be creative.

Now, I like to answer the first question: I understand the difficulty you have comprehending the last scene of this movie. I sympathize with you. But this has been deliberate on my part. In *Taste of Cherry* I have tried to keep a distance between my spectator and the protagonist. I didn't want spectators emotionally involved in this film. In this film, I tell you very little about Mr. Badie, I tell you very little about what his life is about, why he wanted to commit suicide, what his story is. I didn't want the spectators to get engaged in those aspects of his life. For that purpose I had to keep Mr. Badie away from the audience. So he is a distant actor in a way. First I thought to end the movie at the point when he lay down on his grave but later I changed my mind. I was uncomfortable to end it at that point because I was very concerned, and am always concerned, about my spectators. I do not want to take them hostage. I do not want to take their emotions hostage. It is very easy for a filmmaker to control the emotions of spectators but I do not like that. I do not want to see my audience as innocent children whose emotions are easily manipulable.

I was afraid that if I ended the movie where Mr. Badie lay down on his grave the spectator would be left with a great deal of sadness. Even though I didn't think the scene was really that sad, I was afraid that it would come out as such. For that reason I decided to have the next episode where we have the camera running as Mr. Badie was walking around. I wanted to remind spectators that this was really a film and that they shouldn't think about this as a reality. They should not become involved emotionally. This is much like some of our grandmothers who told us stories, some with happy and some with sad endings. But they always at the end would have a Persian saying which went like this "but after all it is just a story!"

[. . .]

Kiarostami: The very last episode reminds me of the continuation of life, that life goes on, and here the audience is confronted with the reality they had hoped that Mr. Badie would be alive and there he is a part of nature and nature still continues and life goes on even without Mr. Badie. And if one could really think about being or not being present in life, or if one thinks about it in terms of the real implication of such presence, one might not in fact engage in committing suicide at all. The person committing suicide might think that s/he is taking revenge from the society, nature, life, powers to be, and so on. But s/he doesn't realize that after a suicide life still goes on and things stay the way they are. I could interpret this in a different way. If my audience is as creative as

I imagine them to be, they can take this in a variety of interpretations and I can sit here and every time make a different interpretation of it, as every time one can creatively reinterpret the reality.

Chapter 12

Mohsen Makhmalbaf

ONCE UPON A FILMMAKER
Conversation with Mohsen Makhmalbaf

Hamid Dabashi: Let me restate my question. What *does* morally and intellectually nourish you as an artist who is obviously concerned with the fate of our society? For example, in *Gabbeh*, which is a film in celebration of life, what provided the moral and intellectual energy for that work?

Mohsen Makhmalbaf: It's hard for me to say – I'm too much inside the matter itself. I can't offer you some manifesto with a list of my demands. I can only give you a summary of my feelings about our predicament. I think that the Iranian people must, on their own and for themselves, pursue a more rational end, not an emotional end. The duality, the schizophrenia of Iranians, in being one thing in public and another in private, exists because our national character has not yet been fully constituted. We can be happy, but one cannot yet be sure that we are happy because of the envy of the rest of the world, or because of an innate inner joy. I see happiness as a right. I think that it is a human right to be joyful. The person who makes a dark, realistic film in India is wasting his time. Gandhi, in the large scheme of things, did very little. Socialism has also failed. Many things must yet change in India before the people's lives become better . . . So why should the people be depressed by movies like that? They must be allowed to have some pleasure in life. The person who has had to sell his body for a morsel of food – you want to make a film for him about social justice? What is he supposed to do after seeing that film? Kill the guy sitting next to him? It's far too simplistic to see films as answering these larger questions. These problems are so complex. I am moved by the problems of humanity, you know, and the meaning of life for me is not just in living for oneself, but in living for everyone else. That's called humanity. However, these problems don't have clear-cut answers – one of the things I am trying to do is speak of relativism in a society that has individualistic and fundamentalist tendencies. As for those who want to follow me instead of someone else, I will do all I can to dissuade them from blindly following me. I teach thinking, thinking for one's self, and I don't want any followers.

In conclusion, in choosing from among religion, politics, and art, I choose art. In the same sense that art has instructed and educated me, I feel that my own responsibility is to continue to educate myself through art, since I thereby become more knowledgeable . . . My hope is that the viewer of my work for an hour and a half will during this time, to a small extent, breathe in an air which is somewhat different from that in which he or she lives. If successful, this will be no more than a very small, almost insignificant, achievement. I don't believe that I am doing anything very significant. But I can do nothing else, and I must do something. But the significance of what I do is not very important to me. Its nature, its quality, is what is important to me . . . My influence is small, and I influence no one more than I influence myself. But, naturally, some people are affected by what I do, in the same way that I am affected by Sepehri. And perhaps some people will be influenced by those whom I affect. But I don't think that I am in any way changing the world. Any person who has tried to take the responsibility of the world upon himself has done nothing but corrupt it in the end. Instead, I criticize myself every day, I try to break myself every day. I am a filmmaker, and I hope that nothing I say will ever lead to an assassination, or to someone being killed in defending what I have said. A single human life is still more valuable to me than all of cinema.

We filmmakers are here only to illuminate, to bring joy to life. All I seek is that, after seeing a film of mine, a person feels a little happier, and acts with a little more kindness towards the world. I don't think that cinema can hope to do much more. But even this little is enough to fulfill my ambitions, which are to a great extent due to historical circumstances. I aspire to be a real person, rather than to represent some ideal, and that's why my films tend to be more realistic than idealistic, although idealism is certainly part of the reality of life, its joys and pains. As for religion, I accept God, in my heart. But I would never want to try to persuade someone else to accept him. This is a personal matter. The things which attract us to the world are the details of living. The prophets of religions all have come to tell us just that.

When, as a child, I started going to the mosque, I wanted to save humanity. After growing a little older, I wanted to save my country; now, I think, I make films in order to save myself. With films I can create a representation of myself that I can then examine, and say "Where have I come to now?" I can see where I have problems, what things I wish to change. I make mirrors, then, to see myself. For example, when I watch the scene in *The Peddler* in which a sheep is slaughtered, I become enraged at myself. I begin to wonder whether the film was worth the life of that one sheep. Or in *Boycott*, someone plucks the wings off a butterfly. I go mad when I see that. I hate it. I've edited it out. Not that I'm not committing injustices every day. By simply walking, I may kill numerous ants. What I'm saying, though, is that I'm interested in changing myself rather than anyone else – not that I'm against others changing. I just don't know what the truth is, so how can I play the soothsayer and try to convince others to change?

There is a wonderful fable that the truth is a mirror that shattered as it fell from the hand of God. Everyone picked up a piece of it, and each decided that the truth was what he saw reflected in his fragment rather than realizing that truth had become fragmented among them all. In my opinion, everyone is confronted by their own particular truth, but there is no need to be too worried about that. People who live under all sorts of stress and tribulations get by and go on living. I simply want people to have hope while they live. And we can all choose our own way of living. Shamlu writes in a poem, "This long road . . . with all of this faith in one's own road." We should have faith in our own road. I don't want to tell anyone to follow mine, to waste people's time with my opinions. A friend of mine once said that certain poets waste the time of words. I replied that certain clerics waste the time of knowledge. And revolutionaries can waste the time of the people. People will find their own ways. There is a peddler you can hear when he calls out his wares in the street. He sells trinkets. Occasionally, he swindles a few people, and he is swindled from time to time. At night he goes home bringing food for his children, and sleeps beside his neighbors. He lives in the depths of reality. For him, life is about washing a dish. About being a small shopkeeper, or working for a pittance. It's all those things that are worth living for. That's all.

Chapter 13

Birgit Meyer

RELIGIOUS REMEDIATIONS
PENTECOSTAL VIEWS IN GHANAIAN VIDEO-MOVIES

S INCE THE BEGINNING of the 1990s one can discern an increasing, explicit alignment of video-films and Pentecostal perspectives in Ghana. Democratization and the liberalization of mass media offered unprecedented possibilities for Pentecostal-charismatic churches to appear in public. By skillfully making use of newly available media technologies – often in hi-tech church-run media studios – these churches (in contrast to more orthodox Protestant churches and the Catholic church) seek to address new followers. Pentecostalism's deliberate use of audio-visual technologies indicates an almost seamless articulation of the religious quest for being able to look beyond the level of mere appearance to the possibilities of new media. At the same time, the adoption of these media into practices of religious mediation marks a significant rearticulation of Christianity in the era of technological reproducibility, instigating new modes of belief that rely on mass membership, spectacle, and a voyeuristic concern with the demonic.

The obsession to stage spectacular struggles against demonic forces for a mass audience is a central point of convergence between video-films and Pentecostal-charismatic churches. Pentecostalism has successfully absorbed popular forms of grassroots Christianity that place a strong emphasis on Satan and the demons that serve him. These demons are held to be behind the gods worshipped in the context of local religious traditions and the power of witch-craft, but also encompass new spirits, such as Mami Water, the erotic goddess at the bottom of the ocean who seduces people with sex and commodities. In the Pentecostal perspective, such demons are responsible for the hardships and problems in everyday life, and thus to be fought by the power of the Christian God. In other words, the obsession with demonic forces is positioned in a dualistic frame of God and Devil. As their struggle, though shaping the material world, by and large takes place in the 'realm of the spiritual', Pentecostals feel compelled to make visible what happens in that realm and to fight a spiritual war. In Pentecostal-charismatic practice, much emphasis is placed on the need to reveal the operations of the powers of darkness. Making demonic forces visible is a necessary device in the fight against them.

To my knowledge, the first movie that explicitly took up Pentecostal views is *Deliverance from the Powers of Darkness*, which spectacularly visualizes how a witch, in the course of becoming a born again Christian, is exorcized from her links with demonic forces, many of which she has embodied spiritually and is made to vomit out. This movie not only offers a visual supplement to Pentecostal-charismatic exorcism practices, but also to the Nigerian preacher Emmanuel Eni's famous, widely circulating tract 'Delivered from the Powers of Darkness', that raised the popularity of Pentecostalism throughout Africa, including Ghana. The filmmaker, director and producer Sam Bea told me that he had first seen this film appear on a white wall, and that pastors had assured him that this had been a God-sent vision. Offering spectacular scenes featuring demonic forces and at the same time asserting the superiority of the Christian God over traditional powers, this movie signaled a shift from spectacular depictions of occult forces towards the incorporation of this kind of spectacle into a Christian dualistic frame in Ghanaian films. Although this film met the protest of established filmmakers and intellectuals, who were not only worried about the endorsement of popular 'superstitions' but also about the celebration of Christianity and demonization of local religious traditions, the 'remediation' of Pentecostal views became a characteristic feature of Ghanaian films. The link with Pentecostalism was more or less outspoken, ranging from an explicit focus on the spiritual war of God and Satan to showing divine power at work in the midst of the profanity of everyday life. The bottom line was filmmakers' realization that a film critiquing Christianity and celebrating local cultural heritage might do well in international festivals such as at FESPACO [Panafrican Film and Television Festival of Ouagadougou] in Burkina Faso, but would surely flop in the local market and hence destroy one's business. They found at least some positive reference to Christianity to be unavoidable. Conversely, the dualism of God and Satan allowed for spectacular representations of occult forces and stunning special effects, provided they were marked as demonic and hence inferior to the Christian God.

This trend has been very much enhanced with the arrival of Nigerian video-films in the Ghanaian market in the late 1990s, which thrive on similar plots, but put remarkably more emphasis on demonic forces, involving computer-made special effects, violence, and the smashing power of God, and which, as Ghanaian actors working on Nigerian film sets and Ghanaian viewers assert, look 'terribly real'. A great number of Nigerian films are produced by Pentecostal churches, which use the medium to attract believers. Having to live up to the new standards set by these Nigerian movies (which are usually made with more money, and hence superior in terms of acting, set design and camera work, in addition to being able to circumvent the strict standards of the film censorship board to which Ghanaian video-movies are to be submitted), Ghanaian filmmakers realized even more the need to satisfy audience expectations, rather than bother about intellectuals' critique of misrepresenting local religious traditions. And hence video-filmmakers, irrespective of their personal conviction, developed modes of depicting the spiritual realm in film that mimicked pastors' oral accounts about this realm. Substituting the eye of God with the camera, many movies were (and still are) framed as Christian revelations and made to remediate Pentecostal concerns in the medium of video. Invoking a Christian frame – articulated through Bible quotes or statements as 'Thank you Jesus!' or 'Glory to God' – video-filmmakers strive to make their movies exceed mere fiction and make believe. In order to appear as genuine revelations of divine power, however, audio-visual representations of divine and demonic power need to be authorized as authentic by the audiences. By explicitly addressing them as Christian viewers in search of revelation, calling upon the Bible to give credence to the film (and by the same token actualizing the Bible), and remediating familiar Pentecostal views, video-filmmakers try to assure that audiences are tuned in such a way that this authorization actually occurs.

Despite these deliberate attempts to transfer Pentecostal views and practices onto the screen, it would be mistaken to assume that video-films fully converge with Pentecostalism. It is important to keep in mind that video-filmmakers, in order to keep the business going, need to attract large audiences. Writing off filmmakers' appeal to popular belief as 'mere' business, however, would be too simple. Such a view suggests an irreconcilable distinction between business as profit-oriented and belief as sincere. It is important to realize that Pentecostal-charismatic churches are run deliberately in a business-like fashion. As the attraction of a mass-membership is key to their survival in the highly competitive religious market, these churches, in their own way, also have to make sure they appeal to a broader public. As is the case with video-films, Pentecostal-charismatic media ministries also appeal to audio-visual mass media so as to secure popular support. Certainly in regard to the spectacular representation of miracles in the context of televised church services and prayer sessions, a striking elective affinity can be discerned between video-filmmakers' and pastors' attempts to use audio-visual technologies so as to make people believe. Both the video-film phenomenon and Pentecostal-charismatic churches are part and parcel of a broader process in which belief and spectatorship, religion and mass entertainment, being born again and making money, are becoming inextricably entangled.

In this sense, video-movies, remediating popular views that are heavily leaning towards Pentecostalism, though not entirely controlled by Pentecostal leaders, are an unavoidable reality to which pastors, too, have to relate. Here we get a glimpse of a paradox: in the course of the popularization of Pentecostal views that goes along with its spread into a Christian mass culture, it is increasingly difficult for Pentecostal pastors to control and streamline popular Pentecostal religiosity. In contrast to more orthodox churches which are organized around the model of congregations that are localized in particular areas and supervised by a pastor or priest, Pentecostal-charismatic Christianity is much more mass oriented. Though omnipresent in public space, this brand of Christianity faces the problem of how to effectively claim religious authority over an ever expanding, dispersed mass audience.

Blurred boundaries

The closeness of the video scene and popular Pentecostal Christianity that I sought to highlight through the notion of remediation also figures in the perceived blurring of boundaries between film and everyday life. This is a central topos in the world of video-filmmaking. I heard numerous accounts, proudly told over and over again, of lead actors being addressed by viewers in town in terms of the role they played. Similarly, video-filmmakers recounted with much pleasure how people took for real their computer-produced special effects, which took a substantial part of the budget, and were the film's key attraction points. Filmmaker Socrate Safo told me how he listened to a radio program about witchcraft, in which people phoning in referred to Ghanaian films so as to prove that Satan truly exists and to explain how witchcraft works. Although filmmakers tend to be bemused about ordinary people's inclination to believe what is deliberately construed as make believe, there is more at stake than the assertion of a neat distinction between false beliefs about occult forces and true knowledge about film technology, or of the idea that the latter will eventually replace the former. Actually, as I experienced over and over again, video-filmmaking is situated betwixt and between the technologically facilitated representation of demonic forces and the fear that these representations become real – a kind of reality effect not confined to the film as a finished product, but also at work in making films.

The point is not simply that spectators would unmask the appearance of occult images as false once they were enlightened about the computer technology that made it possible to depict occult forces and magical powers. Filmmaker Michael Akwetey Kanyi recounted how an old acquaintance who had seen some of his films asserted: 'you have occult powers!' How otherwise could he be able to show a person transform into somebody else, imprison miniature doubles of a bewitched person in a pot in the wardrobe, or let witches fly through the air on a carpet? While in this perspective a filmmaker is attributed with occult powers, a competing perspective views filmmakers as similar to pastors, in that they are found to have the power to look into the invisible – a capacity, as we saw, that is a prerequisite for claiming spiritual power (and in fact, power tout court). Rather than standing in opposition to spiritual power, technology is here called upon so as to affirm this power and make it materialize.

All in all, as in so many other settings, the explanation that extraordinary powers can be depicted thanks to computer-produced effects fails to disenchant these images and turn them into mere representations. Echoing Jacques Derrida's observation that '[t]he critique of televisual mystifications does not prevent them from operating, and from doing so in the form of the spectral noema of "making present" ',[1] here too spectators' knowledge that video-images of demonic forces are produced with the help of audio-visual technologies and special effects does not disenchant them. Instead, spectators are inclined – certainly if they identify as Christians – to authenticate these images as revelations of the invisible powers which hold such a central place in the popular imagination, and as a consequence, in Pentecostal Christianity. Knowledge about technological devices producing special effects and belief in the existence of demonic forces easily go hand in hand, or even appear to enforce each other. 'Technology shows what is there,' would be a common remark. This reality effect occurs because video-films quite successfully appeal to audiences so as to authorize video-images as authentic. In short, film technology itself is considered not to stand in contrast to, but to be fully consonant with supernatural power. This pertains not only to video-films, but to the use of audio-visual technologies at large. Certainly in Pentecostal circles, as indicated above, one may notice a skilled and effective use of modern mass media, which are called upon so as to assert – and indeed produce – the pastor's charisma, or even his power to perform public miracles. TV and video are called upon so as to provide evidence for the truthfulness of spiritual power.

Interestingly, the mediated images of demonic forces do not only have a kind of reality effect for spectators who are outside the context of filmmaking and only see the finished product. Also on the set the visualizations of occult forces and the forces themselves were perceived to come uneasily close. The

camera, and other devices, were viewed as technologies operating in accordance with an inbuilt logic, yet at the same time there was the belief that spirits
or demonic forces are able to work on the camera, so as to stop it, or make
it impossible to make certain shots. Actors, certainly if they were staunch
Christians, were convinced of the necessity to depict the operations of demonic
powers, and yet they felt incredibly vulnerable when doing so, and sought to
protect themselves through prayers. Likewise, set designers felt insecure about
setting up artificial shrines, since, according to the popular imagination,
numerous spirits roam about in the sky, seeking suitable abodes to inhabit. As
Nina Nwabueze, a set designer from Nigeria working in Ghana put it: 'Here the
belief is still there that there are spirits in the sky. When you create an idol, they
can get into the idol.' This is reminiscent of the suspicion of the image pointed
out above. Filmmaking, though defined by producing images, seems not
beyond this suspicion. Paradoxically, movies are made to mimic Pentecostal
vision as a power to make demonic forces appear, yet in the very process of
mimicking, these powers may actually come true. Therefore, every day on set
begins and ends with prayer.

Conclusion

This article has been devoted to exploring the interface of film and religion
through an empirical study of the entanglement of video-films and Pentecostal
Christianity in Ghana. For the sake of staying in the business, video-filmmakers
mimic Pentecostal modes in such a way that audiences are inclined to authorize
these visualizations as authentic. In this setting, film is not confined to mere
representation and the sphere of fake and illusion, but involves an unstable
relationship between representing demonic forces and their actual presence.
Rather than merely representing the visible and invisible dimensions of reality,
video-films embody reality, thereby breaking open the distinction between
representation and presence, as well as that between media and immediacy or
authenticity.

Video-movies' remediations of Pentecostal beliefs and practices give rise to
what I propose to call a 'techno-religious realism'. This techno-religious realism, I would like to stress, does not merely derive from the power of films to
'spontaneously appeal to his [the spectator's] sense of belief', their intrinsic
capacity to 'speak to us with the accents of true evidence, using the argument that "It is so",' but above all from combining films' capacity to appear
'believable' with an appropriation of Pentecostal belief resources.[2] In video-
films technologies of make believe and spectators' desire to believe in, and
receive visual evidence for, the power of God easily go together. Pentecostal

beliefs and technology act so much in support of each other that they become more or less indistinguishable. This being so, it is impossible to maintain a stable distinction between film and religion.

One of the most striking features of this techno-religious realism concerns the fact that video-movies' remediations of Pentecostal views do not so much claim to erase the medium and offer immediate access to the spiritual world out there in the dark. These remediations rather produce, to invoke Bolter and Grusin,[3] a kind of 'hypermediacy' that is generated by merging the medium of video with practices of religious mediation. Audio-visual technologies are mingled ingeniously with the Pentecostal quest for divine vision and fear of being seen by the devil (and the concomitant awareness of the tension between the need to depict the demonic so as to fight it and the potential danger of the image). This mingling suggests not only that these technologies are inalienable parts of Pentecostal mediation, but also that they are highly suited to be vested with spiritual power. Ultimately, this mingling breaks down the distinction between techniques of representation, on the one hand, and the presence of the powers depicted, on the other. This distinction is called upon, yet at the same time perceived to be transcended in the practice of video-filmmaking. By the same token video-filmmaking implodes the distinction between media and authenticity that characterizes, according to Bolter and Grusin, a naïve stance towards transcendent immediacy that views authenticity as a privileged origin situated beyond the sphere of media and remediation. By contrast, in the world of video-movies the authorization of film images as immediate and authentic depends on audio-visual technologies.

Obviously, this use of media for the sake of making appear a supposedly dark, invisible realm, and the concomitant transcendence of the rift between religion and technology implied by it, is not specific to the Ghanaian context. The techno-religious realism outlined here should therefore not be mistaken as an indication for the failure to understand the true nature of media technology as a neutral device. Instead, the particular use of media in the service of religious vision reveals an understanding that has much in common with postmodern practice and analysis. Far from more or less truthfully reflecting a world still held to exist out there, media are able to articulate a reality that features as convincingly true. Here immediacy is achieved not by virtue of the alleged absence of media, but instead is made to depend on them. The fact that media technologies are called upon to visualize the very religious views in the name of which these technologies are to be authorized as authentic, challenges all too simple views of religion and film, and urges us to devote far more attention to their interface than has been the case so far.

Notes

1 Jacques Derrida, ' "Above All, No Journalists!" ', in Hent de Vries and Samuel Weber (eds) *Religion and Media*, Stanford, California: Stanford University Press, 2001, 87.

2 Christian Metz, *Film Language. A Semiotics of the Cinema*, New York: Oxford University Press, 1974, 4.

3 Jay David Bolter and Richard Grusin, *Remediation. Understanding New Media*, Cambridge, MA: MIT Press, 1999.

Chapter 14

Jolyon Mitchell

TOWARDS AN UNDERSTANDING OF THE POPULARITY OF WEST AFRICAN VIDEO FILM

IT **IS AN** unforgettable experience to sit in a packed cinema or video house in Accra and watch a locally produced Ghanaian or Nigerian video film. The audience is rarely entirely silent, and often actively cheers, boos or prays out loud for the characters.[1] This experience stands in sharp contrast with sitting in a Western multiplex watching a Hollywood film, where the audience is usually almost entirely silent. The peace is occasionally disturbed by a cough, or the rustle of sweet wrappers or the crunch of popcorn. Any talking is normally 'shushed' and exclamations are rare, the exception being laughter during comic moments or screams at sudden surprises in horror-movies or thrillers. The silencing of the Western audience is a fascinating story well told elsewhere. Appearances, however, can be deceptive. This comparative silence does not mean that audiences are necessarily entirely passive. Research by Hoover (2006), for example, illustrates how the opposite is in fact the case.[2] Audiences actively weave complex patterns of meaning on the basis of the media that they consume. Nevertheless, precisely which films are viewed and the cultural context in which they are watched remains a significant element for understanding the complex triadic relationship between the spectator, the producer and the media text.

In this essay I focus on these three components of West African video film: the audience, the film producer and films themselves. This is in order to investigate why these video films have displaced Hollywood productions that dominate in so many other parts of the world. Why have these locally produced video films become so popular? I will suggest that these films dominate the market in Ghana partly because they articulate local concerns and customs in highly realistic cinematic forms. More precisely, the popularity of these video films is derived from the fact that they often make concrete and visible the hidden forces of evil that are perceived as lurking behind the modern urban life of cities such as Accra. These feature length films are eclectic, drawing upon a range of cinematic and theatrical traditions: from local street drama to Hollywood action movies. They have evolved considerably over the last decade. In the 1990s the majority of these films focused primarily either on the family (exploring themes such as faithfulness between marriage partners, loyalty between parents, children, siblings or the extended family), or the quest for money and power in relation to the occult. These are morality tales that are invariably played out against the backdrop of spiritual warfare. Sometimes films show how the family can be shattered by involvement in the occult. Initially, the vast majority of Ghanaian video films lacked the suspense or explicit violence embodied in Western horror movies, but with the increased popularity of more violent Nigerian and jointly produced Ghanaian-Nigerian films, the local film industry in Ghana in the late 1990s and early part of the twenty-first century has evolved into producing and marketing movies that have closer parallels with a number of different genres.

Elsewhere I have identified a range of conversations currently taking place in the emerging field of religion and media. By focusing upon these highly popular and religious video films in Ghana and Nigeria, this essay contributes to a number of these ongoing discussions. This unique phenomenon in West Africa merits close attention, and is also pertinent to research into the relationship between religion and film.

[. . .]

Understanding the new wave of West African popular video films

The year 2001 saw over 600 video films produced in Nigeria and nearly 100 in Ghana. The number has increased every year for the last ten years. In 2002, however, most productions in Nigeria ceased for several months. This 'recess' was an attempt to bring order to a market that was becoming saturated with new productions. This was only a brief pause in the production of local films. Given that Francophone Africa remains far more cinematically productive than Anglophone Africa, these video films represent a vital new development in film production in Anglophone Africa. With a lack of investment and scant resources for creating indigenous African films, American films have dominated the cinemas of Ghana and Nigeria until the last few years. 'With the advent of video', Nigerian film historian Frank Ukadike suggests, 'Ghana has been able to cultivate an indigenous film and video culture'.[3]

William K. Akuffo has produced over 30 films in Ghana, and is one of the leaders of the new video movement in Ghana. He was originally a cinema projectionist who approached various filmmakers with the suggestion that they should use video rather than celluloid for film production. In spite of being a vastly cheaper alternative this idea was rejected, so he decided to work on his own. In the early 1990s, he purchased a VHS camera and made his first film *Zinabu* independently, editing on two video machines. No one would purchase this video film so he rented a cinema house, Globe Cinema in Accra, and advertised the video as a Ghanaian film. He assumed that most people had a bias against video at that time. So for the premier he camouflaged the bulky video machine and put it right in front of the film projector so that nobody would actually know where the pictures were coming from. When they started showing the film Akuffo admits: 'I was quite scared because I didn't know how people were going to receive it because of how the professionals were going about it, and to my surprise they [the audience] clapped, they laughed and everything' (Akuffo interviewed by Mitchell, 2000).

The popularity of locally produced video films is clear even after a brief walk through the streets of Accra. These videos are sold not only in video shops and general stores, but also off the back of carts and from stands in the city's markets. Locally produced videos, not the Hollywood films, tend to dominate the shelves. Franklin Kennedy-Ukah has spent several years researching these video films in Nigeria. He points out that there are also video cafés, which become the location for vigorous discussions provoked by the films.

> Often we come together and watch some of these tapes. People, especially young people, discuss these videotapes in groups. Even on [Nigerian] university campuses we have little video cafés, we have group video viewing sessions on campus and each week about four, five sessions are held in the university where young people come together; friends come together to watch these videos. It goes to show how tremendously popular, how tremendously important the people think this aspect, this sphere of popular culture is (Kennedy-Ukah interviewed by Mitchell, 2000).

It is interesting to note how audiences use these films. The sheer ubiquity of video houses and video outlets in Accra and Lagos illustrate that it is by no means only in universities that they provoke discussion. Local people now watch many of these films on television, and sometimes even in churches. Increasingly, films are watched and discussed at home, in front of the VCR. But what aspect of these films generates the liveliest discussions?

Demonizing, marginalizing and exemplifying religious figures

One of the most common areas of debate is the portrayal of religious figures in many of these video films. Traditional African religious leaders are frequently caricatured, stereotyped or even demonized. They can be the cause of sickness, violence or death. They are sometimes portrayed as having direct links with actual spirits, who in turn are depicted as having real power. In the Ghanaian film Namisha (Akwetey-Kanyi Productions, 1999), the protagonist Slobo exerts terrible revenge on those who have stolen his wife and were responsible for the death of his two daughters. He uses Namisha, one of the spirits beholden to the earth spirit Abadzen, to seduce his enemies and then brutally murder them. Ministers from the historic mission churches (such as the Methodists, the Presbyterians or the Anglicans) by contrast, are often represented as well intentioned but ultimately ineffectual and marginal to the outcome of the story. They neither contribute to nor counter the horror. Pastors from the independent Pentecostal or charismatic churches, by contrast, are typically portrayed as dynamic and spiritually powerful. They often use the accoutrements of power, such as mobile phones or computers alongside a large black leather-covered Bible. Frequently, it is they who overcome or at least help to overcome the evil forces, which let loose the agents of horror. At times, the three-way dynamic is simplified to a sharply defined two-way conflict. Africanus Aveh teaches film and video at the University of Ghana in Accra and believes that:

> In most of the videos we see the Christian pastor is always neatly dressed in a suit or in a white cassock. He is always a peace-broker who is welcome in every home, who mends broken marriages, who will be consulted and bring life through counselling, etc, etc. But on the other hand you see the African traditional priest being portrayed as a killer, being portrayed as a fraud, being portrayed as a liar who kills for a fee, who help people achieve all their evil and demonic intentions. For example, if you are a young lady and you see a man that you like and the man is already married, it is portrayed that these young ladies consult the African traditional priest

and then he is able to help them snatch legitimate husbands from other women (Aveh interviewed by Mitchell, 2000).

At other moments the battles between the faiths are more explicitly represented. In the final scene of the Nigerian film *Magic Money*, for example, the Christian pastor and African traditional priest call, even shout, for the help of their respective Gods. They both dance on the spot and gesticulate aggressively, but the traditional priest is literally laid low, overwhelmed by the more powerful force called upon by the Christian pastor.

This literalistic battle scene is taken a step further in *Namisha* where one character commits his life to the elemental spirit Obadzen. He has a secret room to which he adjourns to pray to this spirit. She declines to assist him. So he tries to use his own power. In a scene reminiscent of a science fiction movie, he hurls curses out from his room; with them go super-imposed circles of light thrown towards his opponents in the sitting room. They are accompanied by echoing sound effects. The pastor, who has been praying with three women associates, is knocked down and lands back on the sofa. The praying in tongues does not abate, if anything it continues more vigorously. The pastor recovers and this time rays of light burst from them, and knock out their opponent. This scene is more comic than horrific, with some audiences in Ghana laughing out loud at the weakness of the traditional religionist enacted in this sequence. Intentional and unintentional comic episodes balance moments of suspense, surprise and horror. Only later when Namisha murders her unfortunate victims or turns into a black raven to escape her pursuers is there anything redolent of the more traditional forms of the horror film. Nevertheless, it is clear from the scene described above that the forces are portrayed semi-realistically and that the stronger force is to be found with the prayerful Christians.

These and other similar portrayals provoke fierce criticism from a number of local commentators. Elom Dovlo is head of the religion department at the University of Ghana in Accra:

I think the films should be more authentic in reflecting traditional culture and should be geared more towards how there could be interaction between Christianity and traditional culture, rather than be geared towards condemnation of that culture and the people who follow it. [At present it] simply causes tension within the society (Dovlo interviewed by Mitchell, 2000).

This tension has its roots in Ghana and Nigeria's colonial past, where traditional religion was perceived in particularly negative, even horrific terms.

Historical awareness leads some commentators to be deeply suspicious of these video film portrayals. Elizabeth Amoah teaches at the University of Ghana in Accra:

> For me, it's the content and the images and the impact of these on the audience that I am more concerned about, because there are some of these home-made videos that are very violent, that are very negative to some religious traditions, that are very controversial. This has a long history and it's part of our colonial and missionary history, because if you read how Islam and Christianity came to Africa — these two major religions, because of where they are coming from and their ideology behind their coming, portrayed the indigenous beliefs very negatively (Amoah interviewed by Mitchell, 2000).

Up to this stage in the discussion at least two points have emerged. First, Ghanaian and Nigerian video films have provided an alternative source of entertainment to Hollywood films. In many shops and most video cafés, particularly in Ghana, they have actually displaced Hollywood films as the most popular item for viewing. They offer a rare example of a local industry that, whilst lacking extensive production and post-production facilities and budgets, nevertheless resists the domination that Hollywood exerts in many parts of the world. Second, one regular criticism of these films is the negative stereotyping of traditional African religious figures and the positive stereotyping of Christian leaders. Given these observations and criticisms, and given the lack of technical sophistication, why is it that many of these films are so popular in Ghana and Nigeria?

Explaining the popularity of Ghanaian and Nigerian video films

'Prior to being sold as a video cassette for home viewing, a popular movie can easily be seen by tens of thousands of people in Accra's cinemas in the center and suburbs and become the talk of the town. Often its story is "broadcast" through mobile people such as taxi drivers, street vendors, and traders in Makola market'.[4] The popularity of these video films can be explained from several different perspectives. One of the most persuasive explanations concentrates upon the belief systems that they embody. Many of these films reflect dominant popular beliefs, in particular a belief in the reality of evil powers. From studying particular films and listening to audience responses it is clear that many of these videos are popular because they enact, in highly realistic forms, the horror that evil forces can bring and their ultimate demise in the face of the Christian God.

On the basis of several local interviews, it is clear that many Nigerian and Ghanaian viewers believe that evil spirits, evil characters and evil powers really do exist, and are indeed responsible for bringing about horror and tragedy in people's real lives. Given this belief system, cinematic portrayals may be seen as fictionalized accounts of reality. These portrayals thus reflect common beliefs, common concerns and common anxieties. In the video-film houses of Accra it is common to find audiences applauding and cheering as the Christian character vanquishes the apparently evil witchdoctor or traditional religionist. Another research project would be required to analyse the extent to which the audiences recognize these scenes as genuinely reflecting everyday concerns, practices and experiences of faith, and how this might vary in different parts of Ghana and Nigeria.

Nonetheless, it is valuable to highlight the 'realistic' way in which themes are enacted in these films. For example, consider one scene from Time (Miracle Films, D'Joh Mediacraft and Igo Films, 2000), one of the first jointly produced Ghanaian and Nigerian films. In it one of the key characters has kept the corpse of his wife in his wardrobe in their bedroom. He is following the advice of the traditional healer who had told him that if he does this, she will provide him with all the money that he needs. In the scene under consideration, his son nervously enters the room, crosses himself and then opens the cupboard door. He is shocked by the sight of the corpse of his dead mother and falls back on the bed in horror. The following shots include an image of the corpse essentially vomiting money. There are actual bank notes coming out of the mouth of the corpse. When I saw this in central Accra, there were gasps of shock from the audience. These became louder as the father bludgeons the boy to death with a baseball bat for uncovering the corpse.

[...]

Seeing video films as moral parables

My argument up to this point is that many of these locally produced video films are popular not because they borrow elements of different genres from Hollywood, but partly because they 'give expression to local issues' and 'local perspectives' in highly realistic forms. As anthropologist Birgit Meyer suggests, some films, such as the extremely popular Nigerian produced film Blood Money (OJ Production, 1997), articulate popular anxiety in Ghana about the trade of body parts for ritual sacrifice in Nigeria and Ghana (Meyer 2002). The popularity of many of these videos is clearly a complex phenomenon. It is worth noticing the resonance in some of the films, especially those produced in Nigeria, with traditional Hausa and Yoruba theatrical melodramatic genres, as well as their cultural appropriateness in terms of geographic and social space. In other words, viewers will recognize settings, customs and dramatic genres as their own, rather than as located in a foreign sphere seen only through Hollywood's lens.

This ensures that these films can, in the words of Seth Ashong-Katai, one of Ghana's most experienced producers, continue to act as 'moral parables'. Embedded in many of their narratives are warnings about the dangers of money, ambition or unfaithfulness. According to Birgit Meyer 'many women in fact want their husbands or boyfriends to come along and watch the latest Ghanaian movie in order to see that bad or morally unacceptable behavior really will lead into all sorts of disasters. So these men should learn that it is better not to take a girlfriend out and drink, squander money and so on. So for women they are really moralizing and educating devices' (Meyer interviewed by Mitchell, 2000). As morality tales these films therefore play a vital social function, and are used by many women as a way of showing their partners the right way of living. There is a sense in which some films are Ghanaian or Nigerian versions of *Faust* where the protagonist sells his, and it normally is 'his', soul for immediate benefits. The wages of such a contract is often a horrific end or if he's more fortunate, a painful conversion. Thus horror, though not in the traditional horror genre sense, bolsters the current moral order and shows how people should live. Invariably there is a moral conclusion where good, normally inextricably connected with Christianity, is victorious.

In interviews a number of the producers and directors made it clear that many are not creating film for proselytizing or pastoral purposes. Another one of Ghana's most prolific directors and producers William Akuffo, for example, confided that his thirty films:

> don't reflect my beliefs at all. They've got nothing to do with my beliefs because to start with I don't believe in all the Christianity crap that is going around me, although I don't believe in this Africanian thing so . . . I am not an atheist; but I believe there should be a supreme being somewhere but since I haven't seen him, I don't bother myself very much about him. I don't think my films reflect what I think at all (Akuffo, interviewed by Mitchell, 2000).

For Akuffo the bottom line of making films is to appeal to large numbers of Ghanaians and make himself rich. This is his stated objective. He recognizes that the majority of his potential audiences are Christian and he makes his films accordingly. Horror represents a small, but significant element of his expanding repertoire. In Nigeria targeting films appropriately is more complex as filmmakers face an audience composed of Christians and Moslems. Many make video films with one particular faith group, or even sub-group, in mind. Moreover, as the anthropologist Brian Larkin points out: 'there's a tension in Northern Nigeria between local, Hausa-produced videos and Lagos-based videos. For Hausa filmmakers, they couldn't possibly, nor would they necessarily want to, get away with certain sorts of licentious activity that goes on in Lagos videos' (Larkin interviewed by Mitchell, 2000). Thus audiences exert a significant influence over the practice of filmmakers, often encouraging a moralistic and Christian approach to cinematic story-telling.

[. . .]

Conclusion

I have suggested that there are many explanations for the popularity of these video films in Ghana and Nigeria. Their ability to adapt to the market and to develop new themes and approaches partly accounts for their continued popularity. There is a sense in which these filmmakers are creating a new genre, which breaks open traditional understandings of the horror genre or action genre. It is a genre which has its roots firmly fixed in Western African cultural soil, but still bears fruit in a surprisingly diverse fashion. Several moviemakers have moved beyond producing the simple family drama or occult spectacle to more eclectic and violent representations. The violent scenes in various recent films are but one aspect of these movies. Unlike many Hollywood horror films the horror is not an end in itself.

The elements of religion in these films can be seen as cultural artifacts that provide valuable insight into the moral and religious landscape, the anxieties and the questions commonly found in Ghana and Nigeria. For example, how do the beliefs of the village-dweller change when they come into contact with the city? Does or should such a shift inevitably lead to a violent abandonment of traditional beliefs and practices? Why does Pentecostal-charismatic Christianity have such a tremendous appeal? How do charismatic Christians relate to other Christian, Islamic and African traditional groups? How can these religious groups co-exist when they all have competing claims to the soul of both countries? Alongside these issues the local video film phenomenon is itself evolving.

New sets of questions are raised such as: Why is there now in Ghana a strong preference for Nigerian films, and Ghanaian producers are struggling to meet their own production costs? How far is the reception of these films influenced by the social spaces in which they are watched? Given the extent of the video film phenomenon in Ghana and Nigeria, these and other related questions deserve further investigation.

Notes

1   I am indebted to Birgit Meyer, Rosalind Hackett and the International Study Commission on Media, Religion and Culture for providing the opportunity to experience this first hand in Accra, Ghana. I am particularly grateful to Birgit Meyer who has shared many of her insights from extensive research into this pheno-menon. [See previous reading.] I am also grateful to Brian Larkin for generously sharing his insights about Nigerian video culture.

2   See: Stewart M. Hoover, *Religion in the Media Age*, London and New York: Routledge, 2006; and Lynn Schofield Clark, *From Angels to Aliens: Teenagers, the Media, and the Super-natural*, Oxford University Press, 2003.

3   See: N. F. Ukadike, 'Critical Approaches to World Cinema: African Cinema', in John Hill, John and Pamela Church Gibson (eds), *The Oxford Guide to Film Studies*, Oxford University Press, 1998, 570.

4   See: B. Meyer, 'Money, Power & Morality: Popular Ghanaian Cinema in the Fourth Republic', *Ghana Studies*, 4, (2001): 65–84.

Chapter 15

Elia Suleiman

NOTES FROM THE PALESTINIAN DIASPORA
An Interview with Elia Suleiman

Cineaste: It might be a naïve question to pose, but the title of your film, *Divine Intervention*, seems congruent with the sad reality of life in the Middle East today. Because the situation is now so dire, people can only desperately hope for "divine intervention."

Suleiman: Titles have a lot to do with poetic license. I also get my titles towards the end of the editing process. I make the images in a tableaux-like fashion and then add sound and pigment. And it's the same with the titles. The title might provide a summary of the film's content. Since the title is arrived at just before the film is ready for release, you can hit on some poetic resonance if you're lucky. When this poetic license is present in the title, it can extend itself to various corners of the film itself.

Cineaste: So the audience can provide its own interpretation.

Suleiman: Exactly. I think there's a certain irony and second degree humor. The title *Divine Intervention* is a bit pompous. That's why I had to ground the film with the subtitle – "a chronicle of love and pain."

Cineaste: Did you always intend to open the film with the scene featuring Santa Claus being taunted in Nazareth?

Suleiman: Always. I absolutely wanted that scene. The first time I shot it, it didn't work. The producer even asked me if I could make the film without this scene. But, after thinking about it for twenty-four hours, I said, "No, this scene has to open the film and it's going to give you an idea of everything that will follow." It was originally a joke to list Michel Piccoli as playing Santa Claus, but he eventually agreed to dub the character's heaving breathing.

Cineaste: You've spoken of your childhood hatred for Santa Claus.

Suleiman: I hope that my hatred of Santa Claus will spread all over the world. I associate Santa with a nauseating sweetness. I enjoy the fact that people are a little shocked by this. Every year, Santa Claus comes with his jingle bells and the world is going to its doom. It's a good idea to rupture the sweetness associated with Santa.

Cineaste: And it's ironic, but not at all coincidental, that this assault on Santa Claus occurs in Nazareth.

Suleiman: Nazareth is the best place to stab Santa. When people know that I'm from Nazareth, they say, "Wow, that was where Jesus walked." But you should just go and see for yourself the kids who live in Nazareth today. They lost their innocence years ago and there's nothing left for them to do. So, fuck Santa! But this is just an anecdotal account. In fact, it's a great opening because you get a definite idea of the breakdown in communication that comes later in the film. It lets the audience unfasten their seat belts and helps them become attuned to the humor that comes later.

Cineaste: And perhaps their expectations are frustrated as well.

Suleiman: Well, it's really a question of achieving a flow and some harmony. It's similar to what happens with a symphonic piece. If you start with a bang, you can then proceed to all of the little variations on the main theme. The musicality of the film's structure is important.

Cineaste: To ask another naïve question, many viewers probably wonder how autobiographical this film really is.

Suleiman: It's very autobiographical, but not in a literal-minded, exact way. That's why I refer to the film as a self-portrait. You can't be presumptuous about biographies anyway – they're all inventions. I'm inventing factual moments, and their truth value probably lies in the way that I'm telling (or retelling) them, not whether they actually happened or not. But I can tell you that most of the events actually happened in Palestine, except of course for Santa, (actually Santa did get stabbed there once, but not in Nazareth.) All the stuff about my father and the woman are definitely taken from reality. It's not a realistic representation of my father, but it corresponds to some aspects of him. A lot of this stuff actually happened during my childhood.

Cineaste: Many of these incidents also illustrate the fact that people who feel oppressed frequently vent their anger among themselves and within their own communities.

Suleiman: Yes, and I'm sure what you see in the film is only one one-thousandth of what actually goes on. I recently heard about some gang shoot-outs; it's a true ghetto atmosphere. People are extremely angry and frustrated. They're not nice to each other and there's no tenderness whatsoever or hint of harmonious community.

People complain about the checkpoint scene being implicitly violent. Go and watch the true violence, if you like, and you'll see the sadism that's being exercised every day. But I am against portraying brutality, for moral reasons, within the film frame.

Cineaste: Is this because you don't want to reproduce cinematic clichés?

Suleiman: It's more a question of how can we in fact depict the extent of pain and violence within the frame. You can hint at the extent of pain and violence, but as soon as you contain it within the frame, there is the assumption that you know its extent. For example, if you were to portray an interrogator beating someone being interrogated, the audience wouldn't really understand what the victim was experiencing. Instead of doing that, it's up to the spectator to make the association between the events of the film and the true horror.

For example, I'd say that too much sensationalism concerning the Holocaust really obscured a lot of what the Holocaust really meant for those who lived through it. This kind of reductive history can reach an immoral level. I'm really repulsed by people opportunistically reproducing images of bodies being thrown into big holes and audiences consuming them. If you reduce the Holocaust to these images, you are banalizing it – as opposed to someone like Primo Levi, who is one of my favorite writers of all time. When I read Levi, I understood how I should shoulder moral responsibility for the stories I'm telling.

In The Writing of the Disaster, Maurice Blanchot talked about these issues in a much more complex way – the silence we must maintain if we really don't comprehend certain historical events. But Primo Levi poeticized the little events of daily life and left the horror for the reader to imagine. I've learned a lot from him, both morally and aesthetically. It's funny; some people might question my identity.

Cineaste: It was quite amusing to overhear some conversations at the film festival press screening. A few uninformed critics were asking, "Is he Palestinian or Jewish?"

Suleiman: That's very funny. Factually, of course, I'm not Jewish. But I often refer to my humor as "conceptually Jewish." They just didn't get the humor again. Would it matter if I actually was Jewish? No, but certain cultural particularities would be different. Am I attracted to certain Jewish cultural and philosophical strands? Yes, of course.

Chapter 16

Ousmane Sembene

THE POWER OF FEMALE SOLIDARITY

An Interview with Ousmane Sembene

Cineaste: One thing that makes your films, including *Moolaadé*, unique – and is distinctive within world cinema – is the emphasis on the community rather than individuals. They're radical films inasmuch as there's really no central character and this is of course even more apparent in earlier movies such as *Emitai* and *Ceddo*.

Sembene: Given the current situation in Africa, I don't think you can feature one main character in a story. I'm not making epics dealing with warriors, but am more concerned with daily life. I think this communal approach to film-making enables my audiences to understand the films better when we're engaged in discussions. With a communal approach, people can see themselves on screen. You can't take a character like, for example, Faat Kiné and single her out; it doesn't work. That's the result of my own analysis of the current situation in Africa.

Cineaste: We agree, but so many filmmakers seem to feel that you're obliged to have a single protagonist for the audience to "relate" to. They assume that this strategy brings audiences "into" the film and I wonder if you're consciously going against the grain of the dominant psychological, interiorized approach to narrative.

Sembene: You can start with one individual, but when you get to the reaction to that individual's actions it becomes, for me, a community-based narrative. We are not alone within our communities; there's not one political party or one trade union to consider. There are instead people with differences and points in common.

Cineaste: Does this tendency refer back to the tradition of the griot, the storyteller who's responsible for transmitting values to the community?

Sembene: That's what I would like to accomplish. In our culture, the griot is traditionally a sacred character but he has now become a very banal individual. He used to be a very respected figure and he didn't just sing praises to his society but was a guardian of the past and of the truth. Since he was a master of the spoken word, he was a trustee of society's secrets.

Cineaste: This point also highlights an aspect of your films that is rare in Western cinema. So many of the films feature crises being worked out verbally through communal debate.

Sembene: Africa still needs that. Even though it's undergoing change, I wish it could preserve those values. Unfortunately, in the cities, as I mentioned before, these values are fading away. Most of our leaders are mimicking the West.

Cineaste: Taking up that point: some years ago, you launched a scathing attack on the neocolonial élite in *Xala*. Do you think this critique is still pertinent to the situation in Senegal today?

Sembene: I don't want to make any sweeping generalizations, but, within the Francophone countries at least, I think the situation is worse than it was in the Sixties and Seventies. During the last forty years, more Africans killed each other than were killed by outsiders during the previous hundred years. I'm talking about wars, not deaths by disease. Nowadays, the leadership is even more alienated from the people than the leaders of the previous generation. That's the dangerous situation we're faced with now. And I'm going to deal with this topic in my next film, *The Brotherhood of the Rats*. [holds up script] Even though the situation is worse, you have to bear witness. As far as many issues go, we've actually regressed over the years. Tradition has just become a value people use to escape reality. People merely invoke tradition in order to go backwards.

Cineaste: To return to *Moolaadé*, do you see some hope in the development in an indigenous African media? The Western left often views the media as a means of deception, but your film goes against the grain of Marxism in the West by viewing it as a source of consciousness-raising (particularly since the women's radios that are seized appear to represent a major source of enlightenment).

Sembene: My view is that, without the media, there's no future. It's not the media itself that are of importance – it's the content. I'm dealing with the issue of globalization. In reference to the Western left that you mention, hasn't it become backward and lost ground in recent years in its fight with the mainstream?

Cineaste: Yes, that's true.

Sembene: In Africa, we have a lot of independent radio stations. But our leaders don't like these independent radio stations! Yet now we have radio stations broadcasting in all of the African languages. This is important because of the many African languages and the great geographical distances on the continent. If you speak two or three languages, you can listen to several stations dealing with different topics. For Africans, radio and television are very important tools.

Cineaste: Is this related to the fact that you shot the film in Burkina Faso? Are you making more of an effort to address the problems of African nations outside of Senegal? Is 'Pan-Africanism' still a viable goal?

Sembene: I was working with technicians from France, Senegal, Benin, and other countries. But it was difficult to the extent that they're all from cities and the place we were shooting in Burkina Faso didn't have electricity or running water. And there were a lot of mosquitoes – I can attest to that! In addition to French, the actors spoke Bambara. It's not a majority language or a lingua franca, but most people in West Africa speak it.

It's too easy to speak of Pan-Africanism. Marcus Garvey and Du Bois in the United States introduced the notion of Pan-Africanism. To put in a nutshell, Africa is a vast continent. It's in the interest of Africans, however, to have regional ties because the countries complement each other, both economically and culturally.

Of course, African unity is the ultimate goal. But at the time when the concept of Pan-Africanism was formulated, there were no independent states in Africa – except perhaps Ethiopia. Now that we've had independent states for forty years, we haven't made one step of progress towards Pan-Africanism. All of our heads of state talk about Pan-Africanism, but they all want to preserve their thrones as in monarchies. No one wants to share political power. As far as the Francophone countries go, those leaders spend more time with the French President than they do among themselves. How can you talk about Pan-Africanism in this context? Does Bush hold meetings about his national interests in China? Of course not. We can't even talk about globalization yet in Africa; we're on the periphery of the world. We have raw materials in our soil, but this doesn't make us wealthy; it makes other nations wealthy. If you look at the raw data of the United Nations, there are about 800 million people in Africa – three-fourths live on less than a dollar a day.

Cineaste: This problem was of course the theme of one of your most powerful films in recent years – *Guelwaar*.

Sembene: Yes, you're right. But, again, the role of the artist is to raise issues and trigger discussion.

Cineaste: How much faith do you have in the possibility that these movies will bring about change?

Sembene: I realize that I'm not able to change my society single-handedly. But I have the impression, when I bring students food for thought and conduct discussions with them, that I'm doing my part. I was recently in central Africa, screening *Moolaadé* in the South of Cameroon. In the North, they are Muslims and practice excision. I wouldn't have been able to show the film there – even my friends dissuaded me from doing that. I couldn't have changed anyone's mind there; it's just like the elderly man in the movie who doesn't want the women to listen to the radio because he's afraid that they're being fed subversive ideas. Yet I don't think that Africa can afford to live in isolation nowadays, closed in upon itself.

Chapter 17

Cheick Oumar Sissoko, with Ray Privett

I MAKE FILMS ABOUT THE BIG PROBLEMS OF OUR CONTINENT

MALIAN FILMMAKER Cheick Oumar Sissoko has a taste for excess, and nowhere is this more evident than in the latest film he has directed, *La genèse* (*Genesis*), based on the tales of Jacob, Esau, and Hamor in the first book of the Bible. This is a lavish epic of patriarchs, misbehaving sons, wandering nomads, and onscreen circumcisions.

Genesis is in many ways a continuation of *Guimba* (1995), the previous historical epic Sissoko directed. *Guimba* tracks the abuses of power by a corrupt king, ending with his demise and a resolution that no longer should any one man hold such power over so many. It was clearly an allegory for recent events in Mali, where Moussa Traoré, a dictator who had ruled since the late Sixties, had fallen of late. *Genesis* is based on the story of Jacob in the middle chapters of the book of Genesis, in the time between when Jacob's sons have sold their brother Joseph into slavery and when they go down to Egypt and find him there. Hamor's son Shechem and Jacob's daughter Dinah are suddenly together, and both families struggle to accommodate this. Meanwhile Esau and his clan look on. The sons' actions suddenly become more significant as the aged fathers withdraw their power, creating the ambiguities of a power vacuum that allegorizes post-Traoré Mali, as well as, more generally, post-Cold War Africa.

The power struggle that erupts in this vacuum has many ferocious consequences, including some particularly vicious fratricidal warfare. Jacob's sons agree to Dinah's marriage only if all of Hamor's sons are circumcised;

astonishingly, Hamor's sons agree. After a scene that should bring contortions to all men's faces, Jacob's sons invade the village on horseback, killing the men and raping the women. These acts unmistakably and intentionally evoke recent events in Rwanda, the Congo, and too many other places across the continent.

This kind of 'state of the continent' address seems especially characteristic recently of films made by a handful of West African filmmakers. Children of the independence generation who passed through Europe while developing their craft before returning to become entrenched within African film culture, they include Sissoko and Souleymane Cissé, in Mali, and Idrissa Ouédraogo and Gaston Kaboré, in Burkina Faso, and might be grouped together as Continental Filmmakers. They tend to be involved in some way with every aspect of film culture, from the conception of a film through its development, production, distribution, exhibition, and criticism, as well as the education of young film-makers. Such dedication and perseverance to building national infrastructure is surely among the reasons these filmmakers have been supported by Hubert Bals's Fund at the Rotterdam Film Festival, which supports filmmakers from developing countries, especially projects that help in the development of domestic film industries.

Sissoko himself spent much of the 1970s at a handful of schools in France studying mathematics, history, and cinema, including a course in film semiotics with Christian Metz. He returned to Mali in 1980. Ever since then he has been closely involved with domestic film culture. For several years he was the director of the National Center of Cinema (CNC), an institution that was developed in the 1960s soon after independence. Recently, however, Sissoko left the CNC to devote more time to his production and distribution company Kora Films, named after the large stringed instrument of the Mandé peoples of West Africa.

I spoke with Sissoko, in English and French, for *Cineaste* while he was promoting *Genesis* in New York City in October. – **Ray Privett**

Cineaste: Let's talk about *Genesis*. Why did you choose this story?

Sissoko: All my films are about tragedies – tragedies of children, of the desert, and drought. I make films about the big problems of our continent. Our continent is very rich, but it has so many problems that interfere with our ability to develop. When I made *Guimba*, it was the same year that Africa knew the drama of Rwanda. One hundred kilometers from where I was shooting *Guimba*, people were killing each other. Elsewhere in Africa there were many similar tragedies, many fratricidal conflicts. So I knew I had to make a film that dealt with these kinds of tragedies.

To my mind, fratricidal conflicts come about because of decentralization mandated by the World Bank and the IMF, which makes people struggle among each other for what little power is left. I needed a text to deal with this. Around this same time a friend of mine in France showed me a script proposal dealing with Genesis chapters twenty-three through thirty-seven. I said, my God, it's what we need. Because after Rwanda we heard about Bosnia, Algeria, religious intolerance, and so on. *Genesis* belongs to all humanity. It is the basis of three big religions – Judaism, Islam, and Christianity. I accepted the script and worked on it with the screenwriter. Then we found a location that looked like the Holy Land.

Cineaste: The film is clearly set in the Holy Land, yet it is also very clearly set in the Sahel, as you can see, for example, in the peoples' clothing. Is there something specifically about Mali here?

Sissoko: Today, in Mali, the primary conflict is between the Soninké and the Fulani. This is a fratricidal conflict. I wrote the script of this film about fratricide five years ago, and it shows what is happening in my country right now, in the southwest and in the northeast. Something like one hundred and fifty people died recently in a conflict between the Soninké and the Fulani. There are also conflicts between Arabs and Maures and in the area around Gao. All this is because of decentralization, the economic crisis, and the poor government of Mali. The World Bank and the United States say this is democracy, but that is not true.

I suppose you can say the process is not explicitly represented in the film. What I represent is the outcome of the decentralization, the conflict. In the film, you have peasants and farmers. They live together for centuries. They know each other very well, and they share many things. But because they know each other so well, they also have many reasons to hate each other. In the film, like right now in Mali and across Africa, they are choosing to focus on these. Why? They share customs, they marry together. But because of poverty, because of money, there is all this jealousy and envy and ultimately fratricide.

Cineaste: So you're also not explicitly representing the warring tribes in Rwanda, the Hutus and the Tutsis.

Sissoko: No, in fact, you know the Hutus and Tutsis are the same physically, and they speak the same language. The only similarity is that they live together, as Jacob the farmer and Hamor the peasant live together. They share a lot of problems. They marry together. They have all these things in common, but then they kill each other. I'm depicting the process that leads to this.

A guy from Rwanda saw the film at FESPACO in Ouagadougou. He didn't get a seat, so he stood for the entire one hundred and two minutes. After the film he tracked me down and said, "You related my story as a man of Rwanda. Each second of your film is the story of my country. And I hope this film will be shown in Rwanda." I said to him, "If you want to organize that, I will send you a copy for free." I am waiting to hear from him.

Cineaste: Has it shown successfully elsewhere?

Sissoko: There was a very good reaction in Cannes and a lot of good articles. I understand there was also a good reaction in Toronto. Today, after the screening in New York, we had many questions. Eventually we had to stop because we needed to clear out of the movie theater. People were very happy to see this film.

As for showing in Africa, my production company, Kora Films, has a distributor who makes contacts. We have had some success, and it will be showing soon in countries like Senegal, Mali, Burkina Faso, the Ivory Coast, and Cameroon. We distribute many kinds of films, but it is very difficult to distribute African films.

We have some connections to Southern Africa. In South Africa, some distributors want our film, but elsewhere it is very difficult. We don't have many contacts with Egypt. We go to a film festival in December and that is all. They have a certain kind of film they want to see: Egyptian productions. They don't even like films from other countries in the Arab world. Here, as in other parts of Africa, at least for *Genesis*, I don't think I will be able to have it shown.

Cineaste: This film is in a way about forging such connections.

Sissoko: Yes, it's about connections across different groups on the continent, but it's also about African people going to find other African people who they sold into slavery. You see what I mean? Joseph was sold by his brothers into slavery, and at the end of the film, Jacob sends them to Egypt where they will find Joseph, just like now, I mean as a parable. African people should go to look for their lost brothers in the United States.

Cineaste: There seems to be some symbolism in you giving the first lines of the film to Esau, who is played by Salif Kéïta, the great international musician. He becomes one of the key voices in the film.

Sissoko: He's not the narrator, but he does have the first lines in the film. The narrator is the fool. The fool is a slave who dresses up as a woman in the film – the *buffon du roi*. He is not the same as the griot. It's his voice. When the people sit down and talk to each other, this guy dresses up like a woman and makes fun of everybody.

In our society, only the fool can say what he really thinks to the chief. The griot will flatter whoever pays him money, but the fool does not. He is able to say "no" to the chief and even make fun of him, even though he is a slave of the chief. He has a peculiar position between the lower castes and the chiefs, as a musician existing in the middle space between the two. He is the narrator of *Genesis*.

Cineaste: His position in some ways resembles your own as a filmmaker.

Sissoko: Exactly.

Asian and Australasian Perspectives

INTRODUCTION

NO READER IN RELIGION and film could approach thoroughness without significant attention paid to all that goes on in Asia and Australasia. India's enormous Mumbai-based industry produces over 800 films each year, many of which incorporate themes from Hindu mythologies and/ or have been intended as "devotional films," beginning, as we saw in part 1, with the very first Indian films by D.G. Phalke. Japan's artsy and animated industries have consistently involved significant Shinto and Buddhist religious dimensions, beginning with Kenji Mizoguchi's films in the early days of cinema, and extending to Akira Kurosawa's and Yasujiro Ozu's mid-century works, the recent *anime* of Katsuhiro Otomo and Hayao Miyazaki, and the new crop of "J-Horror" films. Korea's "Buddhist films," by Bae Yong-gyun, Im Kwon-Taek, and Chang Sonu, have turned filmmaking there in several new directions. From productions such as *The Lord of the Rings* trilogy and *Once Were Warriors* to David MacDougall's ethnographic work and Jane Campion's disturbing fictions, films from Australia and New Zealand have tended to display fantasy, alongside ancient and postcolonial clashings of religious cultures. Recent cinemas emerging in Malaysia and Bangladesh offer up a rich hybrid of cultures, languages, and religions. Meanwhile, Indonesia, which is a world leader in cinema production, presents everyday life in a Muslim country in a way that does not fit the sterotypes of Arabic Islam common to most European and American cinema.[1]

That said, the readings in this part, arranged alphabetically by author or director, attempt to cover a significant amount of ground in a short space, and inevitably have to omit many areas in the process. Nonetheless, we provide here a series of readings from filmmakers and scholars on film that begin to hint at the vast array of relations between religion and film in Asian and Australasian histories.

Much of Rachel Dwyer's scholarly work has focused on the visual culture of India. In her book, *Filming the Gods: Religion and Indian Cinema* (2006), she investigates the role of religion, and especially depictions of deities, within a history of Indian cinema. In a wide-ranging account she examines the religious fault-lines found both in the Indian film industry and represented in the films themselves. She locates her discussions in the context of technological developments, television serials, secular filmmaking, nationalist impulses, shifting sexual mores and interreligious conflicts. It is clear from Dwyer's work that the rich and colourful world of Indian cinema is fertile ground, ripe for discovering creative interactions between film and religion (reading 18).

Reading 19 from Geeta Kapur, an art critic and writer living in New Delhi, is taken from a chapter in her book *When was Modernism?* This chapter tells of two classic, though highly distinct, Indian films, *Sant Tukaram* (1936; dir. Vishnupant Govind Damle, 1892–1945) and *Devi* (1960, dir. Satyajit Ray, 1921–1992). The first is part of a tradition of mid-century "saint films" in India that focused on medieval poet-saints from the *bhakti* (devotional) tradition; *Sant Tukaram* was highly successful and won an award at the 1937 Venice film festival. The latter film, by Satyajit Ray perhaps the best known art-film director from India, develops a critique of religious devotion. The excerpt here focuses on Kapur's analysis of *Sant Tukaram*, as she shows how the film's cinematography relies on visual devices borrowed from painting, theater, and other two-dimensional images. Kapur argues that the religious "iconic" way of looking at these images is created through a filmic realism, and discusses how this religious visuality is bound up with nationalistic interests.

Moving to East Asia, an interview in reading 20 with the prominent Korean filmmaker Im Kwon-Taek (1936–   ) reveals ways in which national-cultural history might be preserved through film. Im, who has made nearly one hundred films over the past half-century, points toward the hybrid nature of Korean religion in films such as *Surrogate Mother* (1987). Meanwhile, the 1993 film *Sopyonje* deals with the religio-cultural music tradition called *p'ansori*, and two other films deal very specifically with monastic Buddhism in Korea: *Mandala* (1981) and *Come, Come, Come Upward* (1989). These films "utilize a Buddhist filter in order to address contemporary concerns about class and poverty,"[2] showing again how the religious is screened in ways that intersect with the social and political.

In a critical work on some trends in contemporary Japanese film, religious studies scholar William LaFleur notes even more ways in which a "realistic" approach to filmmaking lends itself to a religious vision (reading 21). LaFleur's work here draws on Paul Schrader's critical examination of the "transcendental style" of the great Japanese director Yasujiro Ozu (1903–1963). LaFleur here picks up on Ozu's style and Schrader's comments, applying them to a more contemporary filmmaker Hirokazu Kore'eda (1962–), and especially his 1995 film *Maborosi*. This is one of those films that says very little about explicit religiosity, but when examined closely unfolds as a great religious drama. Kore'eda's film *After Life* (1998) directly approaches common religious questions of life after death, while *Maborosi* approaches questions of life before death, and what happens to life lived after another person's death.

Back to South Asia, Philip Lutgendorf's critical examination of the 1975 surprise cult hit, *Jai Santoshi Ma* ("Hail to Mother Santoshi") speaks more toward the *bhakti* influence on film viewing (reading 22). Geeta Kapur earlier spoke of the "saint film" genre, while Lutgendorf speaks here of another prominent Indian genre, the "mythological film," of which *Jai Santoshi Ma* is a vital, blockbuster work. Lutgendorf retells the story of Santoshi Ma, and discusses how her story, as told in this film, appealed to many women (especially lower-middle-class women) across India. By invoking traditional ritual structures, the film is made accessible to many religious devotees, and therefore should not be placed within the mythological genre, but rather described as a "devotional film."

Along with Deepa Mehta (1950–), Mira Nair (1957–), has been one of the most internationally prominent, and critically acclaimed filmmakers to come from India. While she spends much of her time now in Uganda and New York, Nair's work retains a strong connection to her Indian roots, especially evident in her treatment of issues such as migration and multiculturalism. Alongside fictional works such as *Monsoon Wedding* (2001) and *Vanity Fair* (2004), she has created a number of documentaries, often in the style of *cinéma vérité*. She does not speak directly of religion, but we have chosen this excerpt (reading 23) because it begins to speak toward a quasi-religious mode of filmmaking itself, merging the art of filmmaking with something akin to a religious practice.

Paul Schrader published a critical study on religion and film called *Transcendental Style on Film* in 1972, just four years before his screenplay for the Martin Scorsese-directed *Taxi Driver* (1976) won the Golden Globe for Best Screenplay. He has gone on to work with Scorsese on a number of pictures, including *Raging Bull* (1980) and *Last Temptation of Christ* (1988). Born into a strict Calvinist home, Schrader has retained a deep interest in Japanese culture, and his work as a director, screenwriter, and theorist sees correspondences in what he calls a "transcendental style" across cultures. This tends toward realism, with austere lighting, long takes, and a carefully crafted use of close ups, even though he is careful to point out how realism itself is a *style*. The excerpt here (reading 24) provides a short definition of the transcendental style, and then applies it to the work of the great Japanese director, Ozu.

Japan's film industry has produced some of the greatest figures in world cinema, and is now producing even more through the genre known in the West as *anime*. *Anime* typically refers to a style of animation that originated in Japan, though, like all styles is a hybrid of others (including, significantly, Disney), and is now produced around the world. Among many others, Osamu Tesuka (1928–1989), Katsuhiro Ôtomo (1954–   ), and Mamoru Oshii (1951–   ) have consistently incorporated religious themes into their works, while the director best known in the West is certainly Hayao Miyazaki (1941–   ). Miyazaki's films, such as *Princess Mononoke* (1997), *Spirited Away* (2001), and *Howl's Moving Castle* (2004), often intertwine Shinto, Buddhist, and other religious mythologies and rituals. Moreover, as the excerpt below (reading 25) from Jolyon Baraka Thomas suggests, his films inspire viewers to recreate rituals that incorporate aspects of the animated films.

The last excerpt in this section comes from an interview with the Australian director Peter Weir, whose films helped define the look of contemporary Australian cinema. Weir is particularly skilled at helping to create cinematic depictions of small closed communities, such as Australian soldiers under fire at Gallipoli during the First World War (*Gallipoli*, 1981), the Amish in late twentieth century USA (*Witness*, 1985), or sailors on board a nineteenth-century sailing ship (*Master and Commander*, 2003). Religion, metaphysics, or mysticism rarely take center stage in Weir films, but are often there in the background, sometimes bubbling to the surface and regularly adding depth to his films. In the introduction to part 3 we briefly considered the puppet scene in Weir's *The Year of Living Dangerously* (1982) and the claim that "the unseen is all around us." The significance of the unseen is a recurring theme both in Weir's Hollywood financed movies and his earlier Australian films such as *Picnic at Hanging Rock* (1975), where three girls and their teacher mysteriously disappear on a St Valentine's Day outing in 1900. There is a hallucinatory and dreamlike quality to this film which hints towards the existence of alternative realities beyond what is actually seen. One Australian scholar, Richard Leonard, has gone so far as to suggest that Weir's work contributes to the creation of a cinematic "mystical gaze."[3] Weir himself has even described how his own mystical experience at Anzac Cove influenced his decision to make the film *Gallipoli* (1981). While walking up Shrapnel Gully he felt that was being watched, but couldn't see anyone. Despite crying out "hello" and "who's there?" no-one replied. Feeling "claustrophobic" he started saying his name, his age and his nationality and then said: "I know who you are and I know you're watching me. . . . I don't know whether to do this film . . . You're strangers but I've been thinking of making a film about you . . . I wouldn't harm what you did here, because I know what you did here. If you are with me, show me your secret things. Help me." The feeling of being watched soon evaporated but a few moments later he discovered "a can opener, a knife and fork, a pair of shoes, some bullets and a bomb, even a bottle of Eno's fruit salts unbroken, which I brought home . . . So I swore a pact with the ghosts that I'd do the film."[4] This memorable story demonstrates Weir's openness to reflecting upon the "unseen" influences upon his own filmmaking. The excerpt provided here is taken from an interview where Weir reflects upon another encounter which changed his own understanding of filmmaking (reading 26).

Notes

1   Good general overviews of each of these national cinemas, including varying attentions to religion, include: Rachel Dwyer, *Filming the Gods: Religion and Indian Cinema*. London and New York: Routledge, 2006; Donald Richie, *A Hundred Years of Japanese Film: A Concise History, with a Selective Guide to DVDs and Videos*. Oxford: Oxford University Press, 2005; Deb Verhoeven, ed. *Twin Peeks: Australian and New Zealand Feature Films*. Melbourne: Damned Publishing, 1999; Albert Moran and Errol Vieth, *Historical Dictionary of Australian and New Zealand Cinema*. Lanham, MD: Scarecrow Press, 2005; William Van Der Heide, *Malaysian Cinema, Asian Film: Border Crossings and National Cultures*. Amsterdam University Press, 2002; Krishna Sen, *Indonesian Cinema: Framing the New Order*. London and Atlantic Highlands, NJ: Zed Books, Ltd., 1994, and Karl Heider, *Indonesian Cinema: National Culture on Screen*. Honolulu: University of Hawaii Press, 1991. Also key to all of this is David MacDougall's *Transcultural Cinema*. Princeton: Princeton University Press, 1998.

2   See Francisca Cho, "The Art of Presence: Buddhism and Korean Films," in S. Brent Plate, ed. *Representing Religion in World Cinema* (New York: Palgrave, 2003), 111; and David James, "Im Kwon-Taek: Korean National Cinema and Buddhism," in *Im Kwon-Taek: The Making of a Korean National Cinema*, David E. James and Kyung Hyun Kim, eds. Detroit: Wayne State University Press, 2002.

3   See Richard Leonard, *The Cinematic Mystical Gaze: The Films of Peter Weir*. University of Melbourne, PhD thesis, 2003. See also Rob Johnston's discussion of the films of Peter Weir in *Reel Spirituality* 2000, 173–195.

4   N. Jillet, "Images of Gallipoli: the day Peter Weir Met the ANZAC Ghosts", *The Age*, 26 January 1978, 17.

Chapter 18

Rachel Dwyer

FILMING THE GODS
Religion and Indian Cinema

Religion, secularism and the film industry

THE HINDI FILM INDUSTRY prides itself on being secular, and it is secular in the sense of 'equal respect' being given to each religion. The diversity of the industry goes back to its earliest days, at least in Bombay, where Bengali Hindus worked alongside Germans (New Theatre), while in other companies many Muslim stars worked alongside Hindus, Jews and Parsis. After independence, when many Punjabi Hindus who had fled the partition came to Bombay, they worked alongside Muslims. A notable example is B.R. Chopra, who left Lahore in August 1947, and, for his 1950s films such as *Ek hi raasta* (1956) and *Naya daur* (1957), had a story-writing team that was mostly Muslim (including Akhtar ul-Imam and Akhtar Mirza); his lyricist was Muslim (Sahir Ludhianvi), his music directors Hindu (O.P. Nayyar, Hemant Kumar), his singers Muslim (Mohammad Rafi) and Hindu (Lata Mangeshkar) while his stars were Muslims (Dilip Kumar, Meena Kumari) and Hindus (Vyjayanthimala, Ashok Kumar).

Manto (1998) also shows how mixed the world of the film people was in terms of religious backgrounds, and there were many deep friendships, affairs and marriages across communities (Raj Kapoor and Nargis; Kishore Kumar and Madhubala) in the 1940s, just as there are today (Shahrukh Khan and Aamir Khan both married Hindus while Hrithik Roshan married a Muslim). This is all well known by the fans, who often regard the stars themselves as gods, even having temples dedicated to them. However, their behaviour, while often accepted, is not seen as something to emulate for the 'ordinary people'.

The film industry does not, on the whole, try to elide the differences between the different religions – nor indeed, between different regional backgrounds – but festivals, life rituals, etc. are celebrated together, whatever the community. However, one notable feature of the industry is the absence, at least at the higher levels, of anyone lower caste or Dalit. There are certainly some castes that are numerically significant in the industry (notably the Punjabi Khatris) but there does not seem to be any other association around caste.

The Hindi film industry's treatment of religion is probably not that dissimilar from Hollywood where everyone knew who was Jewish, Roman Catholic and so on. Although many of the Hollywood moguls were Jewish, it seems their studios celebrated 'national' (often Christian) festivals such as Christmas and Thanksgiving. No eyebrows were raised at the involvement of Jewish people in creating the American dream of the Christian festival through film, notably with songs like the 'secular' 'White Christmas' written by Irving Berlin (Israel Baline).

One much over-hyped feature of the industry is that actors had to 'conceal' their religious identities by changing their names, so Yusuf Khan became Dilip Kumar, Begum Mumtaz Jehan became Madhubala and Mahajabeen became Meena Kumari. However, concealment was not the aim as everyone in the industry and beyond knew these were stage names and no attempt was made to hide people's religious backgrounds. While no one ever changed his or her name to a Muslim name, many Hindus also changed their names (Ashok Kumar Ganguly to Ashok Kumar, Kulbhushan Nath Pandit to Raaj Kumar, Hari Krishna Goswami to Manoj Kumar and so on) in order to have modern, neutral names, as many Hollywood and other movie stars took stage names that sounded more fashionable or less 'ethnic' (Frederick Austerlitz to Fred Astaire, Lucille Le Sueur to Joan Crawford, Camille Javal to Brigitte Bardot and so on). Similarly in the west, there was no attempt to conceal religious origin, as Woody Allen, who changed his name from Allen Stewart Konigsberg, has always played up his Jewish ethnicity.

The industry has many practices which are directly religious. The films themselves often open with religious images, whether RK Film's sequence of Prithviraj Kapoor worshipping Shiva, or Mukta Arts' use of Om and the recitation of the *Gayatri mantra*, or Mehboob Khan's communist hammer and sickle with the popular Urdu verse: 'No matter what evils your enemies wish for you, it is of no consequence. Only that can happen which is God's will.' (The poem is anonymous though variously attributed to Irshad Lucknowi and Agha Hashr Kashmiri.)

The industry itself uses religious practices such as having an auspicious moment (muhurat) for the first shot, which usually incorporates Hindu rituals such as the breaking of a coconut. Many offices have images of Hindu deities in them, which are worshipped. Astrology, which is not exclusive to any religious tradition and whose popular usage in India tends to blend western and Indian forms, is important for working out dates for releases and other significant events, while numerology and other practices lead to the changing of spellings of names of films (such as Rakesh Roshan's 2006 film Kkrish) and of the actors (Kareena Kapoor has changed the spelling of her name to Karriena and Kariena).

In recent years, certain cults have become important in the film industry, notably that of the Venkateswara temple in Tirupati (Andhra Pradesh) and that of Sai Baba of Shirdi (Maharashtra). While the former is more closely associated with the Telugu and Tamil industries, several members of the Bombay film industry are known to be devotees, and Amitabh Bachchan visited for a special ceremony for his sixtieth birthday in 2002. It is the richest shrine in India, with an annual income said to be of around Rs 800 crore (approx. £100 million).

The first major devotee of Sai Baba in the film industry was Raj Kapoor, who made regular visits to the shrine. Sai Baba, who is claimed as a Hindu and a Muslim, is regarded as 'secular' in the definition given above, in that he is held in equally high regard by Hindus and Muslims. It is not surprising that given this 'secular' religiosity, the proximity of his shrine to Bombay, the simplicity of the rituals involved and his granting of miracles, that he has become such a focus of devotion to many in the industry.

[. . .]

In the last fifteen years Indian society has undergone some of the greatest changes it has seen since Independence in 1947. Several key events at the beginning of the 1990s inaugurated the processes that occurred during the decade. These years saw the rise and fall of the political parties who support Hindutva or policies of Hindu nationalism, while economic reforms brought in a new age of consumerism and liberalism that has taken root across the Indian metropolises.

While other major social transformations also took place during this decade, such as the rise of lower castes (Jaffrelot 2003), this period can be said to be one in which a new social group, 'the new middle classes', dominated India economically, politically, socially and culturally (Dwyer 2000a). The impact of these new groups was felt outside of India as they were part of transnational family networks and the diaspora that became increasingly important as a market for Hindi films, alongside other global audiences.

This decade also saw a media revolution (satellite and cable television since 1991), a communications revolution (the mobile phone and the Internet) and new technologies (the audio cassette, the CD, the VCD and the DVD). The dynamics of the interaction of these new media with the film industry have been fast and there has barely been time to analyse them.

Religious genres, which had been phenomenally popular as religious soaps on terrestrial television (notably Ramanand Sagar's *Ramayana* and B.R. Chopra's *Mahabharata*), soon spread throughout the cable and satellite channels along with other religious programming (lectures, music programmes), and now religious channels such as Astha and Sanskar are growing in popularity. Audio cassettes and CDs of religious music have continued to sell well, while VCDs and DVDs have allowed religious films to recirculate. Religious content has also flourished in other media, so the Internet now offers online *pujas* ('worship') as well as access to texts, religious history and so on, while even mobile phones offer SMS blessings and religious ringtones.

Much of this material in the new media is recycled from the religious films. It is impossible to predict where this is all going, and even the present situation remains unclear. One emerging trend is that the consumption of these new media is very different from that of cinema. Although cinema attendance in India has grown with new viewing trends such as the multiplex, the trend for mediated religion is away from an audience in a theatre hall towards a consumer in a domestic space. This must be viewed with caution as the work of Mankekar (1999) on viewing the television *Mahabharata* suggests Indian viewing practices may be different and these new media may allow the creation of new audiences.[1] This is true of other media as audio cassettes and CDs are played in taxis, autorickshaws and other public places, while VCDs are shown on television screens during festivals.

These new technologies allow more rapid dissemination of religious content to the diaspora, and increasingly these groups are active as consumers and producers. Just as Islam has been affected by globalisation, especially among the Muslim diaspora (Devji 2005, Roy 2004), one may expect to see the emergence of a new form of globalised Hinduism as the religioscape spreads through the world, linked by these new media. It remains to be seen what form this globalised Hinduism will take.

Although these new media may have initially been viewed as a threat to film (and the DVD seems to be a particular problem for piracy), they actually reinforce film, which remains more spectacular, has better technology and brings audiences together in pleasant surroundings, notably the new multiplexes in shopping malls. The changes in film technology, especially those of digitally produced special effects, have led to talk of a new film of the *Mahabharata* with superstars Aamir Khan and Shahrukh Khan playing Karan and Arjun (although it remains to be seen if the audience will accept Muslims, albeit superstars, in these roles).

Cinema is part of the wider project of modernisation. It deals with material progress, sometimes with moral progress but it has deep ambiguities which are its strengths and which make its study so rewarding. Lyden (2003) suggests that the very nature of film evokes the religious. I read this with the caution exercised by Asad in his analysis of the proposition that nationalism is a form of religion, where he shows that this widely held view does not stand up to close scrutiny.[2] While there is much that is religious in the nature of film itself, it does not necessarily constitute a religion. The differences between American cinema and religion and Indian cinema and religion are such that great care should be taken in drawing parallels between the two. More research needs to be done into the pleasures of the religious aesthetic, of faith and of belief in a moral universe in India and in Indian cinema.

It may be that Indian cinema has specific traits that incline it more towards the religious than other cinemas. One must consider the aesthetics of Hindi cinema, such as its deployment of the miraculous, stars, *darshan*, tableaux, sets, song and dance, and the aesthetic of astonishment and its evocation of wonder and reverence. Of course it is not just the text itself, but the way the audience perceives it. One only has to think of how Gandhi came to be seen as a divine figure.

While all film stars are different from mere mortals through the mechanisms of stardom, Hindi film stars are often perceived as gods by their fans, who may dedicate temples to them. Research has already shown the close associations in India of religion and performance, though this is yet to be analysed in cinema. Bharucha (1998: 40) notes: 'There is, I believe, an intensely private space in the believer's consciousness that is activated during prayer, worship, meditation or ecstasy.'[3]

Cinema creates a group identity for people who believe in the congregation (*satsang*) and its miraculous effects, and its 'aesthetic of astonishment'[4] for an audience that believes in miracles and in stars as gods. Most people react to cinema as something ineffable: we know cinema, we feel cinema but we find it hard to analyse.

It is promising that the scholarly discipline of film studies is slowly beginning to engage seriously with religion. For some years the dominant paradigms were Freud and feminism, which undoubtedly were productive for engaging with melodrama with its study of the unconscious, dreams, desire, and fantasy. We still do not have a better language than this, and so we persist with it, despite our awareness of its limitations. Of course, for religious films, one has to be aware that psychoanalysis sets itself up as a new religion. The theories of postmodernism and the breakdown of grand narratives are not accepted by the majority, neither in the west nor in India.

In *Filming the Gods*, most of the readings can be said to be meanings that are known to the audience and also based on the views of the filmmakers, critics and audiences, though for the first time they are historicised and contextualised rather than interpreted individually, and as a mistaken teleology.

These films, however cynical critics may be, do create religious sentiment in viewers and audiences and may contribute towards a hybrid Hinduism, whether they are taking it from the world around them or whether they are creating it themselves. The films' focus on the family, on the group, on the nation, on the transnational Indian community is all part of a search for a new morality and a new happiness. This raises the question of a Hindu imagination, for these films suggest that religion is more important than nationalism. As British Muslims now often prefer to define themselves as Muslims rather than as Pakistani or Indian, so perhaps a new Hindu imagination may be emerging where the British or North American person of Indian origin is no less Hindu than an Indian. This does not imply any necessary association with Hindutva or Hindu nationalism but with a form of popular belief that has not been redefined in these Semitic terms, nor in any form of systematic belief. If this is indeed a Hindu imagination, it needs to be defined, analysed and historicised.

[. . .]

Secularist nationalism in India placed the religious in the private not in the public sphere. Yet it is not clear how this division can be made in India where the secular is so different from its western (Christian) form. Secularism is produced by religion and most of our understandings of it are based on European society (Asad 2003). In Hinduism, there does not seem to be a possibility of separate domains for the sacred and profane. The division would be between pure and impure – *pavitra* and *apavitra* – which are by no means equivalent. The gods of Hinduism are here in the everyday world, which is sacred itself, a goddess, known as Bhu, Vasundhara and many other names. It remains to be seen how Hinduism would produce a secular imagination, and what it would be.

The media have created ways of representing religious groups and identities. Some of these draw from precolonial divisions but they also show how profoundly the colonial representation of caste and community has been fixed in the Indian imagination. The cinema, although it rarely mentions caste, has also constructed new religious identities, and I have noted several for women including the worship of Santoshi Maa and the spread in popularity of rituals such as that of Karva chauth (a fast for a husband's welfare).

The discussion [a previous chapter] shows that there is clearly an Islamicate imagination, a depiction of a culture where the Muslim figure is in the centre of the world while God is also present, not just in Sufi shrines and sacred objects, but also has agency and can cause miracles to occur. Even when Muslims appear in 'non-religious' films, they are shown as religious and often devout figures, who belong to this world. The complex relationships between the communities are often alluded to in the films. Hindus are shown to be respectful to Islamicate culture and even to worship at Muslim shrines. Muslims can pay their respects to Hinduism, and some Muslim rulers were known for giving grants to Hindu temples, but they cannot worship the images.

The media have played a major part in forming this Islamicate imagination, of image, text and music, drawing from sources as diverse as Mughal art to Parsi theatre and chromolithographs to popular stories. The Islamicate films have built on these images and created their own representations of beauty, architecture, religiosity and music. The figure of the courtesan has been central to this and now every courtesan's song and dance will have to reflect this world, where even a Hindu, such as Chandramukhi in *Devdas* (2002, dir. Sanjay Leela Bhansali), has to present herself as part of this culture. The beauty and elegance of the 'lost world' of Lucknow is contrasted with a supposed Hindu – and colonial – lack of refinement.

The Hindu imagination seems more elusive, although Greeley's argument for the existence of a Catholic imagination has some clear parallels.[5] One shared feature is that Greeley is looking at the Catholic imagination in a society where Catholics are aware of, and in part defined by, their relations to other religious groups. The films examined in this book also suggest that communities are defined and self-aware in India in part, at least, through their definition against others. In India, while there is some syncretism, the religious communities are also separate but they interact and shape themselves in relation to others (notably Hindu reform movements of the nineteenth century as figures such as Swami Dayanand tried to make Hinduism, at least in the form of the Arya Samaj, follow the religions of the book).

Although it seems too early to posit a well-defined Hindu imagination, cinema is the best place to look for the presence or absence of the Hindu and of the secular imagination anywhere in India. It needs to be examined in conjunction with ideas of other modernities, where one may begin with the fact that although cinema is the art form of modernity, it is never free from religion.

This Hindu imagination must not be confused with Hindu-ness as Hindutva. For many people this eruption of the religious in the most modern forms of media may be frightening and associated with extremism and fanaticism. There is no reason that religion should be a force for evil but it may be a giver of strength, joy and pleasure. The Hindu gods must be worshipped and celebrated and the films go some way to keeping them in the world. Many images of Ram today, in particular those promoted by Hindutva, may be of the warrior king, ready to fight, but for many he remains an object of devotion and love. The history of the images of the gods in the media show the audience is making an active appropriation of meanings for new situations in life.

Pauline Kael at the Arts Club of Chicago in 1975 pointed out the import-ance of Catholic directors in Hollywood (Altman, Coppola and Scorsese), in that their sensuous style was not about religion; rather their work was connected with religious themes and moral conduct. Cinema is an important forum to examine these key issues in western society, which now values emotions and feelings above all else and where sexual identities have become more important than other ways of thinking about oneself. Many of the arts in the west no longer pay attention to minds and souls, virtues, love, duty, self-sacrifice and character, but instead concentrate on bodies, from surfaces to orifices. Hindi films still ask important questions about bodies, souls, morals and selves, and it is these themes which make it so much more interesting than much of Hollywood. Indian cinema's serious consideration of religion is part of under-standing Indian history and society, if one is prepared to engage seriously with it.

Notes

1   Purnima Mankekar, *Screening culture, viewing politics: an ethnography of television, womanhood, and nation in postcolonial India*. Durham: Duke University Press, 1999.

2   See Talal Asad, *Formations of the secular: Christianity, Islam, modernity*. Stanford: Stanford University Press, 2003, 181–201.

3   Rustom Bharucha, *In the name of the secular: cultural practice and activism in India today*: Delhi: Oxford University Press, 1998, 40.

4   See Tom Gunning, 'An aesthetic of astonishment: early film and the (in)credulous spectator'. In Linda Williams (ed.) *Viewing positions: ways of seeing film*. New Brunswick: Rutgers University Press, 114–33.

5   See Andrew Greeley, *The Catholic Imagination*. Berkeley: University of California Press, 2000.

Chapter 19

Geeta Kapur

REVELATION AND DOUBT IN *SANT TUKARAM* AND *DEVI*

IN FILMIC CLASSIFICATION Sant Tukaram, along with other 'saint' films, may be placed in the category of the mythological. However it belongs more correctly to a subgenre of special significance. The saints' lives are quasi-biographical material. Their message of spiritual equality makes these lives legendary as well as expressly adaptable to historical ends. We know of course that in the nationalist ethos saints' lives were especially valorized and made to light the way to social justice. The need to publish new editions of Marathi bhakti poets was emphasized as early as the mid-nineteenth century by M.G. Ranade who, like other middle-class nationalists of the period, saw the seventeenth-century bhakti movement as a kind of Protestant movement wherein caste difference were sought to be softened.

This contextual factor was evidently recognized by the makers of the 'saint' films at Prabhat Studios (Prabhat Film Company). Damle/Fattelal's film *Sant Dnyaneshwar* (1940) propagated among other things nonviolence, truth and national consensus. Contemporary reviews and discussions of the film examined its social content. For example K.A. Abbas, a leftist writer and filmmaker of the Progressive Writers' Association and Indian Peoples' Theatre Association (IPTA), commented on the degree of 'realism' in the film, praising it for its naturalness in the first part while criticizing its devolution into a series of miracles in the second part – the director succumbing, as he put it, to the conventions of the popular mythological. 'A saint is something more than a magician', Abbas wrote in his review. Abbas queried the choice to recoup traditions through the techno-magical possibilities of the cinema and entered the debate about the political import of popular culture as such. The reply in the *Bombay Chronicle* by an unnamed critic confirms that in India, as in Europe, alternation between the magical and realist potential of the cinema was an ongoing polemic. The point I shall be making at some length is that the *bhakti* saints and their portrayed lives have to be seen neither in terms of realism nor in terms of the mass appeal of the miracles that defenders of such films cite. The films have to be seen as socially symbolic narratives. For, like literature, cinema supplements the primary representation of the social with its own narrative representation through a process that may be called 'iconographic augmentation'.

The iconic image

The pictorial convention on which *Sant Tukaram* is based is such as to give its imagery an iconic aspect, taking iconic to mean an image on to which symbolic meanings converge and in which, moreover, they achieve hypostasis. An iconic image, according to this functional definition, may or may not be mythological or religious but it does suggest an iconographic process wherein morphology – a dynamic principle of formal aesthetics – takes on the gravity of the symbolic to thus ground itself in a given tradition.

The immediate antecedents of the Prabhat films, including *Sant Tukaram*, are the films of Dadasaheb [D. G.] Phalke (1870–1944). As the pioneer cinematographer of India, Phalke projected the iconic image in a more literal sense. He drew upon a traditional iconographic repertoire. His express aim was to bring forth the Hindu pantheon through the technical magic of the cinema; to revive the gods of the puranas; to fortify and gladden the masses of India in a moment of national self-affirmation. Stepping into a corridor of antecedents one may ask, what visual sources were tapped for the purpose?

The iconic, at the conjunctural moment of Indian cinema, already includes the naive element – as in early photography where the subject is positioned up front or rather, where subjectivity itself takes on a frontal aspect, the better to allow its magical capture as image. But this in turn includes pictorial iconography, the formal positioning and frontality of Indian photographs of the nineteenth century referring both to icons proper and to the pictorial conventions of idealized portraiture in medieval times. For although medieval portraits are shown in profile there is an aspectual iconicity in the posture offering a deflected grace: the portrait sets up a complementary relation to the icon. Mid-nineteenth century pahari and Sikh miniature portraits (shading into the

Company School) continue to confirm this formal attitude. While abandoning the sacred protocol of the pictorial tradition early Indian photography inherits the humbler version of the artist's idealizing imagination. It reverts the profiled types once again to staid attention and lends a fresh alertness to frontal address. In continuation, early cinematic imagery has the naive boldness to invoke pictorial origins and complete the circle by assuming the attributes of the (pseudo) icon.

Let us look at the characteristics of the image as it comes across in *Sant Tukaram* to recognize how religious iconicity is mediated to secular effect in the filmic process. Repeated over-the-shoulder shots of the devotee first put god and the viewer in contact. But even as Tukaram the saint adores the black-faced Vithoba and witnesses his miracles in wonder the cinematic image is construed to symmetrically reverse the gaze: the saint turns around to let the viewer 'adore' him and witness his sublime speech and song. It is his generosity of address towards all phenomena, real and divine and, with it the alertness and dignity of sacred protocol that help the film in transmitting a nonvoyeuristic gaze to the viewer. But if in this performative about-turn there is a transfer of affect between god, saint and viewer conducted through the very body of the saint, there is also a cinematic rhythm in the reversed gaze which makes for reciprocity, an intersubjective truth-effect that is ultimately secular.

The film *Sant Tukaram* succeeds among other things precisely in the way it develops an *iconic sign*. The iconic in the language of cinema derives its character-istics from painting. Figurative images, especially portraits, rest not only on likenesses or resemblances but equally on an economy of representation, and with that an autonomous logic of positioning and structure. This inevitable distancing between the pictorial image and the real world acquires additional virtues in the transfer between painting and cinematography. The iconic sign, peculiar to cinema, denotes precisely this transfer (of icon-image-sign) and helps in breaking down a rigid assumption: that the cinema upholds ultimate verisimilitude.

In the *Natyashastra* the actor is a *patra*, a vessel, conveying the attributes and emotions of a 'character' to the viewer while remaining intact himself. He is at once deity and man, he is both an iconic and an indexical sign. By virtue of this double coding the 'character' devolves and what is conveyed in performance is body, voice, discourse. In several Indian theatrical traditions, for example the Ramlila at Ramnagar (Varanasi), little boys who are apprenticed to play Rama, Sita and Lakshmana are treated as both deity and child and nurtured on that account for over two months. But their apprenticeship entails training in recit-ing the verses of the *Ramacharita-manasa*, not in acting. Once the performance begins they must simply *be*, and they must simply speak the text. They raise their voices and intone the text in an unvarying but astonishingly clear and lofty manner and they succeed in reaching out to the thousands in the audience. The enunciation is the determining factor, for the text as discourse establishes symbolic paramountcy. The god is sheer presence or, on the other hand, a 'mere' sign.

Narrative movement

It is in the narrative that the content of the discourse, the meaning of the words as they are uttered in passionate verse, is mobilized. In so far as the saints' lives are perceived in the Indian tradition as historically 'true' but also emblematic (closed off by the self-realization of the saint through voluntary death, suicide, *samadhi*, or some form of mythic assumption), the retelling or replaying of these lives will tend to follow the allegorical mode. This is true for *Sant Tukaram*. Consequently, as compared with the phenomenologically rich but overdetermined and unitary 'realism' that Andre Bazin seeks in cinema, we can place *Sant Tukaram* in the genre of the Indian 'mythological' and see in it a different constructional principle. The miracles, for example, are so embedded in the story as to be seen not only as motivating points of the narrative but even, one might say, ideal prototypes of human action. The question of realism is thus always kept a little in abeyance though never quite eschewed, since the pedagogical aspect of the life of a saint requires constant reference to reality. What is interesting is that the *social* is introduced, as in the realism of Bresson and even Rossellini, by opening out the subjectivity of the elect protagonist within the historical. This entry is by way of a saint's acts of transgression; they may be in a political context those of a rebel or a revolutionary.

'Can metaphysics be converted into action? And can action have meaning beyond itself? These are the questions that have haunted filmmakers who do not stop at naturalism.' Kumar Shahani poses this with reference to the saints of Prabhat, going on to say that if the answers are in the negative neither these saint films nor post-Rossellini cinema would have been possible. In *Sant Tukaram* it is the unselfconscious simplicity fusing thought and action which makes for this particular form of didactic narration. Shahani adds that such simplicity can rarely be repeated even by the authors themselves, and asks whether this 'aspiration' to transform the subject-matter itself into form and content is not dangerous when conducted deliberately and in imitation of the naive. The uniqueness of *Sant Tukaram* lies in the fact that 'The legend, the heroic saint himself, dictated the movement of the film.'

The actual movement of the film consists, in the first instance, of Tuka's song and reverie. This releases the spring of miracles which in turn mobilizes the life of the villagers – the peasants and artisans of the village of Dehu – and forms the material environment within which the struggle of Tuka's impoverished wife and children is foregrounded.

Having already mentioned the unique presence of the actor who plays Tuka, Vishnupant Pagnis, a word about his performative style. Shahani points out how Pagnis as Tuka moves only his torso when he sings; the body moves in a subliminal rhythm above the hips and the viewers see him often in close-up, singing to himself as he sings to us. Sometimes we see him in mid-close-up, leading the kirtankars and singing with them as he winds his way in and out of the village streets, weaving a community together. The singing modulates the pace and structure of the moving image. Compare Tuka's style with that of his corrupt rival, Salomalo the priest, who sings the plagiarized verses of Tuka with the body all askew, using the jerky movements of the tamasha actor. One might also compare the pragmatic, uncouth but vulnerable Jijai, Tuka's wife, in her attempted naturalism or spontaneous 'expressionism', with the seductive stylization of the courtesan after the hybrid mannerisms of Ravi Varma's pictorial compositions, and note how a diverse stylistics is consciously used to set off the integral being of Tuka.

The second mobilizing feature of the film is the childlike, indeed childish set of miracles. The stiff idol of Vithoba comes alive smiling as he dances on his little feet, arms akimbo. The wheatstalks in the ravaged fields shoot up of themselves as Tuka sings with his eyes closed. Child Krishna pours grain from the sky with his own two hands to save Tuka. The goddess emerges from the depths of the water with Tuka's bundle of verses intact. Vithoba multiplies the person of Chhatrapati Shivaji, a hundredfold, at Tuka's request, to fool the invading armies. Tuka ascends to Vaikuntha in a chariot flown by Garuda (in the shape of a great hairy bird). The miracles make happy omens for the magical aspect of the cinema since its very inception; there is a never-fading thrill in the technical transformation of contours, substances, bodies, and there is a special thrill in the kinetic transformation of hitherto static iconography.

The fabulous, even where it appears ephemeral, has a narrative function. This brings me to the third aspect of the movement in *Sant Tukaram*. Because the magic is inducted into the everyday life of the little community at Dehu it becomes a motivating impulse towards a materially plentiful existence. The first signs of this are the wholly generous acts of Tuka himself, as for example when he walks through the village like a divine somnambulist letting the plundering army of little children take their pick of his great bundle of sugarcane until by god's grace there is but one each left for his own two children, the poorest of the lot, but made happy so easily.

Then there is Tuka's gracious effect on his community as shown in the sequence where his priestly interrogator, Pandit Rameshwar Shastri, an authority on the vedas, comes to Dehu to indict Tukaram for defiling the scriptures.

Riding into the village, the priest is bewildered to see the villagers engrossed in artisanal tasks by virtue of Tuka's supportive verse and song. There is a wonderful tracking shot parallel to the priest on the horse but taken from the near side, so that you see between the camera and the priest an entire pageant of working people engaged in their craft, trade and domestic chores. Singing all the while, they give rhythm to their daily life. The film here achieves (through remarkable use of a depth-of-field and sustained lateral movement which prolongs the penetrating view) a shift in the viewer's perception – the priest and his cohorts rather than the poor in their hovels are the objects of the viewer's voyeuristic interest and derision. This sequence also achieves a retake on the viewer's attraction to the spectacular miracles. Here is evidence of real emancipation shown to be immanent within a community of unalienated labour. Here life, song and work combine to attain the sustained rhythm of reverie we associate only with leisure. This gift to his people is the saint's true miracle.

The actual miracles in Sant Tukaram are naive to the point of being crude, just as the image and its iconography are construed cursorily and simply signpost the event. But it is also as if the moments of fallibility suggest complementary moments of identification, just as the moments of material want and suffering recall moments of plenty. Take for example the scene where Jijai and her two children succumb to greed and play unabashedly with Shivaji's nazrana but at Tuka's rebuke willingly surrender the ruler's wealth. In another scene the village poor loot god's boon to Tuka, the piles of grain at his door; and in that upsurge you see, inadvertently almost, the glistening energy of muscle and movement mounting up to revolutionary effect. The energy born of need becomes, through the saint's encouragement, a virtual prefiguration of peasant insurgency.

If the film has a Méliès-like magicality (via the example of Phalke), the miracles also initiate a sensuous gain in the daily life of the community and become the mode of social transformation in the film. Ultimately Tuka's ascent to heaven is fairly matched by Jijai's pathetic but real claim to see him back home for his daily meal. We can see the other part of the cinema, the early realism of, say Pudovkin, already moulded into this saint's life on film.

Through the materiality of the miracles and the precise conflation of faith and labour, through a cinematic narrative that interweaves magic and realism, through the physiognomy of Vishnupant Pagnis as Tukaram and the phenomenological elaboration of a life-in-poverty in peasant India – through a propitious combination of these factors given dignity by the national struggle, Sant Tukaram becomes a revelatory text conducive to a hermeneutic of affirmation.

Chapter 20

Im Kwon-Taek, with David James

AN INTERVIEW WITH IM KWON-TAEK

Interviewers: What is the position from which you go back to Korean history? By making historical films, do you tell stories of our society today? Or do you make them to preserve the history we are forgetting?

Im Kwon-Taek: Films could serve the function of preservation, I guess. Could we talk about this using *Surrogate Mother*? Why do we need such representations today? For example, I am the first son in the family, but there is a conflict between my mother and me, because my mother thinks that I won't pay attention to the ancestor worshipping rituals when she passes away. Even though I am responsible while she is alive, my going around making movies and giving them more attention than our ancestors is a potential crisis. Our lifestyle today is such that we can't possibly give as much care as they did in the old days, but my mother still insists I give more. So we still face very traditional questions, and even now there are incredible efforts to have a male child, creating scandals with the doctors and so on. We create massive movements all over the nation around New Year's Day and Autumn Harvest Day, when an estimated twenty million people return to their original homes, to meet their ancestors and to perform the rituals according to the Confucian framework. There is nothing in Confucianism that stipulates itself as a religion except its emphasis on self-restraint and education – and filial piety. The requirement that the descendants guard the parents' graves for three years without doing much else is a religious concept. Three years to demonstrate filial gratitude, that's a scary thing about our national identity. And it's not simply the powers above that force us to place so much emphasis on worshiping ancestors. When people die, they become gods to us, and we think that if we obey them well, we will be blessed. There is no way for us to say, "It's over when we are dead." The ones who live and the ones who die cannot easily be separated. This is why our nation goes through massive migration [during the holidays] and prefers male children. How could we not think that we need a film like *Surrogate Mother?*

Interviewers: Do you then think that there are problems with our national feudal traditions?

Im Kwon-Taek: I think there are many problems. I made *Surrogate Mother* in that belief. I thought that the story of one woman being unjustly sacrificed to bear a son could be used as an element of resistance. But, three years after the film, I told a foreign critic that the film might have been a mistake because I had criticized the process of acquiring a son in exchange for the human sacrifice of a surrogate. I changed my position since the film. Why is that the case? In Korea, we intermix Buddhism with Shamanism and so on, but I had judged other people's religious principles by my own logic. How could I arrogantly make a film and make precipitous statements when the nation itself already has that kind of complex religious mentality? Similarly in *Festival*, I attempted to display how comical our funeral process is.

Interviewers: The fact that it is complicated and cumbersome?

Im Kwon-Taek: It's not that it's cumbersome but that it lacks any logic and is full of contradictions. Traditional Korean religion is made up of Shamanism, Confucianism, Buddhism, and some Taoism. The Confucian philosophy insists that when people die, spirit and flesh become divided. Flesh returns to nature when the body decomposes in the grave, and the spirit lives with us for four generations. But in Buddhism, when people die, a messenger comes and Yama, the king of Hell, then determines whether you belong in hell or nirvana. Shamanism is different again. The function of Shamans is to heal the sick and send the bad spirits of the dead to heaven, so that they don't haunt the living people. Whether they go to heaven or not is beside the point. But in our religion, as you can see in *Festival* when a character climbs up the roof, he calls out, asking the spirit to come back and live again. This must be Confucian since according to Shamanism, spirits should not come back. Then there's a part that concerns Buddhism. For the three messengers who have come to take away the dead, we must prepare three rice bowls, three pairs of shoes – I guess heaven is that far away – and traveling money. But if the dead is taken away, that should be the end of it. But no, they break the rice bowls, preventing the return of the dead spirit. This is Shamanism. Then, after the burial, they carry the ancestor tablet back home. According to Buddhism, the spirit that should have been sent away is carried back into the house. And finally, breaking the gourd while carrying away the dead body is a Shamanist act, to ban the dead from returning home. Nothing works logically here.

Interviewers: Because the three religions are mixed together?

Im Kwon-Taek: Every possible good deed for the dead is done, whether or not it makes sense. I am not being critical, but I am dealing with the subject with the mentality that if we are really concerned with the funeral, then perhaps there could be a change in the social consensus. I think if we use the film to get a "close-up" on the contradictory clements, we could change things that need repair.

Interviewers: There have been some criticisms of Sopyonje. From feminist perspectives some people have pointed out that Yu-bong's blinding of Song-hwa is legitimized and the film ends too ambivalently. What do you think?

Im Kwon-Taek: I am aware of that concern. I argue that you should not see Sopyonje as a film that exploits women. The reason I made a film about p'ansori was because our culture was being toppled by Western culture. Since the Japanese colonial period, our culture has been delegated to the lower class and often regarded as trash. Even I – who since 1978 or 1979 had been thinking of making a film about p'ansori – would switch to other channels when it was on television, searching for something more entertaining. To demonstrate that our beautiful and moving p'ansori is as great as – if not superior to – any other music, was my first objective. Then the question is how to interpret the characters, especially Yu-bong. When our life becomes economically sound and prosperous, our values change, and when life is hard, then our objectives also change. For Yu-bong, training his voice to achieve excellence is the most important objective in his life, and if that's not possible, he wants to do it through someone else. From the perspective of Yu-bong, looking at his child Song-hwa, he thinks that even for her the greatest value in life must be singing a great song. He thinks that whatever the sacrifice, if Song-hwa can acquire an extraordinary voice, then she will be happy. Of course, this is stubbornness and egotism, especially since it entails the abuse of a human being in pursuing its objective, and he is an egotistical bastard. After Song-hwa's brother runs away, he is worried that she might also run away. Therefore he decides to believe the myth that the han entailed in losing one's sight allows one to acquire a great voice. He doesn't know whether this is true or not, but his worry that she may run away and his greed as a man force him to trap her, and so Yu-bong is not a great person. In my films, sometimes there are saints like Ch'oe Hae-wol and Ch'oe

Si-hyong in Fly High, Run Far, but most are ordinary people who make us wonder if we would have done the same thing. Yu-bong's not an ideal figure, and I don't want it to be thought that because he blinded her, men are superior. Human beings are full of contradictions and ironies. Sound was also another thing to consider. In the section where she sings the part of Simch'ong, who goes around begging for rice in the shabby house, the poverty delivered through the song and the images only makes the song more convincing. In Sopyonje, the most important objective was visually to complement the beauty of the singing and transfer it to the audience clearly.

Interviewers: You have made two films that have explicitly dealt with Buddhism: Mandala and Come, Come, Come Upward. What attracted you to this religion?

Im Kwon-Taek: I shot Mandala thinking how beautiful it is to live with intensity. In filming it, I found a little more about the worldview of the monks, which led me to the next project, Come, Come, Come Upward. The Buddhism Korea accepted was the Mahayana sect, whose objective is to bring ordinary people to enlightenment. Many monks, however, do not follow the precepts of Mahayana Buddhism and communicate it to ordinary people. They live as Hinayana hermits in the mountains. If reality is painful for most people, then it is necessary to share ordinary people's pain and struggle by following Mahayana Buddhism. I made Come, Come, Come Upward to ask how the monks could separate themselves from ordinary life and follow Hinayana Buddhist ways.

Chapter 21

William R. LaFleur

SUICIDE OFF THE EDGE OF EXPLICABILITY

Awe in Ozu and Kore'eda

I see the hard, round, whole substance of pain splinter and crack into everything there is.[1]

Religion at a low temperature

AMONG THE MAJOR religions Buddhism has long tolerated, sometimes even encouraged, an agnostic approach in unexpected areas. On certain questions deemed essential by the monotheistic faiths and about which they have claimed to have data from highly placed sources, the earliest Buddhists maintained what was, at least by their own lights, a principled silence. The existence of deity, the origins of the universe, and like matters constituted, for them, questions deemed unanswerable – due not only to scanty data but also because such questions tend to distract humans from attention to the problem of suffering. And it is not unheard of for Buddhists themselves to express skepticism about traditional ideas once taken to be core tenets of the tradition – karma, for instance. Although in recent films such as Bertolucci's Little Buddha karmic rebirth is taken as a staple of Buddhism and a belief which – somewhat conveniently – gives a metaphysical scope to the technique of the 'flashback', such a concept, say some, may not really be an essential of Buddhism after all.

Buddhism in this form would seem to be a clear example of what A.N. Whitehead in 1927 called 'religion at a very low temperature'. His point however, was what might be 'low' should not be misidentified as 'out'. Because we may be far more accustomed to the more high temp prophetic modes of religion, we may need to retrain ourselves to be able to see and feel what is religious about less overt modes. Such an effort may be especially needed in contexts, primarily Japanese, where an aesthetic has been shaped by the Zen form of Buddhism to provide something unusually interesting – even if also very elusive. This is so because already in China Buddhists following this particular trajectory had often turned the possession of non-knowledge into something of a virtue, gaining thereby respect from some. The tomes of both Chinese and Japanese Zen relished the skeptical mode. They are full of accounts of masters resistant to the use of religious language and turning away piety as merely a version of pretence.

Sakyamuni's silence and Kasyapa's enigmatic smile, parts of the foundation story for Zen as a school, have been a peculiar goad to anyone wanting to articulate how this low temp religion became a cultural and aesthetic style in Japan, one also likely to be a feature of certain films. This is a piety which, if not perverse, is at least inverse: It gets expressed through diffidence and disclaimers concerning its very existence. And this surely presents an obvious problem to anyone hoping to *express* what might be meaningful in acts of silence. To articulate the norm threatens, by definition, to violate it. Knowing this while at the same time attempting to work around it is to me one of the most interesting things about Donald Richie's classic study of Yasujiro Ozu. In an effort to further unpack what Paul Schrader had tagged as the evidence of 'transcendental style' in Ozu. Richie wanted to employ terms like *mu* and *mono no aware* – that is, terms linked closely to the Buddhist aesthetic of an earlier era in Japan. But he knew Ozu would have laughed off the very suggestion. '[Ozu] himself never spoke of *mu*, or *mono no aware*, though he knew what they meant, and I doubt he would ever have seriously discussed them.'[2] Nevertheless, Richie noted that Ozu had his ashes buried at a Zen temple in Kamakura and that the graph *mu* engraved on his tombstone suggests 'the nothing that, in Zen philosophy, is everything'.[3]

Paradoxical in this is the move toward affirmation by way of negation. In this mode of being religious the old minimalist dictum holds true: To say less is to say more. A primary teaching of Buddhism had been that *all* things and beings are impermanent. Thus, our attempts to 'comprehend' them – since these involve *prehendere* or grasping by the mind – will ultimately both fail and court futility. Initially this comes across as a negative: the impermanence that is the prime feature of things (*mono*) forces limits on our capacity to know them fully. Just as we cannot physically hold in place or in stasis that which is passing away, so too we cannot *hold in mind* that which ultimately runs far beyond our mental grasp.

But the flip-side of this limitation is positive. The fact that even ordinary things and persons cannot be fully grasped implies their capacity to elude the limitation that our holding efforts would place upon them. The myriad ways in which phenomena interpenetrate implies that they can serve as apertures through which we can glimpse something of the vast network – sometimes called 'Indra's net' – of the universe. And for Buddhists, awe vis-à-vis phenomena is awe and 'transcendence' enough. Mu is the negation that is 'everything', the denial of certainty that opens out into the 'mysteriousness in things' (*mono no aware*).

Mu as a word on Ozu's tombstone suggests that it may also be a key feature of his films. If awe is a posture of the mind, it is also one the body should be expected to articulate. Silences, taciturnity, or even mumbled inanities can characterise the tongue in times of reverie. And the nearly quiescent, *sitting* body – especially when complemented by the famously 'sitting' camera of Ozu – is the apt corporeal mode, one perhaps so enculturated in Japan that an overt reference to it seems hardly necessary to most Japanese. Richie explains how conversational hiatuses operate both in the psychology and aesthetics of Ozu's films: 'They tell us that Ozu characters are people capable of sitting back, of being contemplative'.[4] But it is important to note that the cinematographic techniques were of one piece with that director's core philosophy:

> . . . Ozu usually prefers to break rather than resolve, at least in the middle of his films. An unavoidable inference is that the weather, nature, the world that exists outside man and his petty concerns, is much wider, much *more mysterious*, than we usually think.[5]

This in a most literal sense becomes how the world is viewed.

My ambition here is that this is very much like what is often going on in films made by Hirokazu Kore'eda and especially in his 1998 *Maborosi*. Frequently compared to Ozu, Kore'eda also makes films that open forward into an attitude of awe before the immensity and mysteriousness of the universe and all the particulars within it. In *Maborosi* too the unmoving camera induces a stance of contemplation, one which respects and relishes what may forever remain unknown in things. The stance is one that becomes satisfied with no needing to 'break through' the world of phenomena to locate some entity, some God, or some Being which lies somehow *beyond* the penumbra of the known.

Yumiko's search

Kore'eda, who is more concerned about plot than Ozu had been, also invests more effort in a deliberate undermining of intellectual obstacles to such a vision of the world. He insists that we see what is deeply inexplicable about our universe and our lives and tries to facilitate that by a certain amount of ground-clearing. In Maborosi this matter is focused through the problem of suicide and specifically whether or not it is something which can ever be adequately comprehended by others. To be sure, they make sustained efforts to grasp it. It can become an obsession. As the heroine of Maborosi states near the film's end, her first husband's death had been a matter 'going round and round in [her] head'. But the film strongly suggests that such efforts cannot ultimately succeed.

What, therefore, might be the 'religious' dimension of such a film consists not in doctrinal resonances but in how the film itself, both in its narrative and in its cinematic techniques, accommodates to the deep incomprehensibility of events and, beyond that, adumbrates the mysteriousness of the world itself. The narrative moves in the direction of showing that even in the case of suicide we do well to recognise not only something tragic – that is, the usual approach – but also something finally inexplicable and, to that extent, awesome. But to take up this theme and to value it in such terms constituted a bold and unconventional move on the part of a director. Here I try to pursue the question of why this is so important but at the same time recognise what my close focus leaves unsaid about this rich film. I note that elsewhere Keiko McDonald has provided an analysis of Maborosi that is so attuned to the subtleties of its plot and so attentive to its details that any effort of mine to do the same would be both redundant and embarrassingly inadequate by comparison.

The plot of Maborosi moves on an axis – away from the urban life of the young and happily married Yumiko, through the tragedy of her husband's totally unanticipated suicide under a train, and her subsequent move into a new marriage, one that means she henceforth will live in a rural seacoast community. Through most of the film that is where she lives but the domestic happiness she eventually comes to know there is always qualified by the question that cannot leave her mind – namely, that of the reason for her first husband's death. By the film's denouement it has become her obsession.

Maborosi is a film whose core tension depends in part on a contrast between an ever widening visual spaciousness on screen and what we cannot avoid perceiving as the protagonist's narrowly focused mind. If the external world is wide and free, the ambit of the principal character's mind is tight and constricted. The unresolved problem makes it so. Our insight into the pain of Yumiko is sharpened by a perceptible contrast between what we gather concerning her inner life and the expansive landscape of sea, fields and sky – a landscape to which the camera of Kore'eda is so attentive that it becomes a part of the philosophy of this film. Met and driven to her rural home by Tamio, her second husband. Yumiko seems aghast to see that the sea is so vast. This theme gets reiterated in a later scene where her own child and that of her second husband are at play together in rice-fields. A high-angle shot catches them as small figures next to an endless sea and on a fragile strip of land running next to ricefields that themselves exquisitely mirror the expanse of the sky above. On the road going there one child remarks that the scope of the land is wide and then the other responds, saying that the ocean is even more vast.

Yet, importantly, these are not shots that in any way *reduce* the humans by juxtaposing them to what might be the physical world's capacity to terrorise by virtue of its immensity. Humans are not rendered minuscule: that part of Rudolph Otto's *mysterium tremendum* does not come forth. Even the ocean, audibly and endlessly roaring, is not ever presented as somehow 'indifferent' since even that approach, a favourite of Naturalism in the arts, lays down an anthropomorphic attempt at 'comprehension' whereas what interests Kore'eda's camera takes in a nature that is neither hostile nor friendly. It is a nature that just *is*. And as long as it is so, the manner in which it slides out beyond the epistemic grasp yields what about it is wondrous. The truly meditative stance refrains from writing melodrama over the phenomena of nature. And this, I suggest, is the Ozuesque stance.

What we know about the inner life of Yumiko, however, is that it remains fixed, even at times obsessed, with trying to understand the suicide of Ikuo. This mind and this preoccupation cannot avoid being also those of any viewer of *Maborosi*. He or she is never given privileged access to any information about that death. And, thus, Yumiko's central preoccupation is necessarily that of the viewer as well. If anything, the searched for reason for Ikuo's suicide becomes increasingly more obscure, more unattainable as the story moves forward. Well into the narrative we learn, when Yumiko does, that Ikuo's state of mind during the hours just prior to his death had not shown even a trace of the mentality we ordinarily describe as 'suicidal'. What is remarkable about this film is that it is not one whose narrative tension will be relieved in the end by the provision of some missing datum that makes for 'resolution'. On the contrary, Kore'eda's design is to show that Ikuo's death, perhaps to illustrate something about all suicides, will remain a deeply *incomprehensible* one.

Kore'eda has intended to deprive us of the various ways in which we, notably in the modern era, are accustomed to thinking that we might be able to uncover the exact cause or causes of an act of suicide. Most explicit about wanting to take away what we think of as a socio-economic explanation, he writes:

> What I wanted to do [in *Maborosi*] is explore the sense of loss that
> one woman carried within her, independent of the poverty of the
> time or even her own poverty. I thought that way I would achieve a
> pure portrayal of that loss. For my generation . . . there is a feeling
> of a *lack of certainty* about anything – a universal undefined feeling
> of loss.[6]

Kore'eda states that it was his intention to undercut the way in which an
older contemporary, Kohei Oguri, had suggested in film that suicide is explicable – namely, that once the conditions of poverty or deprivation are presented,
an audience will know why someone chose death. It seems clear that Kore'eda
denied any suggestion of material deprivation in the lives of Yumiko and Ikuo
when the latter went under the wheels of a speeding train.

The collapse of explanatory adequacy, however, goes on. Also taken away is
the likelihood of psycho-pathological motivation. Through much of the film
Yumiko appears to wonder whether some kind of deep depression, one that
Ikuo had hidden from her, had in fact been present and had pressed him to a
breaking point. This lurking possibility, however, gets emphatically discarded
once Yumiko returns to the urban site of her former life for a visit and there
learns that Ikuo had been anything but depressed on the day of his death. From
the coffee-bar proprietor who had seen him just prior to the suicide, she finds
that Ikuo had been upbeat, showing none of the signs of a condition that could
be clinically defined as 'suicidal'.[7] Thus, neither poverty nor pathology – that
is, probably the 20th century's two favoured justifications – were able, according to this director, to bring about a satisfactory explanation for suicide. At least
they fail to do so for what Kore'eda, significantly, calls 'his generation',[8] And
he surely knew he was moving against the stream – something shown in his
statement: 'I really don't think it's bad for people to be attracted to the idea of
death or loss, or to portray it, or to approach it, or to measure one's distance
from it'.

Important to note about *Maborosi*, however, is that its director does not offer
yet another theory as to what might push an individual into a voluntary death.
Instead, he employs a complex play with light to provide a viewer of this film
with his or her own experience of being attracted toward some context which,
however opaquely, promises to provide some intense epiphany of things. Via
this film the trajectory toward suicide is not so much theorised as it is
rehearsed. What is unique in this becomes clear when we realise that our usual
way of explaining suicide is in terms of what conditions or experience might
possibly have been *pushing* an individual toward it. All such theories assume that
being alive as an individual is so obviously preferable to dying that it would
require an immense amount of force – social, psychological, ideological, or

whatever – to push someone to make the opposite judgement and then act upon it. What we mean by the 'breaking point' is the arrival at that point of view and readiness to implement it. All our existing explanations of this process attempt to pinpoint what it is that exerts such a level of pressure. And they assume that, since death by a person's own hand is an unqualified negative and an act with no redeeming features, to remove the conditions that might propel someone toward it must be unqualifiedly positive.

Kore'eda invites skepticism towards precisely that supposition. This is the import of what he says explicitly about how he differs from Kohei Oguri and implicitly about how his own 'generation' differs from its close predecessors. *Maborosi*, consequently, does not offer yet another theory as to what might be the push away from this world. Rather, via the techniques of film itself, it draws a viewer into his or her own experience of what it might feel like to be *attracted* to the moment of dying. Commenting that it need not be '*bad* for people to be attracted to the idea of death', Kore'eda raises a profound question about the correctness and adequacy of what had been the core presupposition in all theories of suicide favoured within the modern epoch. But just to raise the possibility that there might be something profoundly *attractive* in death is to lay emphasis not upon the condition of being dead but upon the experience of dying, one which, however fleeting, is held out as possibly providing an absolutely unparalleled experience of being connected to the panoply of things. Although to the bulk of mankind the price paid is far too much, Kore'eda suggests that for some individuals it is not so. For them the resultant state of being dead does not itself cancel out the value of what might be had in the experience of voluntary dying. To take this point of view is to revive the contention of Yasunari Kawabata, himself later a suicide, offered at the time of his reception of the Nobel Prize for literature in 1968. It was that the person who consciously and intentionally dies has an unparalleled view of things in their awesomeness. Kawabata referred to it as a point of connecting with this world with 'eyes that see it for the last time' (*matsugo no me*).

Seductive light and celluloid trains

Kore'eda does not, however, refer to Kawabata. Instead he builds into his film something with precedent in a body of religious lore handed down from Japan's medieval period. His narrative makes such a connection near the film's end and it comes when Yumiko had returned from her excursion to her former home in the city and had learned there that lkuo had killed himself for no explicable reason. At this point in the film she is finally and totally bereft of explanations. There had been no 'sense' in lkuo's suicide. And she is distraught to a degree not seen before. She takes sudden leave of her usual domestic responsibilities and journeys by bus to a location further removed and by the sea. What follows is a sequence widely recognised by critics as one of extraordinary cinematic beauty. Before a lens positioned in some high location snowflakes appear and then fall with a gradual increase in their rate and volume. In the distance a corpse-bearing group of mourners wends its way slowly out the shore's edge. Next we see Yumiko at a later point and deeply disconsolate, standing alone in protracted fixation on the burning list of the pyre on that strand.

Tamio, the man to whom she has now been married for some years while living far from the city, has searched her out and travelled by car to find her alone and by the sea. When she tearfully blurts out to him her inability to grasp why her first husband had chosen to die, Tamio tells her that a mysterious and beautiful light can sometimes appear in the distance, so alluringly that individuals entranced by it may become willing to die just in order to do so. His own fisherman father, Tamio says, had once seen such a seductive light out over the sea.

This light is the *maborosi* of the film's title, a phantasmagorical kind of light or *maboroshi no hikari* of the original. But there is a profoundly important allusion operative at this point of the film, one easily missed by critics. That is, what Tamio's father had reputedly seen out at sea was something to which Japanese Buddhist writings had referred with some regularity already in the medieval period. And the reference is much more than a bit of arcane trivia. Beginning at least as early as 868 and with examples recorded as late as 1722 there had been within Japan a practice, the *Fudaraku-tokai*, according to which certain Buddhist holy-men would set out to sea in boats supposedly destined to reach Potalaka [Fudaraku], a paradisal location. Potalaka was assumed then to be the abode, an intensely luminous one, of the Bodhisattva of Compassion. Avalokitesvara (Kuan-yin to the Chinese and Kannon to the Japanese).

Medieval and early modern Japanese texts tell of a sequence of persons, often prompted by sights or reports of wondrous light emitted by the distant Potalaka, sailing off, never returning, and assumed by others to have died. Departure dates were often well announced and crowds would gather at the sea's edge to see such persons off and to marvel at such acts of faith and fervor. And, we gather, there was a desire to be on hand just in case of a last-minute weakness of will and an embarrassing trip-cancellation. In a 1961 short-story translated as 'Passage to Fudaraku', the late Yasushi Inoue, Japan's premier writer of historical fiction, recapitulated this narrative tradition in modern prose and for a wide readership.[9]

Within *Maborosi* there is a powerful functional analogue to the Potalaka's alluring light out at sea. It is the glittering stream of passenger train windows that move through the night and through the urban locale that is the home of the newly married lkuo and Yumiko. The film as a whole, of course, is a medley of chiaroscuro. But to take note of that feature and then either praise it as a reason for its beauty or censure it for photoludic overkill is to miss what is unique in *Maborosi*. And that consists in Kore'eda's skill in taking what humans know to be inherently fascinating about light, intensifying its allure to the point of letting it become an invitation to dying to a degree that begins to approximate Potalaka's magnetism, and then positioning these complex dynamics within the film's narrative in an explicit way. Moreover, *Maborosi* raises to a new level what it can mean for a viewer to be stitched into a film. Coordinated with how the plot infoms us that the elegant luminosity of a passing train had sucked lkuo into its path is the film's own incessant but fascinating play with lights and luminosity. This means that the viewer of the film, however likely to be resistant to the idea of there being nothing necessarily 'bad' about suicide, will within the course of viewing this film have, at least in all likelihood, an intense experience of *the seductive power of light*.

Kore'eda, that is, has structured this film so that any possible 'understanding' of lkuo's seemingly irrational act will come, not through some new and alternative theory about a suicide's likely cause but, rather, via its having forced upon us viewers an awareness that, yes, we too could find ourselves caught in the powerful grip of an amazing, alluring play of light. We too are given at least a taste of the fascination that pulled lkuo in. During the course of nearly two hours we not only become conscious that lights and lamps of all kinds feature strongly in *Maborosi* but have also begun to anticipate and even relish every new one. The forge of a steel mill, the lights at street corners, a kitchen gas lamp, shafts of light falling on a staircase, and then surely the funeral pyre's flame rising up against the dark ocean – all these had formed a pattern of fascination. And they collectively merged into the light that is at the core of the film's plot – namely, that of the glittering windows of a train rushing through the night. For even if we cannot in the end claim to have a *single intelligible reason* for lkuo's death, we will have willy-nilly become complicit in its dynamic. We will have tasted something of what Kawabata referred to as seeing the world with *matsugo no me*. The beauty of such lights had registered not just on our retinas but also in some interior place where we ordinarily would have expected to find nothing but resistance to the idea of suicide. Thus, even if our conscious minds cannot locate an adequate explanation for something as 'irrational' as lkuo's suicide, this film as *experienced* suggests otherwise.

The beauty of a world so seen becomes also the beauty of cinema itself, Kore'eda forges this recognition in a way that is unique. The lights of the train drawing lkuo to itself come to be tied closely to what this film reflexively says about what *film itself can do*. The tie-in comes early in the narrative. lkuo and his bicycle have stopped at a railroad crossing in the city. Now himself a stilled spectator, he stands quietly as the segmented but light-drenched windows of the multiple passenger cars flicker past in a manner not at all unlike the way in which the sequential frames of a strip of light-backed celluloid, if slowed, will move before a viewer's eyes. The train itself *has become* a filament of film – and one of startling beauty. And if Ikuo in this scene has become the 'out in front' representative of us who at that precise time are viewing this film, then he also, by implication at least, has become – by the way in which this suturing and the plot itself coalesce – someone who is merely 'out in front' of the rest of us in terms of knowing what might be attractive in the experience of dying. That is, the moment of being transfixed is also one of uncommon beauty. The passing train becomes an aperture into the passing nature of the world. Dying and seeing come together. What moves before the eyes moves away most certainly, but not without first being a sequence of otherwise unattainable beauty.

An earlier version of this essay was presented at a Conference on Religion and Cinema held at Princeton University, 30 March–1 April 2001. I am indebted to the comments received there, especially from P. Adams Sitney. Dudley Andrews, Jeffrey Stout and Christine Marran. Donald Richie graciously read the earlier version and provided multiple helpful criticisms. Errors that remain are entirely my own.

Notes

1   Sheron Cameron, *Beautiful Work: A Meditation on Pain*. Durham and London: Duke University Press, 2000, 72.
2   Donald Richie, *Ozu*. Berkeley, 1974, 175.
3   *Ibid.*, 252.
4   Richie, *op. cit.*, 58.
5   *Ibid.* 57 (emphasis mine).
6   Director's commentary on the DVD version of *Maborosi* (emphasis mine).
7   Albert Stunkard MD, my colleague at the University of Pennsylvania, found nothing distinctively pathological in some of the Japanese war criminals, who were under his medical and psychiatric care in Sugamo Prison after the end of World War II. Although bent on committing suicide out of a sense of honour, these individuals did not show the usual symptoms of being suicidal.
8   It is difficult to ignore what might have been a catalyst for Kore'eda's thinking provided by events and disclosures following the 20 March, 1995 sarin attack in Tokyo subways by the Om shinrikyo organisation. Initial explanations of the clearly suicidal actions of some of that group's members were focused on the concept

'brain-washing' (nósen). Yet this hypothesis collapsed in the face of the group's members' statements recorded in the documentary film titled 'A' and analysed by Richard Gardner in 'Lost in the Cosmos and the Need to Know', Monumenta Nipponica 54 (Summer 1999), 217–247. Donald Richie relates that Distance, the latest of Kore'eda's films, is even more clearly responsive to the sarin attack (Personal communication, 18 September 2001). See Richie's review of Distance in The International Herald Tribune, 15 June 2001.

9   Translated by James T. Araki and published in Theodore W. Goossen (ed.) The Oxford Book of Japanese Short Stories, Oxford, 1977, 206–223.

Chapter 22

Philip Lutgendorf

JAI SANTOSHI MAA REVISITED
On Seeing a Hindu "Mythological" Film

> Audiences were showering coins, flower petals and rice at the
> screen in appreciation of the film. They entered the cinema barefoot
> and set up a small temple outside. . . . In Bandra, where mytho-
> logical films aren't shown, it ran for fifty weeks. It was a miracle.
>
> —Anita Guha (actress who played the goddess Santoshi Ma)[1]

Genre, Film, and Phenomenon

CECIL B. DEMILLE'S cynical adage, "God is box office," may
be applied to Indian popular cinema, the output of the world's largest film
industry, albeit with certain adjustments – one must pluralize and sometimes
feminize the subject of the adage. The film genre known as "mythological" was
present at the creation of the Indian feature film and has remained a hardy
perennial of its vast output, yet it constitutes one of the least-studied aspects of
this comparatively under-studied national cinema, cursorily dismissed (or
more often ignored) by scholars and critics. Yet DeMille's words also belie the
fact that most mythologicals – like most commercial films of any genre – flop at
the box office. The comparatively few that have enjoyed remarkable and sustained acclaim hence merit study both as religious expressions and as successful
examples of popular art and entertainment.

Of the 475 Indian films released in 1975, three enjoyed enormous success.
All were in Hindi, the lingua franca of the entertainment industry based in
Bombay (a.k.a. Mumbai), lately dubbed "Bollywood," which (although it
generates less than a quarter of national cinematic output) enjoys the largest
audience throughout the subcontinent and beyond. *Sholay* (Flames) and *Deewar*
(The Wall), were both heavily-promoted "multistarrers" belonging to the genre
sometimes referred to as the *masala* ("spicy") film: a multi-course cinematic

banquet incorporating suspenseful drama, romance, comedy, violent action sequences, and song and dance. Both were expensive and slickly made by the standards of the industry, and both featured Amitabh Bachchan, the male superstar whose iconic portrayal of an "angry young man" would dominate the Hindi screen for the next decade. Female characters were marginal to both, and this was not surprising given that their target audience was young urban males.

The third "superhit" of 1975 could hardly have been more different, however, and came as a complete surprise to both the industry and the press. *Jai Santoshi Maa* (Hail to the mother of satisfaction) was a low-budget film about a little-known Hindu goddess, featuring unknown actors, cheap sets, and crude special effects, and a plot and audience dominated by women. Yet it became a runaway, word-of-mouth hit, packing cinemas in major urban centers and smaller provincial towns. It also became something more: a phenomenon that gave a new and specifically Indian inflection to the American pop phrase "cult film," for audiences commonly engaged in ritual and devotional behavior during its screenings, and temples and shrines to its titular goddess soon began to appear in many parts of India. As the years passed, the film acquired the status of a cult classic, and was regularly revived, especially for women's matinees on Friday, the day associated with the *vrat* or ritual fast and worship of Santoshi Ma; by all accounts, hundreds of thousands and perhaps millions of women periodically participated in such worship. Media accounts of the sudden emergence of a "celluloid goddess" attracted the interest of scholars interested in the impact of film on religion and popular culture, and as a result *Jai Santoshi Maa* became unique among mythological films by becoming the subject of a modest scholarly literature.

[. . .]

Jai Santoshi Maa *Re-Viewed*

The story opens in what is obviously *dev-lok* – the world of the gods – a setting immediately recognizable to anyone who has seen a mythological film. The basic elements of this heavenly realm, imagined as lying above the clouds, are decorated walls and plinths that rise out of a drifting, dry ice – generated fog. Ganesh and his family are seen celebrating the autumn festival of Rakhi (a.k.a. *raksha bandhan*, the "tying of protection"), when sisters tie string bracelets on the wrists of their brothers and receive from them sweets, gifts, and the promise of protection. Ganesh is receiving a bracelet from his sister Manasa, but his two little sons are distressed because they have no sister to likewise honor them. The divine sage Narada appears, immediately recognizable by his costume and stringed instrument as well as by his cry, "Narayan, Narayan!" (a name of Vishnu, of whom he is a devotee). In Hindu lore, Narada is a mischievous busybody who flits about the worlds eavesdropping and stirring up trouble. He takes up the children's nagging of Ganesh ("Daddy, bring us a sister!"), piously announcing that the god "who fulfills everyone's wishes" must not disappoint his own sons. Ganesh is visibly annoyed by this demand that he sire another child, and his two wives appear embarrassed and downcast. But after additional pleading, Ganesh becomes thoughtful and raises his right hand in the boon-granting gesture. Tiny flames emerge from his wives' breasts and move through space to a lotus-shaped dais, where they form into a little girl, upon whom flower petals rain down. Riddhi and Siddhi are overjoyed. Crying, "Our daughter!" and "Oh, my little queen!" they embrace her affectionately and lead her to her brothers for the tying of the rakhi bracelet. The girl then faces the camera and bows slightly with palms joined while Narada extols her: "This mind-born daughter of Lord Ganesh will always fulfill everyone's desires, will cause the Ganges of gratification to flow and known by the name of 'Mother of Satisfaction,' will promote the wellbeing of the whole world. Hail Santoshi Ma!"

Through this charming scene – which assumes that gods celebrate holidays just as human beings do, and that they may similarly be pestered by their children – the responsibility for Santoshi Ma's birth is diffused over numerous agents: the nagging boys and busybody sage, the wives, Ganesh's sister, and, of course, Ganesh himself. This collective agency of divine figures, acting out of apparently human motives albeit with superhuman powers, and displaying no evidence of omniscience or even of much forethought, will characterize the portrayal of all but one of them throughout the film. It is a style of representation that is entirely "traditional" – attested to by centuries of oral and written narrative, visual and performance art, and now in several decades of mythological films. Whereas the praising of deities in worship or in philosophical discourse may emphasize their "otherness" to the human – their being eternal, all-powerful, all-knowing, etc. – the praising of deities through stories about their "acts" (charitra) or "play" (lila) stresses their humanlike qualities, which are vividly evoked. For the majority of Hindus, such divergent discourses coexist unproblematically in their respective contexts.

It is clear that Ganesh is reluctant to create a daughter; he yields only to placate his sister, sons, and wives. As Kurtz notes (drawing on Lynn Bennett's research), Santoshi Ma is thus established as a "sister-daughter" goddess, filling a role that, in the context of north Indian patriarchy, connotes both auspiciousness and liability. A daughter gives joy to her brothers and female relatives – and the maternal affection of Riddhi and Siddhi is especially evident – but is a worry to her father, who must ultimately provide her dowry, guarantee her chastity, and oversee her transfer to another family. As we witness the "birth" of the little girl-child whom Narada paradoxically hails as a "Mother" of fulfilled wishes, we may recognize the ambivalent welcome she receives – a cooing embrace from her mothers, a somber stare from her father – as representative of the emotions that sometimes attend the birth of a daughter in India.

The scene shifts abruptly to earth, where we witness the fulfillment of Narada's benediction through the joyous worship of Santoshi Ma by a group of singing and dancing women, led by the maiden Satyavati (Kanan Kaushal). The setting is another mythological film staple: a pastel-colored, neoclassical temple enshrining in its sanctum a brightly painted image, here equipped with a glittering motorized halo. Everyone looks well fed and prosperous, bedecked in bright costumes that suggest a non specific north-Indian rural setting. The women's choreographed ensemble dancing is unlike anything one would see in a real temple (where worship is normally individual and idiosyncratic) – again, this is standard cinematic convention. Satyavati stands in the center of the whirling dancers and leads them in the first of the film's three catchy *bhajans* or devotional hymns, *Main to arti utaru* (I perform Mother Santoshi's arti) – referring to ceremonial worship with a tray bearing lamps, flowers, and incense. The emphasis throughout this scene is on the experience of *darshan*: of "seeing" and being seen by the goddess – the reciprocal act of "visual communion" that is central to Hindu worship. The camera repeatedly zooms in on Satyavati's face and eyes, then offers a comparable point-of-view zoom shot of the goddess as Satyavati sees her. Finally, it offers a shot-reverse shot from a position just over the goddess's shoulder, thus approximating (though not directly assuming) Santoshi Ma's perspective and closing the *darshanic* loop by showing us Satyavati and the other worshipers more or less as Santoshi Ma sees them. Each shot in this repeated sequence (which is intercut with the dancing women, musicians, etc.) is held for several seconds, establishing an ocular dialogue further emphasized by the lyrics.

> Satyavati: There is great affection, great love in Mother's eyes.
> Chorus: . . . In Mother's eyes!
> Satyavati: There is great mercy, power, and love in Mother's eyes.
> Chorus: . . . In Mother's eyes!
> Satyavati: Why shouldn't I gaze, again and again, into Mother's eyes? Behold, at every moment, a whole new world in Mother's eyes!
> Chorus: . . . In Mother's eyes!

Such *darshan* sequences contribute to an aesthetic of "frontality" often noted in popular cinema, especially in mythologicals, which often consciously recapitulate the conventions of poster art. But their ubiquity should not obscure their significance: The camera's movements invite the viewer to assume, as it were, both positions in the act of *darshanic* intercourse, thus closing an experiential loop that ultimately moves (as most Hindu loops do) toward an underlying unity. Indeed, the face of Santoshi Ma seen in the sanctum is of a young woman who resembles Satyavati.

[. . .]

Getting "Satisfaction"

Several scholars of Hindi cinema have argued that significant thematic changes occurred in commercial films during the mid-1970s. M. Madhava Prasad has noted the decline, after several decades of dominance, of the type of "social" film that he calls the "feudal family romance," and its replacement by a "populist cinema of mobilization" that attempts to address (and, according to Prasad, to co-opt) the rising expectations of lower-class groups "agitating for the realization of the new nation's professed democratic and socialist ideals."[2] Similarly Kajri Jain notes the shift in leading men from the "soft, romantic" heroes of earlier decades to the unquestioned megastar of the 1970s and 1980s, Amitabh Bachchan, whose lithe and sinewy physique contributed to his effective portrayal, in numerous films, of a "goal-driven, instrumentalized" subaltern hero, a working class "angry young man."[3] Significantly, the major action hits of 1975, *Deewar* and *Sholay*, figure as key texts in both scholars' analyses.

1975 was also, of course, the year when nearly three decades of Congress Party rule suffered its most significant challenge. Amid exposés of widespread bureaucratic corruption and a court decision against the prime minister, activist Jayaprakash Narayan called for a "total revolution," and massive strikes threatened to cripple the country's nationalized infrastructure. Indira Gandhi responded in June by declaring a state of national emergency, suspending constitutional liberties and freedom of the press, and jailing thousands of her opponents. This desperate measure would eventually further weaken the Congress mandate, leading to Gandhi's massive defeat at the polls in 1977 and, in the longer term, to the rise of opposition parties that mobilized religious and local caste- and class-based identities. Though the changes that ensued certainly stopped short of "total revolution," they nevertheless eroded the authority of the elite that had been ruling the nation since Independence and contributed to the political awakening and rising expectations of formerly disenfranchised groups: "scheduled" and "backward castes" and lower-middle-class laborers, artisans, and merchants.

Rather than categorize *Jai Santoshi Maa* as an anomalously successful mythological in a year of violent "mobilization" films, I propose that it too represents part of a larger picture of nonelite assertiveness and agency, but with specific relevance to an audience unaddressed by films like *Deewar* and *Sholay*: an audience mainly consisting of lower-middle-class women. The adaptation of a popular *vrat-katha* to the screen – skillfully preserving key features of its written version while also invoking and in fact demonstrating the representational and narrative conventions of mainstream cinema – helped to incorporate this new audience into the "public culture" of the period. Evoking a rural and lower-class ethos through its setting and themes, and full of clever inter-textual references accessible (and hence satisfying) to its audience, this is a film that addresses viewers' aspirations in several ways.

Above all, it concerns the life experience that is typically the most traumatic for an Indian woman: that of being wrenched from her *mayka* or maternal home and forced to adjust to a new household in which she is often treated as an outsider who must be tested and disciplined, sometimes harshly, before she can be integrated into the family. Satyavati's relationship with Santoshi Ma enables her to endure the sufferings inflicted on her by her sisters-in-law and to triumph over them, but it also accomplishes more. It insures that Satyavati's life consistently departs from the script that patriarchal society writes for a girl of her status: She marries a man of her own choosing, enjoys a companionate relationship (and independent travel) with her husband, and ultimately acquires a home of her own, out of reach of her in-laws.

Moreover, viewers can enjoy her achievement of all this because it is presented as the "Mother's grace," bestowed on a humble, submissive woman who overtly asks little for herself. While appearing to adhere to the code of a conservative extended family (the systemic abuses of which it dramatically highlights), the film quietly endorses goals, shared by many women, that subvert this code.

This oblique assertiveness has a class dimension as well. The three goddesses are shown to be "established" both religiously and materially: They preside over plush celestial homes and expect expensive offerings. Santoshi Ma, who is happy with *gur-chana* and is in fact associated with less-educated, and less-advantaged people, is in their view a poor newcomer threatening to usurp their status. They intend to nip her "upward mobility" in the bud, yet in the end must concede defeat and bestow their (reluctant?) blessing on the *nouvelle arrivée*. The sociodomestic aspect of the film (goddesses as senior in-laws, oppressing a young bride) thus parallels its socioeconomic aspect (goddesses as established bourgeois matrons, looking scornfully at the aspirations of poorer women).

Satyavati's relationship to Santoshi Ma, established through the parallel story of the goddesses, suggests that there is more agency involved here than at first appears to be the case — though it is again the diffused, depersonalized agency favored in Hindu narrative. Satyavati's successful integration into Birju's family, indeed her emergence as its most prosperous female member, parallels Santoshi Ma's acceptance in her divine clan and revelation as its most potent *shakti*. In both cases this happens without the intervention, so standard in Hindi cinema, of a male hero, for there are no exemplary male figures in the film. Birju is a pleasant but clueless hunk who escapes disaster only through the timely intervention of his wife. In heaven, the tridev are likewise amiable gentlemen, yet evidently in control neither of their wives nor of the cosmos. If there is a presiding divine figure (apart from the quixotic prankster, Narada, who pushes the plot forward through whimsical and even malicious interventions) it is the serene and self-possessed "mother of satisfaction," Santoshi Ma.

Yet through its visual treatment of the reciprocal gaze of *darshan* and its use of parallel narratives, the film also suggests that Santoshi Ma and Satyavati — deity and devotee — are, in fact, one, a truth finally declared, at film's end, by the wise and compassionate Daya Ram. As in the ideology of tantric ritual (or the conventions of "superhero" narrative in the West), the "mild-mannered" and submissive Satyavati merges, through devotion and sheer endurance, with her ideal and alter ego, the cosmic superpower Santoshi Ma. Similarly (and only apparently paradoxically), the latter's ultimate incorporation into the "established" pantheon comes about precisely through the persistent agency of her long-suffering earthly counterpart. This is in fact consistent with the relationship between divine and human realms found in much Hindu lore, which reverses the standard Christian formula to present an ultimately human-centered theology that unfolds, so to speak, "in heaven as it is on earth."

In a further theovisual argument, the film proposes that not only is Santoshi Ma available to all women through her *vrat* ritual but that she is, in fact, all women. Appearing as a little girl at the film's beginning, as a self-confident young woman in her manifestations throughout most of the story, and as a grandmotherly crone on the final Friday of Satyavati's fast, Santoshi Ma makes herself available to viewers as an embodiment of the female life cycle, and conveys the quietly mobilizing message that it is reasonable for every woman to expect, within that cycle her own measure of "satisfaction" in the form of love, comfort, and respect.

Notes

1   Nasreen Munni Kabir, *Bollywood, The Indian Cinema Story*. London: Channel 4 Books, 2001.

2   M. Madhava Prasad, *Ideology of the Hindi Film: A Historical Construction*. Delhi: Oxford University Press, 1998, 138–159.

3   Kajri Jain, "Muscularity and its Ramifications: Mimetic Male Bodies in Indian Mass Culture," *South Asia* 24 (2001): 216–221.

Chapter 23

Mira Nair

I WANT MY FILMS TO EXPLODE WITH LIFE
An Interview with Mira Nair

Nair: I am just at the cusp now of realizing an old dream of mine. We purchased the plot of land next door, where we will be establishing Maisha, which means 'life' in Swahili, an East African and South Asian filmmakers lab. It is based on the Sundance model. Our first session will be next summer. We will pick twelve candidates every year: four from East Africa – Uganda, Kenya, Tanzania – four from South Asia, and four from Asian and African kids in the diaspora. For those twelve it will be free. They will be flown here, there will be sixteen rooms, and each year we will fly in eight mentors, qualified people. We raised money for three years and we are investing our own money to build the center, and then it will pay for itself. We have just broken ground, we are slashing into the jungle, and the architect is coming in three weeks. It's amazing! [laughs] We are also going to introduce Iyengar Yoga to Uganda with free classes for the village.

Cineaste: How do you connect this creative project with your films?

Nair: I realized something about myself. I have to make something all the time. The garden is the same thing for me. In the morning I go down to the garden to see what has bloomed, what is happy or what is not happy. As the time and place comes to fix it, I do that. It's not like New York, which is based on productivity – bang, bang, bang. This interview would be very different in New York. I would speak very economically and pointedly.

Cineaste: How does yoga fit into this?

Nair: The garden is also a form of yoga. It's very centering and makes me very strong. It gives me stamina. It teaches me the art of resistance and surrender. In a yoga position, if you take a pose, it's not ever about achieving a goal, but about how to position the body in a correct way. You have resistance in one part of the body in order to surrender in another part of the body. For example, if you do 'down dog' – you know, from the hips to the ankles – it is about having a stiff, rigid support in order to be as supple as possible in the hips, neck, and torso. So it's a kind of union, which is the name of yoga, with fitness and sensuality and giving. Resistance and surrender is a huge lesson that every director should know because making a film is all about solving problems.

One of my worst nightmares, for example, happened on *Monsoon Wedding* [2001]. Two days before we were to begin shooting, the hairdresser's assistant fucked up and dyed the father of the bride's hair a dark orange. We couldn't fix it. His hair was a beautiful natural gray. He's a legendary actor, and was the first person I cast in April. In August he had made his hair like a Punjabi man – they have mustaches and salt-and-pepper hair. Then the assistant dyed it a mud-brown orange! You couldn't bring back the gray, and two days later we were to start shooting. That's resistance and surrender: you look at the problem and ask, 'What can we do now?' It was not going to get undone. So I took him to my childhood hairdresser and had his hair redyed a decent, believable black, and recut his hair to give him an entirely different look.

Cineaste: Do you think of yourself as a political filmmaker?

Nair: My husband doesn't. He says I should be more political [laughs]. I always looked for models and people and ways that art and politics might combine to change the world. Most often, they didn't. The art combined with politics became agitprop, and lacked the sort of inexplicability that makes great art. That is always the challenge for me. I am not good at making pleasant Sunday afternoon movies that you come out of and say, 'Where are you going for dinner?' I prefer to make movies that stay under your skin, that make you question things.

Cineaste: What kind of questions do you want moviegoers to ask?

Nair: It depends on the theme. *Monsoon Wedding*, for example, is a joyful, affectionate study of everything that makes a family stick together and fall apart and work. Every family has its darknesses. The challenge is how you cope with those darknesses and how you make them light.

Cineaste: The father in *Monsoon Wedding* is ideal. He is inspiring, but in my experience I have not come across that many men who have taken on that role.

Nair: Oh, they're rare. I don't say I have one, but I have always looked for people like that. I have always had a strong affinity and respect for older people who have shown us these ways, people who are noble. You think he's going to fall apart, that's the beauty of it, but he surprises even himself.

Cineaste: How does your 'yogic' vision of life compare to Thackeray's more cynical view of class in society? [Thackeray was the author of *Vanity Fair* (1847–8), which Nair adapted as a film (2004).]

Nair: If Thackeray had lived longer, I think he would have become contemplative. His wife sank into madness early in his marriage, and that gave him a philosophical view of life. He looked after her to the end. He was very honorable and a strong father to his daughter. That intimate view he had of madness gave him a depth of insight into the foibles of people – like Dobbin, who develops his love for Amelia.

Cineaste: What is your favorite scene in *Vanity Fair*?

Nair: A scene I really enjoy is what I call my 'pregnant love scene,' where Rawdon is leaving for Waterloo, and Becky is full-blown pregnant. We had struggled so long with Reese's real-life pregnancy in the film, camouflaging it and then revealing it. I had planned that my gift would be that Reese would show me her beautiful, six-months-pregnant belly. I told Reese, I want to go for the whole thing. I want him to see her belly, to caress her belly, to celebrate the whole glory of woman with baby. For a young mother to be caressed on screen by another man, however, who is not the father of her child, is an intimate thing, and a lot to ask for. But Reese said fine. So we made her a special corset, with a slit in the front, and we lit it in such a way that the whole contour of the belly is revealed. It was a beautiful scene in the movie.

Cineaste: Do you think being a mother yourself has changed how you work as a film director?

Nair: Immensely. You just experience things that fuel your work. Another scene in the book, for instance, is when Amelia has given her son away to be brought up by her father-in-law, who does not approve of Amelia because she is poor. The son is growing up like a young Lord Fauntleroy, while his mother has nothing. The mother makes shirts for her son, and one day she goes to give one of the shirts to him. In the novel, the son looks at the shirt and says, 'How can I wear your funny old shirts now, mom?,' and walks away. That's the way it is in the novel. But, as a mother, it's impossible to play that scene so cut and dried. As a mother, the kind of hunger you would have to see your son, that unbelievable physical desire to just hold him, would be impossible to deny.

Cineaste: So being a mother has given you a more profound sense of character?

Nair: Oh my God, yes! In the scene where Amelia sees her son on the street with the grandfather, you see her pain and her love, her emotional devastation. Then we cut back to India where Dobbin is reading the letter, which explains how Amelia has given away her son, and he is pissed off, for her sake, that she has done that. He's in the middle of a wrestling match, and he almost kills this guy. I added this scene because I wanted Dobbin to be somewhat manly, not just a selfless, lovelorn chap who doesn't do much.

Amelia's giving away her son so he can have a better life is the ultimate act of sacrifice for a mother. Another director might have done that differently, had they done it at all. I love that scene because, for me, it is about the choices one has to make in life. When you see adaptations of *Vanity Fair*, it's usually all about Becky Sharp, her rise and fall and la-di-da, but nobody goes into the subplots and their machinations. The studio wanted me to keep the Amelia/ Dobbin subplot to a minimum, but my goal was to keep them both happening.

Chapter 24

Paul Schrader

TRANSCENDENTAL STYLE ON FILM

TR A N S C E N D E N T A L S T Y L E seeks to maximize the mystery of existence; it eschews all conventional interpretations of reality: realism, naturalism, psychologism, romanticism, expressionism, impressionism, and, finally, rationalism. To the transcendental artist rationalism is only one of many approaches to life, not an imperative. "If everything is explained by understandable causal necessities," abbot Amédée Ayfre wrote, "or by objective determinism, even if their precise nature remains unknown, then nothing is sacred." The enemy of transcendence is immanence, whether it is external (realism, rationalism) or internal (psychologism, expressionism). To the transcendental artist these conventional interpretations of reality are emotional and rational constructs devised by man to dilute or explain away the transcendental.

In motion pictures these constructs take the form of what Robert Bresson has called "screens," clues or study guides which help the viewer "understand" the event: plot, acting, characterization, camerawork, music, dialogue, editing. In films of transcendental style these elements are, in popular terms, "nonexpressive" (that is they are not expressive of culture or personality); they are reduced to stasis. Transcendental style *stylizes* reality by eliminating (or nearly eliminating) those elements which are primarily expressive of human experience, thereby robbing the conventional interpretations of reality of their relevance and power. Transcendental style, like the mass, transforms experience into a repeatable ritual which can be repeatedly transcended.

[. . .]

The films of Yasujiro Ozu exemplify the transcendental style in the East. In his films this style is natural, indigenous, and commercially successful, largely because of the Japanese culture itself. The concept of transcendental experience is so intrinsic to Japanese (and Oriental) culture, that Ozu was able both to develop the transcendental style and to stay within the popular conventions of Japanese art. Ozu, often described as the "most Japanese of all directors," gained respect as a genre director and critical and financial success – rewards which no director interested in transcendental style could expect to reap in the West.

Oriental art in general and Zen art in particular aspire to the Transcendent. Like primitive art, traditional Oriental art makes no distinctions between the sacred and the secular. The Orient forged a lasting culture out of what the Neoplatonists and Scholastics hypothesized and in rare cases realized: an anonymous art in which "all that is true, by whomsoever it has been said, has its origin in the Spirit." In Zen, this is expressed by R. H. Blyth: "The poetical and the religious are identical states of mind . . . to the religious all things are poetical . . . to the poetical all things are religious." For thirteen hundred years Zen has cultivated the transcendental experience, and the Transcendent has found expression not only in religion and the arts, but also in a wide variety of "commonplace" activities. This expression of the Transcendent was not the perquisite of an intellectual or clerical elite. It became an endemic part of the Oriental heritage mainly through the arts, and no distinction was made between the fine and the manual arts. Zen dislikes the "odor of abstraction" which comes from a term like "transcendence," D. T. Suzuki points out, because in fact Zen dislikes any appeal to words. Acknowledging this semantic obstacle, it is safe to say, as Suzuki does, that Zen operates within the "realm of transcendence."

Thus Ozu did not need to revive the expression of the Transcendent in Japan, or inject it into the Oriental culture, but only to adapt it to film. Ozu represents traditional Japanese thought and art, and he brings the weight of Oriental tradition to the modern, anarchic film medium. Donald Richie has schematized Japanese film directors, placing Kurosawa on the far left (modern) and Ozu on the far right (traditional). Ozu was markedly conservative in subject matter and method (he was among the last Japanese directors to utilize sound or color), and he strove to put the old tradition in the new format. In Japan "modern civilization is only one hundred years old and is a veneer over a civilization which has endured for two millennia"; in Ozu's films Zen art and thought is the civilization, film is the veneer.

Although the Japanese cultural tradition afforded Ozu some luxuries, his task was not as easy as it may seem. Cinema has been one of the primary

Westernizing influences in contemporary Japan, and in his striving for traditional values Ozu often ran contrary to current trends and is still regarded as reactionary by many Japanese youths. In a sense Ozu bucked fashion in his pursuit of a filmic transcendental style, but the resistance he met was relatively minor compared to the resistance encountered by Bresson who, in France, has to go back to the Scholastics for an aesthetic precedent and on the way forfeited any hope of mass popularity or commercial success.

Ozu's career was one of refinement: he constantly limited his technique, subject matter, and editorial comment. Early in his career (Ozu made fifty-four films over thirty-five years, from 1927 to 1962) he filmed the romantic and social themes insisted upon by Japanese producers, but later in life, particularly after the Second World War, Ozu limited himself to the shomin genre, and within the shomin-geki to certain forms of conflict and resolution.

The shomin genre concerns proletarian and middle-class life and "the some-times humorous, sometimes bitter relations within the family." The shomin-geki, initially a genre of melodrama and light comedy, originated in the later 1920s and early 30s, only after the Japanese middle class had become sufficiently entrenched to laugh at itself. Several critics have pointed out the evolution of Ozu's approach by comparing the 1932 I Was Born, But . . . (Umarete Wa Mita Keredo) with the 1959 remake, Good Morning (Ohayo). Ozu's intentions in I Was Born, But . . . were social and particular; his intentions in Good Morning were satirical and universal. Compared to the remake, I Was Born, But . . . was "active rather than contemplative." Ozu's early films (such as I Was Born, But . . .) were squarely within the original shomin-geki concept: light understated comedies with a tinge of social consciousness. Time, affluence, the war, governmental pressures, and Westernization sobered the shomin-geki in general, and Ozu in particular. When Ozu changed – when his light comedy slowly turned to "resigned sadness" – he took the shomin-geki with him, exerting much the same influence over the shomin genre as John Ford did over the American Western. Ozu's later films were not descriptive of the shomin-geki, but prescriptive of it.

"In every Ozu film," Richie writes, "the whole world exists in one family. The ends of the earth are no more distant than outside the house." In his films the middle class is represented as office workers, and in some films, such as Early Spring (Soshun, 1956), the office "family" replaces the household family unit. Ozu focuses on the tensions between the home and the office, the parent and the child, which are extensions of the tensions between the old and new Japan, between tradition and Westernization, and – ultimately – between man and nature.

Toward the end of his life (he died in 1963 at the age of sixty), Ozu focused his attention on certain forms of conflict within the shomin-geki. This conflict is not drama in Western terms, and it certainly is not plot: "Pictures with obvious plots bore me now," Ozu told Richie. "Naturally, a film must have some kind of structure or else it is not a film, but I feel that a picture isn't good if it has too much drama or action." And concerning *Late Autumn* (*Akibiyori*): "I want to portray a man's character by eliminating all the dramatic devices. I want to make people feel what life is like without delineating all the dramatic ups and downs." In Ozu's mind Japanese life had resolved into certain opposing forces which he repeatedly demonstrated in his films, and although these forces must be reconciled, they would not be reconciled by anything as artificial as plot.

Ozu's later cycle of family–office films (thirteen films from 1949 to 1962) features the estrangement of parents and children. The incidents of estrangement are in themselves remarkably petty: marriage, relocation, bickerings, and at most running away from home. Behind these incidents are the divisive elements of modern Japan: the Second World War (the children are called the *après-guerre* generation) and Westernization (the compartmentalizing effect of office routine). The parent–child estrangement is not a failure to "communicate," as in American juvenile delinquency films. Even in successful relationships Ozu's characters do not communicate, as that word is used in sociological jargon, with commiseration and emotional interchange. The estrangement results from the loss of the traditional family unity which was never verbally communicated in the first place. In his later films Ozu set these opposing forces within a home-office superstructure containing a variety of interchangeable character-conflict infrastructures. One story (really nothing more than an anecdote) could sustain several films. Ozu was notorious for filming the same situation over and over again: the father–daughter conflict of *Late Spring* (*Banshun*, 1949) became the mother–daughter conflict of *Late Autumn* and reverted to a father–daughter conflict in *An Autumn Afternoon* (*Samma No Aji*, 1962).

Just as Ozu settled on certain conflicts to present in his films, he settled on certain people to help him present those conflicts. The majority of the later films were photographed by Yushun Atsuta and all were written in collaboration with Kogo Noda. Ozu and Noda enjoyed a legendary relationship between director and writer: "Although we don't write down the details of the sets, they are in our minds as one common image. We think alike. It is an amazing thing." Ozu and Noda would devise the projected film entirely in their minds, word by word and image by image. After this extensive preparation (which took from four months to one year in seclusion), Ozu would mechanically shoot the preset Ozu-Noda script.

Similarly, Ozu settled on a select group of actors and actresses to appear in his films. The nucleus of this group consisted of Chishu Ryu, Setsuko Hara, Nobuo Nakamura, and Shin Saburi. They were Ozu's filmic "family." In each film they would play slight variations of character, acting out domestic conflicts with the sense of resigned awareness which comes from playing the same roles and feeling the same emotions many times. Ozu chose his actors not for their "star" quality or acting skill, but for their "essential" quality. "In casting it is not a matter of skillfulness or lack of skill an actor has. It is what he is . . ."

But most of all, Ozu refined his technique. Ozu is cinema's consummate formalist; his films are characterized by "an abstentious rigor, a concern for brevity and economy, an aspiring to the ultimate in limitation." Because Ozu's technique is so limited and predictable, it can be examined closely and in depth, a task which Donald Richie has accomplished in a remarkable article entitled, "Yasujiro Ozu: The Syntax of his Films." Richie described Ozu's "syntax" as exemplified in his grammar, structure, editing, tempo, and scene, and there will be need to periodically refer to some of Richie's observations as this section progresses.

Ozu's camera is always at the level of a person seated in traditional fashion on the tatami, about three feet above the ground. "This traditional view is the view in repose, commanding a very limited field of vision. It is the attitude for watching, for listening, it is the position from which one sees the Noh, from which one partakes of the tea ceremony. It is the aesthetic attitude; it is the passive attitude." The camera, except in the rarest of instances, never moves; in the later films there are no pans, no dollies, no zooms. Ozu's only filmic punctuation mark is the cut, and it is not the fast cut for impact or the juxtaposing cut for metaphorical meaning, but the pacing cut which denotes a steady, rhythmic succession of events.

One must not, however, mistake Ozu's "predictability" for superficiality or obviousness. It is not necessarily a virtue – nor necessarily a fault – if a director uses the same techniques repeatedly in film after film. Predictability in Ozu's films does not stem from a lack of initiative or originality, as it does in the films of some directors, but rather from the primitive concept of ritual in which repetition is preferred to variety.

It is possible to define Ozu's style by what it is not. Ozu is the filmmaker who doesn't do certain things. This rarification of technique continued throughout Ozu's lifetime, from his first film to his last. As he got older there were more and more things he didn't do. This can be seen not only by comparing the early and later films (I Was Born, But . . . and Good Morning), but also by comparing the different phases of his later films. Early Summer (Bakushu, 1951) was made in about the middle of Ozu's later (postwar) period, yet it is markedly different from his last films made ten years later, Late Autumn, The Autumn of the Kohayagawa Family (Kohayagawa-ke No Aki, 1961), and An Autumn Afternoon. For example, in his last films Ozu completely forsook certain techniques he had used in Early Summer: (1) the tracking shot, of which there are fifteen in Early Summer, (2) a closeup with emphasis on facial expression, such as an old man's pleasure in watching the theatre, (3) a physical action to express obvious emotion, such as the throwing down of a handkerchief in disgust, (4) a cut on motion, that is, a cut which breaks one action by an actor into two shots, (5) a cut between two different indoor settings without an outdoor "coda" pause, (6) use of chiaroscuro, non-"flat" lighting, although this is very rare even in early Ozu. *Early Summer* also contains techniques which Ozu did not completely discard but came to use less and less: (1) nonfrontal (90°) angles, (2) camera takes of relatively short duration, (3) scenes whose sole purpose was light comedy.

The purpose of this essay, however, is not to define Ozu's style by what is omitted, but by what was left after his unceasing prunings – his final style, which might be called a transcendental style.

[. . .]

The disparity in Ozu's films is primarily internal; man cannot find nature within himself. The disparity in [Robert] Bresson's films is primarily external: man cannot live harmoniously with his hostile environment. In Ozu, there are no futile protests against the fraility of the body and the hostility of the environment, as in Bresson. In Bresson, there is no resigned acceptance of environment, as in Ozu.

The decisive action in Ozu's films is a communal event between members of a family or neighborhood. The decisive action in Bresson's films is limited to a lonely figure pitted against a hostile environment. Bresson stands in the Judeo-Christian tradition of the single redeemer: Moses, Christ, the priests, saints, and mystics who each in his own life righted man with the world. Ozu does not structure his films around a specific Christ or a specific Calvary. In Ozu's films a number of characters can participate in the Transcendent through a number of decisive actions.

The differences between Ozu and Bresson are unified in stasis, the culmination of trascendental style. The Wholly Other, once perceived, cannot be limited by culture.

[. . .]

Spiritual art must always be in flux because it represents a greater mystery, also in flux, man's relationship to the Holy. In each age the spectator grasps for that special form, that spot on the spectrum, whether in art, religion or philosophy, which can take him to greater mystery. At present, no film style can perform this crucial task as well as the transcendental style, no film as well as the films of Ozu and Bresson. To expect or settle for any less from film in general, or the films of Ozu and Bresson in particular, underestimates and demeans them. Transcendental style can take a viewer through the trials of experience to the expression of the Transcendent; it can return him to experience from a calm region untouched by the vagaries of emotion or personality. Transcendental style can bring us nearer to that silence, that invisible image, in which the parallel lines of religion and art meet and interpenetrate.

Chapter 25

Jolyon Baraka Thomas

SHÛKYÔ ASOBI AND MIYAZAKI HAYAO'S ANIME

WE LACK TERMINOLOGY for describing intersections between religion and media in Japan where, although 70 percent of the population claims to lack religious belief, there is a trend to fulfill religious impulses in a variety of ways often only tenuously connected to traditional religious institutions. The extant writing on religion and *anime* (animation) in Japan deals largely with tracing themes from popular film back to traditional religions, while some writers dealing with film and religion outside of Japan have suggested that the act of viewing film might fulfill a religious function. With some rare exceptions, these analyses largely suggest surprise or satisfaction that religion persists in a seemingly secular environment, overlooking the more subtle aspects of the forms that religion is taking and the effects that the conflation of religion and entertainment are having on generations of people in a society where religion has not been secularized so much as diversified and outsourced. This essay takes a different approach by making a case study of the films of director Miyazaki Hayao, exploring the attitudes towards religion, entertainment, and spirituality that underlie their production and consumption.

Definitions

Shûkyô asobi

The artificial distinction between religion and entertainment upon which these earlier analyses are based neglects the historical tendency within Japan for the conflation of, or oscillations between, the two. In many instances, and particularly in the contemporary context, this combined religion-entertainment has been a prevalent part of Japanese culture, and can be seen in a number of products and activities, some of which include *manga* and *anime* and their production. Here, using the words shûkyô (religion) and *asobi* (play/entertainment), I propose the term shûkyô *asobi* to describe this area of Japanese religious culture. Shûkyô *asobi* is a conflation of religion and entertainment which: 1) can be viewed as religious in its production or consumption; 2) can also be said to be one of the many alternative strategies for negotiating spiritual needs in post-war and postmodern social circumstances; 3) draws upon, but also modifies, existing religious themes; 4) can have a moral or spiritual effect on the audience, including an effect on how people view or practice religion, not necessarily limited to sect or a specific doctrine; 5) allows for oscillations between religion and entertainment while nevertheless referring to the space where the two overlap; and 6) therefore isolates those moments where entertainment experiences provide the impetus or environment for religious learning or behavior, or where religious doctrine, ritual and pedagogy act as modes of entertainment.

[. . .]

Case study: Miyazaki Hayao's *Anime*

We can see a clear example of shûkyô *asobi* by examining the work of *anime* director Miyazaki Hayao in more detail. In what follows, I take up four of Miyazaki's *anime* in light of what the director himself says about their production, and also in light of audience responses to them. These responses show that ritual reactions to, and interactions with, Miyazaki's films show a sincere conception of the existence and/or efficacy of the gods, saviors and spirits therein as instructive and inspiring. The ritual of watching film, the rituals enacted vicariously through the film, and the rituals performed in reality but created through the influence of the film all resonate with elements of [Ronald] Grimes' taxonomy of ritual and media. Miyazaki's films serve as religious texts that inspire and exhort people to alterations in behavior; they are sometimes used ritually (repetitively, as liturgical texts, as scripture) for edification as well as entertainment. Furthermore, the cosmology and mythology of the films comes to be interpreted and applied to reality after the films end. At times this results in audience members recreating rituals in reality that they learned through the film narrative; audience members may also identify certain physical places as sacred because they were the alleged inspiration for sacred places found within the narrative realms of the films themselves.

In general, *anime* and the related comic-book genre *manga* often incorporate religious themes ranging from hagiography to criticism of the role of religion in society. Just as *anime* deploys religious motifs, religious institutions and individuals deploy *anime* as a method of affecting audience outlook and behavior. Although the intent of the producers of *anime* and *manga* ranges from proselytization to profit, their products frequently conflate religion and entertainment in ways that have the potential to affect their audience religiously, inviting and promoting faith, ritual action and moral edification.

Miyazaki's work in many ways epitomizes the current state of Japanese popular *anime*. The 1984 film *Nausicaä*, based on a *manga* also written by Miyazaki, is the story of a young princess whose character includes elements of psychic, scientist and messiah. These elements help Nausicaä to reconcile humans and nature in a post-apocalyptic and polluted world. In the 1988 film *My Neighbor Totoro*, the protagonists Mei and Satsuki befriend a benign forest spirit who helps them through a difficult period of transition. The 1997 film *Princess Mononoke* revolves around the intertwined relationships of gods and humans and humans and nature, emphasizing the necessity of strengthening humanity's connections with both. The 2001 film *Spirited Away* shares this pedagogical approach, and takes place in a world populated with a diverse array of gods and spirits.

These films illustrate the fact that: 1) contemporary Japanese are making and watching films that draw upon and modify previously existing religious themes; 2) that moviemakers are creating movies with the intention of inculcating certain values that are at times religious; 3) that the films themselves have the ability to affect future interpretations of religious literature and content; and 4) that audiences can respond to the films in a spiritual fashion, if not a formally religious one.

[. . .]

Shûkyô *asobi* in Miyazaki's thought

While Miyazaki says that "all he wants to do is to entertain,"[1] elsewhere the director's statements suggest that he is at least partially motivated by a type of spirituality largely infused with an environmentalist ethic. Miyazaki's spirituality is largely concerned with environmental issues, and seems to be predicated upon: 1) the existence of an immanent life-force that binds organisms together; and 2) the loss in present times of an idealized past where connections between organisms were both stronger and more respectful. He seems to promote this ethic through film. He states:

> In my grandparents' time . . . it was believed that spirits [kami] existed everywhere – in trees, rivers, insects, wells, anything. My generation does not believe this, but I like the idea that we should all treasure everything because spirits might exist there, and we should treasure everything because there is a kind of life to everything.[2]

Yet despite this spiritual nostalgia, Miyazaki wants to distance himself from formal religion. Wright states: "Essentially, his films attempt to re-enchant his audiences with a sense of spirituality that eschews the dogmas and orthodoxies of organised religions and politics, instead reaching for the original, primal state of spiritualism in human history and how it can be lived today."[3] In an interview for The Village Voice, Miyazaki says:

> Dogma inevitably will find corruption, and I've certainly never made religion a basis for my films. My own religion, if you can call it that, has no practice, no Bible, no saints, only a desire to keep certain places and my own self as pure and holy as possible. That kind of spirituality is very important to me. Obviously it's an essential value that cannot help but manifest itself in my films.[4]

This manifestation, combined with the aforementioned underlying intent to entertain his audience, places Miyazaki squarely in the realm of shûkyô asobi. The act of moviemaking begins as an act of entertainment, but along the way it shades into an expression of spirituality, not only reflecting the director's views, but also attempting to inculcate certain values in his intended audience. Considering that audience in light of this, it should also not go unnoticed that Miyazaki has publicly recognized the consumer demand for spiritual content in Japan, and continues to make movies with this in mind. Miyazaki's moviemaking, therefore, not only reflects his personal spirituality but also the audience's desire for spiritual themes; simultaneously, it reflects his basic desire to entertain and the audience's desire to be entertained. These overlapping desires result in new modes of religious entertainment, or playful religion, shown in the following examples.

Shûkyô asobi in audience reactions to Miyazaki's works

My Neighbor Totoro

Miyazaki clearly draws upon but also modifies preexisting religious themes in his films. The nature spirits in My Neighbor Totoro, for example, seem to be based upon traditional Japanese conceptions of kami. Yet Helen McCarthy reports that although Miyazaki referred to the totoro as " 'nature spirits' of the same kind as those familiar in Japanese religion," the movie has, according to Miyazaki, "nothing to do with that or any other religion."[5] As McCarthy notices, the film makes an active contrast between Miyazaki's fantastic spirits and the cold, inert symbols of traditional religion. The totoro represent a simultaneously new-old type of nature spirit strategically set in contrast to the preexisting (institutional) notions of kami. Whether or not Miyazaki's audiences believe in the existence of the totoro themselves, the film promotes an alternative perception of kami, tactically deploying traditional religious motifs as a foil for the magical, cuddly, and spiritually fecund totoro. The movie's pastoral narrative, combined with this refashioned kami, simultaneously offers a critique of traditional religious institutions and contemporary urban living.

This content alone suggests the power to affect at least a portion of Miyazaki's audience profoundly, and significantly many people who have grown up with Miyazaki's films have referred to My Neighbor Totoro as a favorite or as an influential film in their lives. Casual conversations with many Japanese acquaintances have prompted more than one person to comment on the ability of this film to "soothe" or calm one spiritually (seishintekini). Looking at a Miyazaki-themed fan message board on the Japanese blog site, MIXI, one is quickly struck by the depth and number of audience reactions to the films, including reactions that seem to shade towards the religious. One person, writing on the influence of Miyazaki's films, and about Totoro in particular, states: "Often, with my older sister we would . . . hold an umbrella and try to pray for the sprouts to grow,"[6] mimicking a scene in the movie in which the totoro lead Mei and Satsuki in a prayer-dance to grow sprouts into a giant tree. The children's imitation of the scene suggests the power of film to create ritual outside of movie watching itself.

Nausicaä of the Valley of the Wind

Scholars and critics have identified the manga that is the basis for Miyazaki's 1984 production Nausicaä as religious. Yamanaka Hiroshi places Nausicaä in the category of "*manga* that acts as a religious text" in his description of "religious *manga*." He writes: "As a whole this *manga* [and I would add the *anime* based upon the *manga*] provides the same structure as a religious text like the Bible." *Nausicaä* is a drama about the salvation of the world and humanity; approaching social and environmental catastrophes become the stage for the actions of Nausicaä the savior. Yamanaka concludes his section on Nausicaä thus: "In the midst of this drama of death and rebirth, Nausicaä the protector of the Valley of the Wind is reborn as Nausicaä the guardian angel [divine protector] of humanity."[7] Similarly, Shimizu Masashi points to Nausicaä's messianic status and to her supernatural abilities. To Shimizu, not only is Nausicaä immortal and possessor of supernatural powers (*chônôryokusha*), she is also good, just, and the embodiment of love.[8]

Nausicaä, with its vivid apocalyptic vision, reflects Miyazaki's pedagogical impulse. He states:

> When I started Nausica [sic], my theory was one of extinction; when it ended, my theory was one of coexistence. . . . There is no mighty intelligence that guides the world. We just keep repeating our mistakes. . . . If we want mankind [sic] to live for another thousand years, we have to create the environment for it now. That's what we're trying to do.[9]

While denying the existence of a "mighty intelligence," Miyazaki uses preexisting religious motifs such as clairvoyance, apocalypse, and redemption, as well as the traditional religious concept of *musubi*, an immanent spiritual productive energy that binds organisms together, to influence future outlook and behavior.

The comments of *Nausicaä* fans on fan-based message boards suggest a long-lasting change in outlook based upon watching the film, and, at times, a ritualized way of watching the film, often referring to a sense of connection with other organisms that reflects belief in an immanent spiritual bond existing among all living things. Keeping in mind Grimes' taxonomy of ritual and media, the audience here affirms its connection with all of nature through repetitive viewings of the movie (ritual performed around a media device). The scene of Nausicaä's death and resurrection can be seen as a sort of mediated (vicarious) ritual as well. One person draws a direct connection between *Nausicaä* and Christian ideas of death and resurrection, and suggests that the Ômu (giant insects that protect the fungal forest that has covered the earth) are actually divine.[10] Another person says, "Now Nausicaä seems far away from this reality in which we live, but really [she] is pointing to our current actions (like treating nature disrespectfully)."[11] The act of being entertained is simultaneously hermeneutic; audience members interpret the films and apply their lessons to reality.

Princess Mononoke

Miyazaki said of *Princess Mononoke*: "I've come to the point where I just can't make a movie without addressing the problem of humanity as part of an ecosystem,"[12] and his spiritual beliefs come to the fore when Susan J. Napier states:

> It is Miyazaki's notion that he and presumably other Japanese are the spiritual descendants of the "glossy leafed forests" that . . . once covered Japan . . . and that these vanished forests still exert a spiritual pull on the average urban dweller, and it was this that he attempted to dramatize in his creation of the forest of the *shishigami*. He explains "If you opened a map of Japan and asked where is the forest of the *shishigami* that Ashitaka went to, I couldn't tell you, but I do believe that somehow traces of that kind of place still exist inside one's soul."[13]

For part of the audience, the movie resonates with extant mythology or promotes ritual action, as the posts on a Miyazaki fan board attest. In response to a post entitled: "The Setting of Princess Mononoke" (*Mononoke Hime no butai-chi*), one person wrote: "I really went to Yakushima [the alleged inspiration for the forest], and it seemed as if *shishigamisama* [the main deity in the film] would really appear!" Another respondent wrote: "There [in Yakushima] people really believe in *Mononoke Hime* [Princess Mononoke] . . . [and the other animal gods] whereas [in Kumano, another potential setting] they believe in trees and waterfalls." A third person relates the story of how a friend traveled to Yakushima and had a *kodama* [a kind of small tree spirit that features in the film] appear in a photograph.[14] The first person's comment suggests a kind of pilgrimage, a sort of ritual practice around a conception of sacred space created through the medium of film; the second person's comment shows connections (found or created) between existing mythology and the mythology of the film; the third person's story clearly crosses the boundary between the mythology of the film and reality – the *kodama* that appears in the photograph is an indication of its existence in reality. Many of the commentators express a desire to visit Yakushima in the future, presumably to experience it as a place of mystery, inspiration, or the sacred.

Spirited away

Responses to a leading post, "*Sen to Chihiro . . . ni kakusareta meseeji*" [Hidden messages in *Spirited Away*] on a Miyazaki fan site suggest that some members of the audience have had a spiritual response to that movie as well: from the aforementioned environmental commitment based upon the idea that all organisms are spiritually connected, to a renewed respect for the distinction between divine and human (*kamisama no tabemono wo taberu* [eating the food of the gods/spirits]), to striving for a kind of spiritual love (*sûkô na ai*). Again, the message board posts are interpretive: fans use the films as a basis for determining moral action in their daily life. The other reality of film has come to profoundly affect the audience in this reality; the powerful images and the feelings that they promote persist. More than simply drawing on previous religious themes, Miyazaki has actively changed them by adding an environmental focus, and his fans have responded to the film in ways that can be interpreted as spiritual, if not formally religious.

The production and consumption of shûkyô asobi

These four examples portray *shûkyô asobi* in two important ways. On the one hand, they show how Miyazaki the director is playing with the stuff of religion; he utilizes religious motifs in a calculated fashion to encourage a particular audience response, and modifies traditional religious concepts for his particular pedagogical ends. On the other hand, Miyazaki's films – presumably created solely as a means of entertainment – not only reflect Miyazaki's spiritual beliefs, but also seem to have the power to create responses such as ritualized behavior. In addition, the films appear to generate hermeneutic thinking and exegesis, that is, interpreting films and applying those lessons to daily life. The director's spirituality seems to elicit similar spiritual responses in at least part of his audience, and therefore the movies have the power to create new forms of thought and practice that contribute to and are part of the wider field of contemporary Japanese religiosity.

Conclusions

I would like to conclude with a few final points on *shûkyô asobi*. First, Miyazaki's ambiguous statements make it difficult to associate him with any one particular religion, but they also indicate that the director seeks a simultaneously playful spirituality or a spiritual entertainment. Miyazaki's repeated choice to incorporate religious themes is likely just as much his recognition that "spiritual sells" as it is a reflection of the director's own spiritual views. This pragmatic attitude, apparent I think in Miyazaki and part of his audience, reflects the fact that Japanese religion is based upon a strong sense of responding to mundane needs. This can manifest itself in both fervent religious practice and in a seemingly more "irreverent" usage of religious stuff for mundane ends. *Shûkyô asobi*, broadly viewing religion as inclusive of spirituality, and resisting the artificial distinction between religion and entertainment, allows for and can describe Miyazaki's work.

Second, entries on fan message boards suggest that some audience members respond to Miyazaki's films in a spiritual fashion. While [John] Lyden has suggested that the ritual of film watching can be a religious experience, certainly only some of these fans would actively identify their response to Miyazaki's films as such. As members of the spirituality culture surrounding Miyazaki's films, they "consider themselves part of the audience, information consumers, and have no sense of belonging to a particular organization, sect or church."[15] Yet fans recognize something religious in Miyazaki's films even if they do not consider the films religion. *Shûkyô asobi* refers to that important element of Japanese religion where the mundane desire or need for the experience of entertainment shades into the mundane desire or need for the experience of religion.

A third important element of *shûkyô asobi* in Miyazaki's films lies in the comparisons and contrasts that can be drawn regarding the *manga* and *anime* produced by formal religious institutions. Miyazaki's films subtly underscore his skepticism of formal religion, but formal religions have clearly recognized the proselytizing potential presented by *manga* and *anime*, sometimes producing large numbers of these products aimed at wide audiences. Yet *manga* created by religious institutions are not necessarily always successful, at times being treated with something close to derision. Although the use of *anime* and *manga* as media for expressing and conveying religion is not going to disappear any time soon, it seems that films which serve as religious texts without specific institutional affiliations (like Miyazaki's) are more likely to reach and capture a wide audience than the products created by religious institutions.

Ultimately, the artificial distinction between popular entertainment and religion needs to be replaced with an articulation of the utilization of the common space of religious entertainment – or playful religion – by various interest groups. This is particularly important as established religions utilize popular culture as a vehicle for religious instruction and proselytization; and as pop culture producers increasingly draw upon spiritual/religious themes that obviously attract audiences. The result may be the creation of entirely new religious doctrines, interpretations, rituals, and beliefs. *Shûkyô asobi*, fundamental to properly apprehending the seemingly discrete but conflated modes of religion and entertainment, can presumably be found in other sectors of Japanese religion, and outside of Japan as well.

Overall, in light of the diversification and proliferation of religion occurring at present, *shūkyō asobi* is an apt term for describing an element of religion that has been hitherto difficult to apprehend – the new forms of religious thought and practice arising at the junction between entertainment and religion.

Notes

1   Quoted in Helen McCarthy, *Hayao Miyazaki, Master of Japanese Animation* (Berkeley: Stone Bridge Press, 1999), 89.

2   From the *Japan Times Weekly*, 28 September 2002, cited in James W. Boyd and Nishimura Tetsuya, "Shinto Perspectives in Miyazaki's Anime Film 'Spirited Away,' " *Journal of Religion and Film* 8, no. 2 (October 2004), 5 (my page numbering); online at <http://www.unomaha.edu/jrf/Vol8No2/boydShinto.htm>.

3   Lucy Wright, "Forest Spirits, Giant Insects, and World Trees: The Nature Vision of Hayao Miyazaki," *Journal of Religion and Popular Culture* X (Summer 2005), 2 (my page numbering); online at <http://www.usask.ca/relst/jrpc/art10-miyazaki-print.html>.

4   Quoted in Elisabeth Vintacelli, "Bittersweet Symphonies," *The Village Voice* (27 October–2 November 1999): 3 (my page numbering), <http://www.village voice.com/film/9943,vincentelli,9453,20.html>.

5   McCarthy, *Master of Japanese Animation*, 120–21.

6   MIXI (Online Blog Community) Miyazaki fan site, available by membership only. A person identifying herself as Soppi (post 13) wrote on a thread started by *Yuhi*: *Miyazaki kantoku eiga no eikyô wa?* [What is the influence of director Miyazaki's movies?] *Miyazaki Hayao kantoku eiga no nazo wo tsuikyû/kaimei* [Pursuing and elucidating the mysteries of director Miyazaki Hayao's films], <http://mixi.jp/view_bbs.pl?id=3413393&comm_id=290365>, accessed 2 January 2006. This link is no longer active, and the entire thread has been removed from the community page. Presumably the discussion moderator found some of the content objectionable or outdated. Other threads, cited below, may also become inactive at a later date. The MIXI links cited are fully accessible once one has logged into the MIXI site. Using MIXI requires the ability to read Japanese. Readers who have difficulty navigating the site should contact the author.

7   YAMANAKA Hiroshi, "*Manga bunka no naka no shūkyô*" [Religion in *Manga* Culture], in *Shôhi sareru "shūkyô"* [Consumed "Religion"], ed. SHIMAZONO Sususmu and ISHII Kendo (Tokyo: Shunjusha, 1996), 181.

8   SHIMIZU Masashi, *Miyazaki Hayao wo yomu: bosei to kaosu no fantashii* [Reading Miyazaki Hayao: Fantasies of Maternity and Chaos] (Tokyo: Chôeisha, 2001), 141–42.

9   Interview with Charles T. Whipple, "The Power of Positive Inking," n.d., 8–9 (my

page numbering), <http://www.charlest.whipple.net/mangamiyazaki.html>, initially accessed 15 January 2005. Attempts to contact the author for the date of writing have thus far been unsuccessful. Based on the content of the article, cross-referencing the movies it mentions with their dates of release, it seems to have been written in late 1994.

10   MIXI (Online Blog Community) Miyazaki fan site. Thread by Airinsachi (Kekaha), *Naushika no saigo wa* . . . [The end of Nausicaä . . .], *Miyazaki no nazo wo tsuikyû/kaimei*, <http://mixi.jp/view_bbs.pl?page=1&comm_id=290365&id=1884432>, accessed 1 September 2005. See particularly the series of posts by Hajime (6), Airinsachi (Kekaha) (7, 10), Hibachi (8), and Kenji (9).

11   Airinsachi (Kekaha), "The end of Nausicaä . . .", *Miyazaki Hayao no nazo wo tsuikyû/ kaimei*, <http://mixi.jp/view_bbs.pl?page=1&comm_id=290365&id=1884432>, accessed 1 September 2005. This is post 7, by topic starter Airinsachi (Kekaha).

12   *Asia Pulse*, May 1997, cited in McCarthy, *Master of Japanese Animation*, 185.

13   Susan J. Napier, *Anime from Akira to Princess Mononoke* (New York: Palgrave, 2000), 186–87.

14   Thread by Chunbaa, *Mononoke hime no butaichi* ["The Setting of *Princess Mononoke*"], *Miyazaki Hayao no nazo wo tsuikyû/kaimei*, <http://mixi.jp/view_bbs.pl?id= 2444019&comm_id=290365>, accessed 23 October 2005. See particularly the posts by":) nussy" (4), Naki mushi no amattare (6), HHC (9), and Mamepucchi (13).

15   SHIMAZONO Susumu, *From Salvation to Spirituality: Popular Religious Movements in Modern Japan*. Melbourne: Trans Pacific Press, 2004, 303.

Chapter 26

Peter Weir

UNDER WEIR AND THEROUX
An Interview with Peter Weir

Editor's note:

THE FOLLOWING EXTRACT from an article/interview was done shortly before the release of The Mosquito Coast and was written by Pat McGilligan.

Interviewer: Your films have a preoccupation with dreams and illusions, with the subcurrents of reason, with ancient, forgotten beliefs.

Peter Weir: I must say that is abundantly apparent now, but I can't say that I was aware of it at the time. I'm somewhat uncomfortable with that pattern. It gives me no particular pleasure. I don't think there is anything significant about it. These are just things I got very interested in ten years ago and began to investigate in myself, and to think, read, and talk about. While I did so, I was least in touch with these things. Fortunately, I realized this after some years – that it was best not to talk about them and then they will come back with all of their richness. Of course we all have our dreams as part of our psychic makeup. There are simply unmeasured abilities we have, forms of communication, or ancient

McGilligan, Pat. "Under Weir and Theroux: An Interview with Peter Weir," Film Comment 22.6 (1986): 23–32.

influences that have come through the very genes that make us what we are. It's a subject with no boundaries. But I've explored it consciously enough to decide it's best to leave it alone and to concentrate on craft.

[. . .]

I was making a documentary in Sydney, which I really did as a favor for a friend, a potter – highly regarded, charming, much loved – who was retiring from teaching pottery after many years at a technical college in Sydney. An arts foundation wanted this filmed record of his work, so I said, "All right, if I can make it my own way." I found his story very interesting. He had been a prisoner of war of the Japanese captured in the fall of Singapore; he had endured the hardships and horrors in a Japanese prisoner-of-war camp, and yet, after he came out, he had become a potter. Of course, anyone who becomes a potter has to go to Japan and immerse himself in the history of the great masters of pottery. I found this very interesting – that a man who had experienced prisoner-of-war trauma ended up having this kind of Oriental aspect to his personality, apart from his pots.

Part of this film involved meeting a Japanese potter called Shiga, a master who was living and working in Australia. I filmed him one night when he opened his kiln and brought some pots out. It was very exciting for me. And over many glasses of sake that night he talked about pottery – about art and about craft. That conversation that evening came to change my view about filmmaking, and it remains unchanged to this day. Putting it simply, for him there was no art, it was all craft. He talked about how the great potters didn't sign their pots because it was considered a vanity to do so; how their pots were utilitarian objects rather than something just to be stuck on the wall, like paintings; how you make these vessels to be used, for eating and drinking; how you make each one to the best of your ability – using Head, Heart, and Hand – which is what I called the documentary – in perfect balance. How you should never think about making a work of art because you would be punished if you did. That the gods choose when to touch your hands, and you will never know when that may be. You must keep working, and every now and again, when the gods do touch your hands, out will come this wonderful creation. It was so fundamentally opposed to the European idea of, simplistically speaking, the artist-as-God.

I loved his approach. Here were movies- which were items to be used and consumed in your daily life and then thrown away. When I returned to feature filmmaking, the emphasis for me was clearly on craft, and to forget about the artistic propaganda trip that I felt had been perpetuated. Of course, inspiration is still part of the process – head, heart, and hand. The area of the heart, or presumably, the soul, the unknown area, provides that leap of imagination that touches the fires to the brain. But after talking with Shiga, I found I had a kind of pocket philosophy that would get me through some ups and downs, and threw me back into the fray, trying to understand this wonderful craft I was involved in. And I was free of the curse of thinking of it as an art form.

European Perspectives

INTRODUCTION

GIVEN THE HISTORY OF Europe it is no surprise that Christianity regularly appears in European cinema. It comes into view in various forms, reflecting Europe's fragmented religious past. European filmmakers who interact with Christianity do so in many different ways, reflecting Catholic, Protestant and Orthodox interests. Some directors through their films reflect discontent and even fierce anger with the religious tradition that they were brought up in. For example, this can be seen in the *oeuvre* of one of Spain's leading twentieth-century directors, Luis Buñuel (1900–1983), who had a strict Jesuit education. In films such as *L'Âge d'or* (1931), *Nazarín* (1958), and *Viridiana* (1961) he depicted the Catholic Church in far from favorable terms. As we shall see not all European directors were as critical.

The beliefs of a director, however, do not necessarily determine the final content of a film. It is ironic that one of the most highly respected cinematic depictions of the life of Jesus was produced by Pier Paolo Pasolini, an outspoken Marxist-atheist, whose other films sometimes led to outrage from religious groups. The brief excerpt (reading 27) from the Jesuit scholar Lloyd Baugh's discussion of *The Gospel According to Saint Matthew* (1964) highlights this point. Baugh later describes how this film was celebrated by film juries, recommended by theologians, and even applauded by "eight hundred Catholic bishops assembled in Rome for Vatican Council II." Baugh's essay is part of a larger book which considers in detail both

Jesus-figure and Christ-figure films. The former was the representation of Jesus himself on screen, such as in *The King of Kings* (1927) or *The Greatest Story Ever Told* (1965) and the latter was the portrayal of characters whose depictions resonate with the life or death of Christ, such as the protagonist in *Cool Hand Luke* (1967) or *Pale Rider* (1985). This is one of several books to make the distinction between the Jesus-figure and the Christ-figure in films. As Baugh and other critics acknowledge, identifying a film's protagonist as a Christ-figure may reveal more about the interpreter than illuminate the actual narrative.

Filmmakers are themselves creators, interpreters, and questioners of reality. As we saw earlier, through André Bazin's discussion of Robert Bresson's *Diary of a Country Priest* (1951) in Reading 8, the cinematic narratives and characters can resonate with older religious stories. In spite of these resonances many filmmakers express their relation with religion in highly ambiguous terms. For instance, the Swedish director Ingmar Bergman was the son of a Lutheran pastor, and was brought up in a pious and some would say autocratic home. Especially during the 1950s and early 1960s, Bergman depicted characters wrestling with faith in the midst of despair, anxiety, and suffering. Films such as his trilogy about people living in search of comfort and guidance in the absence of God, *Through a Glass Darkly* (1961), *Winter Light* (1962), and *The Silence* (1963), and his Passion film *Cries and Whispers* (1973), explore several of these existential themes. In Ingmar Bergman's *The Seventh Seal* (1956) the personification of death asks the Knight:

> Death: What are you waiting for?
> Knight: Knowledge.
> Death: You want a guarantee.
> Knight: Call it what you will . . . What will become of us, who want to believe but cannot? And what of those, who neither will nor can believe? . . . I want knowledge. Not belief. Not suppositions. But knowledge. I want God to put out His hand, show His face, speak to me.

The Knight's journey, played with intensity by Max von Sydow, resonates with Bergman and many other European filmmakers' own experience: a search for a silent God in the face of both death and human love. Bergman is a rare example of a director who acknowledges some basis to his cinematic search in theological thinking. This can be seen in the excerpt presented here which is the introduction to the published film script of *The Seventh Seal* (reading 28).

Other European filmmakers have cast a sceptical eye on religious institutions, creating films that highlight the abuses of religion or that satirize it. The Greek-born Costa-Gavras (1933–   ) has been making films since the 1960s that deal with political issues, from Palestine to Chile to U.S. covert operations (e.g., *Z* [1969], *Missing* [1982], *Hanna K.* [1983]). His 2002 film, *Amen.*, is the topic of the interview excerpted here (reading 29). That film deals with the accommodation of Nazism by the Roman Catholic church, creating what he calls an "interrogation" of the ideologies of religion. From another angle, Jean-Luc Godard (1930–   ) moved from the "French New Wave" of the 1960s to what his interviewer here calls the "contemplative, middle-aged Godard" of the 1980s (excerpt 30). During this period he made *Hail Mary* (1985), the story of the Immaculate Conception set in modern times (Mary plays basketball and pumps gas at a gas station). As with *Monty Python's Life of Brian* (1979), it might be easy to see *Amen.* as satire, and yet, as Godard explains, there is something deeper going on. He says he "needed a story which is bigger than myself." In so doing he raises new questions about an old story.

Just as Godard's *Hail Mary* translates aspects of a biblical narrative into a contemporary setting, so the Polish director Krzysztof Kieślowski (1941–96) and his writing partner Krzysztof Piesiewicz drew upon *The Ten Commandments* to structure ten short films. These were originally made for Polish television, though both *A Short Film about Loving* and *A Short Film about Killing* were also produced in longer versions and released before the complete sequence in 1988. Kieślowski's introduction (reading 31) to the script of *Dekalog* (*The Decalogue*, 1989) provides a rich resource for understanding how these films portrayed everyday life in a large housing estate in Warsaw, creating "extreme and extraordinary" situations and tentatively relating each film to one of the Ten Commandments.

Kieślowski's work was highly praised around the world and his premature death was lamented by many reviewers. Newspaper critics, and more recently television and internet film criticism, play an important role in the circuit of cinematic communication. With the rapid evolution of the World Wide Web, reviews from a multiplicity of sources are readily available through sites such as IMDb or *Rotten Tomatoes*. Rarer nowadays are published collections of reviews by film critics. Exceptions include *A Century of Films: Derek Malcolm's Personal Best* (2000). In this collection by a well-known British critic several films by directors featured in this reader appear. For example, Kieślowski's *A Short Film about Killing* was selected by Malcolm as one of his best 100 films. Another review, presented here (reading 33), discusses *Day of Wrath* (1943), a film by the Danish filmmaker, Karl Theodor Dreyer (1889–1968). Dreyer was the illegitimate son of a Swedish farmer and his housekeeper, who spent his formative years in different foster homes before he was adopted by a Lutheran family. Malcolm, who admits in another review that "films about the Christian God are not exactly my cup of tea," celebrates Dreyer's work, putting it into its historical and cinematic context (reading 32). The Danish director, Lars von Trier, is sometimes described as Dreyer's successor. In *Breaking the Waves* von Trier uses the life and loves of a simple girl from a small, "strictly religious community on the west coast of Scotland" to explore cinematically the nature of prayer, the abuses of sex, and the power of self-sacrifice. In the interview offered here he reveals his own religious background and the themes that absorbed him in *Breaking the Waves* (reading 34);.

The religious mosaic of European films is a complex one, with many critics and directors using cinema as a space to express their idiosyncratic beliefs about Christianity or other religions. For example, Andrej Tarkovsky (1932–1986), son of a prominent Russian poet, while rejecting the atheism of the Communist Soviet regime, unconventionally explores aspects of Orthodoxy in his film based loosely on the life (c.1360–c.1430) of the Russian iconographer *Andrei Rublev* (1966, also transliterated as *Andrey Rublyov*). Tarkovsky only produced seven films but his collection of essays on filmmaking, *Sculpting in Time*, reflects his fascination with the spiritual aspects of life and death, the way cinema transforms time and its ability to explore the "most complex problems" of our age (reading 33). In *Andrei Rublev* Tarkovsky uses the life of Russia's most famous icon painter and the bold risk taken by a young boy pretending he knows the secret of forging a bell, to reflect cinematically on the nature of faith, the spiritual power of images and the hardships associated with artistic creation.

Chapter 27

Lloyd Baugh

THE MASTERPIECE
The Gospel According to Saint Matthew

PIER PAOLO PASOLINI'S FILM, The Gospel According to Saint Matthew,[1] in the minds of most serious critics is still the greatest, the most authentic and "the most religious film on Jesus ever made."[2] It was premiered at the International Film Festival of Venice on 4 September 1964. An Italo-French coproduction, it was given important awards at the Venice Festival but unfortunately, for a variety of reasons, it did not receive a wide distribution in the United States, and "got most of its showings on college campuses after its initial theatrical release."[3]

Pasolini's Jesus-film project began two years earlier during a visit to Assisi. While guest of the Catholic cultural organization, Pro Civitate Christiana, in October 1962, and more or less confined to the house by the town's busy preparations for the visit of Pope John XXIII – to whose "dear happy memory" Pasolini later dedicated the film – the director found a copy of the New Testament on his bedside table. He turned to the gospels, and in his own words, "that day . . . I read them from beginning to end, like a novel."[4] The experience was like a bolt of lightning for Pasolini, who describes how he felt "an immediate need to 'do something' – a terrible, almost physical energy."[5]

In 1964, when The Gospel According to Saint Matthew came out, Pasolini was forty-two years of age. A prolific writer and man of culture, he had already published some twenty-eight books of poetry and essays, film scripts and novels, and in cinema he had worked on the scripts of some fifteen films, and had himself made five films. Active also politically, Pasolini had been a member of the Italian Communist party, from which he was expelled in 1952 because of the scandal caused by his publicly-admitted homosexuality and some run-ins with the law in this regard. His short film of 1963, La ricotta, got him in trouble once again: the film was judged blasphemous and insulting to the Catholic faith, the religion of the state. Pasolini was arrested, tried and given a four-month suspended sentence.

It is from this rich, varied and troubled background that Pasolini, a kind of national Italian enfant terrible, came to the project of making The Gospel According to Saint Matthew, and there is no doubt that this background left its mark on the film and on the portrait of Jesus which it presents. For example, Pasolini's past can be sensed in his preference for Matthew's Jesus: he was attracted by "the revolutionary quality of his [Jesus'] social diversity, of his non-violence, of the power of moral thought."[6] One senses it in Pasolini's objections to the other gospels: "Mark's seemed too crude, John's too mystical, and Luke's, sentimental and bourgeois."[7] Further, Pasolini insists that "Matthew is the most 'worldly' of the evangelists . . . and the most revolutionary."[8] And he continues enthusiastically:

> The Christ [of Matthew] who moves through Palestine is really a revolutionary whirlwind: anyone who comes up to two people and says, 'Throw away your nets, follow me, and I will make you fishers of men,' is totally revolutionary.[9]

Clearly, Pasolini was fascinated, inspired by the strong, aggressive Jesus of Matthew's Gospel. He himself confesses that the words of Jesus that struck him and drove him to make the film were: "Do not suppose that I have come to bring peace on the earth. I have not come to bring peace but a sword. For I have come to bring division, a man against his father, a daughter against her mother" (Mt 10:34).[10] Should there be any doubt as to his basic point of view, Pasolini adds: "I had in mind to represent Christ as an intellectual in a world of poor people ready for revolution."[11] Clearly, Pasolini had in mind something quite different from a biography of Jesus: "This film is simply the visualization of one particular Gospel, that of St. Matthew. It's not a life of Christ."[12] He explains further:

> I did not want to reconstruct the life of Christ as it really was. Instead, I wanted to tell the story of Christ plus two thousand years of Christian tradition, because it took two thousand years of Christian history to mythologize that biography . . . My film is the life of Christ plus two thousand years of history told about the life of Christ.[13]

If Zeffirelli created a very free adaptation of all four gospels, in the end producing a work more of fiction than Gospel, and Rossellini, an austere amalgam
of the four gospels, Pasolini, inspired by the raw power of Matthew's text, was
determined to be utterly faithful to it: "My idea is this: to follow the Gospel
according to Saint Matthew point by point, without making a script or adaptation out of it. To translate it faithfully into images, following its story without
any omissions or additions."[14] Regarding the dialogue of his film, Pasolini
insists that "the spoken words should be rigorously those of Saint Matthew,
without even a sentence of explanation or bridging, because no image or word
added can ever reach the high poetic level of the text."[15] Pasolini was faithful to
his intention: in fact, "not one word in the film is Pasolini's invention."[16] The
only exception is his insertion of several passages from the old Testament book
of Isaiah, prophecies regarding the Messiah, additions which Pasolini rightly
justifies by noting that "Matthew's text is full of citations from Isaiah, so I
thought it would be licit to add a couple."[17]

Different from Zeffirelli's Jesus-film, which was intended to reach the
popular public of the mass television audience, and from Rossellini's, whose
purpose was to teach and edify, Pasolini, the poet, saw his film more as "a
poetic work, which would express all his 'nostalgia for the sacred, the mythical,
the epic.' "[18] Given his hopes for his film of the Gospel, clearly in explosive
contrast with all the Jesus-films made to that time, Pasolini was aware of the
delicacy of his situation; he well understood how the critics, both of the left and
the right, would scrutinize his finished work. He explains his dilemma: "I
walked on the razor's edge: trying to avoid, from my point of view, a uniquely
historical and human vision, and from the point of view of the believer, a too
mythical vision."[19]

Pasolini was not the only one nervous about this project. When he asked
the Pro Civitate Christiana group for help, its director sought the advice of the
powerful and conservative Giuseppe Cardinal Siri, archbishop of Genoa, who
courageously encouraged him to promote Pasolini's project, writing: "To further the conquest of culture for God, something indeed has to be risked . . .
in certain cases even prudence counsels daring."[20] As a result of Siri's letter,
Pro Civitate Christiana gave financial assistance to the film.[21] Pasolini's film-in-
progress was also followed by two Jesuits from the Centro San Fedele of Milan
and by the somewhat skeptical theologian Romano Guardini, "who expressed a
systematic lack of confidence in the possibility of representing Jesus through an
actor."[22]

The controversy which had accompanied The Gospel According to Saint Matthew
from its beginning made itself felt on the evening of its premiere at the Venice
Festival. Anticipating a negative reaction from the far right, the police chief of
Venice tripled the usual number of police and carabinieri around the Palazzo del

Cinema at the Venice Lido. Yet the noisy Fascist demonstrators outside did not prevent the overall warm reception of the film and more importantly, did not prevent its being awarded the Special Prize of the Jury. If a Gospel film was a controversial choice for the secular Prize of the Jury, the same film by an avowed Marxist was an equally controversial choice for the prize of the International Catholic Film office (O.C.I.C.), which justified its award to Pasolini in the following statement:

> The author . . . has faithfully translated, with simplicity and piety, and often movingly, the social message of the Gospel, in particular love for the poor and the oppressed, while sufficiently respecting the divine aspect of Christ . . . this work is far superior to earlier, commercial films on the life of Christ. It shows the real grandeur of his teaching stripped of any artificial and sentimental effect.[23]

Giovanni Cardinal Urbani, archbishop of Venice, present at the film's premiere at the Festival, was annoyed by it. A biblical scholar and professor, he complained: "Pasolini hasn't understood the Gospel. Jesus isn't like that."[24] Without realizing it, Urbani was voicing the objection that many Catholics, unfamiliar with the text of Matthew, would make to the film over the years. The Cardinal however, at the suggestion of one of his assistants, then read through the Gospel of Matthew in one sitting and changed his mind about the film: "I realized that, although he was a layman,[25] Pasolini had projected Matthew's very same Jesus on the screen, with great fidelity, word for word."[26]

Notes

1   The original title is Il Vangelo secondo Matteo, "The Gospel According to Matthew." The title was changed – "Saint" added – by the distributors of the English-language version against Pasolini's wishes and protests. As were also changed the titles of the Spanish and French versions of the film. Pasolini considered the change an "outrage." [Pasolini su Pasolini: Conversazioni con Jon Halliday (Parma: Ugo Guanda Editore, 1992), 76.]

2   Maurizio Viano, A Certain Realism: Making Use of Pasolini's Film Theory and Practice (Berkeley: University of California Press, 1993), 134.

3   Campbell and Pitts, 153.

4   Pier Paolo Pasolini, in a letter of February 1963 to Lucio S. Caruso of the Pro Civitate Christiana, published in Pier Paolo Pasolini, Il Vangelo secondo Matteo (Milan: Garzanti, 1964), 16–17, and quoted in Enzo Siciliano, Pasolini, translated by John Shepley. New York: Random House, 1982, 269.

5   Pasolini, in his book of Il Vangelo second Matteo, 14, quoted in Siciliano, 270.

6   Murri, Pier Paolo Pasolini, 53.

7   Pasolini in Marisa Rusconi, "4 Registi al magnetofono," *Sipario* (October 1964): 16, quoted in Naomi Greene, *Pier Paolo Pasolini: Cinema as Heresy*. Princeton: Princeton University Press, 1990, 72.

8   *Pasolini su Pasolini*, 89.

9   Ibid.

10   Viano, 133.

11   *Pasolini su Pasolini*, 78.

12   Pasolini in "Una visione del mondo epico-religiosa," a conversation with Pier Paolo Pasolini, in *Bianco e nero*, v.25, n.6 (June 1964), quoted in Virgilio Fantuzzi, "La 'visione religiosa' di Pier Paolo Pasolini," in *Cinema sacro e profano*. Roma: Edizioni "La Civilta Cattolica," 1983, 316, note 84.

13   *Pasolini su Pasolini*, 82.

14   Pasolini in letter to Lucio Caruso, quoted in Siciliano, 270.

15   Ibid.

16   Viano, 140. Then, in a long note on pages 331–333 of his book, Viano traces very precisely the correspondences between the text of Pasolini's film and that of Matthew's Gospel.

17   *Pasolini su Pasolini*, 90.

18   Luciano De Giusti, I film di *Pier Paolo Pasolini*. Roma: Gremese Editore, 1983, 68. Clearly both Zeffirelli's and Rossellini's films were made after Pasolini's.

19   Pasolini, responding to criticism of the film in Paris, quoted in De Giusti, 69.

20   Stefano M. Paci, "Prudence Counsels Daring," *Thirty Days* v.7, n. 1 (1995), 65. The words are in a letter from Siri to Father Giovanni Rossi, dated 22 February 1963, and quoted in its entirety in Paci's article.

21   Siciliano, 272.

22   Ibid., 273.

23   Sam Rohdie, *The Passion of Pier Paolo Pasolini* (Bloomington: Indiana University Press, 1995), 162. André Ruszkowsky, film scholar and President of the O.C.I.C. Jury at the Venice festival responded to the strong criticism of the Catholic prize given to the film of a Communist by insisting that "Any jury, and especially a jury that is just and impartial as must be that of O.C.I.C., must make its judgment based on the film in question and not on the person and the positions of its director." [*Rivista del cinematografo* nn.6–10 (1964): 439.]

24   Paci, "A Blessed Clapperboard," *Thirty Days* v.7, n.1 (1995), 68.

25   The Italian word, "*laico*," has stronger connotations that the English word. If "layperson" means simply one who is not a member of the clergy, "*laico*" carries suggestions of religious non-belief, and non-practice, perhaps of atheism with political-ideological overtones.

26   Paci, "A Blessed Clapperboard," 68.

Chapter 28

Ingmar Bergman

INTRODUCTION TO *THE SEVENTH SEAL*

PEOPLE ASK WHAT are my intentions with my films – my aims. It is a difficult and dangerous question, and I usually give an evasive answer: I try to tell the truth about the human condition, the truth as I see it. This answer seems to satisfy everyone, but it is not quite correct. I prefer to describe what I would like my aim to be.

There is an old story of how the cathedral of Chartres was struck by lightning and burned to the ground. Then thousands of people came from all points of the compass, like a giant procession of ants, and together they began to rebuild the cathedral on its old site. They worked until the building was completed – master builders, artists, labourers, clowns, noblemen, priests, burghers. But they all remained anonymous, and no one knows to this day who built the cathedral of Chartres.

Regardless of my own beliefs and my own doubts, which are unimportant in this connection, it is my opinion that art lost its basic creative drive the moment it was separated from worship. It severed an umbilical cord and now lives its own sterile life, generating and degenerating itself. In former days the artist remained unknown and his work was to the glory of God. He lived and died without being more or less important than other artisans; 'eternal values,' 'immortality' and 'masterpiece' were terms not applicable in his case. The ability to create was a gift. In such a world flourished invulnerable assurance and natural humility.

Today the individual has become the highest form and the greatest bane of artistic creation. The smallest wound or pain of the ego is examined under a microscope as if it were of eternal importance. The artist considers his isolation, his subjectivity, his individualism almost holy. Thus we finally gather in one large pen, where we stand and bleat about our loneliness without listening to each other and without realising that we are smothering each other to death. The individualists stare into each other's eyes and yet deny the existence of each other. We walk in circles, so limited by our own anxieties that we can no longer distinguish between true and false, between the gangster's whim and the purest ideal.

Thus if I am asked what I would like the general purpose of my films to be, I would reply that I want to be one of the artists in the cathedral on the great plain. I want to make a dragon's head, an angel, a devil – or perhaps a saint – out of stone. It does not matter which; it is the sense of satisfaction that counts. Regardless of whether I believe or not, whether I am a Christian or not, I would play my part in the collective building of the cathedral.

Chapter 29

Constantin Costa-Gavras

FILMING THE STORY OF A SPY FOR GOD

An Interview with Costa-Gavras

Cineaste: Your film [*Amen.*] seems, along with others such as Peter Mullan's *The Magdalene Sisters*, Giuseppe Ferrara's *The Bankers of God*, and Carlos Carrera's *The Crime of Father Amaro*, to be part of a recent group of films highly critical of the Catholic Church. How do you account for this?

Costa-Gavras: Well, there's been no contact between us [laughs].

Cineaste: There goes our conspiracy theory!

Costa-Gavras: I think if we consider that cinema, as a popular art, acts as a sort of antenna receiving the waves of society, there is a widespread perception that there is something wrong with religions today, and particularly with the Catholic religion. It is perhaps the most important religion because it is the only one organized as a state, with a centralized power.

Cineaste: How would you respond to charges that your film engages in 'Catholic bashing'?

Costa-Gavras: The film has nothing to do with Catholic bashing. *Amen.* is about the leaders of the Catholic Church who acted not out of the Catholic or

By Gary Crowdus and Dan Georgakas, *Cineaste*, 28/2 (Spring 2003): excerpt from pp. 19–20.

Christian philosophy but with the logic of a state. The film is not opposed to the Christian religion but is in favor of it because the two main characters are Christians.

Cineaste: In one of our early *interviews* with you, you stated that ideology, whether political or religious, can be one of the most destructive forces on the face of the earth.

Costa-Gavras: Yes, I believe it, I believe it very deeply. Today we hear that all ideologies are dead. But how can we live in a society without ideology. Ideologies live and die like human beings. The problem is when ideology becomes a dogma. When it becomes a dogma, the absolute truth, then people die for it, or, what is even worse, they kill for it.

When the Pope went to Africa, he preached against the use of condoms, but something like 5,000 to 7,000 people die every day of AIDS in Africa. He also preached against abortion, which shows that Catholic dogma is more important than the happiness and well-being of the people. Consider what happened in Rwanda in the Nineties, when about a million people – a number that comes from *The New York Times*, so we have to believe it – were killed in three months. Can you imagine how many people were killed every day? Those were Catholics killing other Catholics, essentially – a chief of one of the tribes engaged in the killing is a Cardinal in the Church – but the Pope said nothing.

Cineaste: It should be acknowledged that the Vatican was not unique in its failure to protest the extermination of the Jews during the war. In the film, Gerstein meets with a similar response from his Protestant coreligionists, each of whom has his or her own reason why they can't get involved in a protest.

Costa-Gavras: Yes, that scene was inspired by Pierre Joffroy's book on Gerstein, *A Spy for God*. Joffroy worked for three years on his book, both in the archives and by interviewing friends of Gerstein who survived the war.

Cineaste: In fact, the Vatican's stance of noninvolvement and silence was pretty much representative of most of the allied countries.

Costa-Gavras: Churchill never spoke about this issue, nor did De Gaulle or Roosevelt. The allies were engaged in fighting the war, of course, but there's long been a debate about whether they could have bombed the railroads or the gas chambers. Sometimes they did bomb the railroads, but for military reasons. But during the three and a half years of deportations, with something like six million people being deported, there were clearly a lot of trains going back and forth. The gas chambers were separated from the camps. They were one to two kilometers away, so they could have been bombed.

Some people complained about what they felt were 'anti-American' touches in the movie, but we only show the historical position of the U.S. What the American Ambassador says at one point in the movie, in response to allegations about the operation of the extermination camps – "We must win the war and then all that will be over" – is defined very clearly in Wyman's book.

Cineaste: Your film has a brilliant ending, a sort of scorpion's tail, with a reference to the "Vatican Ratlines," whereby the Vatican assisted the escape of Nazis from Europe to America or Argentina.

Costa-Gavras: Yes, Bishop Hudal, the character you see in that last scene, was the Episcopate for German-speaking Catholics in Italy and wrote several books, in one of which he explained how the Nazi system could be used to eliminate the 'corrupt Jewish element' from the European community. He helped people such as Franz Stangl, the chief of the Treblinka concentration camp, as well as Adolf Eichmann, to escape. Thousands of Nazis left Europe through the monasteries.

Cineaste: Although *Amen.* is clearly a historical film, its implications about denial and noninvolvement, or, at worst, complicity with evil, clearly have broader contemporary social implications.

Costa-Gavras: Absolutely. For me, the movie is a metaphor about our silence today, about our indifference or silence about other violence and genocides during the last twenty to twenty-five years. But it was important to make a film about this subject because historically everything's proven for me, and I think also for most historians, and, given the historical distance, it's easier to speak about these events today.

But films are not history books or universities. The Italian historian, Carlo Ginzburg, explains it well when he says that movies can bring the audience into the historian's chamber, where they can then try to learn more if they wish. He says that the distance between history and the moviegoer is too huge, but a movie can broach a historical subject by not attempting to provide all the elements.

A book is read by how many – 10,000, 30,000? A movie is seen by hundreds of thousands of people, sometimes millions, and when it's shown on television, it'll reach three to four million more. That's why the Church has reacted to *Amen.* If it were a book, they'd say "Forget it." But I'd never say that I'm a historian. And I'm not a judge, either, although people have said that for me the Pope was clearly guilty. The movie asks questions, it's an interrogation, but it's not a courtroom.

Chapter 30

Jean-Luc Godard, with Katherine Dieckmann

GODARD IN HIS FIFTH PERIOD

Katherine Dieckmann: Are you a Catholic?

Jean-Luc Godard: No, I was raised a Protestant, but I don't practice. But I'm very interested in Catholicism. I think there's something so strong in the way the Bible was written, how it speaks of events that are happening today, how it contains statements about things which have happened in the past. I think, well – it's a great book! And somehow I think we need faith, or I need faith, or I'm lacking in faith. Therefore maybe I needed a story which is bigger than myself. I like it that *Hail Mary* is being really discussed. Instead of people saying, "Oh, it's directed by Godard," people are talking about the subject of the film first. Later they say, "It's by Godard."

Katherine Dieckmann: It's a sincerely spiritual film. What about it do you think is offending the Catholics most? The obsessive nudity?

Jean-Luc Godard: Probably. But you know, our purpose was to try and shoot a woman naked and not make it aggressive, not in an X-rated-picture way. There are several shots which have more the purpose of an anatomical drawing. Maybe the nudity's a bit much. It encounters the risk of becoming sinister. Or sin, even. Perhaps that's too big a word. But it was difficult to know how to

From *Film Quarterly* 39/2 (1985), 2–6. © 1985 by The Regents of the University of California. Reprinted by permission of The University of California.

show it. Very often in painting, the Virgin is depicted half-naked, or at least with the breast naked or revealed, because of the Christ child. This has always caused problems: In the time of Martin Luther, there was a great deal of opposition to Raphael, for instance. The German soldiers came to Rome and scratched up many Raphael paintings. They thought it was offensive, too much of a *Playboy* style of painting. In *Hail Mary* I was trying to make the audience see not a naked woman, but flesh, if that's at all possible. And the difference between – a feeling of something fleshy. And we had thought of having Joseph be naked also, as we had a nude male in *First Name: Carmen*, but decided the audience wouldn't understand, they would immediately think Mary and Joseph were going to have intercourse. So it was absolutely impossible. And I'm a man, still, I like to look at women naked!

Katherine Dieckmann: You're dealing with this opposition between science and nature, or logic and illogic, in this movie. The men are associated with the logical, the women with the intuitive. And you're using a very different set of symbols. Usually your films are full of quotations from popular culture, with bits of traffic signs, neon, advertisements, cartoons. The signs in *Hail Mary* are very pure: a moon, a sun, water. Apples. Some of the images are even a little corny, like *National Geographic* photography.

Jean-Luc Godard: Well, women are more casual. They accept more things. Whereas men always feel they have to master, to understand. As for these symbols, we shot exactly like the old-time Walt Disney documentaries were shot. We set up a camera and were waiting, waiting, waiting until a certain time when you got the exceptional in everyday, natural things. I mean, we shot the sun, but we needed to have a plane cross the sun, and it doesn't happen every second! It's a one-time thing. That's why we went over budget with *Hail Mary* and had to stop and shoot *Détective* to make some money, and then go back and finish *Hail Mary*, which was very disruptive. I didn't want to make *Détective* at all, though I don't mind it now that I've done it. But it was an unwanted child, and then what do you do? You have to take care of it. What we wanted to show in *Hail Mary* was signs in the beginning. Signs in the sense of signals, the beginning of signs, when signs are beginning to grow. Before they have signification of meaning. Immaculate signs in a way. And not just to give a feeling of nature, in order to be poetic, but to show the physical process of making nature possible. A philosophy of nature, just as we tried to show the spirit and flesh of Mary. Also to bring science close to the natural, not to show them as oppositions. Because there's a scene where the professor is talking about creation – the text comes from the work of a British physicist – and it sounds very Biblical or religious. We are an extraterrestrial people, as it says in the film. We come from the sky. And it's not by chance, but by design.

Katherine Dieckmann: And you have so many images of the circle, in nature and elsewhere, which gives the movie a strong feeling of unity.

Jean-Luc Godard: Yes, the circle. We used it metaphorically: the woman as circle, and the plane flying toward it. That's one signal: coming to a woman's center. But at a certain point there's no difference between metaphor and actuality. I had no idea we'd shot the moon so many times, but then suddenly we had all these shots of the moon, and I discovered then that the moon was like the basketball in Mary's games. So it was the same: Mary was playing basketball with the moon.

Katherine Dieckmann: Tell me about the use of sound, because it's very complex.

Jean-Luc Godard: I try to work not with an idea of vertical sound, where there are many tracks distinct from one another, but horizontally, where there are many, many sounds but still it's as though every sound is becoming one general speech, whether it's music, dialogue or natural sound. *Hail Mary* had more of a documentary use of sound than other films I've done. It's simple in a way: There's dialogue, direct sound and music. The story was known, more or less. And I knew that the only music that would work would be Bach. I tried to put in all sorts of Bach: violins, church music, piano, choral. The picture could be described also as a documentary on Bach's music. And it couldn't have been Beethoven, or Mozart, because historically Bach was the music of Martin Luther. And as I was saying before, Martin Luther was attacking the Catholic church, specifically the way the Catholic church makes images. Probably in his time Bach was immensely popular, because his music was played in churches that had no heat, and it was probably very cold in church, and you needed a strong and passionate music. It's a strange thing, but if you have good speakers and play Bach very, very loud – even if it's just a smooth piano piece – it sounds like rock music. Bach's music can be matched to any situation. It's perfect. When you play it in reverse, it sounds almost the same. It's very mathematical. You could play it in the elevator, like Muzak. It blends itself. Bach is the perfect musician for the elevator.

Katherine Dieckmann: Before you shot *Hail Mary*, you said, "It will be about what Mary and Joseph said to each other before having a child." Does this still apply now that the movie's done?

Jean-Luc Godard: Yes, exactly. What could they say to each other? It's a major problem, because from the Bible we know of only two or three words that Mary spoke, and from Joseph absolutely nothing. And they must have talked together! So it was difficult to invent the dialogue, because nobody knows.

Katherine Dieckmann: You've also said that one film always leads directly into the next with you. So how does the story of Carmen become the story of Mary?

Jean-Luc Godard: Well, Carmen leads to Mary, though of course they're very different. Carmen is more what men imagine women to be. And with Mary, it's more a matter that a man *can't* imagine what a woman is. And, of course, one story ends well and the other ends quite badly.

Katherine Dieckmann: What about your *King Lear* project with Golan and Globus? What do you think about working with producers in America who make mostly commercial, action movies?

Jean-Luc Godard: Well, *Lear* I'm not sure about yet. It's just a project at this point, and I'm going to do another movie in between, though that isn't decided either. I've never read it, you know.

Katherine Dieckmann: Oh, come on!

Jean-Luc Godard: I don't know much. I'm not a very good pretender. [Laughs] I just know it's about some old man and his young daughter, or three daughters, but one specifically. Of course I'll read it before I shoot. People tell me it's a great story, but it's just one I've heard of, like the story of Carmen or the story of Mary. I met Golan and Globus just crossing the street one day at Cannes. And they approached me. I'd never talked to them before. And we crossed the street together, and in crossing the street we made a fast deal. It's a very specific agreement, so I'm not worried about it. They are the only people now who aren't pessimistic about the future of motion pictures, and that's good enough for me. I haven't seen any of the movies they financed, but I really want to see the Chuck Norris movie. I'll wait until it comes to Paris.

Katherine Dieckmann: Do you go to the movies a lot? I know when you were young and writing for *Cahiers du Cinéma* in the '50s you were notorious for spending all day in the cinema.

Jean-Luc Godard: No, no, I don't go very much at all. I have a feeling these days that just by knowing the names of the directors and actors involved, and by looking at the ads in the paper or on the street, I've already seen the pictures.

Katherine Dieckmann: Are you still living outside Geneva? And why did you choose to shoot *Hail Mary* in Switzerland?

Jean-Luc Godard: Yes, I live in Switzerland, though I have a company located in Paris. I've shot there before – *Every Man for Himself* was shot in Switzerland, and parts of *Passion*. I've been there since my childhood. I was raised there, had family there, though I also have family in Paris. I've always been crossing borders. I belong to two countries, even if I have only one passport, Swiss. I choose Switzerland to shoot in because – I don't know, already I've used Paris and Parisian streets so much, in my earlier films.

Katherine Dieckmann: Let's talk about your work in general, or the way it's been periodized. In 1970 a lot of books came out dealing with your work on the '60s: there was this impulse to talk about Godard. And then in the '70s the image is that you drifted off, got involved in video and political projects. Then when Every Man for Himself came out in 1980 you described it as "your second first film."

Jean-Luc Godard: It works in periods of ten years, yes, because we live in a decimal system. We have ten fingers. So we always invent in periods of ten. Ten years after ten years. I'm past 50 now, so I speak of myself as being in my "fifth period." I began shooting in 1960, I mean really shooting, and then in 1970 I changed more or less, and then in 1980 started up again . . . I'm very regular! Now it's 1985. I have to wait until 1990.

Katherine Dieckmann: You're at the midpoint of the third chapter, because now you've amassed an entire second set of feature films: Every Man for Himself, First Name: Carmen, Détective, and Hail Mary.

Jean-Luc Godard: I'll use the same words as Picasso, not to compare myself to him, but because they fit. He said, "I will go on painting until painting refuses me and doesn't want me anymore." I'm trying to do this with motion pictures. To go until motion pictures refuse me. Not an audience, and certainly not the industry – the industry already did! But to go until the screen says: No. I had the feeling in making Hail Mary that there was an immaculate screen, and it was saying to me, "Don't stray too far, or don't come too close. Or come closer. Or don't come." I had the feeling of a voice there.

Katherine Dieckmann: Have your working methods changed after 25 years of making films?

Jean-Luc Godard: I am closer to images now. Part of this comes from having worked in video, which I'm doing more and more. I use video to help me see and work better, because I can shoot something and see it immediately, all the while imagining a real screen behind. Video lets me look first, and then I can begin to write from what I see. Before – just like most moviemakers and industry executives – I always wrote first, and then let the image come. I would write about you: "She sat in the corner, she looked at me with such a face," then I'd imagine the face and direct it. Now I look at you and imagine first, and take notes from that. Most people think they work only when the camera is rolling, but that's not it. When the camera rolls, everything is done already. It's like life. Take this hotel room. When two newlyweds enter this room, they know what they are going to do, they've written it before, in the elevator or on the street. And the real work's been done on the street or in the elevator. Here's the completion of the work: The camera's rolling. Cinematographers shoot a movie, and then for six months they don't touch a camera! What makes them think they're still working when they're not looking? Images are like life. And images can show you something in your life you don't want to see, which is probably why people react violently to *Hail Mary*. If you're jealous, you don't want to see the image of the other man or the other woman right away. Things like that. The image is something very strong when it comes at you. That's why movies are so popular. But it's not dangerous. A lot of people don't want to go to the doctor. They don't want to know what kind of disease they have, or how a disease might look. Maybe I can look because my father was a doctor. I was raised not to be afraid of certain categories of truth.

Chapter 31

Krzysztof Kieślowski

INTRODUCTION TO *DECALOGUE:*
THE TEN COMMANDMENTS

Of course, the simplest answer to the question why make a series of films about the Ten Commandments would be: 'because they are there'. Such an answer would also perhaps be the most truthful, since essentially it contains all the reasons for our decision to undertake the project. Of course there are other, more complicated reasons. But in order to go into these we would have to analyse why the films are the way they are and not different, and what caused certain choices to be made; in short, the road that we took.

Krzysztof Kieślowski

I BELIEVE FATE is an important part of life. Of all our lives, my own included. How many twists of fate must there have been for me to be sitting here in Warsaw, writing an introduction to the English-language edition of the *Decalogue*? Naturally, a person may select his or her path through life and so to a certain extent determines what happens along the way. But to understand where you are in the present, it is necessary to retrace the steps of your life and isolate the parts played by necessity, free will and pure chance.

Immediately after completing film school in Lodz, I started making documentary films. I loved the form and believed it was capable of describing the world. I made films about life as it is, not how it might exist in the imagination, and continued to make such films for the next twelve years. It was entirely natural that when martial law was declared in December 1981 I wanted to record the tanks, clandestine news-sheets, and anti-communist slogans daubed on walls. Severe jail sentences went hand in hand with these activities. I was keen to set up my camera in the courts where the sentences were being delivered and hoped to film the faces of both accusers and accused. Getting permission for such a project was difficult, and was eventually granted as late as August 1982.

The camera was received coldly in the court room at first; it was a witness, with an extremely long memory. The judges were never quite certain of my intentions, while the defence lawyers and their clients probably suspected that I was working on behalf of a completely compromised institution, state-controlled television, and refused to co-operate with me. But this did not last long. After only a few days, the lawyers noticed that whenever the camera was present during the hearings there were either no jail sentences at all, or they were suspended by the judges. There was a simple explanation for this. The judges were afraid that the reels of film recording their faces at the very moment they delivered unjust prison sentences could one day be used as evidence against them. The lawyers then started to tell me in advance of their clients' cases, calculating that they were likely to get off with a shorter sentence. The camera in the court room had become a desirable and welcome presence for them. There were several such cases taking place in military or civilian tribunals every day, and so in order to satisfy all my 'bookings', I had to try to get hold of a second camera. While it was still officially possible, I used to set up the two cameras in the courts without even bothering to check whether they were loaded with film or not.

After a while, unsurprisingly, permission to carry on filming was withdrawn. I never made the film because, although I had been present at several score court cases, I had not managed to record one single jail sentence. But one of the lawyers who had been quick to understand the function of the camera in the court room was Krzysztof Piesiewicz.

Two years later, I was thinking of making a feature film based on my experiences in court. I knew next to nothing about the legal intricacies of political trials, and at that moment thought of Piesiewicz. Together we wrote the screenplay for No End and became friends as a result. The film had a rough reception. The authorities were furious because it clearly wasn't sympathetic to them; the Party newspaper Trybuna Ludu wrote that it was an 'instruction manual for the underground', and for purely malicious reasons the film was badly distributed. The political opposition regarded the film as compromised and alien; they wanted to be portrayed as triumphant heroes, whereas everyone in this film hangs their heads in shame. The message was that in this war there were no winners. The third powerful force on the Polish political scene, the

Catholic Church, criticized the film because there was a suicide and the leading actress was shown on several occasions without a bra, and once without any underwear at all. While all this was going on, I happened to bump into my co-scriptwriter in the street. It was cold. It was raining. I had lost one of my gloves. 'Someone should make a film about the Ten Commandments,' Piesiewicz said to me. 'You should do it.'

It was not a good time. This was a few months before three state security officers were put on trial for the murder of Father Jerzy Popieluszko, with Piesiewicz as one of the prosecuting lawyers in the case, but already there was an ominous sense of foreboding in the air. The country at large had sunk into chaos and disorder; nothing and no one was spared. One could detect a certain tension, a feeling of hopelessness and fear of yet worse to come – indeed, it was glaringly obvious that something was about to happen. By this time I had begun to travel abroad a little and also observed a general uncertainty in the world at large. I am not thinking about politics here, but of normal, every-day life. Behind every polite smile I detected indifference. I had the over-whelming impression that more and more I was seeing people who didn't really have a clear idea of why they were living. I came to the conclusion that perhaps Piesiewicz was right, but realized that the task of filming the Ten Commandments would not be an easy one. I asked him how we should go about it. 'I don't know,' he said.

We still didn't know for quite a long time after that. Should it be one film? Several films? Maybe ten films? A serial, or rather a cycle of ten separate films, based on each of the Commandments? This concept seemed most faithful to the very idea of the Decalogue. Ten propositions, ten one-hour films. Initially, while we were at the stage of writing the screenplays, I wasn't too concerned with the problems of direction. One of the reasons for starting work in the first place was the fact that for several years I had been assistant artistic director to Krzysztof Zanussi in the Tor Film Studio. Since Zanussi was working mostly abroad, he took only general decisions and left the day-to-day running of the studio to me. One of the functions of the studio is to help young directors make their first film. I knew several such directors who deserved to make a break-through and I also knew how difficult it was to find the money. For a long time television had been the natural home for a directorial début – TV films are shorter and less expensive, and so there is less risk involved. But the problem was that state television was not interested in one-off films, only serials, although if pushed it sometimes accepted cycles. I thought that if we were to write ten screenplays, we could present them as a cycle based on the Ten Commandments and allocate one each to ten up-and-coming directors. Only much later, when the first screenplay versions were ready, did I realize rather selfishly that I wanted to do the whole lot myself. I had already become quite attached to several of them and was sorry to let them go. I had been keen to direct a few of them anyway and so it seemed logical to do all ten.

From the very beginning, we knew the films would be contemporary. For a while we toyed with the idea of basing them in the world of politics, but the problem of getting them past the censor made this impossible. There was certainly no lack of material in Poland for films about the dramatic, tragic, criminal and often ridiculous mistakes of the authorities; each of the Ten Commandments could have been adequately illustrated. But in reality this was all hypothetical because by the mid-1980s, politics had ceased to interest us. On a day-to-day basis they were tedious and trivial, and, from the historical perspective, hopeless. We didn't believe that politics could change the world, even less so for the better. We also realized that few people were really in a position to understand its subtle twists and turns, and we were not too confident of our own ability to understand them either. So we decided to ignore the world of politics in the films. Also, we began to suspect intuitively that we could market *Decalogue* abroad.

We ignored very Polish specifics, in other words, the daily grind of life around us: queues, meat ration cards, petrol shortages, a bureaucracy which reared its ugly head in even the most trivial of matters, the noisy public on the buses, the price increases as a constant topic of conversation, the ill dying in hospital corridors and so on. Everyday life was unbearably monotonous and terribly uninteresting. We knew then that we had to find extreme, extraordinary situations for our characters, ones in which they would face difficult choices and make decisions which could not be taken lightly. We spent some time deciding what sort of heroes they should be. They had to be credible and recognizable to the extent that the viewer would be able to think: 'I've been in that position. I know exactly how they feel,' or 'Something very similar occurred to me once.' And yet the films could not in any way be an account of ordinary life – on the contrary, they had to take the form of highly compact, streamlined bullets. It very quickly became clear that these would be films about feelings and passions, because we knew that love, or the fear of death, or the pain caused by a needle-prick, are common to all people, irrespective of their political views, the colour of their skin or their standard of living.

I believe the life of every person is worthy of scrutiny, containing its owns secrets and dramas. People don't talk about them because they are embarrassed, because they do not like to scratch old wounds, or are afraid of being judged unfashionably sentimental. Therefore we wanted to start each film in such a way that would suggest that the lead character had been chosen by the camera almost by accident, as if one of many. The idea occurred to us of showing a huge stadium in which, from among the hundred thousand faces, we would focus on one in particular. There was also the idea of the camera picking out one person from a crowded street and then following that person for the rest of the film. Finally we decided to place the action of Decalogue in a large housing estate, with thousands of similar windows framed within the establishing shot. Behind each of these windows, we said to ourselves, is a living human being, whose mind, whose heart and, even better, whose stomach is worthy of investigation. This approach had several advantages. The television viewers following the cycle from the beginning would be able to recognize in the individual films people from other parts of the series, encountered only fleetingly in a lift, a corridor, or appearing only with a request to borrow some salt.

The most important problem still remained – how to adapt the action of each film to illustrate the relevant Commandment. We read everything it was possible to read in libraries; a mass of interpretations of the Commandments, discussions and commentaries on the Bible, both Old and New Testaments. But we decided fairly quickly to dispense with all this. Priests draw upon it every day and we weren't here to preach. We didn't want to adopt the tone of those who praise or condemn, handing out a reward here for the doing of Good and a punishment there for the doing of Evil. Rather, we wished to say: 'We know no more than you. But maybe it is worth investigating the unknown, if only because the very feeling of not knowing is a painful one.'

Once this approach had been decided, we found it easier to solve the problem of the relationship between the films and the individual Commandments: a tentative one. The films should be influenced by the individual Commandments to the same degree that the Commandments influence our daily lives. We were aware that no philosophy or ideology had ever challenged the fundamental tenets of the Commandments during their several thousand years of existence, yet they are nevertheless transgressed on a routine basis. Or to put this more simply: everyone knows it is wrong to kill another human being, yet wars continue and police forces the world over find dead bodies in cellars and parks with knives in their throats. One cannot put the question whether it is good or evil to kill without being suspected of naïvety or stupidity. But it seems to me that one can put the question of why one human being may kill another without reason, especially if one voices doubts over whether the law has the right to punish one form of killing with another. We endeavoured to construct the plot of this film so that the viewer would leave the film with the same questions in mind which we had asked ourselves when the screenplay was only an empty page fed into the typewriter.

For a long time we were worried about the dimensions of Decalogue, though not in the sense of the work it entailed for us as the scriptwriters and for myself as director. We were afraid of something else. Did we have the right to deal with a subject of such universal significance, a subject which even for many of those who break the Commandments is something deeply sacred? These fears are easy to comprehend in a Catholic country like Poland, where the Church is a powerful force in shaping public opinion. Our fears subsided when we suddenly realized that all writers, painters, playwrights and film-makers indirectly deal with themes which are central to the Commandments – they had done so in the past and would no doubt continue to do so in the future. Doesn't Shakespeare's Richard III covet something which is not rightfully his? The Karamazov brothers had few good reasons for honouring their father, and Raskolnikov had none at all for killing the old woman. Brueghel painted robbers and thieves, and in his films Woody Allen seems unable to stop himself from trying to jump into bed with another woman; it is also not uncommon for someone else to leap into bed with his film-wife. The same applies precisely to second-rate crime films and third-rate melodramas, and it applies also to Beethoven, who praised and at the same time questioned God, sometimes in one and the same symphony. It effects all those who describe a life, a mood or a frame of mind, and we were simply taking our places in the queue.

It took us more than a year to write the scripts, one after the other, in succession. We spent many evenings sitting either in Piesiewicz's kitchen or in my small, smoke-filled room. The next year and two months were taken up with filming. But this was all a long time ago. We are left now with the films themselves, which have been received much better than we could possibly have imagined, although it is not really clear to us why.

Krzysztof Kieślowski, Warsaw, spring 1990

Chapter 32

Derek Malcolm

A CENTURY OF FILMS

Day of Wrath

IT IS QUITE COMMON to hear film buffs, even critics, acknowledge Carl Dreyer's greatness with the merest hint of a yawn, as if this Danish director of The Passion of Joan of Arc, Vampyr, Ordet and Gertrud was a film-maker relevant to history but not to us today.

Yet Godard paid tribute to him in Vivre Sa Vie when Anna Karina is moved to tears by Falconetti in The Passion of Joan of Arc, and Antonioni, Resnais and other directors who came into prominence in the sixties freely acknowledge their stylistic and moral debt to him.

Nothing could be further from the truth than characterising him as a close relative to Shakespeare's gloomy Dane and his films as too slow and lingering, too concerned with martyrdom and suffering and too intent on marketing a gaunt spirituality to reach out to modern audiences. Vampyr, for instance, was one of the most poetic horror films ever made, and Day of Wrath one of the most physically terrifying.

The fact is that almost all his films, stretching through the silent era into sound, etch themselves in the memory. And if they deal with the kind of subject matter today's film-makers, and some audiences, find largely beyond them, that is surely not to his discredit. He stands amongst the greatest, most profound artists of the twentieth century.

Day of Wrath is about the persecution of witches in the seventeenth century and is sometimes seen as an allegory on the German occupation of Denmark.

Anne, the second wife of an old pastor, has given refuge to an alleged witch, and discovers that her own mother, also accused of witchcraft, was saved from the stake by the pastor in exchange for her hand. Falling in love with her stepson, she is wracked with guilt and confesses to her husband. When he dies from the shock, she herself is denounced as a witch and burnt at the stake.

The film, in looks sometimes reminiscent of Dutch painting, examines the tortuous cruelty of the time, supposed to be the workings of divine law, and also the two central characters – one of whom admits under torture that she is a witch and the other who volunteers to die, convinced of her own evil.

Dreyer's measured pace and stark visuals – long horizontal pans and close-ups of riven faces – accompanied as they are by acting of intense realism, make this a morality play of enormous power. And the scenes of torture and burning, though discreetly handled, are almost unbearable, at least partly because the torturers and burners are not mere hysterics but stolidly convinced they have divine justice on their side.

What Dreyer achieves is the sense that, for these sternly Protestant people, their inscrutable faces concealing great passion, witchcraft was a frightening reality. He does not argue for or against it but simply, as a critic has said, evokes the dark night of the soul through an intensely physical world.

Most directors refine their style towards the end of their lives, and Dreyer did so with Gertrud, which some regard as one of the dozen or so greatest films ever made and others as an impenetrable bore; just as The Passion of Joan of Arc is regarded either as a masterpiece of the silent cinema or a film saved by the luminous face of Falconetti. Dreyer was indeed not everybody's director. He was, however, over some 45 years of work, a unique and innovating talent.

Chapter 33

Andrey Tarkovsky

SCULPTING IN TIME

THERE ARE FEW PEOPLE of genius in the cinema; look at Bresson, Mizoguchi, Dovzhenko, Paradzhanov, Buñuel: not one of them could be confused with anyone else. An artist of that calibre follows one straight line, albeit at great cost; not without weaknesses or even, indeed, occasionally being far-fetched; but always in the name of the one idea, the one conception.

In world cinema there have been many attempts to create a new concept in film, always with the general aim of bringing it closer to life, to factual truth. Hence pictures like Cassavetes' *Shadows*, Shirley Clarke's *The Connection*, Jean Rouch's *Chronicle of a Summer*. These notable films are marked, apart from anything else, by a lack of commitment; complete and unconditional factual truth is not consistently pursued.

The artist has a duty to be calm. He has no right to show his emotion, his involvement, to go pouring it all out at the audience. Any excitement over a subject must be sublimated into an Olympian calm of form. That is the only way in which an artist can tell of the things that excite him.

I am reminded of how we worked on *Andrey Rublyov*.

The film is set in the fifteenth century, and it turned out to be excruciatingly difficult to picture 'how everything was'. We had to use any sources we could: architecture, the written word, iconography.

Had we gone for reconstruction of the picturesque tradition of the picturesque world of those times, the result would have been a stylised, conventional ancient Russian world, of the kind that at best is reminiscent of miniatures or icons of the period. But for cinema that is not the right way. I have never understood, for instance, attempts to construct mise en scène from a painting. All you will be doing is bringing the painting back to life, and duly being rewarded with superficial acclaim: 'Ah, what a feeling for the period!' 'Ah, what cultivated people!' But you will also be killing cinema.

Therefore one of the aims of our work was to reconstruct for a modern audience the real world of the fifteenth century, that is, to present that world in such a way that costume, speech, life-style and architecture would not give the audience any feeling of relic, of antiquarian rarity. In order to achieve the truth of direct observation, what one might almost term physiological truth, we had to move away from the truth of archaeology and ethnography. Inevitably there was an element of artificiality, but this was the antithesis of that of the revived painting. Had someone from the fifteenth century suddenly appeared to witness it, he would have found the filmed material a strange enough spectacle; but no more so than us and our own world. Because we live in the twentieth century, we have no possibility of making a film directly from material six hundred years old. I remain convinced, nonetheless, that it is possible to attain our objectives, even in such difficult conditions, provided we go the whole way, unswervingly, along the path we have chosen, despite the Herculean labour involved. How much simpler it would be to go into a Moscow street and start filming with a concealed camera.

We cannot reconstruct the fifteenth century exactly, however thoroughly we study all the things that remain from it. Our awareness of that time is totally different from that of the people who lived then. But nor do we think of Rublyov's 'Trinity' in the same way as his contemporaries, and yet the 'Trinity' has gone on living through the centuries: it was alive then, and is so now, and it is a link between the people of that century and this. The 'Trinity' can be taken simply as an icon. It can be taken as a magnificent museum piece, perhaps as a model of the style of painting of that particular epoch. But this icon, this memorial, can be seen in another way: we can turn to the human, spiritual meaning of the 'Trinity' which is alive and understandable for us who live in the second half of the twentieth century. And this is how we approached the reality which gave birth to the 'Trinity'.

Given such an approach we had deliberately to introduce elements that would dispel any impression of archaism, of museum reconstruction.

The script includes an episode in which a peasant, who has made himself a pair of wings, climbs up on to the cathedral, jumps, and crashes to the ground. We 'reconstructed' this episode, checking its essential psychological element. Evidently it was a case of a man who all his life had been thinking of himself flying. But how would it really have happened? People were running after him, he was hurrying. Then he jumped. What would this man have seen and felt as he flew for the first time? He didn't have time to see anything, he fell and was shattered. The most he could have known was the unexpected, terrifying fact of falling. The inspiration of the flight, its symbolism, were eliminated, for the meaning was straightforward and basic, and related to associations which are perfectly familiar to us. The screen had to show an ordinary, dirty peasant, then his fall, his crash, his death. This is a concrete happening, a human catastrophe, observed by onlookers just as if now, as we watched, someone were to dash out for some reason in front of a car and finish up lying there crushed on the asphalt.

We spent a long time working out how to destroy the plastic symbol on which the episode was built, and reached the conclusion that the root of the trouble was in the wings. And in order to dispel the Icarus overtones we decided on an air balloon. This was a clumsy object put together from skins, ropes and rags, and we felt it rid the episode of spurious rhetoric and turned it into a unique happening.

The first thing to describe is the event, not your attitude to it. Your attitude has to be made clear by the film as a whole, to be part of its total impact. In a mosaic each separate piece is of a particular, single colour. It may be blue, or white, or red – they are all different. And then you look at the completed picture and see what the author had in mind.

. . . I love cinema. There is still a lot that I don't know: what I am going to work on, what I shall do later, how everything will turn out, whether my work will actually correspond to the principles to which I now adhere, to the system of working hypotheses I put forward. There are too many temptations on every side: stereotypes, preconceptions, commonplaces, artistic ideas other than one's own. And really it's so easy to shoot a scene beautifully, for effect, for acclaim . . . But you only have to take one step in that direction and you are lost.

Cinema should be a means of exploring the most complex problems of our time, as vital as those which for centuries have been the subject of literature, music and painting. It is only a question of searching, each time searching out afresh the path, the channel, to be followed by cinema. I am convinced that for any one of us our film-making will turn out to be a fruitless and hopeless affair if we fail to grasp precisely and unequivocally the specific character of cinema, and if we fail to find in ourselves our own key to it.

Chapter 34

Lars von Trier, with Christian Braad Thomsen

TRIER ON VON TRIER

Christian Braad Thomsen: *Breaking the Waves* took five years and 42 million kroner to make. Where did the original idea for the film come from?

Lars von Trier: I prefer working with extreme ideas, and I wanted to make a film about 'goodness'. When I was little, I had a children's book called *Guldhjerte* (*Goldheart*), which I had very clear and happy memories of. It was a picture book about a little girl who goes into the forest with some slices of bread and other stuff in her pockets. But at the end of the book, when she's got through the forest, she's standing there naked and with nothing left. And the last line in the book was: ' "But at least I'm okay," said Goldheart.' It seemed to express the ultimate extremity of the martyr's role. I read the book several times, in spite of the fact that my father thought it was absolute rubbish. The story of *Breaking the Waves* probably comes from that. Goldheart is Bess in the film. I also wanted to make a film with a religious theme, a film about miracles. And at the same time I wanted to make a completely naturalistic film.

The story of the film changed a lot over the years. To begin with, I wanted to shoot the film on the west coast of Jutland, then in Norway, then Ostende in Belgium, then Ireland, and in the end Scotland. It's probably no coincidence that a lot of the film is set on the Isle of Skye, where a lot of painters and writers went during the Romantic period in Britain in the 1800s. I worked a lot on the script of *Breaking the Waves* over the years. I've been a bit like Dreyer, cutting bits out, condensing and refining it. But then just before we started filming, I lost my enthusiasm for the piece. It had taken so long to get the film made that I was tired of it. I'd already moved on from it.

Christian Braad Thomsen: [. . .] Breaking the Waves has a strong religious background. What made you include that in the film?

Lars von Trier: Probably because I'm religious myself. I'm Catholic, but I don't pray to Catholicism for Catholicism's sake. I've felt a need for a sense of belonging to a community of faith, because my parents were committed atheists. I flirted with religion a lot as a young man. In your youth you're probably more attracted to more extreme religions. Either you disappear to Tibet or you seek out the strictest faith available, with total abstinence and so on.

I think I've developed a more Dreyeresque view of it all now. Dreyer's view of religion was primarily humanist. He also tackles religion in all his films. Religion is attacked, but not God. That's what happens in Breaking the Waves.

Christian Braad Thomsen: In the film, religion is described as a power structure. The mechanics of power and its problematics is something you've tackled in several of your previous films.

Lars von Trier: My intention was never to critize any particular faith, like the one in this Scottish setting. That doesn't interest me at all. It's too easy, and that's not something I want to get involved in. Cultivating a point of view that's easily accessible and generalized, it's like fishing in shallow water. In many ways I can understand people who are obsessed by spiritual issues, often in a very extreme way. It's just that if you're going to create a melodrama, you have to include certain obstacles. And religion struck me as being a suitable obstacle.

Christian Braad Thomsen: Bess's conversations with God have a directness and an intimacy that gives a human voice to the religious theme.

Lars von Trier: Bess is also an expression of that religion. Religion is her foundation, and she accepts its conditions without question. In the funeral scene at the beginning of the film, the priest condemns the deceased to eternal damnation in hell, which is something Bess finds completely natural. She has no scruples about that. But we, on the other hand, do. Bess is confronted with a lot of other power structures, like the power exerted by the hospital and the doctors. And she has to adopt a position using the inherent goodness that she possesses.

Christian Braad Thomsen: [. . .] Was that [difficulty finding well-known actors] because of the sex scenes?

Lars von Trier: It was probably the story as a whole. It's a strange mix of religion and sex and obsession. The well-known actors we approached didn't want to lay their careers on the line, like Helena Bonham-Carter, who pulled out of the project at the very last minute. So it felt important to find actors who really wanted to be involved. And I think it shows that the actors we chose in the end are wholeheartedly committed to the film.

We auditioned several actresses for the role of Bess. Then I looked at the video of the auditions together with Bente [*Lars' partner*], and she thought it was obvious that Emily Watson ought to get the part. I was also very taken by Emily's acting, but it was mainly her enthusiasm that convinced me. I remember that Emily was also the only one who came to the audition without any make-up and barefoot! There was something Jesus-like about her that attracted me.

Christian Braad Thomsen: [. . .] At the end of *Breaking the Waves*, in the scene where the wounded and expelled Bess comes into the church, she contradicts the church council's rule that women must remain silent in the congregation and says: 'You can't love the Word. You can only love a person.' That's a line that could be interpreted as both an *hommage* and a response to Dreyer.

Lars von Trier: That might be taking it a bit far, but it's actually one of the few lines that I rewrote on location. In the script there was something far more wordy and generally unformed. The idea of her outburst was to pick up something that the members of the congregation said and stood for – and to contradict it. The priest talks about loving the Word and the Law. That was the only thing you had to obey. That's what would make a person complete. But Bess twists the concepts and says that the only thing that can make a person complete is loving another person. This is really the formulation of the film's moral.

Christian Braad Thomsen: [. . .] In one response to that, Maria Bergom-Larsson, who is both a radical feminist and a Christian, described the film as the story of a modern saint, and proposed the hymn of the Virgin, the Magnificat, as a motto for the film: 'He hath put down the mighty from their seats, and exalted them of low degree.'

Lars von Trier: It's a beautiful thought, one that I wholeheartedly agree with. Danish feminists, on the other hand, would hardly offer religious interpretations. A hymn is something that they would instantly attack. It's just something that would make them even more angry. Mind you, Danish feminists have probably become better behaved over the years. A decade ago they had more gumption. They'd probably have liked to see me castrated then.

South and North American Perspectives

INTRODUCTION

THE UNITED STATES, and "Hollywood" more specifically, has tended to dominate the world cinematic market; not because they produce more films (as India does), nor because they are necessarily better aesthetically, but simply because more money is spent on the production and distribution of U.S. films than anywhere in the world. Apart from the sheer entertainment value of Hollywood's multi-million dollar films with their multi-millionaire stars, millions of viewers around the world are regularly enamored with the fantastical stories of romance and crime set in the United States. These movies allow the chance to escape to another world, to dream of life "over the rainbow," to shed the cares and concerns of the so-called real world.

Yet, there are of course other dimensions to cinema in the United States and the rest of the Americas, and many films deal seriously and carefully with the impact of religion. Independent filmmakers from the United States such as Jim Jarmusch (1953–) and John Sayles (1950–), and the Canadian Atom Egoyan (1960–), tend to tell small stories that nonetheless unfold to larger, even mythical dimensions. In many ways due to the influence of Roman Catholicism on Latin American cultures, and considering its continual presence in the films of the region, many critical volumes might be written on the religion–film relation in Latin American cinema alone. And so, here too there are inevitably lacunae, which is partly because of the lack of availability of works in English and partly because there are fewer critical works on Latin American filmmakers in ways that usefully cover religious concerns.

That said, we have assembled here a dozen readings from across the Americas, from both filmmakers and scholars. Many are well known in the English speaking world, and others not so much, even though recognized in their own regions. In some regions we were once again spoilt for choice, and with more space would have liked to include discussions related to American filmmakers like Terrence Malick, who in his films such as *Days of Heaven* (1978) or *The Thin Red Line* (1998) draws together religious themes through metaphysical questioning or Buddhist or Jewish references. Many of the filmmakers included here are at first sight non-religious, even though they acknowledge the importance of religious beliefs and practices when filming narratives about people's lives. Other American filmmakers critique religion, or cast a weary eye on its institutions, even though they incorporate it into their films.

One of the best-known filmmakers to give religion a sideways glance is Woody Allen (1935–) who for over three decades has cinematically explored the themes of love, sex and death, and how they can sometimes interact with religious beliefs in his comedic and dramatic work. He plays on his own Jewish heritage at several points (e.g., *Annie Hall*, 1977), shows signs of a search for faith at other points (e.g., *Hannah and Her Sisters*, 1986), and deals with deep, dark ethical quandaries in other of his films (e.g., *Crimes and Misdemeanors*, 1989). The reading (reading 35) here is taken from one of a series of interviews of Allen by the Swedish filmmaker and writer, Stig Björkman (1938–).

Like Allen, the Mexican screenwriter Guillermo Arriaga (1958–) personally rejects any religious affiliation and yet cannot escape the questions raised (and answered) within religious structures. Arriaga has worked with Alejandro González Iñárritu on several films that intersect with religious concerns, *Amores Perroes* (2000), *21 Grams* (2003), and *Babel* (2006), all written in tripartite storylines that reveal deep interconnections between characters seemingly quite distant from each other. In the interview below (reading 36), he contemplates the role of fate in life, and how our stories and connections to others are basic to being human.

The history of African-Americans on film, and films made by African-Americans is a troubled history. The 1920s and 1930s saw a huge industry of black filmmakers, with black actors, creating films for black audiences. Key here was the work of Oscar Micheaux (1884–1951). However, as filmmaking was consolidated into a handful of big commercial companies in the 1930s, black filmmaking all but disappeared. Into the twenty-first century there is a smaller African-American presence in cinema than there was eighty years ago. One current filmmaker who has continued to push issues of race in film is Spike Lee (1957–). Sometimes he does this blatantly, sometimes it is more subtle, but he always does it with a great knowledge of the filmic medium. He also understands the role of religion in the history of racism, for better and worse, and in the reading below (reading 39) Lee briefly describes his own religious experience and beliefs. While not as well known as Lee, Julie Dash (1952–) also confronts African-American identity through a retelling of history in her *Daughters of the Dust* (1991). The story is of a Gullah family living on the Sea Islands off the coast of South Carolina at the turn of the twentieth century, and the interview here with bell hooks tells of the use of mythology for understanding one's past, what hooks calls "mythic memory." The reading by religious studies scholar Judith Weisenfeld (reading 46) notes the importance of visuality in the construction of race, and how film is a prime actor in this construction. She turns to look at the 1929 film *Hallelujah* (dir., King Vidor, 1894–1982) for its intriguing depictions of "racialized religion," and for the ways such a big-budget film can have lasting implications on a society's understandings of race, and of religion.

Some of the most prominent and successful U.S. directors in the history of cinema have regularly incorporated religious themes into their films. Steven Spielberg (1946–), George Lucas (1944–), and Martin Scorsese (1942–), all emerged as key figures in the midst of radical changes in U.S. cinema in the 1970s. They have won multiple critical awards, and their films remain some of the highest grossing of all time (especially Lucas and Spielberg). Part of what makes their work so appealing is their ability to take timeless mythical stories and retell them through adept artistic filmmaking processes. They each understand the power of narrative, and understand how film creates a unique audio-visual experience of narrative, not confined to words alone. Spielberg's work has ranged from science fiction (*Close Encounters*, 1977; *E.T.*, 1982; *A.I.*, 2001) to historical drama (*Schindler's List*, 1993; *Amistad*, 1997) to fantastic adventures (the "Indiana Jones" series) as he constantly pushes questions about the limits of the human and natural world, and where something other – aliens, supernatural forces, altruism – might break through. The excerpt describing Spielberg's energetic filmmaking while making *Schindler's List* also provides an insight into his own interactions with and growing respect for Judaism (reading 44).

In 1999, over two decades after the first *Star Wars* film (1977), Bill Moyers sat down with George Lucas and asked about the ways myths are regenerated for each new generation (reading 40). Lucas tells of how he merges Taoist, Buddhist, Christian, and other mythologies into his films, and these stories include both the "good side" and the "dark side." In the full interview the discussion highlights Lucas' indebtedness to the author of a *Hero with a Thousand Faces*, Joseph Campbell. Martin Scorsese's "dark side" is found on the streets rather than, outer space, in the personal, shattered lives of common people. He spent a total of sixteen years in the Catholic education system, including one year as a fourteen-year-old at a seminary school in New York. While he toyed with the idea of ordination he eventually decided to make films instead, and here too the great old stories serve a contemporary focus, well seen in his controversial remake of the Nikos Kazantzakis' novel, *The Last Temptation of Christ* (1988). As he tells it in this reading from 2005 (reading 41), he wanted to make a contemporary gospel story, but in ways distinct from the previous filmmakers such as Pasolini who had done so. He wanted to retain the gritty, street life that can be seen in *Mean Streets* (1973), *Raging Bull* (1980), or *Gangs of New York* (2002), and found that ability through Kazantazkis' story.

If Spielberg looks towards the limits of human identity, the Canadian David Cronenberg (1943–) consistently looks at the limits of the human body, its mutability, its separation from other bodies, and its relation to death. With such a topic taken on in a filmic context, one is also confronted with horror, especially religious horror, since confrontations with the human body are also about one's mortality. In a series of films since the 1970s, Cronenberg has investigated bodies that morph into other creatures (*Naked Lunch*, 1991; *The Fly*, 1986), attach themselves to technology (*Videodrome*, 1983; *Crash*, 1996; *eXistenZ*, 1999), or to other people (*Dead Ringers*, 1988). Perhaps his greatest investigation of horror is in his *A History of Violence* (2005), created after the interview took place, showing the banality of evil. In all of these, religion is a constant presence (reading 37).

The Brazilian filmmaker Walter Salles (1956–) generally sets his sights on Brazilian and Latin American issues, but realizes again and again how it is impossible to do this without also taking seriously the role of religion in political environments. Films like *Behind the Sun* (2001) deal with identity set alongside ancestral traditions, while the topic of this short reading (reading 43) is his 1998 *Central Station*. In this film he re-creates a pilgrimage that is personal and political at the same time, showing the realities of life in contemporary Rio de Janeiro. Like Salles, the Cuban director Tomás Gutiérrez Alea (1928–1996) also sees the intertwined structures of religion, culture, politics, and economics. The best known and most accomplished filmmaker in post-Revolutionary Cuba, Gutiérrez Alea, has offered a string of films that mix humor and drama with the fantastical and everyday. Santeria becomes a critical force in films such as *Guantanamera* (1995), while the history of Christianity's impact on the island is restaged in *The Last Supper* (1976). Theologian Antonio Sison discusses Gutiérrez Alea's film in his book *Screening Schillebeeckx* (2006), from which the reading is taken (reading 42).

Finally, a look at religion and film in the Americas would not be complete without giving some attention to the role of Walt Disney in the shaping and reshaping of contemporary myths. A reading by film studies scholar Anna Lee Ward from her *Mouse Morality* (2002) discusses the impact Disney has on the consciousness of young and old, and looks specifically at *The Lion King* (1994), one of Disney's most successful animations ever.

Chapter 35

Woody Allen, with Stig Björkman

WOODY ALLEN ON WOODY ALLEN

Stig Björkman: So, you think you want to try and deal with death again in a poetical way?

Woody Allen: I was trying with *Shadows and Fog*, but . . . Yes, I would like to. Because, first off, the so-called – it's become such a tiresome phrase – existential subjects to me are still the only subjects worth dealing with. Any time one deals with other subjects one is not aiming for the highest goal. One can be aiming at some very interesting things, but it's not the deepest thing for me. I don't think that one can aim more deeply than at the so-called existential themes, the spiritual themes. That's probably why I'd consider the Russian novelists as greater than other novelists. Even though Flaubert, for example, is a much more skilled writer than, I think, either Dostoyevsky or Tolstoy – he was surely more skilled than Dostoyevsky, as a technician – his work can never be as great, for me, personally, as the other two. Very often people avoid making value judgements, but I think the opposite. I think it's very important to make them; it's almost an obligation. One can say, 'I appreciate Flaubert more than Kafka or Stendahl more than Tolstoy.' But I don't. I myself don't. I just feel that you must – if you're operating at the maximum of your capabilities – aim at very, very high material. And that to me would be the spiritual, existential realm. It's great when it's done realistically, and it's great when it's done poetically. But poetically is more intriguing for me. Take, for instance, a movie like *In Cold Blood*. It's full of natural, existential material. This little town which suddenly finds these brutal killings. Everybody's lives change. It's done realistically, and it's a fascinating story. It was fascinating in the novel and it was pretty fascinating on the screen as well. But I just appreciate it more, when it's done poetically. To me, *The Trial* would be great fun to be able to do, because you're able to deal with some very substantial and profound feelings and intuitions and ideas and deal with them in a very poetic way. It's very seductive.

Stig Björkman: I mentioned romantic literature in connection to *Crimes and Misdemeanours*. In Wordsworth's play *The Borderers* he creates what one could define as the first existentialist, a man who through his deeds creates not only his autonomy and unique self but also his own scale of values. In this respect Judah in your film resembles him.

Woody Allen: Absolutely. He has a set of values and they are his values. And we live in a world where there's nobody to punish you, if you don't punish yourself. Judah is someone who does what's expedient for him when he has to. And he gets away with it! And leads a wonderful life after, presumably. If he doesn't choose to punish himself then he's gotten away with it.

It's just like the conversation around the dinner table at Judah's parental home, when they're talking about the Nazis. We happened to have won the war. But if we didn't win the war, then history would have been created differently.

Stig Björkman: Why did you name the central character Judah?

Woody Allen: Because I thought it was biblical, and I thought it had wisdom to it. It suggested weight and wisdom. It made him more of a patriarchal figure in the story, and I wanted that.

Stig Björkman: In *Crimes and Misdemeanours* we see the Jewish background in a more explicit way than in most of your other films.

Woody Allen: Well, Judah's problem and its relation to religious teachings and religious belief is significant, and the only religion that I feel I can write about with any kind of accuracy is the Jewish religion. I have no feel for the details of Christianity.

Stig Björkman: One thing which struck me in the film is the conversation between Judah and the rabbi, when Judah discusses the eventual murder of Dolores. Why doesn't the rabbi react more strongly against these thoughts?

Woody Allen: You mean in the scene in the study, during the lightning storm?

Stig Björkman: Yes.

Woody Allen: Because the rabbi doesn't really exist there. It's just in Judah's mind. He's just utilizing the rabbi to have this mental dialogue.

Stig Björkman: One central theme in the film is about seeing and sight. Not only does the rabbi go blind, we see Dolores get completely blinded through the killing. In the scene when Judah goes to her flat and finds her dead, you have a very intense close-up on her face, and he closes her eyes. Eyes and sight are shown or discussed throughout the film. Was this an important subject for you in the film?

Woody Allen: Well, eyes were a metaphor in the story. Judah was an eye doctor who heals people on the one hand, but is willing to kill on the other. And he doesn't see well himself. I mean, his vision is fine, but his emotional vision, his moral vision is not good. The rabbi is blind to other things, to the realities of life. On the other hand, he can triumph over it because he has spiritual substance. *Crimes and Misdemeanours* is about people who don't see. They don't see themselves as others see them. They don't see the right and wrong of situations. And that was a strong metaphor in the movie.

Stig Björkman: One thing which is being discussed throughout the film as well is the relationship of love between the sexes. At some point you show a piece of interview with the philosopher in the film, Louis Levy, to Halley (Mia Farrow). And there he says, 'What we are aiming at when we fall in love is a very strange paradox. And the paradox consists of the fact that when we fall in love, we are seeking to refind all or some of the people to whom we were attracted when we were children, and then we have to attempt to return to the past and at the same time to undo the past.' Is this your belief as well?

Woody Allen: Yes, I think that's true. We spend our whole life trying to do that. We try to go back and rectify our problems.

Stig Björkman: An important character in the film is, of course, the rabbi, Ben. He says at one point, 'I can't go on living, if I didn't feel with all my heart a moral structure with real meaning and forgiveness and some kind of higher power.'

Woody Allen: Yes, my own feeling about Ben is that, on the one hand, he's blind even before he goes blind. He's blind because he doesn't see the real world. But he's blessed and lucky because he has the single most important lucky attribute anyone could have, the best gift anyone could have. He has genuine religious faith. It's not artificial. He genuinely believes what he's saying. And so even in the face of the worst adversity, he is OK. He goes blind. He still loves everybody and loves the world and loves life and loves his daughter. Judah's father has faith. And Ben also has faith. They have faith in God, real faith, and it takes them through all kinds of adversity. The worst kind of adversity can be surmounted with faith. But as the author, I think that Ben is blind even before he's blind, because he doesn't see what's real in the world. But he's lucky, because he has his naïvety.

Stig Björkman: All this really comes through Sam Waterston's performance as well.

Woody Allen: Yes, because he's basically a sweet actor.

Stig Björkman: Is this why you wanted to end the film on him, on Ben dancing with his daughter at the wedding?

Woody Allen: Yes, because I thought that he's one of the people that triumphs in the film. Cliff loses out. Lester remains a pompous fool. Judah gets away with murder. And doctor Levy commits suicide. Life is really quite hard for everybody, they're really having a tough time of it. But Ben triumphs over it because I think the only thing, or the best thing, that gives you a chance to triumph in life is religious faith. It surpasses even earthly love between a man and a woman. Because even if that's very sustaining and wonderful, there comes a time when one of them dies. Then all you have is your spiritual content. So unless you have a strong spiritual feeling, spiritual faith, it's tough to get through life. Ben is the only one that gets through it, even if he doesn't really understand the reality of life. One can argue that he understands it more deeply than the others. I don't think he does myself. I think he understands it less, and that's why I wanted to make him blind. I feel that his faith is blind. It will work, but it requires closing your eyes to reality.

Stig Björkman: What about your own religious faith? Is it like that of the average person?

Woody Allen: Worse! I think that at best the universe is indifferent. At best! Hannah Arendt spoke of the banality of evil. The universe is banal as well. And because it's banal, it's evil. It isn't diabolically evil. It's evil in its banality. Its indifference is evil. If you walk down the street and you see homeless people, starving, and you're indifferent to them, you're in a way being evil. Indifference to me equals evil.

Chapter 36

Guillermo Arriaga, with Warren Curry

BASIC

An Interview with 21 Grams
Screenwriter Guillermo Arriaga

Warren Curry: Why the title 21 *Grams*?

Guillermo Arriaga: 21 *Grams* refers to the weight a person loses at the exact moment of death. I can't say this is a corroborated specific fact. Some doctors have weighed dying people, and at the exact moment of death they lose 21 grams. I wanted to use this as a metaphor about the way a person who dies weighs over the ones that survive them. Sometimes you carry this weight all of your life.

Warren Curry: You've been quoted as saying that your work is about the dead influencing the living. Why is that?

Guillermo Arriaga: Almost all of my work has that theme. It has to do with almost all of my novels and my short stories. My grandmother died when I was 15 years old – you can never understand death. Something that this death brought to me was understanding that our identity is created by who we're surrounded by. For example, in 21 *Grams*, this woman's identity – her family's identity. The moment she loses her family, her identity is broken. Many times, when people die, your identity turns to another direction, has another meaning. You can't forget these dead people – they belong to you as much as the living ones. These people are sometimes much more powerful in their absence than in your presence.

Warren Curry: Both of your films examine morality, and you seem to be specifically interested in the elusiveness of the concept. Especially in 21 *Grams*, where the characters are neither good nor bad, and the film doesn't present traditional protagonists and antagonists.

Guillermo Arriaga: Something I learned very early in my work as a novelist is that you can never judge your characters. You need to always love and understand them in order to make them believable. I think that what is the essence of humanity is contradiction. The more contradictory a character is the more humane he is. In life, there is never black and white. In *Amores Perros*, for example, I wrote horrible, awful characters with awful motivations, but people understand them. To understand a hit man — a hit man is always a terrible person, but I wanted the audience to understand the other side of the hit man. In 21 *Grams*, Jack runs over a family, but it is an accident. What is sad is that he left them dying in the street — he had the decision to stay there. The post-accident decision was his, but he decided to run away. That choice has a consequence, and the consequence is huge guilt. You can do nothing about accidents, they happen, but how you behave after the accident is how the real character of a person is revealed. I wanted to have these kinds of contradictions, and I love contradictions in my characters, so people will not say this is the good guy and this is the bad guy. They will say these are people.

Warren Curry: Amores Perros can definitely be seen as a bleak film, and in my opinion 21 *Grams* taps into even deeper levels of darkness. Is this a reflection of your view of the human condition — that all human beings are, as you put it, in a constant state of contradiction?

Guillermo Arriaga: I think in both films it's clear that we're always in a state of contradiction. Characters that have no contradictions are not appealing to me; people that have no contradictions are not appealing to me. I hate these, as we say in Mexico, "one block" people — people who are very coherent with everything, and you can always expect the same from them. I think that they are dark films, but I think that they are very hopeful films also. It's easy to talk about hope when we have these feel-good movies, but what about hope when you are deep in hell? That's very interesting, and I think that in these times we are having very dark moments. September 11 was a very dark moment. The Oklahoma City bombing was a very dark moment for the United States, and the Columbine killings. Where can you find hope? In the end, I think that both films are quite optimistic. What I want to say with 21 *Grams* is that life has enormous power — it can teach us that life is worth it and that life has more power than death. Even though they are dark films, they are hopeful films. They are love stories, both of them.

Warren Curry: Fate also plays a big role in 21 *Grams*. How much of what happens to the characters is a result of their actions, and how much is out of their control?

Guillermo Arriaga: There is a Spanish philosopher Jose Ortega y Gasset, and he says that a person is defined by his circumstances and by his own decisions. I am obsessed with this – how much is our circumstances and how much is our own decisions? What I try to portray in all of my characters are ones that decide. If even the circumstances take them to deep hell and dark places, they can decide to continue with their lives.

Fate is important, but much more important is the capacity of human beings to make decisions. I'm an atheist – a lot of people think this is my Catholic film. I'm not Catholic, I have no Catholic background at all. I have not a single bit of Catholic education – no religious education. I think life is our only chance; our only chance to tell people we love that we love them. This is the only chance we have to demonstrate how much we love them, and this is the only chance we have to take advantage of. I am always obsessed with people who know that this is the only chance, and they use their decisions to correct the directions in their life. Even if circumstances push it to another place, you have the decision to turn your life again.

Warren Curry: Is there a reason you didn't set the film in a specific city? I know you shot in Memphis, but you never name the city in the film?

Guillermo Arriaga: I want to tell the story very basic with very basic feelings. Our idea is that it's so basic that it doesn't need a specific place to happen – it can happen anywhere. It can be a nightmare for everyone everywhere in the world. I don't think for this particular movie that the setting was important. What's important is to make a person feel that it can happen to you. Even where you're living – in New York, L.A., Memphis, Seattle, Boise, Idaho, it can happen to you.

Warren Curry: So the idea of it being universal?

Guillermo Arriaga: Not so universal – very basic. I don't want to be pretentious and say it's universal. These are basic feelings and basic situations. To lose somebody is one of the situations, and that you're responsible for the death of someone is another basic situation that can happen anywhere. The feelings that this brings is love, hate, revenge, guilt, forgiveness – I think they are very basic.

Chapter 37

David Cronenberg, with David Breskin

THE ROLLING STONE INTERVIEW

David Breskin: Were your parents both atheists?

David Cronenberg: Yeah, they were. The word "atheist" almost suggests you buy the religious system. Beyond atheism, they were simply non-believers. To me, to say you're an atheist almost suggests theism. You can't have atheism without theism, and I'd go beyond that. Non-belief. Period. And therefore all the structures that go with it. And this does not mean that my parents had a disdain for Jewish North American culture. They didn't. Quite the contrary. But it was really totally secular.

David Breskin: So what was celebrated was humanism and science, the rational mind?

David Cronenberg: That's right. Maybe with an emphasis on the humanism, because neither parent was anything like a technocrat.

[. . .]

David Breskin: [In the past you've mentioned] that you are "afflicted" by the curse of balance.

David Cronenberg: Well, maybe this is what people mean when they say my films are conservative. Theatrically, it's wonderful to see someone who's un-balanced. Actors would always prefer to play a villain, because it allows them to express that obsessive craziness which, despite the danger of it, is still rather admired in our culture.

David Breskin: Evil is usually more interesting, cinematically, than good.

David Cronenberg: But I'm not even thinking in terms of evil. Evil is a whole other thing. The minute you say evil, I think: Christianity. I don't throw that word around, and it may not be something I even believe in. But let's say cinematic evil. Okay, I'm willing to go that far. Yeah, it's more interesting. Because it illuminates things, partly, and partly because it's cathartic. A villain in a bizarre, twisted way is always a Christlike figure: You know he's going to die, and he's dying for your sins, for your rage, for your craziness; he's doing it for you so you don't have to do it.

[. . .]

David Breskin: You've said that all the horror springs from the Latin phrase "Timor mortis conturbat mea" (the fear of death disturbs me). Was there any way for you to resolve your fear of death other than by making movies about it, or have you not resolved it even with the movies?

David Cronenberg: I don't know if it's really resolvable for me, but we'll see. I think it would have to be through art, and I think in one sense that is what all art is. I don't mean to be reductive, but I don't think that's so reductive, because the question of death is not a simple question. It's not just fear of death, it's meaning of life – it's the same question. [. . .] If you're religious, you talk about what God might be like, what the nature of God is. The question of human mortality is not a simple question.

David Breskin: Are you positing "art against death"?

David Cronenberg: I'm positing art as a means of coming to terms with death. Yes. I guess I'm putting art in opposition to religion, or as a replacement for religion, in the sense that if religion is used to allow you to come to terms with death, and also to guide you how to live your life, then I think that art can do the same thing. But in a much less schematic way, in a much less rigid and absolute way, which is why it appeals to me and religion doesn't.

[. . .]

David Breskin: [Your particular kind of horror] has never been situational horror (the-man-in-the-basement-with-the-knife) as much as existential, philosophical horror. Where does that come from?

David Cronenberg: I really think it comes from what I need art for. I don't need the story around the campfire; there's a couple of great campfire-type horror stories. But they are basically the man-in-the-basement-with-the-knife. To the extent that that can be cathartic and entertaining, fine. But it's not enough for me. I want, I need more from what I do: I need more complexity, I need more philosophy, and I need more of a struggle in my art than that. More of a struggle with myself.

David Breskin: If there's a horror in confronting the inevitability of death – and we all carry our little mini-horror film around with us in the shape of our own deaths – wouldn't eternal life be an even greater horror?

David Cronenberg: Oh, yeah. There's no way out, that's one of the problems. No one *really* wants to live forever, not really. But on a theoretical level, by apposition, you don't want to die, so you are really saying you want to live forever – even though you know that's not really going to work.

[. . .] I've had moments where the inevitability of death is an absolute strength, it's an escape, it's a freedom. And certainly for people who find themselves in a hideous situation, like the concentration camps, there's a point where death is truly a release. So, the idea that death is merciful, that's not only a schematic concept to me, I can feel it as an emotional reality as well.

At the beginning of *Naked Lunch* is the quote: "Nothing is true, everything is permitted." Although I don't think it was originally conceived by Hassan I. Sabbah as an existentialist statement, in a way it is. It's saying, because death is inevitable, we are free to invent out own reality. We are part of a culture, we are part of an ethical and moral system, but all we have to do is take one step outside it and we see that none of it is absolute. Nothing is true. It's not an absolute. It's only a human construct, very definitely able to change and susceptible to change and rethinking. And you can then be free. Free to be unethical, immoral, out of society, an agent for some other power, never belonging.

Ultimately, if you are an existentialist and you don't believe in God and the judgment after death, then you can do anything you want: you can kill, you can do whatever society considers the most taboo thing.

[. . .]

David Breskin: [I want to touch on catharsis.] You routinely insist on catharsis in your films as a benefit and a *raison d'etre* for horror as a genre, and yet I've rarely consumed an artist's work that leaves me feeling less catharsis than yours.

David Cronenberg: Yeah. Yeah. Well, it's the catharsis of the ambivalent. Maybe that's what I'm selling to you here. If you're simplistic, or your work is simplistic, or you choose to make it simple, then there can be a simple catharsis; and you get that in soap operas, you get it in the traditional comedy, where things are tied up in the end and everything feels all right after you've gone through some perilous moments. And maybe, the catharsis in my films is more complex, in that it is my reconfirming that things are not simple, not easily – perhaps not ever – resolvable. When I need a book, [. . .] I don't want a book in which everything is sweet and neat and nice. What book do you take to the island with you? What really consoles you? Is it something that tells you everything is all right? Is that really consolation? I feel that it's not.

David Breskin: [But even with the intellectual ramifications of doubt, which your work provides, it seems like one could have those and still provide the audience more release and recovery.]

David Cronenberg: This sounds like trout fishing. [Laughs.] [. . .] You catch them, say "Hi!" and throw them back.

David Breskin: You've caught them in the theatre – the audience as trout!

David Cronenberg: And maybe I don't want to let them go. Maybe catharsis is, literally, letting them off the hook too easily!

I'm not insisting that catharsis is the be-all and end-all, I'm just pointing out that it's a mechanism that seems to be there. And obviously, it can vary hugely from work to work. But certainly when you begin to mix your blood with the characters in the film, or if it's a scary film, you're mixing your own anxieties with the anxieties that are being played out in the film, the catharsis does not purge, it makes clear. I suppose my version of it is not totally classical. It's like the frame isolating things out of the chaos on the set. It's sort of saying, "For the moment we're going to concentrate on this. I'm not saying this is the whole world, but for the next two hours it's going to be your world, it's going to be our world together, we're really going to dive in deep, and we're going to explore all the aspects of it." To me, that is cathartic, right there. It doesn't have anything to do with whether there is a happy ending . . .

Chapter 38

Julie Dash, with bell hooks

DIALOGUE BETWEEN BELL HOOKS AND JULIE DASH

bell: Part of the challenge of *Daughters of the Dust* is that it brings us what could be called ethnographic details, though in fact it's set within a much more poetic, mythic universe. I would like you to talk some about your sense of myth and history.

Julie: It's interesting that you say mythopoetic, because *Daughters of the Dust* is like speculative fiction, like a *what if* situation on so many different levels.

Like *what* if we could have an unborn child come and visit her family-to-be and help solve the family's problems.

What if we had a great-grandmother who could not physically make the journey north but who could send her spirit with them.

What if we had a family that had such a fellowship with the ancestors that they helped guide them, and so on.

Myth, of course, plays a very important part in all of our lives, in everyone's culture. Without myth and tradition, what is there? So there is the myth of the Ibo Landing, which helped sustain the slaves, the people who were living in that region.

bell: Tell people what that myth is.

Julie: Okay. The Ibo Landing myth – there are two myths and one reality, I guess.

Ibo captives, African captives of the Ibo tribe, when they were brought to the New World, they refused to live in slavery. There are accounts of them having walked into the water, and then on top of the water all the way back to Africa, you know, rather than live in slavery in chains. There are also myths of them having flown from the water, flown all the way back to Africa. And then there is the story – the truth or the myth – of them walking into the water and drowning themselves in front of the captors.

I was able, in my research, to read some of the accounts from the sailors who were on the ship when supposedly it happened, and a lot of the shipmates, the sailors or other crew members, they had nervous breakdowns watching this. Watching the Ibo men and women and children in shackles, walking into the water and holding themselves under the water until they in fact drowned.

And then interestingly enough, in my research, I found that almost every Sea Island has a little inlet, or a little area where the people say, "This is Ibo Landing. This is where it happened. This is where this thing really happened." And so, why is it that on every little island – and there are so many places – people say, "This is actually Ibo Landing"? It's because that message is so strong, so powerful, so sustaining to the tradition of resistance, by any means possible, that every Gullah community embraces this myth. So I learned that myth is very important in the struggle to maintain a sense of self and to move forward into the future.

bell: It's interesting that whenever an artist takes a kind of mythic universe and infuses it with aspects of everyday reality, like the images of women cooking, often the cinema audience in this society just isn't prepared. So few of the articles that I've read about *Daughters of the Dust* talk about the mythic element in the film, because, in fact, there is this desire to reduce the film to some sense of historical accuracy. It is relevant for moviegoers to realize that you did ten years of research for this film – but the point was not to create some kind of documentary of the Gullah, but to take that factual information and infuse it with an imaginative construction, as you just told us.

Yesterday I interviewed a young black woman, a graduate student, and she said, "This was our paradise that we never had." And I found that exciting, because she wasn't relating to the film, as "Dash was trying to create this ethnographic memory." No, you were giving us a mythic memory.

Julie: Right, because life on the Sea Islands was very hard. Most people didn't live very long. There are extreme changes in temperature there, and life was very harsh. But the particular day that I presented in the story was a day that every family member would never forget. And I think that even within our lives – which are also very difficult – we remember these kinds of ceremonies and family dinners as being something very special, and that's all you remember. Of course it becomes mythologized.

bell: And there is a certain hyperbolic quality when we retell stories.

Julie: Exactly. They become more so.

bell: They become larger than life, and to some extent what you do is create a film where many of the images are larger than life. And the object isn't to create any kind of accuracy. I was very moved by what you said in the *Transition* interview about indigo and your sense, as an imaginative creative artist, that you wanted to have something atypical be seen as the scars of black people.

Julie: I worked with Dr. Margaret Washington Creel, who is an expert on the Gullah. She was my historical adviser on the project, and she reminded me that, of course, indigo was very poisonous and all that, but that the indigo stain, the blue stain, would not have remained on the hands of the old folks who had worked the indigo processing plant. And I explained to her, that yes, I did understand that fully, but I was using this as a symbol of slavery, to create a new kind of icon around slavery rather than the traditional showing of the whip marks or the chains. Because we've seen all those things before and we've become very calloused about them. I wanted to show it in a new way.

bell: I think of Victor Slosky's notion of "defamiliarization," where you take what may be an everyday image and you present it in such a way that people have to think twice. As a spectator, when I saw that I immediately thought about the permanent imprinting of wounds in flesh. But I didn't have to pause and ask, "But is this real?" because that isn't the point.

I think one of the major problems facing black filmmakers is the way both spectators and, often, the dominant culture want to reduce us to some narrow notion of "real" or "accurate." And it seems to me that one of the groundbreaking aspects of *Daughters of the Dust*, because it truly is a groundbreaking film, is its insistence on a movement away from dependence on "reality," "accuracy," "authenticity," into a realm of the imaginative.

Could you say more about your sense of memory? What does it mean, if you're not going to work in a documentary form, to emphasize so much the idea of memory and time?

Julie: After I concluded my research on *Daughters*, I sat back and digested all of that information and said, okay, I want to maintain historical events and issues and the integrity of this region, of these people. But I also want to do something very different, and that's where we get into the poetic thing. I want to show black families, particularly black women, as we have never seen them before. I want to touch something inside of each black person that sees it, some part of them that's never been touched before. So I said, let me take all of this information that I have gathered and try to show this family leaving a great-grandmother in a very different way. And that was when I realized that I could not structure it as normal, Western drama. It had to go beyond that. And that's when I came up with the idea of structuring the story in much the same way that an African griot would recount a family's history. The story would just kind of unravel. This very important day would unravel through a series of vignettes, if you want to call them that. The story would come out and come in and go out and come in, very much the way in Toni Cade Bambara's work one character would be speaking to another and then it goes off on a tangent for several pages and then she brings it back and goes out and back again.

I remember learning about poetry in school; the teacher said, "Well, what makes good poetry is that poets will say things using words that you use every day but they say them in a way that you have never heard it said before. And then it means so much more."

bell: And then, for example, the film's focus on Islam reminds us that, indeed, African Americans draw upon numerous religious traditions. It just so happens that the focus on Islam in the film coincides with the rebirth of nationalism and a renewed focus on Black Muslim identity in America. Some people may see you as drawing on trends in the culture right now, but in fact your thinking about those things predates the resurgence of that interest.

Julie: Oh, absolutely.

bell: Somebody recently raised the question with me – were you a black nationalist, or were you an Afrocentric? And I myself wasn't sure why they were gleaning that from the film. I suppose for them it was your focus on Islam. So, could you talk a little bit about that question? What you wanted to show in terms of religion in the film.

Julie: Well, when I came to the project, I assumed that I already knew a lot about it from my family and from the little research I had done early on. But as I got deeper and deeper into it, I learned a hell of a lot. For instance, I learned about Bilal Muhammed. Actually, he lived earlier than the time of my story. He was in the Sea Islands during slavery, but by the turn of the century, his five daughters who were also Muslim, were still carrying on the tradition of Islam. He was an actual person, a Muslim, and his diaries and his papers are on permanent exhibition at the Smithsonian Institution in Washington. He had been a boy of twelve when he was taken from the Sudan, which shows that the African slave trade was more widespread than we thought – because he had memories of growing up in Sudan. He was also fluent in French, having worked as a slave in the West Indies before being brought to the Sea Islands. And he never stopped practicing his faith. As a slave in the Sea Islands he prayed five times a day. People thought he was just an odd fellow, but it really goes to show the persistence of tradition.

bell: Wow!

Julie: So it was very important for me to include this man in the story, even though I knew *actually* that he was living and practicing his faith in the 1800s. I wanted him to be a part of this day too, to include him because he meant so much to me. No one else has dealt with him to this point. Strange . . .

bell: Yes. I was also interested in Viola's sense of Christianity in the film, as a kind of counterpoint to Islam. History for her begins not with what has happened in the slave past or what is happening on the islands, but at that moment of crossover. And in that sense, she represents a kind of premodern figure for me, because she's the one that says, essentially, "When we cross over to the mainland we are going to have Culture." That's capital-C culture.

Julie: Exactly. Viola is someone who hides within Christianity. She hides her fears, her lack of self-esteem, her womanhood, within the cloak of the Christian missionary. But it's interesting that this particular character chooses to be a Baptist, because Baptist worship is so close to the ecstatic seizures evoked in lots of West African religions. So a lot of African American people will hide within this Baptist religon, but they're really practicing the same thing. They're just hiding their gods, hiding their rituals within Christianity, which for them was modern.

bell: I think she definitely stands – as does Haagar – for a force of denial, denial of the primal memory. I keep thinking about violation when I think about Viola because it seems to me that if she had her way, she would strip the past of all memory and would replace it only with markers of what she takes to be the new civilization. In this way Christianity becomes a hidden force of colonialism.

Julie: Uh-huh, exactly.

bell: The film really touched upon the question of domestic colonization and how black people, like Haagar and like Viola internalized a sense of what culture is.

Julie: Right. And she brought her photographer with her to document "them." She pays the photographer to come document her family. He being a part of the "talented tenth," a scientist. But I see the character of Mr. Snead as having a secret mission. He has another agenda. He's going to take pictures of these very, very primitive people and go back and have a showing of what he's photographed, you know. For me, he also represents the viewing audience.

Chapter 39

Spike Lee, with David Breskin

INNER VIEWS

Filmmakers in Conversation

David Breskin: GIMDAD – "God is my defense and deliverance." You would write that when you were really up against the wall trying to raise money to make *She's Gotta Have It*.

Spike Lee: Oh, that was given to me by a woman, one of my mother's close friends, Amy Olatunji, the wife of Baba, the African drummer. She's a very spiritual person. You write it down – GIMDAD. It worked, and it's been working.

David Breskin: What's your spiritual hookup?

Spike Lee: I've never been a very religious person, as far as going to church. The only time I really went to church was when I spent the summers down South, where we had to go to church with both my grandmothers. My parents in New York never made us go to church.

David Breskin: Nonetheless, you have some relation to –

Spike Lee: Yeah, I do believe that. For me it's a very personal thing. I do believe that there is something greater than us.

David Breskin: Greater than Spike Lee? You're going to blow your image.

Spike Lee: Greater than humanity. [Laughs.] You're just fucking with me.

David Breskin: What were the prayers you were saying every night? You referred to them a number of times.

Spike Lee: "Where are we going to get this money? Please, Lord, please."

David Breskin: Now, you weren't asking the blond, blue-eyed Jesus Christ for that?

Spike Lee: Hey, Buddha, Allah, Jesus – we weren't risking anything! [Laughs.] I think if She's Gotta Have It had been a failure I still would have been successful, but it would have taken another three, four, or even five years to rebound from that.

David Breskin: What's your feeling about organized religion? A lot of religious themes bubble up in Jungle Fever.

Spike Lee: Well, that's really because of who I wrote it for. Ossie Davis is an ordained minister. So I really wanted to bring that flavor to this film. You see that more in older black people. That's all we did: get on our knees and pray, and sing to the high heavens. But I'm not too up on organized religion.

David Breskin: You think the Church was used to hold black folk down in this country?

Spike Lee: All over the world. The Bible in one hand and the gun in the other.

David Breskin: But it kind of backfired, because –

Spike Lee: Backfired? How?

David Breskin: Because in some ways the white Southerners, who forced Christianity down the slaves' throats, didn't realize that the personal empowerment Christianity gave the slaves led to a kind of self-esteem that the white people themselves didn't get from the religion, because they didn't take their religion as seriously as the slaves did.

Spike Lee: Well, it gave us something. It gave us the strength to go on. I don't know that it backfired. But it also kept us praying to Jesus and worrying about the hereafter instead of what was happening now: getting our asses kicked! We were worrying about trying to get into heaven. Malcolm said the white man's heaven is the black man's hell. We want our heaven here on earth! So in a lot of ways religion has been used to oppress people.

David Breskin: Speaking of saviors, one of the things you wrote even before She's Gotta Have It became a hit was that you were "determined not to let other people turn you into a savior."

Spike Lee: Well, that just happens when any black person is successful in any field – there's so few of us that when we do break through, the weight of the whole race is thrust upon our shoulders. And it can't be done by one person.

David Breskin: Do you feel the burden of that responsibility?

Spike Lee: Not as much as I used to, because now I'm not the only one out there. I'm so happy that everyone else is coming up now. I never wanted to be the only black filmmaker, because no one of my films can satisfy thirty million African-Americans. Our taste is just as diverse as anybody else's. A lot of people do not like my films but nonetheless still want to go to see movies. Black parents talk to me all the time, and they wish I would make children's movies – movies they could take their children to – but that's not the type of movies I've made up to this point. I mean, the Hudlins' *House Party* was made specifically for black teenagers. That was a need that should be fulfilled and it was. That's why it made $29 million.

[A young white woman comes over to us and says, "I know you guys are doing an interview, but thanks for *Do the Right Thing*. It's one of the best movies I ever saw."]

David Breskin: You wrote an op-ed piece for *The New York Times* in response to accusations that you were anti-Semitic. Will you share what you related in that?

Spike Lee: I'm trying to remember. I just gave various examples of double standards. I just listed several recent instances where no charges of being a racist were leveled against these films and these filmmakers, and why is it you can never have any negative Jewish characters in a piece of art? [Pause.] I forget what I wrote, most of it.

David Breskin: Were you aware as you wrote and shot those scenes that you were playing with a stereotype that was going to inflame people?

Spike Lee: To me, I did not see that as a stereotype. First of all, that's like when the NAACP came out with that statement that most of Hollywood is run by Jewish people. Jewish people were upset. I don't see what the big deal was. It's the truth. Now the Japanese are buying it up, but the people that run things are Jewish. The entertainment industry, and particularly the film industry. And in this particular case, Moe and Josh, these guys owned the Beneath the Underdog club, were Jewish, and were tight, and they exploited artists. And this was not to say that every single Jewish person exploits artists, or that every single Jewish person in the world is like that. In this case, these guys were. And that's all there was to it.

David Breskin: Did they strike you as caricatures, more than characters?

Spike Lee: Not me.

David Breskin: Not to make it overly simplistic, but did you feel there was a message in Mo' Better Blues about the demands of art?

Spike Lee: That the great artists probably have a very hard time with their personal life. 'Cause a great artist is going to devote every single waking minute to their art, and that family is always going to suffer for it.

David Breskin: Present company excluded?

Spike Lee: Well, hopefully, it won't be the same for me. Knock on wood. [Raps the table.] With the whole Moe and Josh thing: if people want to say that the characters were flat, you know, that's all right. But to say that Spike is anti-Semitic, and "Don't you know that Jews walked side by side with Martin Luther King during the civil rights movement?" and all that other shit, that has nothing to do with the movie. I really didn't want to be swept up in that whole black-Jewish relations thing.

You know, I think there's a thinking among a lot of Jewish people that there's some great black conspiracy against Jewish people. First of all, black people don't see it like that: it's not just Jewish people, for the most part it's just white people. Because how do you know who's Jewish? You just can't look at somebody.

Chapter 40

George Lucas, with Bill Moyers

OF MYTH AND MEN

Excerpts of a conversation between Bill Moyers and George Lucas on the meaning of the Force and the true theology of Star Wars

Moyers: Joseph Campbell once said all the great myths, the ancient great stories, have to be regenerated in every generation. He said that's what you are doing with *Star Wars*. You are taking these old stories and putting them into the most modern of idioms, the cinema. Are you conscious of doing that? Or are you just setting out to make a good action-movie adventure?

Lucas: With *Star Wars* I consciously set about to re-create myths and the classic mythological motifs. I wanted to use those motifs to deal with issues that exist today. The more research I did, the more I realized that the issues are the same ones that existed 3,000 years ago. That we haven't come very far emotionally.

Moyers: The mesmerizing figure in The *Phantom Menace* to me is Darth Maul. When I saw him, I thought of Lucifer in *Paradise Lost* or the devil in Dante's *Inferno*. He's the Evil Other – but with powerful human traits.

Lucas: Yes, I was trying to find somebody who could compete with Darth Vader, who is now one of the most famous evil characters. So we went back into representations of evil. Not only the Christian, but also Hindu and other religious icons, as well as the monsters in Greek mythology.

Moyers: Do you know yet what, in a future episode, is going to transform Anakin Skywalker to the dark side?

Lucas: Yes, I know what that is. The groundwork has been laid in this episode. The film is ultimately about the dark side and the light side, and those sides are designed around compassion and greed. The issue of greed, of getting things and owning things and having things and not being able to let go of things, is the opposite of compassion – of not thinking of yourself all the time. These are the two sides – the good force and the bad force. They're the simplest parts of a complex cosmic construction.

Moyers: I think it's going to be very hard for the audience to accept that this innocent boy, Anakin Skywalker, can ever be capable of the things that we know happen later on. I think about Hitler and wonder what he looked like at nine years old.

Lucas: There are a lot of people like that. And that's what I wonder. What is it in the human brain that gives us the capacity to be as evil as human beings have been in the past and are right now?

Moyers: What do you make of the fact that so many people have interpreted your work as being profoundly religious?

Lucas: I don't see *Star Wars* as profoundly religious. I see *Star Wars* as taking all the issues that religion represents and trying to distill them down into a more modern and easily accessible construct – that there is a greater mystery out there. I remember when I was 10 years old, I asked my mother, "If there's only one God, why are there so many religions?" I've been pondering that question ever since, and the conclusion I've come to is that all the religions are true.

Moyers: Is one religion as good as another?

Lucas: I would say so. Religion is basically a container for faith. And faith in our culture, our world and on a larger issue, the mystical level – which is God, what one might describe as a supernatural, or the things that we can't explain – is a very important part of what allows us to remain stable, remain balanced.

Moyers: One explanation for the popularity of *Star Wars* when it appeared is that by the end of the 1970s, the hunger for spiritual experience was no longer being satisfied sufficiently by the traditional vessels of faith.

Lucas: I put the Force into the movie in order to try to awaken a certain kind of spirituality in young people – more a belief in God than a belief in any particular religious system. I wanted to make it so that young people would begin to ask questions about the mystery. Not having enough interest in the mysteries of life to ask the question, "Is there a God or is there not a God?" – that is for me the worst thing that can happen. I think you should have an opinion about that. Or you should be saying, "I'm looking. I'm very curious about this, and I am going to continue to look until I can find an answer, and if I can't find an answer, then I'll die trying." I think it's important to have a belief system and to have faith.

Moyers: Do you have an opinion, or are you looking?

Lucas: I think there is a God. No question. What that God is or what we know about that God, I'm not sure. The one thing I know about life and about the human race is that we've always tried to construct some kind of context for the unknown. Even the cavemen thought they had it figured out. I would say that cavemen understood on a scale of about 1. Now we've made it up to about 5. The only thing that most people don't realize is the scale goes to 1 million.

Moyers: The central ethic of our culture has been the Bible. Like your stories, it's about the fall, wandering, redemption, return. But the Bible no longer occupies that central place in our culture today. Young people in particular are turning to movies for their inspiration, not to organized religion.

Lucas: Well, I hope that doesn't end up being the course this whole thing takes, because I think there's definitely a place for organized religion. I would hate to find ourselves in a completely secular world where entertainment was passing for some kind of religious experience.

Moyers: You said you put the Force into *Star Wars* because you wanted us to think on these things. Some people have traced the notion of the Force to Eastern views of God – particularly Buddhist – as a vast reservoir of energy that is the ground of all of our being. Was that conscious?

Lucas: I guess it's more specific in Buddhism, but it is a notion that's been around before that. When I wrote the first *Star Wars*, I had to come up with a whole cosmology: What do people believe in? I had to do something that was relevant, something that imitated a belief system that has been around for thousands of years, and that most people on the planet, one way or another, have some kind of connection to. I didn't want to invent a religion. I wanted to try to explain in a different way the religions that have already existed. I wanted to express it all.

Moyers: You're creating a new myth?

Lucas: I'm telling an old myth in a new way. Each society takes that myth and retells it in a different way, which relates to the particular environment they live in. The motif is the same. It's just that it gets localized. As it turns out, I'm localizing it for the planet. I guess I'm localizing it for the end of the millennium more than I am for any particular place.

Moyers: What lessons do you think people around the world are taking away from *Star Wars*?

Lucas: *Star Wars* is made up of many themes. It's not just one little simple parable. One is our relationship to machines, which are fearful, but also benign. Then there is the lesson of friendship and symbiotic relationships, of your obligations to your fellow-man, to other people that are around you. This is a world where evil has run amuck. But you have control over your destiny, you have many paths to walk down, and you can choose which destiny is going to be yours.

Moyers: I'm not a psychologist, I'm just a journalist, but it does seem to me there's something autobiographical with Luke Skywalker and his father – something of George Lucas in there.

Lucas: Oh, yes. There is, definitely. You write from your own emotions. And obviously there are two sides to the redeemer motif in the Star Wars films. Ultimately Vader is redeemed by his children and especially by having children. Because that's what life is all about – procreating and raising children, and it should bring out the best of you.

Moyers: So while *Star Wars* is about cosmic, galactic epic struggles, it's at heart about a family?

Lucas: And a hero. Most myths center on a hero, and it's about how you conduct yourself as you go through the hero's journey, which in all classical myth takes the form of a voyage of transformation by trials and revelations. You must let go of your past and must embrace your future and figure out what path you're going to go down.

Moyers: Is it fair to say, in effect, that *Star Wars* is your own spiritual quest?

Lucas: I'd say part of what I do when I write is ponder a lot of these issues. I have ever since I can remember. And obviously some of the conclusions I've come to I use in the films.

Moyers: The psychologist Jonathan Young says that whether we say, "I'm trusting my inner voice," or use more traditional language – "I'm trusting the Holy Spirit," as we do in the Christian tradition – somehow we're acknowledging that we're not alone in the universe. Is this what Ben Kenobi urges upon Luke Skywalker when he says, "Trust your feelings"?

Lucas: Ultimately the Force is the larger mystery of the universe. And to trust your feelings is your way into that.

Moyers: One scholar has called *Star Wars* "mysticism for the masses." You've been accused of trivializing religion, promoting religion with no strings attached.

Lucas: That's why I would hesitate to call the Force God. It's designed primarily to make young people think about the mystery. Not to say, "Here's the answer." It's to say, "Think about this for a second. Is there a God? What does God look like? What does God sound like? What does God feel like? How do we relate to God?" Just getting young people to think at that level is what I've been trying to do in the films. What eventual manifestation that takes place in terms of how they describe their God, what form their faith takes, is not the point of the movie.

Moyers: Wendy Doniger, who is a scholar of mythology at the University of Chicago, says that myths are important because they remind us that our lives are real and our lives are not real. We have these bodies, which we can touch, but we also have within us this omnipotent magical world of thought.

Lucas: Myths tell us these old stories in a way that doesn't threaten us. They're in an imaginary land where you can be safe. But they deal with real truths that need to be told. Sometimes the truths are so painful that stories are the only way you can get through to them psychologically.

Moyers: Ultimately, isn't *Star Wars* about transformation?

Lucas: It will be about how young Anakin Skywalker became evil and then was redeemed by his son. But it's also about the transformation of how his son came to find the call and then ultimately realize what it was. Because Luke works intuitively through most of the original trilogy until he gets to the very end. And it's only in the last act – when he throws his sword down and says, "I'm not going to fight this" – that he makes a more conscious, rational decision. And he does it at the risk of his life because the Emperor is going to kill him. It's only that way that he is able to redeem his father. It's not as apparent in the earlier movies, but when you see the next trilogy, then you see the issue is, How do we get Darth Vader back? How do we get him back to that little boy that he was in the first movie, that good person who loved and was generous and kind? Who had a good heart.

Moyers: In authentic religion, doesn't it take Kierkegaard's leap of faith?

Lucas: Yes, yes. Definitely. You'll notice Luke uses that quite a bit through the film – not to rely on pure logic, not to rely on the computers, but to rely on faith. That is what that "Use the Force" is, a leap of faith. There are mysteries and powers larger than we are, and you have to trust your feelings in order to access them.

Moyers: When Darth Vader tempts Luke to come over to the Empire side, offering him all that the Empire has to offer, I am taken back to the story of Satan taking Christ to the mountain and offering him the kingdoms of the world, if only he will turn away from his mission. Was that conscious in your mind?

Lucas: Yes. That story also has been retold. Buddha was tempted in the same way. It's all through mythology. The gods are constantly tempting. Everybody and everything. So the idea of temptation is one of the things we struggle against, and the temptation obviously is the temptation to go to the dark side. One of the themes throughout the films is that the Sith lords, when they started out thousands of years ago, embraced the dark side. They were greedy and self-centered and they all wanted to take over, so they killed each other. Eventually, there was only one left, and that one took on an apprentice. And for thousands of years, the master would teach the apprentice, the master would die, the apprentice would then teach another apprentice, become the master, and so on. But there could never be any more than two of them, because if there were, they would try to get rid of the leader, which is exactly what Vader was trying to do, and that's exactly what the Emperor was trying to do. The Emperor was trying to get rid of Vader, and Vader was trying to get rid of the Emperor. And that is the antithesis of a symbiotic relationship, in which if you do that, you become cancer, and you eventually kill the host, and everything dies.

Moyers: I hear many young people today talk about a world that's empty of heroism, where there are no more noble things to do.

Lucas: Heroes come in all sizes, and you don't have to be a giant hero. You can be a very small hero. It's just as important to understand that accepting self-responsibility for the things you do, having good manners, caring about other people – these are heroic acts. Everybody has the choice of being a hero or not being a hero every day of their lives. You don't have to get into a giant laser-sword fight and blow up three spaceships to become a hero.

Chapter 41

Martin Scorsese

ON REAPPRECIATING KAZANTZAKIS

IT WAS MY FRIEND Barbara Hershey who recommended that I read Nikos Kazantzakis's novel. She mentioned it for the first time in Arkansas, when we were shooting my film *Boxcar Bertha*, and then she brought it up again in Los Angeles. I'll never be able to thank her enough. I took my time reading the book. And as I always do whenever I get excited about a novel, I started to make notes. I realized, quickly, that I wanted to make a film based on *The Last Temptation of Christ*.

I had dreamed of filming the story of Christ in a contemporary setting – downtown New York, to be exact, where I grew up. When I saw Pasolini's *The Gospel According to St. Matthew*, I felt that he had basically made that film – *Gospel* may have been set during the time of Jesus' life on earth, but it felt completely comtemporary, from the casting to the point of view to the music.

When I read the Kazantzakis novel, with its magnificent language and its restlessly probing spirit – that tone, at once so frank and so tender – I felt that I'd found another way of approaching Christ. Not to work from the gospels, but from a novel that attempted to pinpoint the key conflict of His short life – where did His humanity end and His divinity begin? Kazantzakis understood something that few have ever understood as keenly in a work of art, be it a novel

From Darren J.N. Middleton, ed. *Scandalizing Jesus?* (New York: Continuum, 2005).

or a film. He understood that Jesus must have felt as much of an obligation toward His own humanity – that is, an obligation to fulfill His life as a man, in the way we all feel it – as He did toward His divinity.

Jesus is often pictured as serene, somewhat like Siddhartha. In the Pasolini film, He is often angry – the sermon on the mount is delivered as a fiery call to arms in that film. But in the Kazantzakis novel, He is no longer just a figure, but a uniquely complex character as well – serene at some moments, angry at others. And, at all times, conflicted. Perhaps even confused, in the same way that any of us is confused at times about who we are, and where we're going. About our intuitions of what we want to do with our lives, which light a spark within us – we don't know where they will lead, we don't fully understand them, but we know that we must fulfill them, and see through to the end. I'm reminded of Stanley Kubrick's comment that when you're making a film, or any work of art, you have to preserve the original spark. That's what life is like, I believe. And it was that way for Jesus, as Kazantzakis so brilliantly imagined it.

I had always thought that if Jesus had returned to walk among us, He would be living with the hookers, the junkies, the bag ladies. He would be trying to set the world aright, one soul at a time. And it's certain that many among us would be laughing at Him. Scorning Him. We would be upset that someone was calling attention to the misery around us, insisting that we not look away. And He would be suffering.

I found this longing to make a connection between our present and Jesus' present, to make us one with Him and Him one with us, in Kazantzakis' novel.

It took many years and a great deal of effort to get my film of The Last Temptation of Christ made. It's a long story which doesn't bear repeating – most of the details were exhaustively reported at the time. But in the end, despite the difficulties, not only in getting the film made but in the uproar that followed its release, despite the fact that we were forced to go into production with a small budget and rush through the editing process, despite all those things, I think our film honored the spirit of Kazantzakis's book. Many people accused me of making a film that attacked belief, that attacked faith – just as Kazantzakis himself was accused. As if belief and faith were that flimsy. As if the image of Christ could not withstand interpretation.

If Christ were to walk the earth today, He would be nothing more or nothing less than one of us. He is one of us. Whenever you see someone helping a fellow human being who is weaker than he or she, you're seeing His example. Forgiveness and compassion – the best we can expect of ourselves, and the best we can expect of others. It was Kazantzakis who helped me to understand that Christ's teachings were eternally, radically new. That was the gift he gave me with The Last Temptation of Christ.

Chapter 42

Antonio Sison

SCREENING SCHILLEBEECKX

Cuba: Tomas Gutiérrez Alea's *The Last Supper*

THE CIRCUMSTANTIAL BACKGROUND that informed the sensibility of Tomas Gutiérrez Alea as a filmmaker was the Cuban Revolution, the propitious event that ended the U.S.-backed dictatorship of Fulgencio Batista and catapulted the communist regime of Fidel Castro. Gutiérrez Alea was a founding member of the *Instituto Cubano de Arte e Industria Cinematográficos* (ICAIC), an organization established by *Nuestro Tiempo* in 1959 – three months after the revolution – for the intention of pooling together talent and resources to form a national cinema. *Nuestro Tiempo* was a cultural society that played a key role in the rise of communism. Gutiérrez Alea and his colleagues moved to repudiate the influences of Hollywood in their search for a more socially relevant form of artistic expression. They were drawn toward experimental and anti-commercial tendencies even as they acknowledged their indebtedness to the European avant-garde. They were also fueled by an idealistic vision and were not afraid to dream. The passion and commitment of ICAIC's early members ushered in the development of a vital Cuban national cinema.

Following a Marxist trajectory, Gutiérrez Alea developed a distinct filmmaking style, rooted in his early training in Italian neorealism and the influence of the works of the father of cinematic surrealism Luis Buñuel, but with its own stylistic identity and revolutionary theoretical bed. Unlike his peers, Gutiérrez Alea remained loyal to the ideals of the Revolution but refused to be an obedient servant to them. His filmmaking was not hamstrung by his political affiliations. He successfully drew a balance between his commitment to the Revolution and his critique of its flaws, the ferment of which is sophisticated film making that resists being stigmatized as sheer political propaganda.

Gutiérrez Alea's film philosophy can be derived from the theoretical propositions of his 1988 manifesto *Dialéctica del Espectador* ("The Viewer's Dialectic"), which he wrote twenty years after the Cuban Revolution. Gutiérrez Alea expresses the need to subvert the conventions of documentary filmmaking as Cuban film artists mature politically and aesthetically:

> Cuban Cinema confronts that new and different way of thinking about what social processes are going to hold for us because our film draws its strength from Cuban reality, and endeavours, among other things, to express it. Thus we find it no longer sufficient just to take the camera out to the street and capture fragments of that reality ... The filmmaker is immersed in a complex milieu, the profound meaning of which does not lie on the surface.[1]

For Gutiérrez Alea, Cuban filmmaking is no longer about mouthagape acceptance of the "spectacular transformations" of the Revolution; it has become a task of interpreting the many layers that make up the complexities of social reality, indeed, a task of critical hermeneutics. As such, cinema lends itself to being an instrument of sociopolitical awareness – "Film not only entertains and informs, it also shapes taste, intellectual judgment, and states of consciousness."[2]

Gutiérrez Alea's work tackles a variety of subjects but the Revolution and its continuing impact on the lives of Cubans is a recurrent theme. His internationally recognized films include *La Muerte de un burócrata* ("Death of a Bureaucrat," 1968), *Memorias del subdesarollo* ("Memories of Underdevelopment," 1968), *La Ultima Cena* ("The Last Supper," 1976), *Fresa y Chocolate* ("Strawberry and Chocolate," 1994), and his last film *Guantanamera* (1995).

Memories of Underdevelopment, his most significant opus in terms of narrative inventiveness, demonstrates Gutiérrez Alea's Third Cinema perspective, which casts a gimlet-eye on social reality as such. This is personified in the central character of Sergio who is fox-holed in his social class and his neo-European perspective so that he remains apolitical in the midst of the sweeping revolutionary changes in Cuba. Gutiérrez Alea presents his point by negation – Sergio is impotent precisely because he is detached from the collective. Curiously, critics, both "establishment" and "leftist," missed the film's ironic signification. The film had also been noted for its complex narrational strategies that fuses documentary conventions, cinema vérité, extradiegetic inserts, and dynamic editing.

Gutiérrez Alea's other masterpiece is *The Last Supper*. A period piece on slavery in eighteenth-century Cuba, the film is one of only two titles in Gutiérrez Alea's filmography that are historically farthest from the context of the Revolution and are thematically invested on the subject of religion, the other being *Una pelea cubana contra los demonios* ("A Cuban Struggle Against Demons," 1971). Gutiérrez Alea based his story on a historical anecdote about a 1790 slave owner who performs Jesus' foot-washing act on twelve of his African slaves in a pietistic effort at ritualized humility during Maundy Thursday. Kindred with other historical "slavery" films of the decade, *The Last Supper* sees the issue of slavery in the dual categories of master-slave and colonizer-colonized or what is known as the "Calibán" theme. The motif draws from the 1971 essay of Cuban poet Roberto Fernández Retamar entitled *Caliban*, a term etymologically indebted to the name of a merman in Shakespeare's *The Tempest*. The Calibán theme came to symbolize slavery and the colonial project in Latin America.

In *The Last Supper*, Gutiérrez Alea departs from the dissonant stylistic experimentalism of *Memories of Underdevelopment* and employs an uncharacteristic visual style seen nowhere else in his corpus of films. Uniquely, the generation of meaning and sociopolitical comment occurs within the controlled, visually static, arm's length irony of the sustained supper scene. In this tour de force, the film's Third Cinema optic becomes apparent as it fearlessly confronts the role of religion in preserving the subjugated status of slaves and perpetuating the master-slave social hierarchy.

The Last Supper opens with downtrodden African slaves toiling in a Havana sugar mill. The mill is owned by a wealthy count and run by Don Manuel, a brutal overseer. Today, a runaway slave had just been captured. As punishment, Don Manuel cuts off his ear and feeds it to the dogs, after which he has him lashed a hundred times. The count's visit to his mill falls on this ominous day and he is a witness to the scene. Holy Week approaches and to placate his scruples, the count decides to host a meal modeled after Christ's last supper with twelve randomly chosen slaves as his honored guests. But prior to that, he wishes to conduct a foot-washing ceremony. Much to the overseer's chagrin, one of the chosen ones is Sebastian, the runaway slave he had tortured.

The slaves undergo a Bible crash course about the promise of paradise from a priest who plays a pacifist role in the social equation. The priest then takes them to the river and makes sure they are bathed in preparation for the ceremony. In the chapel, the visibly repulsed master washes the disciples' feet and flinchingly kisses them.

The slaves take their place at the count's table. As the meal progresses, the count shamelessly brandishes blasphemous Biblical rhetoric with the obvious intention of justifying the master-slave equation as the slaves gorge on the food. But the slaves are more clever than he thought and as they voice their recriminations, he lectures them with nonsensical logic. They in turn tell stories and ask him for favors.

The count, now drunk, falls into a slumber and the slaves share their mutinous thoughts among themselves. When the meal is over and the master awakens, he declares Good Friday a non-working day for the slaves. The next day, the overseer barks back-to-work orders at the slaves, and the count, realizing that this would all redound to more profit for his mill, reneges on his promise. A mutiny ensues. The slaves burn the mill and slay the overseer and his wife. The count is enraged and orders for a manhunt of the twelve slaves. In the aftermath of the maelstrom, eleven bloody heads of African slaves are sticking on wooden stakes; the twelfth is empty. The film closes with a defiant Sebastian running freely uphill.

In The Last Supper, Gutiérrez Alea's stylistic option leans more toward vérité camerawork, unobtrusive editing, and, for the sustained segment of the supper, a controlled, chamber-like composition and atmosphere. As I noted earlier, this is a departure from the intentionally discordant fusion of stylistic techniques that had been his signature in Memories of Underdevelopment. The Third Cinema resonance of The Last Supper's stylistic strategies lie mainly on the level of mise-en-scène. Visual composition, costuming, symbolic elements, and the characters' actions work together to generate meaning as the film essays the oppressive master-slave dynamic. Some notable camera angling and editing strategies are used in the latter part of the film and I reserve comment on them for later.

A great part of The Last Supper takes place at the dinner table and this is where strategic mise-en-scène becomes markedly significant. The section is embedded in a matrix of pious Catholic imagery and allusions. It opens with the dinner setting where the count and his slaves are properly seated and ready to partake of the meal. The symmetrically composed table arrangement is an overt reenactment of the last supper of Jesus Christ with his apostles. The assignment of roles is clear. The count, playing host at the center of the table, is Jesus Christ, while the twelve slaves obviously correspond to the twelve apostles. The scene immediately brings to mind the last supper sequence of the Hollywood Jesus-movie The Greatest Story Ever Told (George Stevens, 1965), which was mimetically based on Leonardo da Vinci's fresco. In this painterly scene, Gutiérrez Alea gives a striking irony, a visual representation of what the master-slave relationship is not. There is nothing in the character of the count that is remotely Christ-like. In fact, he is an egocentric Pharisee blinded by the trappings of power and privilege. Neither are the twelve gathered around the count beloved disciples pastured in paths of salvation; they are slaves, stripped of dignity, imprisoned in a life of toil and servitude, and made to live like animals. This is definitely a tragi-comic jab at the role of religion in the master-slave asymmetry, a direction that carries on throughout the long supper scene.

An earlier scene symbolically presents the distorted mode of relationality at work in the master-slave equation when it shows the count talking to his caged pet bird:

COUNT: Now that I've fed you, you must sing for your master!

The scene is a key iconic representation of the rationale of the feast. The slaves are made to feel indebted to the master's "benevolence" and are therefore bound to obedience. The analogy is not subtle – the slaves are caged animals completely subject to the caprices of the master. As the count continues his lecture on the many blessings of being a slave, one elderly bond slave who is about to complete payment for his freedom asks the master to set him free. When he obliges, the slave could not leave; he has so internalized his caged existence that every trace memory of freedom has been obliterated. He has known no other life but slavery and has nowhere to go. The count milks the moment for everything its worth and continues his litany on the benefits of slavery. The referent of the iconic symbol of the caged bird is thus confirmed in the feast – "Now that I've fed you, you must sing for your master!"

Additionally, the very costuming demarcates the master-slave equation vividly. The count is pompously dressed in upper class finery, complete with powdered wig. Contrastingly, the slaves are dressed in filthy rags and look weary and weather-beaten. For sure, this is no gathering of equals.

The center of gravity of the film's Third Cinema vision is worked out in the leitmotiv of resistance and emancipation enfleshed in the character of Sebastian, the tortured runaway slave. At the preceding foot-washing ceremony, he kicks the basin of water as the count attempts to wash his foot. In the supper scene, his conspicuous appearance at the table – with an eye beaten-shut and a glazed-over, defiantly knowing expression – already works as an indictment of the feast and a visual foreboding of eventual turn of events. In contrast to the rest of the slaves who seem oblivious to the manipulative overtures of the count, Sebastian looks intelligently perceptive and self-aware. His missing ear is yet another borrowed biblical image of the high priest's slave whose ear was cut-off by a protective Simon Peter, whom Jesus rebuffs for using the sword and resorting to violence. Jesus miraculously restores the ear in the gospel story but in Gutiérrez Alea's version, miracles are hard to come by. An open, bleeding wound lies on the spot where his ear was. But Sebastian's defiance makes it clear that this is a symbol of the masters' shame, not his. At one point, Sebastian, still in a stupor after his ordeal, collapses face down on the table. The count immediately has him sit at his right side and offers him a drink. He then proceeds to interrogate him. It is interesting to note that the count cribs from the gospel of Mark and appropriates Jesus' question to his disciples – "Who do you say that I am?"

> COUNT: Look, Sebastian, who am I? Come on, identify me. Who am I, Sebastian? Well, recognize me . . . I ask you in the name of Christ: Who am I?

In the Markan pericope, Peter declares "You are the Messiah." In *The Last Supper*, Sebastian gives no answer and spits on the face of the count. Unlike his fellow slaves who are vaguely aware of the fraudulence and malice of the meal, Sebastian, despite one eye beaten-shut, is clear-eyed. He is very much aware that they are being fed with lies.

All these signs of protest and resistance segues to Sebastian's strongest and most lucid indictment of slavery. The count retells the story of the fall of the first man and woman as found in the Biblical account of Genesis with the intent of justifying toil and labor as God's established order. When the count dozes off at the table after one drink too many, Sebastian speaks for the first time in the film. He invokes the Afro-Cuban folk religion known as Santeria and appropriates the story of how the supreme being Olofi created both good and evil. Mise-en-scène plays a key role when Sebastian grabs the head of the roast pig on the table and lifts it to his face. In this strikingly bizarre image, he appears like a man who has a pig's head as he relates how the body of Truth walks around with the head of the Lie. The allusion exposes the master's duplicity, names him a liar, and denounces him for his inhumanity – quite literally, for being a pig. Here, Sebastian subversively draws from folk religion and not the institutional Catholic religion, which had itself become enslaved to his master's self-serving schemes. It is notable that the pig's head was in the foreground of the earlier shot when Sebastian spat at the master.

Gutiérrez Alea satiricizes religion, exposing it as an instrument utilized by society's powerholders to sacralize the status quo. Institutional religion functions to cloak the oppressive master-slave structure with the veil of piety and perpetuates a culture of passivity among the enslaved. The priest, who personifies institutional religion, attempts to moralize the situation and pays lip service but he is emasculated by the powers that be and fails to bring about social change. Teshome Gabriel rightly points out that *The Last Supper* configures Christianity as "the dominant ideology from which the oppressed classes must break away, and both examine the profound impact of that ideology and the difficulty involved in making that break."[3]

The Last Supper has an open-ended denouement suggesting an alternative future for Sebastian. In the final scene, we learn that Sebastian is the missing twelfth slave who escapes execution. He is shown running through the dense forest. Dynamic editing plays a role here. The take showing Sebastian running through the forest is intercut with shots of an eagle in flight, a rushing river, rocks on a landslide, and freely running wild horses. Unfettered, he is moving toward his birthright as an agent of his own destiny. We also get a low-angle view of Sebastian as he takes a leap, emphasizing even more the length of his stride. Additionally, the drumbeats and chants of the rousing musical score convey a kinetic movement. The final shot shows Sebastian running uphill to an undisclosed destination. The syntagmatic elements coupled with the open-endedness of this segment allude to a utopic direction. *The Last Supper* does not paint an image of what the utopic reality might look like but its rumblings are present in indexical fashion, the way smoke signifies a fire.

More to the point, Sebastian is enroute to "destination freedom."

Notes

1   Tomás Gutiérrez Alea, "The Viewers Dialectic", trans Julia Lesage in *New Latin American Cinema*, ed. Michael T. Martin. Detroit, MI: Wayne State University Press, 1997, 109.

2   Ibid, 110.

3   Teshome Gabriel, *Third Cinema in the Third World*. Ann Arbor, MI: UMI Research Press, 1982, 18.

Chapter 43

Walter Salles, with Anthony Kaufman

SENTIMENTAL JOURNEY AS NATIONAL ALLEGORY
An Interview with Walter Salles

THE FILM I DID before, called *Foreign Land*, is a road movie set in that change of decades from 1989 to 1990, which was a time of complete chaos. It's about that moment when the country ceased to be a country of immigration and started to be a country of emigration. It follows a generation of young people in their early twenties that try to lead a second life in Europe. In fact, what they find there is a situation very similar to the one they left in Brazil, one of rejection and the incapacity to belong to something. In that film, the characters were led by events that were foreign to their own decision. The political situation was so oppressive that they could not really define their own destiny. In *Central Station*, the change is that, for the first time, the boy redefines his own destiny, he rebaptizes himself and, in doing so, he becomes a sort of transforming angel. This is what attracted the immense public that we had in Brazil to the film. There is a real need for that kind of change.

Cineaste: Christianity is prevalent in many of the film's scenes, but I wasn't sure if you were mocking it or praising it.

Salles: Neither. I think that, as a documentarian, you learn to at least try to portray things as you see them, and to reproduce this intention with a desire to show with respect and dignity what exists. So, as you enter the part of Brazil that is more anachronistic at first, but which, in fact, is more rich and more complex than the neoliberal, urban Brazil that we have built, you soon realize that religion is something derived from necessity. When there is no one to ask things for in real life, you soon look to higher spiritual elements that can somehow bring you the support you don't find on earth. In this sense, I was very moved by the incredible, spiritual force, the density and verticality of faith, in those areas. I really tried to respect this as much as I could.

In fact, we initially experienced the pilgrimage scene in the film during the research period, which took almost one year. What we did was to try to reenact what I had originally filmed with a VHS video camera. Once we started shooting, however, it stopped, little by little, being the representation of a pilgrimage, and it became the thing itself. For example, the two or three people who addressed the other pilgrims improvised that on the spot. This was not part of the screenplay. It just happened because they were so intimately moved by that experience. This is when cinema becomes interesting to me, when it stops being the representation of something and becomes the thing itself. This is also why I like to work with nonprofessional actors, and mix them with actors, like Kiarostami does, because if you have proper time to rehearse, it brings a richer texture to the film.

Now, this requires a system very different from the normal film production experience. What I learned, little by little, is that a specific technique had to be put into place in order to get the filmic result that I wanted. It basically involves a long rehearsal period, seven to eight weeks, but knowing the geography of where you're going to film prior to the rehearsal. I do the location scouting personally. Then, once the geography is defined, I rehearse the actors and nonprofessional actors in a place, in a theater, and draw the same geography. In this way, I get to know the characters much better, and the actors have a sense of the whole film, which they rarely do when they're parachuted into a film and work for two or three days. It creates a homogenous climate that permeates the film as a whole. It allows you to polish dialog, and change things little by little.

It also helps the nonprofessional actors get closer to their characters and it helps the actors de theatricalize their interpretation, to get rid of all the Stanislavskyian background, in order to get something that is fresher, more interesting, and nontechnical. This allows you to improvise tremendously because you know the material so well. Everyone knows so well what they're talking about that, when you put the camera in an actual geography, small miracles sometimes occur. Antonioni used to say that geography changes character and he's right. You can immediately weigh that, gauge that, in the light of what you had in the rehearsal period. It creates a really interesting system.

Chapter 44

Steven Spielberg

STEVEN'S CHOICE

AS HE SHOOTS, Spielberg talks. And talks. Maybe it's having spent five weeks in Kraków; maybe it's the prevailing mood of testimony. He says talking helps him burn off nervous energy. Much of his conversation is in the way of historical exegesis – he's become quite a scholar of the Holocaust. At other times it is more personal. Growing up Jewish in Arizona was tough, he says. "They threw pennies in the study hall, you know – in a real quiet room, they threw pennies at me."

He was raised Orthodox for part of his childhood. "I kept wanting to have Christmas lights on the front of our house so it didn't look like the Black Hole of Calcutta in an all-Gentile neighbourhood – our neighbourhood used to win awards for Christmas decorations. I would beg my father, 'Dad, please, let us have some lights,' and he'd say, 'No, we're Jewish,' and I'd say, 'What about taking that white porch light out and screwing in a red porch light?' and he'd say 'No!' and I'd say, 'What about a yellow porch light?' and he said, 'No!' "

Spielberg and Universal Pictures bought *Schindler's List* eleven years ago, shortly after it was published. "In my burning desire to entertain," he says, "I kept pushing it back." At one point he fobbed it off on Martin Scorsese, and when he changed his mind, he ended up trading him *Cape Fear* to get it back. Part of the problem was dramatizing Schindler's gradual conversion from a Nazi party member to a hero who kept Jews alive by inventing jobs for them at his factory – he saved small children, for example, by telling the Nazis that only their tiny hands could polish the insides of bombshells. Several screenwriters worked on the script before Steven Zaillian tamed the sprawling narrative by paring it down to what cast members half-jokingly call "a buddy movie," focusing on the friendship between Schindler and Itzhak Stern, a Jewish intellectual played by Ben Kingsley. Stern fights with a charming Nazi killer named Amon Goeth for the soul of Schindler. "It's the perfect dramatic shape," observes Kingsley, "with Stern the good angel and Goeth the bad angel and Schindler in the middle."

As the script matured, so did Spielberg. Becoming a father helped prepare him. "I'm much more political than I was before," he says. "Ten years ago when people interviewed me about E.T., I was proud to say that I was a kind of political atheist, that I was six years late getting the Beatles, and that Vietnam went right over my head."

Spielberg also realised he'd gone somewhat astray in recent years, having been "seduced by my own success. I had always played to the adult audience who were able to remember their childhood and enjoy the movies along with their own children," he says, "but when I began playing to the kids directly, I found that I stumbled on my own shoelaces. Then I realized, when you're making movies, you can't do things consciously."

Schindler is different from anything Spielberg has done before, as far from the "movie" movie universe of Jaws as it possibly could be. Even Empire of the Sun was seen through the eyes of a boy and therefore was much more of a "visual feast," as Spielberg puts it. To make Schindler right, he knew he would have to try a radically different palette. "The authenticity of the story was too important to fall back on the commercial techniques that had gotten me a certain reputation in the area of craft and polish," he says.

This took a certain struggle. It ended up, as emotional struggles often do, with a new technique: "I threw a whole bunch of tools out of the toolbox. One of them was a crane. One of them was color film. I just limited the utensils, so the story would be the strength of the piece. There's nothing flashy in this movie at all . . ." He pauses. "I hope it's not too dull."

[. . .] While waiting, Spielberg speaks of his grandfather, a Jew from Odessa. As a boy, he says, his grandfather was prohibited from attending school. "They did allow Jews to listen through open window to the classes, so he pretty much went to school – fall, winter, and spring – by sitting outside in driving snow, outside of open windows."

He pauses, recalling his grandfather in America putting on a leather phylactery every morning and praying in Hebrew. "I was so ashamed of being a Jew, and now I'm filled with pride," he says. "I don't even know when that transition happened."

Chapter 45

Annalee Ward

MOUSE MORALITY
The Rhetoric of a Disney Animated Film

Film background

WE LIVE, WE DIE. The children live and die – all part of the great "circle of life," as The Lion King's theme song implies. A Disney animated film aimed at children, The Lion King features a cast of animals who represent a society in harmony, then in a struggle for survival, and finally in a climactic battle resulting in renewed peace for the lion kingdom. More specifically, the story focuses on the life of lion cub Simba, son of Mufasa, the king. But it is also a story that relies heavily on myths, archetypes, and rituals as rhetorical means to communicate moral values.

In recent years, the Disney conglomeration has emerged as a significant storyteller of our cultural myths. At one time the sources for myth were diverse but almost always included religious institutions. Now that is less common, and people turn to popular culture to satisfy spiritual hungers. For increasingly harried parents, Disney serves brightly packaged, nutritious, "safe food" in convenient locations, including their own home (in the form of videos). The Lion King in particular, however, invokes transcendent elements as it entertains.

[. . .]

Myth as sacred

The link between the sacred and myths is important to this study, for the primary myths from which The Lion King draws are religious, with roots in biblical stories. They include the stories of paradise, the fall, desert wandering, the reign of Satan, the need for a savior, and the cataclysmic destruction of the earth, followed by the return of the savior who restores peace and the beginning of his full reign as rightful king.

Even the creators at Disney admit that they were trying to do something deeper, something "allegorical" in this film. Critic Perri Klass observes that The Lion King "is an interesting mix of Hamlet, Bambi, and The Jungle Book, all shot through with some contemporary sensibility about men who can't grow up"[1]. I believe there is more to it than this and that the creators' desire to add depth to the film is reflected in the use of biblical myths, relying on archetypes and ritual to raise spiritual consciousness. In most instances this consciousness relates to traditional spirituality, but as Klass notes, New Age messages are also included. Director Rob Minkoff is quoted by Jamie Bernard about the film's spirituality: "the movie attempts 'a level of spirituality, something slightly metaphysical' "[2].

That the director chose to add a spiritual dimension raises questions of intent. Davies et al. offer one possible explanation: "The heroes and gods, or god-like beings, of the mythic fantasies . . . may well be efforts to fill a psychic void created by the rational emphases of modernity"[3]. Real observes that "myths reflect and make sacred the dominant tendencies of a culture, thereby sustaining social institutions and lifestyles"[4]. Most likely, following in the Disney tradition, the film aspires to offer a positive lesson for children about behavior that Disney values by associating itself with deeper myths; in a sense it is sacralizing Disney's (some would say American) values.

Myths in The Lion King

The first myth to which The Lion King alludes is the biblical narrative of life in paradise before the fall into sin. The movie begins with a diverse group of animals that normally prey on one another, joyfully meeting together at Pride Rock to witness shaman Rafiki's blessing of Simba, the new cub of lion king Mufasa and queen Sarabi. The king – Mufasa here, God in the Bible – rules the beautiful land, and all appear to be happy and at peace.

A second reference to the Garden of Eden myth comes when Simba is a frisky lion cub. Just as Adam and Eve are forbidden to eat of the fruit of one tree, Mufasa places a limitation on Simba. He says, "Everything the light touches is our kingdom". When Simba asks about the "shadowy place," Mufasa replies,

"You must never go there, my son". The allusion continues when a tempter, in this case jealous Uncle Scar, suggests that "only the bravest of lions" go to the land of shadows.

In a 1990s feminist reversal, Simba, the male, is tempted and recruits his best friend, female Nala to go with him, as opposed to Eve's recruitment of Adam. Both know it is wrong. Both proceed. And the consequences are that it is the beginning of the downfall of nature's operating in harmony and the inauguration of the reign of evil for, unknown to Mufasa and Simba, Scar has hatched a plan with his evil cohorts, the hyenas, scavengers of the shadow land who periodically prey on Pride Land animals. They intend to kill both Mufasa and Simba, thus allowing Scar to ascend to the throne.

Their plot succeeds in that Mufasa is killed saving Simba from a wildebeest stampede. Scar manages to convince Simba that he is guilty of causing his father's death and tells him he must leave Pride Land and never return; Simba is in essence banished from the beautiful Garden of Eden. Scar then takes over, allowing the hyenas to roam freely. The result is nature out of balance and destruction of the land. In the biblical narrative, that means that evil is in the world and Satan is alive and at work, a reality in which Christians believe.

The route by which Simba leaves is the desert. Aimlessly running until exhaustion and thirst take over, Simba would probably die if it were not for the care he receives from Pumbaa the warthog and Timon the meerkat. This part of the narrative resembles biblical stories of desert wanderings or journeys. Perhaps the most common is the story of Moses, who fled to the desert after killing an Egyptian and was there ministered to and taken in by the family of Jethro (Genesis 2). Another biblical desert wandering is the story of the nation of Israel. God and Israel covenanted together, each with responsibilities to fulfill, but Israel frequently disobeyed and did not live up to its obligations. In the same way, Simba, in taking up life with Timon and Pumbaa, fails to live up to his obligations to his father and to the Pride Land.

While Simba lives his carefree life in the jungle, things grow worse for the animals at home, and Nala finally runs away to the jungle, where she finds Simba. With the help of the ancestral spirit of Mufasa in the sky and the work of mystic Rafiki, Nala succeeds in convincing him that he is the rightful king and must return to Pride Rock. Mufasa appears in the sky, calling to Simba to take his "place in the Circle of Life," to "remember who you are". Compare this event to God's speaking directly to Moses out of the burning bush. God reminds Moses of his ancestors and of his care for the oppressed people of Israel, and he sends Moses back to Egypt to lead Israel (Genesis 3).

When Simba returns to the Pride Lands, he encounters a bleak, desperate land. Ingoglia describes the sight:

Everything had been touched by the drought. The trees were almost leafless. Starving giraffes, stretching as high as possible, had eaten the branches bare. The enormous ancient baobabs were stripped, their stringy bark devoured by desperate, hungry elephants.

The dry wind picked up, and threatening clouds gathered overhead. . . . A blinding lightning bolt scorched the earth, and the dry grasses caught fire.[5]

Not only has the land suffered, but Zazu, Mufasa's faithful servant, is also confined to a cage; the hyenas, having exhausted the herds meant for the lions are about to riot; and Scar is trying to stop a rebellion by the starving lionesses.

Compare this description to the one in the book of Matthew, telling of "the last days" before the return of Christ. Christ tells his disciples:

You will hear of wars and rumors of wars. . . . Nation will rise against nation, and kingdom against kingdom. There will be famines and earthquakes in various places. . . . Immediately after the distress of those days "the sun will be darkened, and the moon will not give its light; the stars will fall from the sky, and the heavenly bodies will be shaken." (Matthew 24:6–7, 29)

Once again the use of biblical myth is evident.

The final comparison is to the biblical description of the savior's rescuing humanity through the conquering of Satan, and Christ's reign over a new heaven and a new earth as the rightful king. The story of The Lion King concludes with Simba, the victor of the battle with Scar, vindicated of responsibility for his father's death. Jung observes, ". . . the myth of the hero is the most common and the best known myth in the world. . . . The essential function of the heroic myth is the development of the individual's ego-consciousness – his awareness of his own strengths and weaknesses – in a manner that will equip him for the arduous tasks with which life confronts him".[6] In one possible stage of the heroic myth, the hero becomes the culture's savior Simba is the hero of Pride Land, for he has saved its inhabitants from chaos and possible extinction.

In the final scene, it is dawn, the Pride Lands have been restored to beauty, the animals once again have gathered in harmony to witness the blessing of a new cub – this time Simba and Nala's – and the circle of life continues. As Eliade observes, "The myth of the end of the world is a universal occurrence; . . . This is the myth of the periodic destruction and re-creation of worlds, the cosmological formula of the myth of the eternal return"[7]. This has obvious references to New Age philosophy in its beliefs in cyclical history, in the intimate relationship of nature and culture, and in ancestors' life after death; all things are related in the "circle of life." But the cyclical understanding of life is present in biblical myth as well. For example, the Christian understanding of salvation is based on understanding birth, life, death, and rebirth. Biblical descriptions of the end of time include a new heaven and new earth, with a tree of life in the new Jerusalem. Northrop Frye's work on myths and archetypal criticism also confirms the presence of "cyclical movement" in myth. The Lion King speaks in sacred myth to communicate its message. In so doing, it relies on archetypes.

Notes

1   Perri Klass, "A Bambi for the 90's, via Shakespeare." New York Times 19 June 1994, Late ed., see 2: 1.

2   Jamie Bernard, " Disney's Lion King Roars Out of Africa". New York Daily News, 12 June 1994, NewsBank, Art, 16: 93–95.

3   Robert A. Davies et al, "The Dream World of Film: A Jungian Perspective on Cinematic Communication." Western Journal of Speech Communication 46 (1982): 326–343, 342.

4   Michael R. Real, Mass-Mediated Culture. Englewood Cliffs, N.J.: Prentice-Hall, 1977.

5   Gina Ingoglia, Disney's The Lion King. New York: Disney Press, 1994, 83–84.

6   Carl G. Jung and M. L. von Franz (eds) Man & His Symbols. New York: Dell, 1968 [1964], 101.

7   Mircea Eliade, Myths, Dreams, and Mysteries: The Encounter Between Contemporary Faiths and Archaic Realities. New York: Harper Torchbooks, 1960 [1957], 243.

Chapter 46

Judith Weisenfeld

PROJECTING BLACKNESS

African-American Religion in the Hollywood Imagination

FILM AND OTHER ASPECTS of visual culture prove very effective in helping to produce and maintain race because of the profoundly visual nature of racial construction. Those of us who have been formed in the cultural context of the United States, for example, are trained to look and, through looking, to discern the racial location of the people we view. And, for most of us, what we believe we learn from this internalized and often unconscious way of looking helps us decide how to proceed in relation to the people our eye evaluates. Even those who resist acting in ways that are expected in a racially stratified system (e.g. by accepting and internalizing racial hierarchy) are, nevertheless, aware of the power of the structuring mechanism of race. Once inside a racialized system, the gaze of some racialized people is necessarily empowered and empowering while others are not permitted to look, or to define the terms for visual interaction. Those empowered to look also assume the power to categorize and racialize. Because "race" as we know it is so fundamentally an epistemological product of the West, it certainly makes sense that it relies profoundly on the visual – generally taken to be the most privileged sense in the Western consciousness. Oyeronke Oyewumi argues that the West privileges the body (a move that is a prerequisite to the development of racial categories) because "the world is primarily perceived by sight. . . . The gaze is an invitation to differentiate." But the centrality of the body in Western thought also stands alongside the insistence that Western rationality has subordinated the body, which then becomes the province of the non-rational other. " 'Bodylessness,' " Oyewumi writes,

> has been a precondition of rational thought. Women, primitives, Jews, Africans, the poor, and all those qualified for the label "different" in varying historical epochs have been considered to be the embodied, dominated therefore by instinct and affect, reason being beyond them. They are the Other, and the Other is a body.[1]

The "film eye" has participated fully in this process of racializing through differentiation and through the privileging of some perspectives over others, and by valuing as aesthetically pleasing some bodies and not others.

Historians of American religion have only just begun to explore the impact of the moving image on twentieth-century American religious life. Recent scholarship on religion and American visual and material culture has focused, for example, on Protestant iconography, on the functions of material culture in the homes of religious individuals, and on understanding particularly religious ways of viewing. Film, which is such a profoundly affecting medium, and one in which filmmakers have often engaged religious themes, has been comparatively less studied. In addition to producing scores of Bible films and religious epics, Hollywood studios and independent filmmakers have utilized religious issues, characters, and conflicts as subject matter for American movies since cinema's earliest days. The variety of uses of religion in American film, particularly in relation to the projection of racial categories, calls out for serious attention. Margaret Miles has rightly argued that we must be careful to differentiate between the power of the devotional image and that of images from mass media, but at the same time she insists that we must take seriously the ways the conventions of mass media influence viewers with regard to religious issues. There are, in fact, many instances in the history of American film in which filmmakers have produced movies with explicitly religious goals in mind, presenting them as devotional images for use with confessional audiences. More commonly, the commercial film industry has deployed images of religiosity as part of its "crucial role in [the] construction . . . representation/re-presentation, and . . . transmission" of particular understandings of American identity.

[. . .]

In this essay, I use Metro-Goldwyn-Mayer's 1929 film *Hallelujah* – a significant signpost on the Hollywood landscape of representations of blackness and black religiosity in this period – to disclose and examine patterns in American popular culture traditions of racializing religion. *Hallelujah* marked both a solidi-fying and a transformation of a set of traditional approaches to representing blackness in American popular culture, moving away from using black religion almost exclusively for comedic or horror purposes and instead exploring its dramatic possibilities. Metro-Goldwyn-Mayer's strategy of presenting this nar-rative dramatic film as "authentic" and as containing documentary truth based on the observation of blacks by a Southern white man is indispensable to the pattern that it set. The aesthetic of primitive black religion that *Hallelujah* presents becomes immediately sanctioned by this discourse of authenticity. In signifi-cant ways *Hallelujah* conformed to the conventional ways in which American literature, art, and theater have figured people of African descent as "natural," as opposed to reasonable; childlike and therefore unfit for full citizenship; and inherently religious in ways that are inextricably linked to sexual expression. *Hallelujah* stands as an instructive example of the Hollywood approach to encod-ing religion as a central constitutive component of the construction of race. In this, and in the other "all-colored cast" films of the period, understanding African-American religion is fundamental to interpreting the moral valence of blackness in the United States. The film encourages viewers to believe that they cannot properly locate African Americans on the American social and political landscape without first consuming the spectacle of black religious practice. The conclusion toward which the film propels viewers insists that a true under-standing of African-American religious expression requires that whites forever exclude African Americans from access to full citizenship.

[. . .]

Religion, race, and sexuality

When viewers first meet Zeke (Daniel L. Haynes), Vidor's [King Vidor was the director of *Hallelujah*] main character, he is not seeking to become a religious leader – a status he achieves in the course of a wake for his brother, whose death has resulted from Zeke's neglect – nor does he seem to desire anything other than simple pleasures and his family's happiness. Early in the film, Vidor estab-lishes Zeke's family context as one in which daily life needs are simple and religion is important, as he shows the members of the family reading the Bible aloud after a long day's work in the cotton fields. The interactions among Mammy (Fanny Belle DeKnight), Pappy (Harry Gray), and their children in these early scenes situate the family as generally religious. Vidor establishes Pappy's position as a religious leader in a larger community when Adam and Eve, along with their eleven children, visit and ask him to officiate at their wedding. Pappy notes with some dismay that "the damage is all done" but relents, concluding that "it's never too late to do the will of the Lord."[2] When Mammy congratulates them on finally getting around to "doing the right thing," Eve ties the decision to marry to her sense of herself as a respectable woman, insisting that she has always been so and wants to avoid any implication otherwise.

In this opening framing sequence, Vidor appears to be particularly interested in the question of whether the moral character of blackness can be accommodated to American national identity. Zeke, Mammy, and Pappy become central to his exploration of this issue, and his conclusion requires the characters to remain located in the strangely utopic cotton fields of the deep South, which he understands to be the natural environs of the American Negro. In this view, urbanization and cultural transformations that move blacks away from the rural can only be damaging because these processes might lead African Americans to imagine themselves as other than a primitive subculture within American society. Mammy's response to Eve's assertion of respectability strikes one of the film's central themes for the first time and emphasizes the film's perspective that the character of blacks is fixed and irredeemable despite their best efforts to act in ways contrary to that fundamental racialized nature.

In the context of the wedding, Vidor first reveals Zeke's inexorable conflation of religion and sexuality. As Adam, Eve, Mammy, and Pappy prepare for the wedding, Zeke follows Rose (Victoria Spivey), his adopted sister, into the living room. When Zeke enters the room, Rose is sitting at a small organ and begins to play the wedding march. We see Rose from behind as she sways from left to right on the stool and as Zeke advances toward her. Rose, unaware that Zeke is behind her, completes the song and leans toward the window to listen to Pappy performing the ceremony. Vidor cuts to a close-up of Zeke's face as he approaches Rose from behind. He breathes heavily and the expression on his face is clearly one of desire. We see Rose listening, still unaware that Zeke is in the room. Then, in a particularly intense sequence, Vidor shoots from Zeke's point of view and we see his hand reaching out to Rose's shoulder. Innocently, Rose turns around and looks in Zeke's direction. At first she seems happy to see him but alarm soon registers on her face. As Vidor cuts to a wider shot of Rose sitting and Zeke standing, we hear Pappy outside explaining to the bride and groom that marriage is like the mystical union between Christ and his church. Just then Zeke insists that Rose kiss him and, as she stands up and begins to back away, grabs her and draws her to him. As Rose begs Zeke to let her go, he pulls her close and kisses her, and, while she is clearly uncomfortable, she does not struggle. Zeke suddenly backs away from Rose and clutches his chest, looking shocked at what he has done. When they are called to come outside to celebrate the conclusion of the wedding ceremony. Zeke apologizes to Rose, saying, "It looks like the devil's in me here tonight." Rose readily forgives him.

The wedding segment is characterized by a number of powerful juxtapositions between marriage understood as a sacred institution on the one hand and the desire for illicit sexuality on the other. As I have already mentioned, Vidor introduces the encounter between Zeke and Rose in connection with Adam and Eve's announced desire for a wedding ceremony, despite having been together long enough to have produced many children. Pappy conducts the ceremony under a tree in the backyard, no doubt a reference to the tree in the Garden of Eden, given the deliberate selection of the names Adam and Eve. The sanctification of the couple's relationship, one already marred by illicit sex, takes place in the shadow of the symbol of the fall of humanity. Vidor may also have made subtle reference to the ascendancy of sexual desire over the sanctity of marriage in his positioning of Zeke and Rose in relation to one another. When Rose sits at the organ with her back to Zeke, an inverted broom leaning against the wall divides the frame with Rose to its left and Zeke to its right. The broom is a potent symbol in African-American history. Denied legally recognized marriage ceremonies, enslaved African-American men and women frequently conducted a ritual to mark their commitment to one another that involved jumping a broomstick. Vidor's use of an inverted broom in the frame emphasizes his view that sexuality compromises these characters' religious commitment.[3]

Vidor does not remain at the level of simply noting an association between religious and sexual expression for African Americans – as in the wedding scene – but proceeds to locate a profoundly sexualized religion at the center of African-American ritual. For example, when Zeke baptizes Chick after she is converted under his preaching at a revival, she interprets her religious experience in sexualized terms and in terms of her relationship to Zeke rather than to God or Jesus. As she is being dunked in the river, she cries out, "I have been a wicked woman. Oh, I've been a wicked woman but I'm sanctified now. Hallelujah. All because of you, brother Zekiel. Keep me good, keep me good, don't let me sin no more." And later, when Hot Shot (William E. Fountaine), her former lover, ridicules her conversion, she tells him that her soul has been "washed in the spring of the Lamb." He responds that she's been "washed in fires of the devil," insisting that she mistakes sexual desire for spiritual transformation. Chick objects to Hot Shot's attempt to convince her to continue in the con game with him and insists that no one will "keep [her] from the protecting arms of Brother Zekiel." At her baptism Chick becomes completely lost in religious ecstasy, and, to the dismay of his family and followers, Zeke carries her out of the water and into a nearby tent. He is clearly affected by his proximity to Chick and by her sexualized moans. Vidor cuts to the interior of the tent as Mammy enters. We cannot see Zeke and Chick but hear her persistent moaning. The camera cuts to Chick lying on a cot, moaning in religious and sexual ecstasy, and Zeke embracing her and wildly kissing her neck. Mammy sends Zeke off, ashamed of himself, and chastises Chick, calling her a hypocrite and telling her that she's got more religion than is good for her. From this point on, neither Zeke nor Chick can seem to separate sexual expression from religious experience.

The most striking and profoundly articulated section of the film in which Vidor weds African-American religion to sexuality takes place at the evening revival following the baptism. The set for the revival is a large, open, barn-like structure with a stage at the front, on which Zeke and his family stand. The room is darkened, but the available light casts shadows on the walls. Zeke preaches a short sermon promising to fight the devil on behalf of his people. Following the sermon the people begin to sing, from a circle, and move slowly around the room in a counterclockwise direction. We hear the sound of women wailing with emotion as it becomes clear that Chick stands at the center of the crowd, deeply involved in the emotion and physicality of the worship. Chick bounces in time to the music, with her arms raised, moving up and down, bending her knees. Following a close-up of Chick dancing ecstatically, Vidor cuts to a medium close-up of Zeke looking down at Chick from his position on the stage, his eyes wide with desire. Vidor then repeats this exchange, following with a close-up of Rose, and later one of Mammy and then of Pappy, all clearly suspicious of Chick's intentions. Chick moves toward Zeke, stands directly in front of him, and grasps his leg, as he attempts to control himself. Chick motions with her head for Zeke to join her, and he steps down from the platform, bobbing up and down in the same manner that Chick has been. Zeke and Chick are now at the center of the circle, bending their knees in time to the music and moving in a clearly sexual manner. At one point, Chick looks at Zeke intensely, takes his hand, and puts the base of his thumb in her mouth, emphasizing the sexual nature of this worship. Eventually, Chick leaves the building, with Zeke following close behind, and the two run off into the woods. This scene serves as the culmination of a number of scenes in which Zeke and Chick commit themselves to resisting sexual temptation and yet find that religious expression leads them, inevitably, to sexual expression.

Music is an integral part of the way the film insists on African Americans' conflation of religion and sex in ways that Vidor argues necessarily marginalizes them from American political and social power. Music inaugurates and accompanies much of the religious frenzy and, outside of the religious contexts in the film, helps to present the characters as carefree children. At the same time, however, the film's music is often extremely compelling and enriches the high-quality visual elements. As a folk musical, *Hallelujah* integrates music into the story in a seamless way, relying on contexts in which people might naturally sing – at work in the fields, performing household chores, at religious services, and so on.[4] With the exception of "At the End of the Road," written by Irving Berlin, most of the film's music comes from African-American contexts, particularly traditional spirituals and blues. Vidor hired Eva Jessye, a college-educated former teacher and former member of the editorial staff of the *Baltimore Afro-American*, as the film's musical director. In an article published some months before the film's release, Jessye argued that music would be central to the film's power and took special pride in the variety of "Negro music" included and in her work as arranger and conductor for Baltimore's Dixie Jubilee Singers, featured on the soundtrack.[5] Many black commentators on the film noted its effective use of spirituals. W. E. B. Du Bois, in his review in the NAACP's paper *The Crisis*, longed for even more traditional music instead of the Irving Berlin "theme-song" but conceded that "the world is not as crazy about Negro folk songs as I am."[6] Berlin's song "At the End of the Road," which tells of happiness and redemption in the future, anchors the film's presentation of music, and in some ways the film positions Berlin's interpretation of "jazz" or of black music as being just as authentically black as the spirituals.[7]

Spirituals and the blues function in expected ways in the film to draw a contrast between religious life and worldliness, as well as to authenticate *Hallelujah*'s portrayal of black life. In addition, the film contains a number of extremely moving moments in which Mammy sings traditional folk songs or sings extemporaneously, both underscoring the potential of the folk musical to tap "the transforming power of memory."[8] Early on, Mammy sings "All the Pretty Little Horses" while rocking her small children to sleep, each in turn. Later in the film, she vocalizes her distress as she senses something amiss (and will soon learn of the death of her son), chanting, "Lord, have mercy on my soul."[9] At the same time that folk songs and spirituals lend an air of dignity to some of the characters, the coupling of the spirituals with "tom-tom" drums signals the danger of sexuality. Indeed, the first sound one hears as the film begins – even as the screen remains black – is that of a distant drum, marking the characters and narrative to follow as primitive and probably unable to be redeemed or elevated.

[. . .]

Regardless of the particular stylistic or ideological approach, Hollywood imaginings of African-American religion, along with its representations in literature and music, became especially contested ground, as black intellectuals negotiated their varied relationships to black folk cultures and did so in light of mainstream popular culture's commodification and re-presentation of elements of that culture. Writing in *The Crisis*, Loren Miller, a Los Angeles based civil rights attorney, bemoaned the nagging presence of "Uncle Tom in Hollywood" in a system that resulted in black audiences cheering for the white hero who rescues the blonde heroine from "savage" Africans and consuming newsreels that "poke fun at Negro revivals or baptisings." Miller argued forcefully that African Americans should take very seriously the impact of media on American political and social life.

> The cumulative effect of constant picturization of this kind is tremendously effective in shaping racial attitudes. Hollywood products are seen in every nook and corner of the world. Millions of non-residents of the United States depend almost entirely on the movies for their knowledge of Negro life, as those who have been abroad can testify. Other millions of white Americans of all ages confirm their beliefs about Negroes at the neighborhood theaters while Negroes themselves fortify their inferiority complex by seeing themselves always cast as the underdog to be laughed at or despised.[10]

While *Hallelujah* did not inaugurate the American cinema's exploration of racialized religion, the film did help to define critical patterns for early sound film that have contributed to the medium's ongoing engagement of race and of religion. The complicated issues that many critics of *Hallelujah* raised with regard to film's impact on Americans' understandings of race remain with us today, as American popular culture frequently uses religious contexts as primary settings for African-American characters.[11] As with *Hallelujah* and the other classical Hollywood "all-colored cast" films, the religious context in these modern iterations serves both to attempt to chart the place of African Americans on the U.S. political and social landscape and to explore the moral valence of blackness. Such projections of black religion have participated in the maintenance of racial hierarchy and in the process of defining American religion in ways that explicitly marginalize – politically, socially, and religiously – forms of religiosity linked with blackness. Never simply inconsequential entertainment, American film has been a vitally important arena for inculcating understandings of racialized religion, both for Americans and for audiences of American films around the world.

Notes

1   Daniel Bernardi, ed., *The Birth of Whiteness: Race and the Emergence of U.S. Cinema* (New Brunswick, N.J.: Rutgers University Press, 1996), 7. I use the term *racializing* to insist on the ongoing process of constructing racial categories and to avoid any implication of races as "natural" entities. Also see Daniel Bernardi, ed., *Classic Hollywood, Classic Whiteness* (Minneapolis: University of Minnesota Press, 2001); Matthew Bernstein and Gaylyn Studlar, eds., *Visions of the East: Orientalism in Film* (New Brunswick, N.J.: Rutgers University Press, 1997); Lola Young, *Fear of the Dark: "Race," Gender and Sexuality in the Cinema* (New York: Routledge, 1996); James Snead, *White Screens, Black Images: Hollywood from the Dark Side*, edited by Colin MacCabe and Cornel West (New York: Routledge, 1994); Randall M. Miller, *The Kaleidoscopic Lens: How Hollywood Views Ethnic Groups* (Englewood, N.J.: Ozer, 1980). Very few of these works recognize religion as an integral part of the constitution of racial categories in the movies, which is the major concern of my forthcoming full-length study on African-American religion in American film from 1929 to 1950 (University of California Press).

2   The classical Hollywood cinema is defined by both stylistic markers and particular practices of production and exhibition. Although the boundaries of the period can be set in a variety of ways, Bordwell, Staiger, and Thompson argue that the classical Hollywood system was in place from 1917 until 1960. They assert that the system involved a particular style of narrative that emphasizes character and motivation, causation, and the creation of a coherent world in the use of space, composition, sound, and editing and that the style emphasizes a realistic presentation of the narrative. In addition, the vertically integrated studio system in which studios controlled production, distribution, and exhibition of films prevailed. See David Bordwell, Kristin Thompson, and Janet Staiger, *The Classical Hollywood Cinema: Film Style and Mode of Production to 1960* (New York: Columbia University Press, 1985).

3   See Robyn Wiegman, *American Anatomies: Theorizing Race and Gender, New Americanists* (Durham, N.C.: Duke University Press, 1995), for a sustained discussion of the development of racial categones in the United States.

4   Young, *Fear of the Dark*, 40.

5   Oyeronke Oyewumi, *The Invention of Women: Making an African Sense of Western Gender Discourses*. Minneapolis: University of Minnesota, 1997, 2.

6   Oyewumi, *The Invention of Women*, 3, 14.

7   John Belton, ed., *Movies and Mass Culture*. New Brunswick, N.J.: Rutgers University Press, 1996, 1.

8   Quotations represent my own transcriptions of the dialogue from the film.

9   W.E.B. Du Bois, "Hallelujah: King Vidor's All-Talking Picture," *Crisis*, October 1929.

10   Rick Altman, *The American Film Musical*. Bloomington: Indiana University Press, 1978, 272.

11   Loren Miller, "Uncle Tom in Hollywood," *Crisis*, November 1934, 329–330.

PART 4

Theological and Biblical Approaches to Analyzing Film

INTRODUCTION

ONE OF THE MOST RAPID areas of growth in the study of religion and film is related to theological and biblical studies. Numerous academics trained as theologians or biblical scholars have turned their critical attention towards the cinema. This is often born out of a passion for movies and a desire to draw upon a communicative form which their students and readers already know well. Many of the readings in the first part of this section (Theological Dialogues) are founded on the assumption that films have the potential to provoke theological dialogue and questioning. Many of those in the second part (Biblical Connections) are examples of writers who believe that films have the capacity to illuminate scriptural texts and vice versa. By contrast with some of cinema's most vocal critics, such as those who spoke of the "Devil's Camera" in part 1, many of these writers explore film's ability to contribute to theological education and to thoughtful interpretations of biblical texts.

Nevertheless, this is far from a triumphalistic pilgrimage to Hollywood or other centers of film production. Several of the following authors highlight the illusory quality of the flickering screen as a place to find God or even signs of the sacred. For example, in *Catching Light: Looking for God in the Movies* (2004) (reading 47), Roy Anker, a professor of English, suggests that many of the films he discusses eschew attempting to name God explicitly, and instead show glimpses of what he describes as the Light. The illusory quality of film is also highlighted by Clive Marsh in his book *Cinema* and Sentiment (2004). The suspension of disbelief is willingly undertaken by many viewers as they enter what Marsh describes as the "house of illusions." For Marsh illusion is only one of several elements in the reception process, which also include: emotion, embodiment, visuality and attentiveness. Part of the significance of Marsh's overall argument is that he explores the theological significance not only of what the film does to the audience, but also what the audience does with the film. In the reading offered here we provide one of Marsh's three case studies, in which he explores the theological significance of film-viewing habits and predispositions towards specific genres such as romantic comedies (reading 50).

The turn towards the audience is also to be found in the work of Christopher Deacy. In Faith in Film (2005) he seeks to "demonstrate, some of the most fertile and intellectually challenging sites of religious significance in contemporary western culture can be located in the medium of film" (reading 48). Deacy's claim is balanced by his suggestion, earlier in his book, that escapist, populist films which are steeped in illusion may "preclude a theological reading", whereas films which "evince social or psychological realism or offer authentic character development" provide a richer ground for exploration. While Marsh and Deacy may agree over the importance of understanding the diverse nature of audiences, they appear to have different views as to the usefulness for theology of blockbuster films which rely on illusion. Another theologian, Gerard Loughlin, goes further and acknowledges that cinema "can be viewed as a quasi-religious practice" (reading 52). In his book, Alien Sex: The Body and Desire in Cinema and Theology, Loughlin explores the possibility of doing "theology in and through film, and through writing on film." He does this through considering specific parallels between church and cinema, particularly in relation to desire, sexuality and the body. The way in which the cinema can re-present saintly bodies and lives is considered in detail by Theresa Sanders in Celluloid Saints (2002). Sanders offers her readers numerous examples for reflecting critically on the ways in which cinema contributes to the "contemporary process of saint-making" (reading 54).

The approach which dominates these and many other recent studies, which bring together film and theology, is best summed up by one word: dialogue. This process is at the heart of Robert Johnston's book, Reel Spirituality: Theology and Film in Dialogue (2000). He provides a matrix for categorizing different approaches, from avoidance or caution to appropriation or belief in cinema as a place of divine encounter (reading 49). The dialogical process is not without its critics,[1] but the attempt to demarcate distinct approaches is a common one and reflects an increasing desire to bring some order to a disparate area of study. In his edited collection of essays, *New Image of Religious Film*, May also provides a map for "contemporary theories regarding the interpretation of religious film." He sets them out in what he believes is their "order of emergence." They are religious discrimination, visibility, dialogue, humanism, and aesthetics. May's particular contribution is in this final category of "religious aesthetics," which moves beyond concern with cinematic morality, "explicit religious elements or humanistic themes" to highlight the "religious significance in terms of cinema's art." This move places him closer to Marsh's inclusive vision than to Deacy's critical analysis and allows May to conclude that "any film, even those without explicit religious elements, can still be considered as potentially religious" (reading 51). No reader on religion and film would be complete without some consideration of one of the most successful religious films in the history of cinema: *The Passion of the Christ* (2003). Jolyon Mitchell and S. Brent Plate consider how this movie provoked lively debates in a number of spheres. They investigate not only the controversies over its supposed anti-Semitism and use of extreme violence, but also the way in which many scholars have entered into critical dialogue with this film (reading 53).

The metaphor of dialogue is not far from the surface of the essays in the second part of this section on biblical connections. Here are several different examples of intertextuality. Adele Reinhartz uses *Scripture on the Silver Screen* (2003) to assist in the development of "biblical literacy" (reading 59). Larry Kreitzer is by training a biblical scholar, but has has made his name through exploring the ways film and fiction can illuminate biblical texts. To date Kreitzer has produced four books which aim to enable "a dialogue to take place between the biblical text, great works of literature, and that most persuasive of modern art forms, the cinema." He describes this process as "reversing the hermeneutical flow." In essence this triadic approach means using classic works of literature and their cinematic interpretations as a way of shedding fresh light on biblical passages (reading 58). Robert Jewett is another biblical scholar who has immersed himself in the world of film criticism. His stated motivation and method are different from Kreitzer's. In his first two books on film he uses St Paul as a conversation partner with specific movies, claiming that, given Paul's missionary desire to be all things to all people, if there had been film in his day Paul would also have engaged with film criticism. Instead of Kreitzer's triadic approach he uses a two-way "interpretative arch," which intends to treat both biblical and cinematic texts with exegetical respect (reading 56). He often moves the reader from the world of the film text to the world of the biblical text and back again. This dynamic movement is to be found in Eric Christianson's essay connecting Film Noir with narratives in the Hebrew Bible (reading 55), J. Cheryl Exum's piece on David and Bathsheba and the male cinematic and literary gaze (reading 57), and Erin Runions' consideration of "identification and resistance in the bible and film" from her book entitled *How Hysterical* (reading 60). These accounts of film have partly emerged out of the careful study of Jewish and Christian texts. While this literary predisposition of many of the writers inevitably informs their interpretations, there is an increased awareness of the importance of treating film on its own terms rather than imposing standards from the worlds of literary or textual criticism.

Note

1   See, for example, Melanie Wright, *Religion and Film*, 2007, 15–16

PART 4.A

Theological Dialogues

Chapter 47

Roy Anker

CATCHING LIGHT
Looking for God in the Movies

IN CONTEMPORARY CINEMA, most encounters with Light happen to quite ordinary people who seem to stray into its path, and Light, literally or metaphorically, encompasses them, usually much to their surprise. That is not to say that they walk away blind or dumb, as was the case with St. Paul or the father of John the Baptist. It is not news to anyone that there are very rare instances of breathtaking displays, at least in Western culture, when God has made God's presence known – has shown up and shown off, as it were – conspicuously and undeniably: in floods and rainbows, in burning bushes and plagues, in wine from water and healings aplenty. Yet, instead of trying to catch the miraculous and unmediated Light for the screen, filmmakers have for the most part taken a different approach, one more complex, demanding, and cogent. In short, instead of big displays, filmmakers have largely focused on chronicling and analyzing the encounter of ordinary people with the divine. The filmmakers' gaze fixes on how God comes and how the divine presence affects those it strikes. Very often it is only by tracking the response of recipients of that presence that the reality and nature of God is made clear. In the depiction of human behavior, the filmmaker and audience detect the presence of the divine by witnessing some event, such as in Spielberg's *Close Encounters of the Third Kind*, or by deducing its nature from the kind of response God evokes. This is the drama of the apprehension of God, the reaction of people as they run into the different displays of the Holy in innumerable ways. In other words, Light refracts through a human prism, and the filmmaker refracts that light through the lens.

Light works its way through to recognition, and audiences see Light as the characters themselves come, by some means or another, to see or sense Light (or it may be in sound, as in Krzysztof Kieslowski's *Three Colors: Blue* [1993] or David Puttnam's *The Mission* [1986]). The camera makes known the reality of God by trying to portray what the character perceives and by tracking the visible consequences as the characters wrestle with it in mind, heart, and soul, that subjective domain "where the meanings are," as Emily Dickinson put it. That is a demanding venture because the camera cannot see very far into personal interior realities; as witness and narrator, the best the camera can do is suggest the tangled psychic realities that contend and roil within mind and soul. But astonishment, anguish, tears, and especially laughter can show a great deal about the nature of the God who has variously whispered, sung, blinded, warmed, or rescued ordinary people as they've traveled their way. The human response functions as a kind of photographic plate, hazy and distorted though it may be, on which light has registered. Indeed, people themselves are far from ideal receptors, because they are vain, overeager, expropriating, tough-skinned, thick-headed, or, as is sometimes the case, all of the above.

Furthermore, there is the problem of the chariness of God: as we have seen, God showed Moses but the hem of his raiment – for reasons of safety. Or God speaks in the still small voice that is barely distinguishable from the thousand other mutterings of the noisy self. In Christianity, for example, Jesus' miracles tended to be small-scale and personal, and Jesus went out of his way to keep them quiet, studiously avoiding the melodramatic poses of Moses in Egypt or on Sinai. Quiet revelations often make a profound difference in the recipient's experience of life itself. Many of the world's religions argue that when this Light comes, even in quiet inward measures, it fully overtakes the self, clearing the mind, warming the heart, exulting the soul, and, in the process, fundamentally reorienting the self toward hopefulness, love, and ecstasy.

Even so, religious fear and trembling or ecstasy in union with God do not usually look plausible on the screen. Words in screenplays go a way to dissipate the divine improbability or the soul's opacity; but many words in movies soon overwhelm or violate the medium, quickly turning it into a stage play or a novel, and viewers usually complain about it. In filling this expressive "void," cinema as an art form features other avenues of conveyance: events and images carry the burden of telling the tale (this does not mean that filmgoers are particularly patient with a film's absence of verbal explanation either). Acting helps as well, giving credibility to the playing of Light in the self. And the language of the medium itself carries the rest: production design, setting, costuming, music, lighting, and a host of camera strategies – all helping to make visible those interior apprehensions that the camera cannot record. No matter how much viewers want movies to both show and tell, that is, using sufficient words to make everything clear (as if words alone can do that), it is important to allow filmmakers to tell their stories as they wish, giving the benefit of the doubt long enough for a particular manner of cinematic "speech," or what is often called "style," to work its way with the viewer. Needless to say, storytelling strategies differ greatly from film crew to film crew, sometimes resulting in legendary fights and firings.

The same is true for the differences between writers and directors (though many of the filmmakers whose works I discuss here are "auteurs," those who take on both tasks of writing and directing). Even though they may share thematic similarities, filmmakers with common interests can differ greatly in subject matter and cinematic style, as is the case with, say, Spielberg and Lawrence Kasdan. Film is an expansive and plastic medium, and thus it is able to flex and stretch, potentially at least, to as many different "takes" on human experience as there are writers and directors. In this regard – again, as many of the films treated here suggest – the medium is very much in its infancy, exploring and innovating the formal capacities of cinematic storytelling in sometimes astonishing ways. The best filmmakers show wonderful adventurousness in the stories they try to tell and in the means they improvise to make their stories enticing and affecting.

Usually when Light does show, the display tends towards the fleeting, subtle, and elusive, so much so that many characters wrestle with the authenticity of their own experience, and what largely ends up on the screen is a filmmaker's impression of individual apprehension and pursuit of the divine. Fortunately, despite its limitations, film has at its disposal virtually all the resources of all the fine arts: storytelling, drama, the visual arts in form and color, and music – all brewed together in one aesthetic kettle. As a highly collaborative enterprise, filmmaking marshals a startling variety of the traditional arts in limning humanity's multitudinous engagements with Light and uses them within the seemingly limitless capacities of modern technology. So the art piece becomes a tool of analysis, of reflection and understanding, going as far as possible with available representational or logical tools to comprehend the mystery. Artists seem to have the special impulse to recapture or represent Light itself as fully as possible – or at least the experience of being enveloped by Light, which is above and beyond the ordinary. Re-creating that experience allows them and their audiences to hang onto something of the original glowing ember.

Chapter 48

Christopher Deacy

FAITH IN FILM

New ways forward

WHILE IT WOULD be facile to suggest that to read film through a Christian or theological lens amounts in any way to a definitive or authoritative reading, it has been my aim in this book to demonstrate how, where and to what extent a theological interpretation of film may be seen to be both tenable and as having much to offer to scholarship. At the end of the day, audiences will read films in a multiplicity of different ways, and some interpretations will carry more weight and influence than others. But, it is hoped that a study such as this can help to redress the balance whereby, for far too long, the study of film from a religious or theological point of view has been comprehensively overlooked – if not, indeed, shunned – by many commentators, critics and academics. As Joel Martin observed in 1995, if religion is dealt with at all in film studies it is as a purely 'peripheral phenomenon in contemporary social organization' (Martin, 1995, p. 2) where the forces of secularization are taken for granted. Likewise, in the words of Gaye Ortiz, writing three years later, whenever a new book on theology and film is published – and there were at least five in 1997 alone – 'the academics in film studies titter and scornfully dismiss churchy types who dare to bring God into the rarified presence of cinematic discourse' (Ortiz, 1998, p. 173). Although the field of religion and film has advanced significantly in the years since then, it has yet to make an impact on the way film studies is practised as a discipline. I hope that this state of affairs will change in due course. No matter how felicitous readings of film through the lens of feminism, poststructuralism, postmodernism, homosexuality or Marxism happen to be, there is a substantial amount of empirical evidence to demonstrate that a religious reading of film should be at the cutting edge, rather than on the periphery, of contemporary scholarly activity.

Once it is accepted that film and theology can be very creative dialogue-partners, all sorts of fecund possibilities are opened up. While it is not surprising that overtly religious films such as Mel Gibson's *The Passion of the Christ* (2004) receive the lion's share of publicity, it has been my aim in this book to outline alternative sites of religiosity, and to suggest that, if a line of demarcation can be drawn between an 'objectively' religious film and an ostensibly 'secular' movie – the classic sacred versus profane distinction – it is a very blurred, broken and permeable one. Questions of religious faith arise in some of the most surprising and unexpected places, even to the point that Scorsese's *Cape Fear* (1991) – which examines the theme of redemption through suffering in the form of Robert De Niro's Bible-spouting ex-convict who exacts divine vengeance in order to coerce the lawyer who betrayed him into confessing his sins – and M. Night Shyamalan's *Signs* (2002) – in which Mel Gibson plays a lapsed Pennsylvanian minister who has to face a metaphysical and spiritual conundrum of literally extra-terrestrial magnitude – are no less deserving the attention of the theologian or religious studies specialist than the somewhat hackneyed and predictable controversies induced by Gibson's *Passion* and Scorsese's *Last Temptation*. Any further research that is undertaken in this area needs to fully embrace what the secular marketplace has to offer. By all means utilize the likes of Gibson's *Passion*, but do not think for a moment that any creative conversation that has the potential to take place between theology and film should operate within such narrow and confined parameters.

The important thing is to view each film on its own merits. That way, one does not fall into the trap of having to make false and unworkable distinctions between different films, whereby one film is deemed more worthy of the theologian's attention than another simply by virtue of the fact that its subject matter is, superficially at least, 'explicitly' theological. As I have sought to demonstrate in this book, to categorize one film as being 'explicitly' religious and another as either 'implicitly' religious or even 'non-religious' is overly simplistic and, taken to the extreme, ends up with the situation whereby only biblical epics or films which are made for polemical or confessional purposes are deemed suitable for discussion, while everything else simply does not warrant serious scrutiny. I encountered this problem of 'labelling' at first-hand when, in August 2000, I sat on the Ecumenical Jury of the 53rd Locarno

International Film Festival in Switzerland. In awarding our prize at the end of the competition to a Chinese film, *Baba* (Wang Shuo, 2000), what struck us most is that there appeared to be a clear exposition within the picture of Christian symbolism and values, including the use of the Christmas carol 'Silent Night', the backdrop of a Christian cathedral and the theme of sacrifice and atonement. Yet, when we spoke to the director, Wang Shuo, afterwards, he commented that the film's appropriation of such motifs was merely accidental and unintentional. This in no way diminishes for me the impact and power that the film has, but it does illustrate just how tenuous and discordant the distinction can be between the 'religious' and the 'secular'. In the past, when the primary focus of the academic study of film was on the auteur, any reading which went 'against the grain' of the director's vision would have been accorded a subordinate status. What I propose, however, is that if a 'secular' filmmaker creates a film which is perceived by some audiences to be redolent in theological significance, then, irrespective of the degree to which such an interpretation is alien to that filmmaker's aims and intentions, the efficacy and integrity of that testimony must not be disregarded.

This is not to say, however, that the insights presented in this book will be of use to all practitioners in the fields of theology and religious studies. Although a viable case can be made that the use of film can transform the way in which theology and religious studies is carried out, a word of caution is required. For the religious studies scholar interested in, say, Hindu life-cycle rituals, early Japanese Buddhism, medieval Jewish mysticism or any other of the host of specialisms that make up the discipline, it would be most inappropriate to suggest that films can, or should, be employed in their research in the same way as they might for, say, the Christian theologian seeking to gain an insight into the way in which a creative and challenging theological vision may be discerned in the midst of contemporary popular culture. Even within Christianity itself, there is by no means a universal acceptance that it is appropriate to enter into a dialogue with secular culture. The origins of this position can be traced back to the early Church, where, for Tertullian in the third century, Christianity should not allow itself to be contaminated by the environment around itself and should maintain its distinctive identity. Nowadays it finds expression in what William Romanowski identifies as the 'Condemnation approach' to popular culture, whereby film and pop music are deemed to be evil and must therefore be boycotted by God-fearing Christians (Romanowski, 2002, p. 12). Sympathy for this position can be found in Steve Peters' *Truth about Rock* (1998), as well as in the following observation by David Noebel with respect to The Beatles:

> They wanted to subvert Western culture. They were pro-drugs, pro-evolution, and pro-promiscuous sex; anti-Christ and more . . .

Rock music is a negation of soul, spirit and mind, and is destructive
to the body . . . The muscles are weakened, the heartbeat is affected,
and the adrenal glands and sex hormones are upset by continued
listening . . . It's also been shown that rock music destroys house
plants. If it destroys God's plants, what's it doing to young people?
(Quoted in Joseph, 1999, p. 3)

As Mark Joseph puts it, 'From the moment Elvis first swayed his hips and Bill
Haley rocked around the clock, rock and roll has been on a collision course
with millions of Americans . . . It was seen as the Devil's music and to be
avoided at all costs' (Joseph, 1999, pp. 1–2). Although I find this a dangerous
position to take – after all, it can lead to the Christian imagination being
constrained and impoverished, and it is hard to see how the Church is going to
perform its mission effectively if it is not able to communicate in the language
of the people – it does illustrate that there is a considerable diversity of perspectives within Christianity alone as to the manner and extent to which the secular
media can serviceably be used.

Moreover, it would be disingenuous not to acknowledge that, salient and
productive though a theological reading of film might be, there are countless
other disciplines which are capable of, and amenable to, entering into a creative dialogue with film. For example, many of the same texts that I have
employed in this study have much pertinent value for scholars working in the
field of philosophy. Although earlier I made a strong case for examining
Groundhog Day in the light of the Christian theme of redemption, there is no
reason why, say, a Heideggerean existentialist should not find in this film 'one
of the most cogent and intelligent extended metaphors for the central tenets of
humanist existentialism ever presented on a cinema screen' (Coniam, 2001,
p. 10). Rather than suggest, as Robert Jewett does, that Groundhog Day bears
witness to one of the central insights of Pauline theology, in that Phil Connors
is faced with the dilemma of either 'reaping the corruption of emptiness' or
'sowing to the spirit' and in so doing having the opportunity to reap eternal
life, from a philosophical point of view the film could be seen to epitomize
what Matthew Coniam calls 'the existential picture of life in a Godless universe' (ibid.). There is no right or wrong reading. Provided that a case can
be made for utilizing film as a resource in whatever academic discipline,
it is possible that all manner of new and innovative ways of 'doing' theology
or 'doing' philosophy (or for that matter 'doing' mathematics or 'doing'
archaeology) can be encountered.

From the point of view, however, of theology and religious studies, there is,
ultimately, something immensely significant about a 'secular' medium that has
the capacity to raise vital questions about the spiritual landscape and normative

values of western society at the turn of the millennium. Indeed, as this book has sought to demonstrate, some of the most fertile and intellectually challenging sites of religious significance in contemporary western culture can be located in the medium of film. The western religious consciousness has undergone an immense restructuring in recent decades and, despite its reaching its culturally definitive form in Christianity, scholars are being faced with a new challenge, one which involves coming to terms with the fact that people's hopes, fears, aspirations and anxieties – as traditionally expressed within Christianity through the language of sin, alienation and redemption – are increasingly being articulated through new vehicles of expression and outside traditionally demarcated boundaries of religious activity. It is quite possible for human beings to be inundated with religious stimuli without ever having attended a church service or belonged to a religious organization or community. Religion is, rather, implicit in many aspects of human life, to the extent that the film industry is one of many contemporary secular agencies that have taken on many of the functions that we would historically associate with traditional religious institutions.

It may be the case that not all Hollywood films amount to fertile repositories or conveyors of theological or religious significance, but it is in the medium of film that prominent expressions of religiosity and rich models and exemplars of Christian activity can be seen to flourish. Without disputing that there is much in popular culture that is trivial and banal, film has the capacity to stimulate serious theological reflection. *Groundhog Day*, *The Apartment*, *Nobody's Fool* and *The Crossing Guard* may not contain any explicitly religious subject matter but they do act as an agency through which audiences can come to a fuller understanding of how to address and engage with some of the fundamental issues and dilemmas that lie at the heart of human experience, and in particular with the universal human experience of sin, alienation and suffering. Accordingly, irrespective of whether a filmmaker is Christian or not, different audiences may choose to interpret a given film through a Christian lens just as a given novel or poem will always be susceptible to a plethora of different interpretations by its readers, regardless of whether those readings are sanctioned or expressly intended by the author. Escapist, fantasy films may be more in keeping with the interests and predilections of the majority of filmgoers, but, as the experience of *American Beauty* has shown, films which turn Hollywood convention on its head are not only capable of doing well commercially, provided that they receive a viable distribution, but they also have the capacity to resonate with and provoke the religious sensibilities of audiences. So long as there are films which enable an authentic encounter with our basic human condition to take place, then filmmakers will continue to be capable of making a serious and judicious contribution to theological and

religious reflection. There are thus viable grounds for supposing that theological activity has the capacity to be discerned and apprehended in the
so-called 'secular' arena, and that, in the medium of film in particular, robust
instances and manifestations of Christian activity may be found to be available
to cinema audiences.

Chapter 49

Robert K. Johnston

REEL SPIRITUALITY
Theology and film in dialogue

Theological approaches to film criticism [excerpts]

SINCE THE INVENTION of motion pictures a century ago,
one can observe five differing theological responses that the church has
made to film as it has learned from and has sought to influence Hollywood.
In the class on "Theology and Film," which I taught with Robert Banks, we
labeled these avoidance, caution, dialogue, appropriation, and divine encounter.[1]

These theological responses by the church to moviegoing can be shown
graphically on a linear timeline:

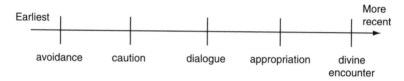

Figure 3.1 The Theologian/Critic's Posture

Although these approaches developed more or less chronologically over
the last seventy-five years or so, one can still find good contemporary representatives of all five of these types of theologian/critic. Moreover, as each approach
is more a type than a firm category, some theologians have adopted over time

multiple perspectives, while others have proven somewhat eclectic in their approach. Despite this fluidity, these options are nonetheless identifiable.

These same five theological approaches to Hollywood can also be graphed, using a matrix in order to show whether a given theologian/critic begins his or her reflection with the movie itself or with a theological position, and whether a given response centers on the movie ethically or aesthetically:

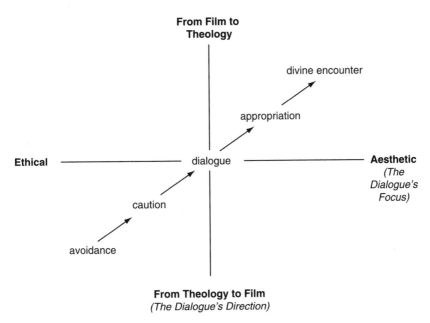

Figure 3.2 The Theologian/Critic's Approach

Theologians who articulate an avoidance strategy do so from an ethical posture (often their books even have words like "morality" and "values" in their titles) and always move from their given theological perspective to the film under consideration, not vice versa. On the other hand, those interested in exploring a divine encounter through film begin with the film itself and only in light of the film attempt to make theological judgments. When they do, moreover, the criticism is first of all aesthetic, not ethical, in nature.

Spread out along the diagonal that one can draw between these contrasting approaches are the three other positions. Those expressing caution take the film as film more seriously but still focus their responses on the film's ethical stance, beginning their deliberations from a biblical/theological posture. Those wishing for theological dialogue want theology to inform their filmviewing and filmviewing to inform their theology in a lively two-way conversation that is both ethical *and* aesthetic in nature. Those wanting to appropriate the movie's meaning start in their deliberations with the movie itself but bring their outside theological perspective more strongly into the conversation than those who would explore divine encounters. Both Jewish and Christian theologians/critics have often proven more eclectic in their approach than the graph might suggest. They have in practice made use of more than one of these approaches depending on the films being considered and the audience intended. (That not all persons fit neatly into a given category is typical of any typology, for these are simply artificial constructs to help organize data.) But many have tended in their theological criticism to use a dominant perspective toward the movies.

It is worth looking at each of these positions in some detail, for they will inform the remainder of our reflection in this book.

Avoidance

The stance of some Christians has been to continue the boycott mentality that characterized conservative Protestantism and Roman Catholicism of an earlier era. Writing in the forties in an introduction to Herbert Miles's book *Movies and Morals*, Hyman Appelman labeled movies to be "next to liquor, the outstanding menace to America and to the world."[2] Miles, if anything, was even stronger in his condemnation: "They [movies] are the organ of the devil, the idol of sinners, the sink of infamy, the stumbling block to human progress, the moral cancer of civilization, the Number One Enemy of Jesus Christ."[3] The best that Miles could say about Hollywood was, "There are some good teachings in the movies. Yes. And there is some good paper in the waste basket, but it is only to be used when it is impossible to secure paper from any other source."[4]

Such rhetoric seems to come from a bygone day, certainly one before the advent of television. But Carl McClain, writing for a Nazarene publishing house in 1970, expressed a similar sentiment: "I submit that a frequenter of the theatre or movie house cannot at the same time be a spiritual force for good, a vital Christian leader or Sunday school teacher."[5]

More typical today than such blanket condemnation, however, is the argument for a selective boycott of films judged morally objectionable. For example, writing to the organizers of the City of Angels Film Festival, Dr. Ted Baehr, chairman of the Christian Film and Television Commission, complained that the Festival had chosen to show Peter Weir's *The Year of Living Dangerously* (1982) and Martin Scorsese's *Taxi Driver* (1976). He attached to his memorandum several pages for the *Communist Manifesto* and complained that Weir's film "takes the side of the Communists in the Indonesian struggle for freedom from Communism. I was there at the time," he writes, "and can tell you first-hand that the communists were killing thousands of people, particularly Christians, and were not the good guys as portrayed in the film." He continues, "My question for *Taxi Driver* would be: What was it about the movie that influenced John Hinkley to shoot President Reagan? When you start to answer that question you will start to understand the spiritual significance of the movie, as you well know."[6] For Baehr, there is a great divide between much of Hollywood and the church. The religion portrayed is not Christianity but "materialism, consumerism, eroticism, hedonism, . . . humanism, . . . the cult of violence."[7] Many films should just not be shown, thinks Baehr. Or if they are, Christians should protest by not going to movie theaters and instead relying on videotapes, which they can selectively choose.

Similarly, Larry Poland has written of his leadership in boycotting *The Last Temptation of Christ* (1988). In his book *The Last Temptation of Hollywood*, which was rushed to press just months after the release of Martin Scorsese's film, Poland chronicles what he calls "this century's most passionate conflict between Christians and Hollywood."[8] What he calls "the hideous distortions of the person and work of Jesus," both in the novel by Nikos Kazantzakis[9] and in the screen-play by Paul Schrader, caused Poland and a small group of other concerned Christians eventually to organize a boycott that was partially effective.

Caution

A more common attitude among contemporary conservative Christians is that of caution, not avoidance. With the advent of television, few Christians continued to argue for abstinence as a viable strategy. But many remained worried over the entertainment industury's influence. Writing in 1974 for InterVarsity Press, Donald Drew asked whether a Christian should even go to movies. He answered with a cautious affirmative: "It is my conviction that a Christian, providing that his foundations are firm, should see films and become involved in the arts and other forms of knowledge. The Lordship of God in Christ must be seen to extend into all areas of life."[10] Having said this, Drew also advised his readers that "a Christian should enter the cinema with a solid grasp of who man is and what truth is."[11] The Christian viewer can watch movies, but carefully, from a clearly defined ethical and religious stance.

Lloyd Billingsley's book's title, *The Seductive Image*, suggests its content and approach. He writes that his "expectations of film are low" and rarely disappointed: "My basic posture toward film as a medium is increasingly skeptical, and any list of all-time favorites I could put together would be rather short. That said, I stress the medium's power, and add that to ignore it would be folly."[12] John Butler is similarly cynical and introduces his discussion of movies by saying that "the second part [of the book] goes to the movies with a look at some of the moral issues served up in between the popcorn and candy bars. Tips on choosing a movie and possibly saving up to five dollars by skipping that new movie, depending on where you live, are examined in chapter ten."[13]

In their arguments, Billingsley and Butler stay tightly within the Christian sphere, but their skeptical rhetoric is self-defeating with regard to influencing any serious moviegoer. I say this despite the obvious strength of their position in arguing for a necessary moral discrimination when it comes to critiquing a movie.

Michael Medved serves as a good example of a cautious but thoughtful critic of Hollywood's values. Although a faithful Jew, Medved does not assume a Jewish readership as he argues that by constantly pushing the ethical envelope, the entertainment world "encourages" (even if it does not cause) antisocial activity.[14] Though moviemaking might function within a contemporary cultural consensus of values, Hollywood also seeks to transform it. In chapter after chapter of his book Hollywood vs. America (1992), Medved wages war with Hollywood because he sees that movies promote promiscuity, malign marriage, encourage illegitimacy, and belittle parents. They are hostile to heroes, bash America, use foul language, often offend, and gravitate toward violence.

In his section entitled "The Attack on Religion," Medved argues that there is today a one-sided vicious stereotyping of the church. In the thirties and forties we had handsome stars who were lovable priests (e.g., Spencer Tracy in Boys Town [1938] and Bing Crosby in The Bells of St. Mary's [1945]), and there was a feeling of religious uplift in many movies. In the 1980s, by contrast, it was more typical to see Christians portrayed as crazed killers and the clergy as vicious, morally corrupt, and bizarre looking. Hollywood seems intent on affronting the religious sensibilities of ordinary Americans. Medved asks rhetorically, If movie after movie shows this, will not viewers begin to believe it? Anti-religious movies typically lose money, Medved notes, but moviemakers do not seem to care. They have an axe to grind.

Perhaps Medved has overstated his case.

[. . .]

In a 1997 essay, Medved recognizes recent positive changes since he wrote Hollywood vs. America in 1992. He notes that in the 1990s faithful Christians and Jews assumed prominent positions in Hollywood. After the "relentless religion-bashing of the last fifteen years" there has been a "shift to more supportive on-screen treatment of religious themes and characters." He concludes with this assessment: "Hollywood's current status still leaves vast room for improvement, but an exhilarating spirit of change – if not outright rebirth and revival – is already in the air."[15]

It is not just those on the religious "right" who suggest caution, however. Those on the religious "left" are sometimes equally suspicious. Margaret Miles, the dean of the Graduate Theological Union in Berkeley, seeks to identify and analyze the values imaged in films.[16] Hollywood, Miles recognizes, continues to shape our attitudes toward race, gender, class, and sexual orientation through its patterns, stereotypes, and symbolic markers. For example, it is often the male gaze that is captured by the camera's point of view. Even as a child, Miles understood from movie marquees that fat people were laughable, people of color were subservient, and beautiful heterosexual people were the norm. The portrayal of a set of values in this way is not "accidental or incidental to religious perspectives," she argues, "but, *as a concrete way religious perspectives are articulated*, are central to religious values."[17] Miles also notes, with Medved, that in its direct portrayals of religion, Hollywood is typically hostile to Christianity. A student of iconic art, Miles chides the motion picture industry for its inability to inspire religious devotion through the images it projects. Often, it seems able only to caricature fundamentalism, as in *The Rapture* (1991) and *The Handmaid's Tale* (1990).

Miles, like Medved, comes to film from an ethically driven theological stance, but she also seeks to be a student of the films she considers. Few films escape her critical pen. She understands *Thelma & Louise* (1991) to be a cautionary tale about the consequences of women trying to escape a male-dominated world. She castigates two recent "Jesus" movies, *Last Temptation of Christ* (1988) and *Jesus of Montreal* (1989), for not offering heroes to their audiences. And so on. Hers is a hermeneutics of suspicion. She views movies from her ethical/ theological point of view and judges whether or not they fit. Though she seeks to be a student of film, she does not try to see a movie on its own terms.

Miles and Medved have a sense of style and discrimination with regard to their movie judgments, even if this reader finds them overly suspicious and does not always agree with their conclusions on particular movies. Butler and Billingsley, on the other hand, seem overly controlled by dogma. All, however, come to film from a defined theological perspective and see a one-sided imbalance between Hollywood and the church, between movies and theology. For the most part, they see that movies are too often in the business of theological subversion. They thus advise caution for the religious viewer.

Dialogue

My comments about avoidance and caution should have been sufficient to signal the direction I believe Christian film criticism must go. Although theoretically the critical dialogue can begin anywhere along the continuum from avoidance to encounter, the danger of theological imperialism is high enough in practice that I would argue that Christian moviegoers should first view a movie on its own terms before entering into theological dialogue with it. The movie experience, like all play activities, functions best when it is a parenthesis within life's ongoingness. That is, when people enter the theater (or go to the opera or the ballpark, or play handball, or dance), they must, when at play, set aside the issues of the larger world around them and be caught up in the movie experience itself. Whether listening to Mozart or looking at a Woody Allen film, the audience must focus exclusively on the "present" of the experience, if it is to be authentic. In a sense, the real world must for a time "stand still." Moviegoers must give to the screen their "as-if" assent and enter whole-heartedly into the movie's imaginative world, or the experience risks being still-born. With motion pictures, moreover, this happens naturally, as the darkness of the theater and the community of viewers, not to mention the surround sound and oversized screen, combine with the images and story to capture the audience's attention.

To give movie viewing this epistemological priority in the dialogue between film and theology – to judge it advisable to first look at a movie on its own terms and let the images themselves suggest meaning and direction – is not to make theology of secondary importance. Religious faith is primary. In fact, I argue that the nature of both moviegoing and religious faith demands that filmviewing be completed from a theological perspective. But such theologizing should follow, not precede, the aesthetic experience.

We thus turn from those approaches which begin theologically and judge movies from a predetermined norm to those critical perspectives, which first view a movie on its own terms. The first of these options I have labeled "dialogue."

Even those who express caution with regard to filmviewing recognize that there are some movies that have identifiably religious themes or elements and thus invite/demand dialogue with them from a theological perspective. Like *Jesus of Montreal* (1989) they might be about Jesus, or like *Sister Act* (1992) might center their story on the nature of the church. They might portray a preacher's redemption, as in *The Apostle* (1997), or someone going insane out of jealousy at another's gifts, as with *Amadeus* (1984). Their posture can be either that of renunciation, as in *Hardcore* (1979) or *Bull Durham*'s (1988) portrayal of the church, or of affirmation, as in *Chariots of Fire*'s (1981) focus on Christian vocation or *Tender Mercies*' (1983) story of salvation. The religious elements in these films might be thematically central or supportive. Theological critics are not imposing an outside perspective on these movies when they enter into conversation with such films. Rather, the movies themselves explicitly deal with religious matters and thus invite a theological response.

Appropriation

The title of Neil Hurley's book, *Theology through Film* (1970), offers a good example of a book written from the perspective of one seeking to appreciate film's vision of life. Hurley seeks to learn from the religious wisdom and insight that film can offer. Will movies simply confirm our prejudices, he asks, or will they "serve that reason which, after all, is the universal spark of the divine which the Stoic philosophers believed to bind all men together in some mysterious cosmic fraternity?"[18] It is telling that when the book was reissued in 1975, the title was changed to *Toward a New Humanism*.

Those, like Hurley, who see a material overlap between film and theology, believe that film is capable of expanding the theologian's understanding. They see this happening particularly with regard to a religious humanism that is embedded within film itself. Movies can tease out of their viewers greater possibilities for being human and present alternative selves not otherwise available to the moviewatcher. Thus, it is not to theology that the critic must first turn, but to a film itself. And the goal in relating theology and film is not, first of all, to render moral judgments, as was the case with earlier options we considered, but to achieve greater insight. Only in light of a movie's own vision of the nature of the human can the theologian effectively enlarge his or her horizons as movie and critic engage in conversation.

James Wall provides us another example of appropriation. He concludes his reflections on "Biblical Spectaculars and Secular Man" by commenting optimistically about the secular person who is no longer interested in pietistic presentations of Jesus: "He will, however, be open to the evocative power of a film which celebrated humanity, and thereby calls us all to receive the gift of life. His openness, I submit, is further indication that secular man is deeply religious, so long as he is permitted to define his religion in terms of meaningful living."[19]

Wall, the editor of *The Christian Century* for more than a quarter of a century, is an advocate for dialogue between Hollywood and the church. This dialogue can take several forms, but chief, perhaps, is his belief that a film's vision "can be said to be 'religious' in the Christian sense if it celebrates humanity or if it exercises with conviction a strong agony over moments where humanity is actually distorted."[20] There is no need for explicitly religious symbols or forms. If a movie speaks to the human situation with an authenticity shared by those who are religious, it is enough. Thus, for Wall, *Who's Afraid of Virginia Woolf?*

(1966) was a "religious" movie because it celebrated humanity in a manner compatible with how Wall himself viewed humanity, given his location within the historic Christian community.

Though I understand Wall's intention as he seeks to let a movie's vision of life deepen and extend his theology, I would refrain from calling such a film "religious." Such labeling seems dishonest about the intent of the movie. It is better to describe the film as "religion-like" or simply to say that the film invites dialogue from (or even an appropriation into) a Christian viewpoint, given its portrayal of the nature of the human – given, that is, its informing vision of life.

Joel Martin and Conrad Ostwalt Jr. have been influenced by the judicious perspective of Wesley Kort, and in their book Screening the Sacred (1995), they caution against baptizing film as unconsciously Christian. It is enough to say that movies can and do perform religious functions in culture today as they communicate a society's myths, rituals, and symbols and provide a web of fundamental beliefs. They are in agreement with Thomas Martin when he writes that "no story can develop without some underlying construct. . . . [A]ll constructs, even in the most banal of stories, are seen as presenting one with a fundamental option about life. And, therefore, every story one encounters has some effect on or challenge to one's sense of reality."[21] Appropriation is inevitable.

Divine encounter

John May has provided a helpful typology of the responses that theologians and Christian film critics have developed, starting from the 1960s. There are differences in his schematic structure from the one I have just presented, but the two overlap. May sketches out five distinct approaches to the religious interpretation of film, which he lists in their order of emergence recognizing that all five theological approaches continue to be practiced. He labels these "religious discrimination," "religious visibility," "religious dialogue," "religious humanism," and "religious aesthetics."[22] [See May in this volume.]

May sees that over the last forty years there has been a general shift in emphasis in theological discussion of film. From an earlier concern with (1) the morality of films and (2) the explicitly recognizable religious elements in a film, theological critics have turned to (3) a desire for theological conversation with film, and a more recent focusing on the (4) humanistic and (5) aesthetic sensibilities of movies. In particular, May believes that "religious aesthetics,"[23] what Robert Banks and I have called "divine encounter," is the most fruitful arena for current inquiry. Movies have, at times, a sacramental capacity to provide the viewer an experience of transcendence. This was my experience with the movie *Becket*, and so too Father Gregory Elmer's.

The emphasis of May on divine encounter is what you might expect from a leading Roman Catholic scholar in the field. For, as Andrew Greeley writes, "Catholicism has always believed in the sacramentality of creation." The Catholic Church has held that God is known through the experiences, objects, and people we encounter in our lives. Greeley would have us know that "grace is everywhere."[24] For Greeley, moreover, film is especially suited for the making of sacraments and the creating of epiphanies, because of its "inherent power to affect the imagination." Moviemakers might not call their intention the celebration of grace, but that is what Christians recognize it to be. Greeley even goes so far as to posit that the filmmaker as artist can at times disclose God's presence "even more sharply and decisively" than God has chosen to do through creation itself. Be that as it may, "the pure, raw power of the film to capture the person who watches it, both by its vividness and by the tremendous power of the camera to concentrate and change perspectives, is a sacramental potential that is hard for other art forms to match."[25]

Other Catholic theologians and film critics argue in similar ways. Neil Hurley, for example, believes that both theology and motion pictures work with transcendence, the difference being that theology appeals to the elite while movies are oriented to the masses. I am not sure theology should be consigned only to the elite, but Hurley is right when he asserts that "moviewatchers are often exercising transcendental faculties of insight, criticism, and wonder that come remarkably close to what religion has traditionally termed faith, prophecy, and reverence. A wedding of the two is overdue, although, happily, the matchmakers are growing in number."[26]

Thomas Martin provides still another supporting voice for this methodological approach as he argues that Christian witness must engage the larger society at a deeper level than that of ideas alone. Film, as "an art of moving pictures," has "a greater ability to produce a total environment than either painting or photography because it can include in its form more of the ingredients of a normal setting."[27] As a visual medium that occupies a large part of the average person's life, it has a tremendous impact on the images that govern one's awareness. Moreover, film as a medium has the ability to dramatize, celebrate, and present experiences that are not open to human experience prior to seeing it. It extends human vision to include that which would otherwise pass unnoticed. In these ways, movies have the "ability to awaken a sense of awe and wonder in the beholder."[28]

Notes

1   The original categorization was developed by Robert Banks and has been expanded over several years by the two of us.

2   Hyman Appelman, introduction to *Movies and Morals*, by Herbert Miles. Grand Rapids: Zondervan, 1947.

3   Miles, *Movies and Morals*, 20.

4   Ibid., 20,95.

5   Carl McClain, *Morals and the Movies*. Kansas City: Beacon Hill, 1970, 25.

6   Fax from Dr. Baehr to Todd Coleman, 3 October 1997.

7   Theodore Baehr, "A Cacophony of Prime Time Religions?" in *Religion and Prime Time Television*, ed. Michael Suman. Westport, Conn.: Praeger, 1997, 117.

8   Larry W. Poland, *The Last Temptation of Hollywood*. Highland, Calif.: Mastermedia International, 1988, 6.

9   *The Last Temptation of Christ*, trans. P.A. Bien. New York, Simon & Schuster, 1960.

10 Donald J. Drew, *Images of Man: A Critique of the Contemporary Cinema*. Downers Grove, Ill.: InterVarsity, 1974, 106.

11 Ibid, 102.

12 K.L. Billingsley, *The Seductive Image: A Christian Critique of the World of Film*. Westchester, Ill.: Crossway, 1989, xii.

13 John Butler, *TV, Movies, and Morality: A Guide for Catholics*. Huntington, Ind.: Our Sunday Visitor, 1984, 10.

14 Michael Medved, *Hollywood vs America: Popular Culture and the War on Traditional Values*. New York: HarperCollins, 1992, 242.

15 "Hollywood Makes Room for Religion," in *Religion and Prime Time Television*, ed. Michael Suman. Westport, Conn.: Praeger, 1997, 111–17.

16 Margaret Miles, *Seeing and Believing: Religion and Values in the Movies*. Boston: Beacon, 1996, 4.

17 Ibid., 15, italics original.

18 Neil P. Hurley, *Theology through Film*. New York: Harper & Row, 1970, 3.

19 James M. Wall, "Biblical Spectaculars and Secular Man," in *Celluloid and Symbols*, ed. John C. Cooper and Carl Skrade. Philadelphia: Fortress, 1970, 51–60.

20 Ibid., 56.

21 Thomas Martin, *Images and the Imageless: A Study in Religious Consciousness and Film*. Lewisburg: Bucknell University Press, 1981, 63.

22 John R. May, "Religion and Film: Recent Contributions to the Continuing Dialogue," *Critical Review of Books in Religion* 9 (1996): 105–21.

23 Ibid., 117.

24 Andrew Greeley, *God in Popular Culture*. Chicago: Thomas More, 1988, 250.

25 Ibid.

26 Hurley, *Theology*, x.

27 Martin, *Images*, 46.

28 Ibid., 52.

Chapter 50

Clive Marsh

CINEMA AND SENTIMENT

Film's Challenge to Theology

Film genres and the habit of cinema-going

ONE WAY IN WHICH film-watching patterns can be shaped is
by viewing particular types of film. There are fans of horror films, science
fiction, disaster movies, romantic comedies, westerns, action movies, thrillers,
period dramas, erotic films, historical dramas, and war movies. Each of these
genres offers to a viewer in a standard format a sustained engagement with a
particular range of themes. Films within a particular genre work by satisfying a
viewer's expectations, whilst seeking to offer a novel enough plot and convincing enough characters to maintain fresh interest. I go to a horror film in
order to be scared, though within a safe environment. I watch a period drama
to become lost in the history and culture of the period in question. I watch a
romantic comedy in order to laugh and to weep. In each of these cases, if my
expectations are not satisfied then I am likely to be disappointed by the film.
Locating a film within a genre is an important aspect in film-making, and above
all in film-marketing and distribution.

For the purposes of this present book, the influence of film-watching
according to genre upon the shaping of a viewer's experience is highly significant. Some form of emotional impact of film remains constant across the
genres. What differ are the particular emotions aroused and their intensity. Fear
may be experienced in horror, in thrillers or war films. Sadness and happiness

may mingle in different proportions in 'weepies' and romantic comedies. Anger may be kindled in certain types of thriller, or in historical dramas, where injustices are portrayed. As important as emotional responses are, however, watching films within genres proves significant also due to the regular exposure which viewers experience to particular questions and issues. Cinema-goers who are regular watchers of thrillers expect to be confronted not simply with a battle of good and evil, but with uncertainty, unpredictability and ambiguity. The shock element within the genre guarantees unexpected plot twists and fosters mistrust of leading characters. The thought that human beings really are very complex is consistently reinforced for a person who is a regular watcher of thrillers.

There is a parallel with the world of theology here. In its cognitive aspect, Christian theology requires people constantly to engage with a range of themes. God (as Trinity), Jesus Christ, Holy Spirit, creation, salvation, human being, church, ministry and sacraments are standard headings addressed in theology textbooks. A feature of theological discussion is which of these themes, if any, controls the others, or on which more emphasis should be placed. But to leave any one of them out of the picture altogether would be seriously to distort a theology. It is, then, as wrong to neglect one as it is to over-emphasise any one at the expense of others. Each needs the other to form a coherent whole.

The range of film genres does not function in exactly the same way, but there are similarities. It is simply not true that you have to like all genres. Personality type and life experience may influence a person not to like a particular genre of film. A person haunted by a war experience may not be able, for example, to watch a war movie. There is, however, a similarity between the range of genres and the themes of theology insofar as the restriction of the film-watching experience is likely to distort a person's perception of human experience. Science fiction films are always also 'about' contemporary human experience even whilst provoking the imagination. They may not, however, be able adequately to cover all the emotions and life-issues which the habit of watching a range of genres would address. Horror films rarely only have the purpose of taking a viewer through a range of types of fear. The ones that work best (*The Shining* is a prime example) also have a good storyline to enable the fear experience to be connected with apparent normality. But they are not likely to tap the viewer's experience of loving relationships and family life in quite the same way as, say, a romantic comedy. Attention to film genre as an aspect of the habit of film-watching is therefore, like attention to the range of themes with which Christian theology is required to deal, two-edged. In keeping with the theoretical line emerging throughout this book I want in this short case study to refer to romantic comedies as an example of both the strength and limitation of 'keeping with a genre' when watching films.

Romantic comedies are perhaps the quintessential form of feel-good movie for adults. Often also functioning as films which arouse emotions and raise questions about family life, they usually turn out happily, endeavour to make the viewer feel warm and affirmed, and connect with whatever loving relationships a viewer currently enjoys. They are positive, life-affirming films which usually play down the negative aspects of ordinary life, brush over life's complexities in their desire to show that life really is largely about dating and mating, though also therefore about 'love, actually'. The charge of escapism is thus sure to be levelled at the cinema-goer who enjoys a regular diet of romantic comedies. Watching *When Harry Met Sally, Sleepless in Seattle* and *You've Got Mail*, or *Four Weddings and a Funeral, Notting Hill* and *Love Actually* will produce a very different view of life from frequent encounter with the films of Ken Loach and Mike Leigh, for example.

In a report of a 2000 lecture given by the then Archbishop of Wales (now Archbishop of Canterbury) – 'Trite films fail to show true love, says bishop' – Rowan Williams is quoted as criticising the portrayal of relationships in *Notting Hill*. Challenging the implication that the 'clumsy courtship' between Anna Scott (Julia Roberts) and William Thacker (Hugh Grant) should be held up as a romantic ideal, Williams commends as 'far more erotic' the relationship between Max (Tim McInnerny) and Bella (Gina McKee). The latter is paralysed and unable to have children, yet 'every word and gesture they come out with is full of absolute mutual joy'.

Williams is surely right in his judgment. The scene where Max carries Bella up the stairs of their house, an ordinary daily ritual, is a powerful expression of both the nature and practical outworking of their love for each other. It is not a customary feature of romantic comedy. But this is also, I think, a point at which screenplay-writer Richard Curtis shows he has managed to subvert elements of the comedy/romantic comedy genre. Whilst maintaining the feel-good factor which is central to such films, he has also shifted from the sentimental to the poignant in each of the three comedies he has written. And, as this book is making clear, I am hesitant about the 'sentimental' being too easily used as a negative term anyway. Romantic comedies are too easily labelled 'trite'. When interpreted and explored in the context of their function, there is much more to them than first meets the eye. Williams' criticism is thus in danger of paying too little attention to the complexity of the practice of film-watching, with regard to watching a whole film, to respecting a film's overall emotional response, and to acknowledging that a film is often reflected on in the company of others. Furthermore, it gives little credit to the intelligence of film-audiences.

I wish to suggest a simple but crucially important function for the regular watching of romantic comedies: they focus on the centrality for human life of loving relationships. Whatever the strengths and limitations of any particular films, so long as there are some high quality films amongst a batch watched – and *Four Weddings and a Funeral, Notting Hill* and *Love Actually* are certainly that – then the stimulus for enjoyment of and reflection upon loving relationships pushes well beyond 'feel-good escapism'. To conclude that regular watching of romantic comedies is inevitably distorting of real human relationships is as crass an oversimplification as saying at the opposite pole that those who attend Christian worship, and say a prayer of confession on a regular basis, become depressed individuals. The latter can happen. But both such over-simple judgments overlook the broader context (social and psychological) within which each activity occurs.

Romantic comedies are, in fact, a challenge to 'feel-bad religion'. To respect the way in which this happens, however, requires a broad understanding of how feel-good movies work, and a recognition that religion does not, on the whole, make people feel bad. There is bad religion about. But good religion knows what to do with romantic comedies. Rather than religion and romantic comedies being viewed (negatively) under a banner of 'sentimentality', I suggest that enjoyment and critical reception of each can be recognised as cultural ways for shaping experience and approaching the future positively.

Good religion in a Christian form knows, however, that there is a critical voice that must be raised against a sole diet of romantic comedies. A film-watching habit which meant a person watched little else might render a person incapable of registering negative aspects of life. The significance of the tough parts of the Curtis films, for example, would be overlooked. In theological terms, this would be like trying to live life as a constant reflection of resurrection without death (which would then be no resurrection at all). This simple case study of romantic comedies therefore serves as a reminder that a film-watching habit too tightly focused on a single genre may prove unhelpful in terms of film's contribution to personal development. Admittedly, the viewing patterns of an individual viewer are rarely so clear-cut. It may be that without some sort of reflective process being encouraged, regular cinema-goers are less clear about their watching patterns or the impact of particular genres upon them. But more research is clearly needed here.

Chapter 51

John R. May

CONTEMPORARY THEORIES REGARDING THE INTERPRETATION OF RELIGIOUS FILM [EXCERPTS]

SERIOUS SCHOLARLY INQUIRIES into the interpretation of religious film arose in the U.S. in response to the acknowledgment of film as art, generally coinciding with the worldwide popularity of certain European and Asian masters in the late 1950s and early 1960s, especially Bergman, Buñuel, Fellini, Truffaut, Ray, and Kurosawa. Their films, on limited distribution at art movie houses and on university campuses, introduced a small but highly influential audience to an artistic freedom in cinema that had not been enjoyed by American directors for over four decades, while the so-called Hays Office exercised control of film production and distribution. The freedom experienced by the immensely popular international directors was not to be experienced in the United States until the Motion Picture Association of America, under the direction of Jack Valenti, abolished the production code in 1966. The following year, Hollywood released two films – *The Graduate* and *Bonnie and Clyde* – that permanently altered the tone and content of America films. The combination of the demise of the production code and the universal popularity of foreign films signaled the need for broader approaches to the discernment of "religious" films among pastors, theologians, and church-related critics of cinema.

1. Religious discrimination (heteronomy)

The classic text in religious discrimination is surely Frank Getlein and Harold C. Gardiner's *Movies, Morals and Art* (1961) – "classic" at least in the sense that it antedates by a decade the flood of books that responded to the new freedom in American film. It is also classic in the way it parallels T. S. Eliot's seminal essay "Literature and Religion," which is considered by many as heralding the founding of the academic discipline of religion and literature.[1] After Getlein's history of the emergence of film as art, Gardiner begins his theory of the moral evaluation of movies with words that ape Eliot's famous defense of Christian orthodoxy as the ultimate norm by which great literature would be judged: "I hold – and many agree with me – that the total artistic judgment, the complete critical evaluation of a piece of art, includes a moral dimension."[2] Insisting that only one act is involved, not two, Gardiner explains that "the 'artistically well done' includes the morally sound conception and the morally good effect" (104). Film, like any work of art, "gives pleasure," and pleasure's reasonableness "resides in the fact that art appeals to man as man," that is, to "those emotions that can legitimately (morally) be exercised" (106). Before he has finished his exposition, Gardiner reverts to the traditional Catholic moral norms for judging the appropriateness of films for audience viewing, discerning occasions of sin and using the principle of the twofold effect.

Regretting the moral indifferentism of most cinema, Gardiner borrows a marvelous phrase from Rene Ludmann, "*phénomène de sédimentation*," to describe the baleful effect of cinema on the audience.[3] "Little by little the moral sense silts over" (161), Gardiner warns, because movies fail to take a moral stand, indeed too often suggest that there is no moral problem at all. In the final analysis, religious films for Gardiner, appealing to John Ford's *The Informer* (1935), are those that "do two things . . . they can bring home to the viewer a sense of his own combined majesty and frailty; and they can broaden the horizons of his natural charity so that the widened love can be transmuted into a supernatural charity" (174).

2. Religious visibility

Religious visibility as a theoretical approach limits the consideration of religious films to those that appeal to identifiable religious elements; and where recognizable religious elements are sought, there has been little genuine change over the past twenty-five years, though very recently a subtle shift in emphasis can be noted. The chapter titles in Ivan Butler's *Religion in the Cinema* (1969) run the gamut of possible explicit Jewish-Christian elements: Bible stories and biblical blockbusters, early Christians, crusades; Christ in cinema, priests, ministers, and the church; preachers, evangelists, missionaries; monks and nuns; churches; saints, visionaries, legends and miracles; and the like.[4] Although Butler's approach begins descriptively, implied norms of religious orthodoxy emerge when he offers a superficial reading of certain "anti-religious" films, including most of Buñuel and Pasolini.

3. Religious dialogue

Within American Protestant churches, the obvious need for education to the emerging reality of film as art took the form of theological dialogue with film rather than of direct moral assessment as it had among Catholic theologians. *Celluloid and Symbols* (1970), a collection of essays edited by John Charles Cooper and Carl Skrade, supported the thesis "that theology needs to be in dialogue with the cinema but must never regress to a monologue which would seek to 'baptize' the film-maker or impose any kind of theology on him."[5] Skrade's "Theology and Films," the lead essay, insists that "films can help us regain, in contemporary form, the basic questions which we affirm Christianity can answer – or at least permit us to live with these questions as we honestly and openly await the answers" (3).

Although religious dialogue as an approach toward the evaluation of religious films is surely continuing today, the bases for film education have shifted in the ensuing two decades, as we shall see, from the implicitly defensive to the ecumenically inclusive ("religious humanism") and the explicitly aesthetic ("religious aesthetics").

4. Religious humanism (theonomy)

No theological critic of film to date can match Neil Hurley's comprehensive and prophetic grasp of worldwide film culture. Will the moving image confirm our prejudices, Hurley asked in *Theology Through Film* (1970), or will it "serve that reason which, after all, is the universal spark of the divine which the Stoic philosophers believed to bind all men together in some mysterious cosmic fraternity?"[6] Hurley readily admitted that his view "presupposes religious transcendence in some form as a constant of man, society, and culture" (8). "A religious principle" that he discovers at work in films assumes that "people will identify negatively with forms of evil and villainy and positively with sacrifice, suffering, and selfless forms of love" (6).

Eight years later (1978), when Hurley published *The Reel Revolution: A Film*

Primer on Liberation, he actually began by asserting that "film is the new humanism and . . . in speaking to literates and illiterates alike it can tease out of us a sense of greater possibilities, alternative selves, and new horizons."[7] His contention is that "movies as 'the reel revolution' meet the requirements of true education – which is to aid in the escape of the best possible self among the many latent personalities in each of us" (xii). Whereas in his earlier work all films seemed at least potentially religious, not all films are genuinely liberating; this narrowing of possibility is perhaps to be expected since in Hurley's view "liberation films" are a species of the genus "religious."

5. Religious aesthetics (autonomy)

General theories

It was not until 1981 that an extensive study by an American theologian appeared that sought to move beyond morality, explicit religious elements, or humanistic themes to define religious significance in terms of cinema's specific art. Thomas M. Martin's *Images and the Imageless: A Study in Religious Consciousness and Film* is the sort of harmonization of concerns that Lynch had in mind in *The Image Industries*, except that Lynch sought active cooperation among the participants. Martin notes that although sophisticated interdisciplinary methodologies were emerging by mid-century in religion and literature, "the discipline [of religion and film] is young and the methodologies are at best in their formative stages."[8] In his brief survey of the earlier scholarship, he notes with justification that even where the emphasis was not on themes, but on film as a medium, "the focus [was] not broad enough" (ii-iii). "This small volume," he goes on to promise, "attempts to relate the film medium to religious studies by means of the spatial interpretation and orientation (the image, the sense of direction) that is common to both forms of reflection" (iii).

Martin contends with good reason that "the persistent experience of electronically transmitted stories has a profound impact on the basic notion of oneself as it relates to one's religious sense of reality" (3). Four terms are pivotal to the development of his thesis: "image, imaginative construct, story, and religious [consciousness]" (3). Martin explains: "Where images are generally in response to immediate situations, imaginative constructs are geared more toward absorbing direction as a whole" (17). Stories are the flesh and bones humans give to images and constructs, he goes on to say; they result from the individual's need to "work out the issues of the self in dramatic forms, not necessarily to fit some established order but to establish some emotional order or integration" (21). Finally, for Martin, "religious consciousness is the sense of relatedness that the human has with the others of the world as all are rooted in a common greater whole" (29).

Film as the art of moving pictures, Martin writes, "has a greater ability to produce a total environment than either painting or photography because it can include in its form more of the ingredients of a normal setting" (46). Taking examples from slow-motion, time-lapse, microscopic and satellite photography, he explores cinema's uniqueness as a source of images: "It is precisely this ability to awaken a sense of awe and wonder in the beholder that is necessary in laying the foundation for religious consciousness in a culture which tends to reduce experience to 'one damn thing after another'" (52). "Human consciousness cannot be the same today as it was prior to the extension of its vision through film. Neither can religious consciousness ever be the same" (55), he observes, while cautioning that "Awareness of the mystery and awesomeness of all existences, of all beings, of all the expressions of life forces does not necessarily lead to a sense of their radical interrelatedness but is a prerequisite for this extraordinary sense of reality [as part of a common greater whole]" (57).

"No story," Martin demonstrates, "can develop without some underlying construct" (63). Moreover, he adds, "all constructs, even in the most banal of stories, are seen as presenting one with a fundamental option about life. And, therefore, every story one encounters has some effect on or challenge to one's sense of reality" (63). Martin discovers five basic models affecting human consciousness – supernatural, process, romantic, secular and depth – and explains them in this way (the names in brackets are the principal figures in intellectual history he associates with each): "The supernatural model [Calvin, Aquinas] with its layered hierarchy to existence challenges the human life to make itself correspond to the higher governing forms if it wants fulfillment. The process model [Whitehead, de Chardin] places the human life in an ever fluctuating process that entails an intricate interplay in all facets of the process that is interacting with a whole which is dependent on but not reducible to the sum of its parts. The romantic model [Schleiermacher, Coleridge] is seen as the reverse of the process. One must go back to the pulsating source of nature if one wishes to attain an experience of fulfillment. The secular context [Bonhoeffer, Cox] offers a picture of more isolated entities set by their outward structure while the depth model [Freud, Jung, Campbell] insists on a unique inner space that must be probed if one wishes to have an authentic existence" (108).

"Human consciousness," Martin admits, "has reached sufficient sophistication to realize that it is not discovering the structure of reality as it is in itself. Rather, it is probing for insight through its systems of symbolic reflection" (114). Moreover, "stories are an important step forward in achieving a stability and texture for a people, for they have the ability to introduce a cohesive world view with a minimum of violence to the particulars of life. Such a cohesive force is necessary for a stable society" (119). Yet "the religious sense," Martin reminds us, "cannot exist if there is no identity with a greater whole" (130). Because the camera makes available radically new sources of consciousness and because "films present a dimension of beings not open to human experience prior to film, this new experience is bound to transform one's sense of oneself and the basic relationship to Being in general" (134). Finally, Martin concludes, "when one is living in a cultural juncture in which the public imagination is fractured, then art forms can supplement the images of one's private imagination by making available the creative integrations of artistic geniuses" (151).

Michael Bird, in his essay "Film as Hierophany," provides another general theory of the aesthetic interrelationship of religion and film, appealing to Paul Tillich's theology and the realist theories of André Bazin and Amédée Ayfre. Because of film's special affinity with reality, he explains, it must direct us to discern "the holy within the real. . . . While many films have portrayed ostensibly religious subjects, these films have too often erred precisely in their disregard for the medium's stylistic virtues."[9]

Specific approaches

The particular approaches to the religious interpretation of film that fall within the category of religious aesthetics can, I believe, be grouped conveniently under four headings: archetypal patterns, mythic orientations, the analogy of action, and visual story. At this point in our survey, it is clear that theory yields specific methodology, which readily lends itself to the practice of religious interpretation.[10]

1   Archetypal Patterns: In Film Odyssey (1976), Ernest Ferlita and I, applying the archetype of the quest, tried to isolate those "elements of the art of film [that] are parents and children of hope."[11] Aside from the obvious appeal to visual imagery related to journey – the celebration of the road as a metaphor for our human search for meaning – we attempted to show how composition of frame, movement of the camera and movement within the frame, types of visual continuity (i.e., narrative), and finally editing could contribute to cinema's celebration of hope. Religious films, in the best artistic tradition, we concluded, are "a celebration of life's promise that transcends the individual to reach out to and sustain the aspirations of others" (4).

2   Mythic Orientations: Neil Hurley, in his essay "Cinematic Transfigurations

of Jesus" (1982), was the first theological critic of film to offer an overview of cinema's fictional appropriations of the Jesus story,[12] anticipating by almost a decade Peter Malone's more comprehensive treatment of the subject in *Movie Christs and Antichrists* (1990).[13] Following the distinctions proposed by Theodore Ziolkowski in *Fictional Transfigurations of Jesus*,[14] Hurley abandons the reference to Christ figures in favor of the terminology of Jesus transfigurations. Inasmuch as Christ is a title that faith applies to Jesus, Ziolkowski recommended reserving "Christ" for the context of faith and using the personal name "Jesus" for fictional variations of the evangelical narrative. Malone preserves the traditional literary terminology of the "Christ figure" for fictional characters in film, but uses "Jesus figure" for cinema's realistic presentations of the Gospel story. Christ figures, he proposes, are either redeemer figures (who suffer unjustly) or savior figures (who liberate others). Malone's mythic analysis of film is based on the assumptions that emotional response precedes our initial intellectual grasp of film's moving images, and that content draws response from the audience, while technique enhances response. Values, Malone says, are discovered in a film's content, especially in the treatment of the basic human drives to live, love, live socially, and transcend self.

3   The Analogy of Action: Ernest Ferlita's "The Analogy of Action in Film" (1982) demonstrates convincingly that the possibility of religious meaning in film like drama is often effectively realized through analogy of action, a dramatic device at least as old as the Greeks but perfected by Shakespeare. The unity of his plays is discovered, Ferlita claims, not in "that single plot line which Aristotle preferred and the neo-classicists canonized, but in the analogy of action, in the interdependence of several stories so juxtaposed one to another that each elucidates the central action, first by its similarity but finally by its difference."[15] Utilizing the insights so admirably expressed in William Lynch's *Christ and Apollo*,[16] Ferlita observes that "in its passage through the finite on its way to insight, [the analogy of action] makes everything radiate the same light and yet its own proper light" (55). *Wild Strawberries* (1957) and *Seven Beauties* (1976) in Ferlita's exposition become excellent examples of the way in which screen-writer-directors have created plots that illumine the spirit through the analogy of action.

4   Visual Story: In my essay "Visual Story and the Religious Interpretation of Film" (1982), I attempted to connect film and religion through the theology of story. My principal assumption about film is the unassailable one, I think, that all feature films are stories. Story in cinema, however, is discerned in terms of film's unique formal elements – composition,

movement, and editing – rather than simply in terms of those formal structures that film shares with literature; namely, setting, character, dialogue, dramatic tension, and plot.[17] Taking the extremes of story as explored by John Dominic Crossan – myth and parable – I tried with assistance also from the works of Huston Smith and Herbert Richardson to construct a paradigm for the interaction of the extremes of story and the fundamental religious questions.[18] Between myth and parable, as Sheldon Sacks demonstrates in *Fiction and the Shape of Belief*, there are three intermediate forms of story – apologue, action, and satire – that can profitably be analyzed as reflectors of religious concerns, although no one has done this yet, to my knowledge.[19] Since the publication of *Religion in Film*, which I edited with Michael Bird, I have continued to explore the shared cinematic and religious dynamics of story, with emphasis in the 1992 collection of essays, *Image and Likeness*, on the reflections of Jewish-Christian belief in classic American cinema.[20]

6. Conclusions

It seems to me that this survey of the serious academic works on the religious interpretation of films has demonstrated, perhaps not surprisingly, that early concern with the "morality" of films has not altogether faded, despite a decade and a half of efforts to discover the cinematic equivalents of religious sensibility. Nor has the marked tendency to reserve the term "religious film" for those films that exhibit explicit, recognizable religious elements; in fact, outside of the United States, it may even be the dominant approach to the identification of religious film.

There is, I think, an irony in this delineation of the discussion. Originally, when the basis for religious evaluation of films was morality, all films were considered at least potentially religious insofar as morality judges behavior and all feature films involve action of some sort. The tendency to limit the discussion, as we have seen, grew out of the developing desire to avoid the narrow discrimination of morality as a norm for deciding what was or was not religious in favor of the greater intellectual stimulation of theological issues. There were and still are, however, too few directors who like Bergman or Fellini raise explicit theological questions.

There are, nonetheless, solid and convincing grounds for asserting that any film, even those without explicit religious elements, can still be considered as potentially religious, if not Jewish or Christian or Catholic. Where this is defended with reason, the basis for religious interpretation is sought in terms of cinema's analogues for religious insights. Just as the advocates of morality as a norm for evaluating film from a religious perspective began with the assumption that cinema is an art form and that morality was bound up with the aesthetic, so too the proponents of "religious aesthetics" necessarily root their discussion of the religious implications of film in the formal elements of cinema itself.

Notes

1   T. S. Eliot, "Literature and Religion," in *Essays Ancient and Modern*. New York: Harcourt, Brace, 1936; reprinted in *The New Orpheus*, ed. Nathan A. Scott, Jr. New York: Sheed and Ward, 1964, 223–35.

2   Frank Getlein and Harold C. Gardiner, *Movies, Morals and Art*. New York: Sheed and Ward, 1961, 103.

3   Rene Ludmann, *Cinéma: Foi et morale*. Paris: Cerf, 1956.

4   Ivan Butler, *Religion in the Cinema*. New York: A. S. Barnes, 1969, 7.

5   John Charles Cooper and Carl Skrade, *Celluloid and Symbols*. Philadelphia: Fortress, 1970, ix.

6   Neil P. Hurley, *Theology Through Film*. New York: Harper and Row, 1970; republished as *Toward a Film Humanism*. New York: Delta Paperbacks, 1975.

7   Neil P. Hurley, *The Reel Revolution: A Film Primer on Liberation*. Maryknoll: Orbis, 1987, xii.

8   Thomas M. Martin, *Images and the Imageless: A Study in Religious Consciousness and Film*. East Brunswick: Bucknell University Press, 1981, ii.

9   Michael Bird, "Film as Hierophany," in *Religion in Film*, ed. May and Bird, 13.

10 Works on individual directors that are sensitive to film as a medium while exploring the religious dimension include two on Ingmar Bergman – Arthur Gibson, *The Silence of God: Creative Response to the Films of Ingmar Bergman*. New York: Harper and Row, 1969 and Charles B. Ketcham, *The Influence of Existentialism on Ingmar Bergman*. Lewiston, PA: E. Mellen Press, 1986 – and one on Lina Wertmuller – Ernest Ferlita and John R. May, *The Parables of Lina Wertmuller*. New York: Paulist, 1977.

11 Ernest Ferlita and John R. May, *Film Odyssey: The Art of Film as Search for Meaning*. New York: Paulist, 1976, 4.

12 Neil P. Hurley, "Cinematic Transfigurations of Jesus," in *Religion in Film*, ed. May and Bird, 61–78. For cinematic variations on the myth of the loosing of Satan, see John R. May, "The Demonic in American Cinema," ibid., 79–100.

13 Peter Malone, *Movie Christs and Antichrists*. New York: Crossroad, 1990.

14 Theodore Ziolkowski, *Fictional Transfigurations of Jesus*. Princeton, NJ: Princeton University Press, 1972.

15 Ernest Ferlita, "The Analogy of Action in Film," in *Religion in Film*, ed. May and Bird, 45.

16 William F. Lynch, *Christ and Apollo*. New York: Sheed and Ward, 1960.

17 John R. May, "Visual Story and the Religious Interpretation of Film," in *Religion in Film*, ed. May and Bird, 23–43.

18   John Dominic Crossan, *The Dark Interval: Towards a Theology of Story*. Niles: Argus Communications, 1975; Huston Smith, *The Religions of Man*. New York: Harper and Row, 1958; Herbert W. Richardson and Donald R. Cutler, eds., *Transcendence*. Boston: Beacon, 1969.

19   Sheldon Sacks, *Fiction and the Shape of Belief*. Berkeley: University of California Press, 1966.

20   John R. May, ed., *Image and Likeness: Religious Visions in American Film Classics*. New York/ Mahwah: Paulist, 1992.

Chapter 52

Gerard Loughlin

ALIEN SEX
The Body and Desire in Cinema and Theology

Christ's cave

CINEMA CAN BE VIEWED as a quasi-religious practice. It is this not only in its use of religious symbols and themes, but in and through its social practice, which congregates people in the dark for visions of desire. Like church, cinema creates social bonds through the projection of other forms of life that exceed the mundane, through the production of visions or dreams that can be sustained only through their repeated attendance. Of course, one might want to say that cinema as religion is an impoverished substitution for what the church offers, even if it is as close as many people now come to the latter. One might also want to question the longevity of such a socio-religious practice much beyond the twentieth century, for it is possible that we are now living in the last days of cinema. Technological developments promise new media, which will intensify what is increasingly for many their only social bond, the consumption of infinitely commodified pleasures. Nevertheless, movie going has enjoyed a rebirth in recent years, with the advent of video, DVD and pay-TV enhancing rather than diminishing the communal viewing of film.[1] It is as if the video of the film, usually only available sometime after the release of the picture in the movie house, has become part of household devotion, not supplanting but supplementing communal worship. It is like the candle blessed in the church, taken home and used for apotropaic effect, which in the case of the video is to avert tedium and constitute a socio-sacral memory of the film through repetitious viewing of it in whole or in part, alone or with partners and friends.

One might want to say that the church is more akin to theatre than cinema, since its visions are not merely presented in word and image, but dramatically enacted, both liturgically and charitably, in the services and sacrifices of common life. Indeed, insofar as modern Western theatre has its roots in the liturgies of the medieval church, we may properly think the church's worship theatrical: the staging of a story for the edification of an audience.[2] The religious play-cycles of late fourteenth and fifteenth-century Europe, dramatized and supplemented the biblical story, and were performed in the civic spaces of town and city. They had been developed from early, more obviously ecclesial performances. The most influential of these were the Palm Sunday and then the Corpus Christi processions, that were staged with enthusiasm throughout fourteenth-century Europe.[3] The progress of the consecrated host, the Blessed Sacrament, out of the church and into the marketplace, or around the bounds of the parish, came to be accompanied by increasingly elaborate tableau vivants, mimes of the Christian mysteries (mystères mimés) that were performed on wagons and drawn through the streets. Such mobile theatrical scenes largely predated the later and more sophisticated mystery and miracle plays, such as those performed at the end of the fourteenth century in York (England), and that used elaborate props and scenery, requiring stationary staging.[4] The civic performance of these divine dramas became the pride and joy of the craft-gilds and fraternities that financed and sustained them, and in England they lasted until the Reformation. The York Corpus Christi cycle was last performed in 1569.[5] Such plays have been revived in the twentieth century, but more for entertainment than edification, celebrating 'heritage' rather than corporate salvation. At York, in 2000, the mystery plays were staged within the Minster, and though this location was unhistorical, it reminds us that even before the development of such dramas in the fourteenth century, the church had already come to understand its liturgy as a dramatic enactment of the one true drama of God (re)making the world in Christ.

In the ninth century, Amalarius of Metz (c. 780–850/1), in his Liber officialis had produced an account of the Mass as liturgical drama, with its various parts representing moments in the passion and resurrection of Christ. 'He understands the Mass as a real repetition of the Passion, but also as an imaginative dramatisation of the Passion narrative. What happens on the altar is real; what the celebrants and the people are instructed to do around that reality is a play-pretend game.'[6] The plan of Byzantine and Romanesque churches, with apse, chancel and nave, provided a stage and auditorium, and the decoration of the grander basilicas, showing the saints and Christ in majesty, constituted scenery for the drama, accentuating its cosmic significance. In the eleventh and twelfth centuries, the developing use of music in the liturgy led to the Mass becoming a stylized music-drama, with some passages of plainsong explaining or expanding upon others, the sense of which might otherwise be lost through their enhancement with contrapuntal melodies. In time, the more prosaic recitatives were themselves elaborated as dialogical exchanges. But the attraction of these explanatory tropes was their emotional power, permitted by the use of a single note for each syllable. The music and the singer could imitate and evoke the intensity of the drama. In the twelfth century, Aelred of Rievaulx (1109–67) would complain of monks who too passionately mimicked their characters, with groans and sighs, and overtly theatrical gestures.[7] From the tenth century came one of the most popular tropes, the 'Quem quaeritis?' ('Whom do you seek?'), which expanded on the story of the three Marys and their meeting with the angel at the tomb of Christ, and which was first developed as an introit for the Easter Mass and then later used at the end of Matins. In St Ethelwold's tenth-century directions for its proper performance, one monk was to sit with palm in hand by the sepulchre-altar, imitating the angel at the tomb, while three others, with their thuribles, were to approach delicately, being the three women with their spices, arriving to anoint Christ's body. The angel-monk was to sing with a dulcet tone.[8] All delighted in the acting out of this story, because it announced the resurrection of Christ, the culmination of the Easter week liturgy, which was and remains the most theatricalized part of the ecclesial calendar.

Insofar as the cinema repeats the theatre as drama, the comparison of church and cinema merely locates a more populist analogue for the church as acting-space, as the locus of a social practice in which God's truth is dramatized. It is a nice fact that just as the medieval church provided the story for later, more secular dramatics, so some of the earliest films presented scenes from the Bible, and in much the same way as in the Corpus Christi processions and later play cycles. As early as 1897, a five minute Passion of Christ was filmed in Paris, while two Americans, Walter Freeman and Charles Webster, filmed The Horitz Passion Play in Bohemia. In the following year, Henry Vincent and William Paley filmed The Mystery of the Passion Play of Oberammergau on the roof of the Central Palace Hotel in New York. The revelation that the film was home produced had no effect on its popularity in the USA, and it was welcomed enthusiastically by both Catholics and Protestants.[9]

Like the development of medieval religious drama, from silent mimes to elaborate performances with special stage effects, so the cinematic Bible developed from short, silent scenes, into extended dramas, eventually presented in colour, stereophonic sound and cinemascope. Just as the medieval play cycles could vary in length, from sometimes only one to many scenes from the biblical story, so the early films could be shortened or lengthened, depending on theatrical schedules and audience interests. Sidney Olsott's *From the Manger to the Cross* (1912) came with optional scenes for Catholic audiences, picturing Jesus meeting his mother and then Veronica on his way to Calvary.[10] And just as the medieval plays expanded on certain moments in the biblical story, so films would elaborate on various scriptural scenes.

The early films of Christ's life partook of the liturgical in a manner akin to the relationship between the medieval plays and the church's ritual pieties. This is perhaps nowhere better seen than in Cecil B. DeMille's religious staging of the production of his 1927 *King of Kings*. DeMille not only hired a Jesuit, Father Daniel A. Lord, as an advisor on the film, but also arranged for the celebration of Mass every morning on the set, as well as daily prayers for other religious groups.[11]

The potential rivalry of church and cinema is suggested by the fact that both can be understood as parodies of one another, both being places where dreams are projected; 'inside' places where images of an 'outside', other than that from which the viewers have come, are shown. When the lights go down, one can see other imagined worlds, other ways of being human. This is to repeat the identity and distinction already drawn between Christian and pagan in the ancient world. In all three places, temple, church and cinema, we can detect the shadow of the cave, which establishes the distinction between the illusory and the real. And. . . . that distinction is itself shadowy, suspending the real and revealing its identification to be a venture of the imagination.

At the same time, what makes any particular image compelling, inviting trust, is not the image alone, but the power with which it is invested by others. By demons, the apologists claim of pagan statuary; by medical technicians, Burgess and Kubrick claim of Alex's 'show of horrors'; by society, we might say, of the films that at any one time grip the public imagination; and by the Holy Spirit in the community, we might further say, of the images proffered in the church, as when in David Lodge's *The Picturegoers* (1960) Mark Underwood comes to see the 'real presence' through the eucharistic practice of the 'drab, smug, self-righteous people' of Brickley, 'who coolly lined up to snap their dentures on the living Christ'.[12] It is thus a matter of discerning the context in which an image can nourish its viewers, feeding their imaginations and ethos.[13]

[. . .]

No less than Freud's dreaming, cinema also deals in wishes, in the secret desires of its audience. And no less than the cinema, the church proffers the fulfilment of wishes, that are themselves formed and tutored through the sacramental realization of what is yet anticipated, hoped for and desired. Fundamentally, the Christian cave projects that which is alone truly desirable, the projected image enticing the gaze of the congregation by whom it is projected, caught up in the power of the Spirit, the trinitarian 'apparatus'. As with *The Exorcist*, to see is to be seen and possessed, and indeed to see the crucified Christ might be to react with an equal horror and terror; but to see the crucified become the risen Christ, is to have terror give way to wonder; and to see Christ present in the Eucharist, in the bread and the wine and the gathered community, is to have wonder transfused with joy and the hope of once more walking in the garden.

Then one is the viewer who has become like a little child, enamoured of the screen, unable to tell shadow from flickering shadow. One has become like the most saintly character in *The Picturegoers*, who is envied for the 'primitive intensity of her dramatic experience' when at the pictures. Clare Mallory is a devout Catholic, who in church or cinema is a happy inhabitant of the cave. 'Any dramatic or cinematic performance, however crudely executed, seemed to draw from her the same rapt, child-like attention. To her, as to a child, what she saw on the screen was real'.[14] Only such a gaze can believe the beatitudes.

Notes

1   In both North America and Britain film going was at its height in 1946, with 1,635 million cinema admissions in Britain alone. Cinema attendance declined markedly in the 1950s with the growth of TV ownership, and continued to decline throughout the the 1960s and 70s, reaching a low point in 1984 with only 54 million British admissions. However, since then there has been a steady increase in cinema admissions, with 123 million in 1996 (UK). See *BFI Film and Television Handbook 1998*, edited by Eddie Dyja (London: British Film Institute, 1997), 42.

2   On the ecclesial origins of the medieval theatre see Glynne Wickham, *The Medieval Theatre*, London: Weidenfeld and Nicolson, 1974 and John Wesley Harris, *Medieval Theatre in Context: An Introduction*, London: Routledge, 1992. See also Francesca Aran Murphy, *The Comedy of Revelation: Paradise Lost and Regained in Biblical Narrative*, Edinburgh: T. & T. Clark, 2000, ch. 6, especially 254–80.

3   See Miri Rubin, *Corpus Christi: The Eucharist in Late Medieval Culture*. Cambridge: Cambridge University Press, 1991, 243–71.

4   See Rubin, *Corpus Christi*, 271–87.

5   Eamon Duffy, *The Stripping of the Altars: Traditional Religion in England 1400–1580*. New Haven and London: Yale Univesity Press, 1992, 581.

6   Murphy, *Comedy of Revelation*, 254.

7   See William Tydeman, *The Theatre in the Middle Ages: Western European Stage Conditions c. 800–1576*. Cambridge: Cambridge University Press, 190.

8   See Wickham, *The Medieval Theatre*, pp. 39–40.

9   See Lloyd Baugh, *Imaging the Divine: Jesus and Christ-Figures in Film*, Kansas City: Sheed and Ward, 1997, pp. 8–9. For an overview of the 'Christ film' see William R. Telford, 'Jesus Christ Movie Star: The Depiction of Jesus in the Cinema', in *Explorations in*

Theology and Film: Movies and Meaning, edited by Clive Marsh and Gaye Ortiz. Oxford: Blackwell, 1997, 115–39.

10   Baugh, *Imaging the Divine*, 9–10.

11   Baugh, *Imaging the Divine*, pp. 12–13. On *King of Kings* (1927) see Bruce Babington and Peter Evans, *Biblical Epics: Sacred Narrative in the Hollywood Cinema*. Manchester and New York: Manchester University Press, 1993, 110–26.

12   David Lodge, *The Picturegoers*. Harmondsworth: Penguin Books, [1960] 1993, 110. The worshipping community is the 'screen' on which God appears, and worship is to be a daily undertaking. A thematically related novel is Walker Percy, *The Moviegoer*, New York: Alfred A. Knopf, 1961, also a first novel.

13   Thus censorship is not so much about denying people the right to view images, as judging the context of their showing. This is why film censorship is always a judgement on audiences, rather than films; and why what is deemed passable changes with time. Censorship also assumes that there is at least one audience with clear vision, the censors; and it is their implied judgement on the rest of us that causes affront.

14   Lodge, *The Picturegoers*, 54. For a Thomistic account of the childish vision nurtured in the ecclesiacinema see Denys Turner, *How to Be an Atheist*, Cambridge: Cambridge University Press, 2002, especially 34–9.

Chapter 53

Jolyon Mitchell and S. Brent Plate

VIEWING AND WRITING ON *THE PASSION OF THE CHRIST*

EVEN BEFORE ITS release Mel Gibson's cinematic rendition of the final twelve hours of Jesus' life had provoked controversy. The Anti-Defamation League (ADL), originally founded in the early twentieth century partly to challenge the stereotyping of Jews in films, had joined forces with an adhoc group of Jewish and Catholic scholars to request that the film avoid any anti-Semitic representations. Their concern was heightened by an awareness of the history of passion plays. Some of the most extreme anti-Jewish violence in Medieval Europe came after Holy Week dramas, which sometimes portrayed the Jews as being collectively responsible for "deicide." Following pre-release viewings the ADL declared: "We are deeply concerned that the film, if released in its present form, could fuel the hatred, bigotry and anti-Semitism that many responsible churches have worked hard to repudiate."[1] In response to such concerns Mel Gibson asserted that "*The Passion of the Christ* is not anti-Semitic" and is instead about "faith, hope, love, and forgiveness."[2]

From many other public statements it is clear that Gibson had no intention of stirring up anti-Semitic feelings. Unlike Cecil B. DeMille, who made several changes to *The King of Kings* (1927) in response to complaints, Gibson made very few changes to the *The Passion* in the light of the criticisms.[3] Gibson had no way of controlling the responses of a vast global audience, which after only four months had paid over 250 million dollars to see his film (*Screen International*). Up to May 2006 it had grossed over 610 million dollars worldwide, making it the highest R-Rated movie in the USA of all time. It was also very popular in parts of the Middle-East, topping the box office charts in Egypt, Lebanon and Turkey for three successive weeks, though it was far less successful both in Western European nations such as Germany and France, and globally when it was re-released as The Passion Recut in 2005, with five minutes of the most graphically violent sections edited out. While some viewers did not find the film anti-Semitic, others found the portrayal of many of the Jewish characters to be deeply problematic, believing that the film trampled over guidelines set out by the American Catholic bishops on dramatising the Passion.[4]

These diverse responses illustrate the gap between directorial intention and audience reception. Powerful cinematic signs will be interpreted by viewers in a myriad of ways irrespective of what the director and production team have hoped to create. The mise-en-scène of the trial and scourging had the Jewish leaders wearing imposing costumes and stern countenances, showing an indifference towards the suffering that indirectly they were responsible for. Like most films The Passion was able to sidestep textual debates, such as how far elements or readings of the New Testament are themselves anti-Semitic. Partly because film can offer rich visual details to audiences, The Passion had the potential to portray the first-century Jewish people as more heterogeneous than "the Jews" of John's gospel. According to several critics, the film failed to take this opportunity, and resorted instead to cinematic stereotypes which showed many of the Jews to be without compassion and sadistic. Admittedly, a few within the Jewish hierarchy and crowd were portrayed as deeply uneasy by the weight of violence thrown against Jesus, but the film does little more than gesture towards the divergence of beliefs to be found within second temple Judaism. Whichever way that Gibson's work is interpreted, The Passion has provoked considerable debate around anti-Semitic representations, contributing to a resurgence of awareness of this deeply problematic practice.[5]

The second significant area of controversy emerged after the release of the film. The violence was unforgiving and in particular the scourging scene leaves nothing to the imagination. Partly created by CGI (Computer Generated Imagery) it showed layers of Jesus' skin being taken off by a brutal and sadistic flaying by several Roman soldiers. Some viewers saw this depiction as "pornographic,"[6] while others commended a de-sanitized truthful representation of the Passion. Even though Gibson and the director of cinematography, Caleb Deschanel, carefully studied the paintings of Caravaggio, the depiction of Jesus' brutalized body is closer to Matthias Grünewald's 1515 'Isenheim Altarpiece', than Caravaggio's 'Flagellation of Christ'(1607), which leaves Jesus comparatively unscathed. There is little mercy shown to the viewer, as the film takes them along a cinematic Via Dolorosa, showing a bloodied Jesus stumble, fall, and then for over twenty minutes die an excruciating death on the

Cross. One irony is that the film found a loyal and large following from many conservative Christians, who are often among the loudest critics of the violence to be found in Hollywood movies. In contrast to Quentin Tarantino's Kill Bill: Volume 1 (2003) Gibson has avoided any hints of comic-book violence, offering his audience instead a cinematic depiction of "how it was." Why so much graphic violence? Was it to make a drama with Aramaic and Latin speaking characters more understandable to audiences raised on Mad Max (1979) and Lethal Weapon (1987) movies, and ever more explicit war films? The realism of the violence in The Passion is not only a claim to authenticity, but also an expression of how both audiences and directors have become increasingly used to gazing upon dismembered limbs and blood-spattered wounds. "I wanted it to be shocking," Gibson explained. "And I also wanted it to be extreme. I wanted it to push the viewer over the edge . . . so that they see the enormity — the enormity of that sacrifice — to see that someone could endure that and still come back with love and forgiveness, even through extreme pain and suffering and ridicule."[7] The execution scene of William Wallace in Gibson's Braveheart (1995) intimates towards this desire to shock and to display sacrificial martyrdom.

This leads to a third controversial area: Gibson's theology as expressed cinematically. The Passion represents a forceful cinematic account of Gibson's beliefs, which puts significant emphasis upon the sacrificial nature of Jesus' death. As it stands this cinematic attempt to recreate first-century Judea mixes together elements from the four gospels, strands of post-medieval Roman Catholic European theology, and the writings of an Augustinian German nun and mystic, Sister Anne Emmerich (1774–1824).[8] As with so many other Jesus films The Passion also draws upon the long tradition of Christian art to express theology visually. Many, if not all, of the fourteen stations of the cross, so frequently artistically represented, find cinematic expression in Gibson's film. This film resonates with the individualistic piety that draws the believer to focus intently upon the suffering, the wounds and the death of Christ. This sacrificial death is for the individual viewer's sins as much as it is for the sins of the world. The fact that the film gives such sparse attention to the resurrection echoes those Christian pieties and theologies which tend to drive a wedge between crucifixion and resurrection. A further irony is that the film was embraced so whole-heartedly by many fundamentalist Christians, with many churches pre-booking entire cinemas, when these very groups often also believe the Catholic theology as represented by Gibson is deeply flawed. This idiosyncratic alliance helped put The Passion at the top of the global film charts. The marketing was skilfully done, with the emphasis upon its "veracity" and the severe criticism, even the "torment" and "persecution," that its director faced were used to good effect in heightening support for the film.

There was also a fourth controversial, and often unnoticed area: scholarly response to *The Passion*. There are at least eight scholarly volumes devoted entirely to discussing the film and the surrounding controversies, plus a number of articles published in the *Journal of Religion and Film*, endless online interviews, as well as other publications that used the film as an evangelistic or pedagogic device, making for a veritable cottage industry of publishing. One of the deeper ironies abounding here is the often heard scholarly critique of the film's franchising of faith, including everything from "The Passion of the Christ Tear Bottle" to T-shirts and evangelism kits all being sold at online websites, overlooked how much we scholars were also participating in an academic franchise ourselves. There is enough written material around for someone else to step up and produce another spin-off: *Mel Gibson's Passion: The Reader*.

By and large, most of the authors and editors realized there were much deeper implications to the film, that the *event* of Gibson's production became a kind of litmus test for contemporary North American culture (the vast majority of articles in these books are from scholars working in the United States and Canada). It reaffirmed old boundary lines – especially between theological conservatives and liberals – even as it tore down others – especially between evangelicals and Catholics. Some of the popular debates surrounding the film provided further worrying evidence of historical and biblical ignorance among some communities. As we suggested earlier, it raised anew the millennia-old, often-hostile relation between Jews and Christians.

One of the recurring themes to be found in this ever-expanding collection of written material about the movie is the assertion that inter-religious dialogues have been initiated as a result of the film. While some feared the film would upset the ongoing conversation between many Jews and Christians, a number of these academic accounts indicate that threat was overcome by discussions about the film, at churches, synagogues, in civic spaces, and in the columns of newspapers. Such conversations, which go beyond the usual enclaves of academia, highlight at least one positive contribution scholars of religion and film, as well as other academics, can make in an increasingly religiously fragmented world.

Several scholars, with classical backgrounds, commented on the unlikelihood of having Jesus speak such perfect Latin, as it was not in wide use by the general public at the time. Such a linguistically sensitive critique of the film leads to a deeper concern with the books (one of ours included). What some scholars, including ourselves, failed to do to varying degrees, was to make imaginative leaps into the experiences of the people in the cinema who sat weeping, who left the theater and talked with their families and friends about what an impact the film had. Many of the authors of these scholarly accounts describe how they sat in the theater and were surrounded by distraught, disturbed, crying people. Powerful experiences were described but rarely considered in detail. Often their crying became a platform to discuss the cinematic reliance on Emmerich or the androgynous sexuality of the Satan character. Indeed, the importance of the filmic event is that it allowed a dialog about these things, but what about those people sitting next to the "knowing" scholar? *Why* did they cry? What moved in them? What did *they* see? And what did they *see*? Is it possible that at times we scholars lacked compassion in the face of the *Passion* spectacle. Chris Deacy who discusses the "Passion" of the audience, particularly as expressed on the web, is a comparatively rare example of a scholar who attempts to investigate these kinds of questions.[9]

We are not arguing against critical interventions or historical descriptions which question the use of violence, the resonances with history of art, the characterization of the women, and, most importantly, the anti-Semitic dimensions to the film; but, if we scholars really do want to contribute to more peaceful and sympathetic debates then perhaps we can risk going beyond questions solely related to critical-historical themes. And instead of starting from on high, from solely laying out the historical context, the history of the inter-religious dialogue, the theological debates of 1,500 years ago, we might also turn to the person next to us, to ask why they are weeping and what they saw.

Notes

1   ADL Press Release, 11 August 2003.

2   Gibson interviewed by Diane Sawyer for ABC's *Primetime*, 14 February 2004.

3   The most significant change was the line based upon Mtt.27:25, where the crowd says "His blood be upon us and upon our children." The original line was kept in the film, spoken in the original language; however, the subtitle was removed.

4   See, for example, John Dominic Crossan's review 'Hymn to a Savage God', at www.beliefnet.com. See also, National Conference of Catholic Bishops, *Criteria for the Evaluation of Dramatizations of the Passion*, 1988.

5   See Terry Goble, "When Lightning Strikes Twice: Signal Graces, Mel Gibson and The Passion of the Christ," *Borderlands: A Journal of Theology and Education*. Issue 3, Summer 2004, 46–9.

6   James Caroll, "An Obscene Portrayal of Christ's Passion," in *The Boston Globe*, 24 February 2004.

7   Gibson interviewed by Diane Sawyer for ABC's *Primetime*, 14 February 2004.

8   See *The Dolorous Passion of Our Lord Jesus Christ from the Meditations of Anne Catherine Emmerich*. Rockford, 1994.

9   Christopher Deacy, *Faith in Film*, Aldershot, UK: Ashgate, 2005, 106–133.

Chapter 54

Theresa Sanders

CELLULOID SAINTS

Images of Sanctity in Film

Celluloid Saints

WHAT ROLE DOES cinema play in the contemporary process of saint-making? In the earliest days of Christianity, people were recognized as saints simply through popular acclamation. When martyrs were slain, people spontaneously gathered at their graves and built shrines, venerating the deceased as God's fortunate ones and petitioning them for favors. The popularity of martyrs was directly proportional to the excitement generated by their *passios*, or the stories of their deaths. As Saint Gregory of Tours explained in the sixth century, Saint Patroclus of Troyes had been all but forgotten because his *passio* had been lost: "It is the custom of the man in the street to give more attentive veneration to those saints of God whose combats are read aloud." Only when a military expedition returning from Italy brought back a document claiming to be "The Passion of Saint Patroclus" did the saint's popularity take off.

The purpose of martyrdom tales was to make the saint present to the living once again. As historian Peter Brown observes, "When the *passio* was read, the saint was 'really' there. . . . Without a *passio* the *praesentia* of the saint lacked weight." In the ancient culture of early Christianity, the human voice could conjure up realities that were otherwise absent. Storytelling not only called to mind but brought into being the deeds of ancestors and heroes, inviting listeners to relive the past in the present. In our day, movies perform this function. We participate vicariously in the exploits of people real and imagined, far away or far in the future, by watching them on screen.

Thus movies are our modern *passios*. Paulist priest Ellwood Kieser recalls that when the movie *Romero* (which he had produced) was released, the slain archbishop's friends were stunned by its power: "For a while I thought Oscar was alive again," one commented. Some who viewed it characterized the film as being the most powerful cinematic experience of their lives; others said that it brought about an experience of God. Concludes Kieser, "What more could a priest-producer want?"[1]

The ability of a film to affect those who view it is not necessarily a blessing, however. When the made-for-television movie *The Courage to Love* (2000) was released, those promoting the cause of Henriette Delille were apprehensive. Mother Delille was the first person of African-American descent to have had her cause officially opened by the Catholic Church. A free woman of color who lived in New Orleans in the nineteenth century, Delille founded the Sisters of the Holy Family, an order of religious, mostly African-American women. The *Courage to Love* tells the story of how the Servant of God gave up a life of relative luxury to work among the poor and sick of New Orleans.

In the movie, the role of Delille is played by Vanessa Williams, a former Miss America whose nude photographs were published (notably, without her consent) in *Penthouse* magazine. The postulator for the saint's cause for canonization commented that Williams "was not the most appropriate actress to have played the role of Henriette Delille," and, pointing out several historical inaccuracies in the film, alleged that its producers "fictionalized many things to excite the audience and for viewer appeal." Though he doubted that the movie would "desanctify" the Servant of God, he clearly wished that it had never been made at all.[2]

Movies are powerful. They shape our world and our perception of the people in that world. That is why it is so important to view cinematic portrayals of saints with an appreciative and yet always-critical eye. Viewers should ask themselves about the relation between what they see at the theater and the historical record, paying as much attention to what the film leaves out as to what it chooses to include. They should be aware of the theological assumptions underlying a work and take note of any discrepancies between those assumptions and their own. In a world saturated by images, we cannot afford to accept passively whatever appears to us on the big screen.

Notes

1   Ellwood E. Kieser, *The Spiritual Journey of a Showbusiness Priest*. New York: Paulist Press, 1996, 322.
2   Clinton J. Doskey, "Readers Respond: Delille Piece Fictional." *Clarion Herald*, 2 March 2000. See clarionherald.org/20000302/artltr.htm.

PART 4.B

Biblical Connections

Chapter 55

Eric Christianson

CINÉMA DIVINITÉ

Religion, Theology and the Bible in Film

Why film noir is good for the mind

A **YOUNG SOLDIER**, Mitchell, hides out in an all-night movie-house. His face occasionally lit by the screen, bewildered at the fact that he is being framed for murder and resigned to finding no way out, he shares his dilemma with his sergeant, Keeley:

> **Mitchell:** Keeley, what's happening? Has everything suddenly gone crazy? I don't mean just this, I mean everything. Or is it just me?
> **Keeley:** Ah, it's not just you. The snakes are loose. Anyone can get 'em. I get 'em myself, but they're friends of mine.

Like Mitchell, in Edward Dmytryk's film noir, *Crossfire* (1947), the shady characters who inhabit the dark corners and wet streets of noir are invariably troubled. And as the films themselves are played in retrospectives and (probably more often than we realize) on television, their gritty people with their hard-boiled words become even more deeply embedded nostalgic icons, signs for coping with the uncertainty of dangers long gone and yet strangely familiar. André Bazin captured it in his own eulogy to noir icon Humphrey Bogart, who was important because 'the *raison d'être* of his existence was in some sense to survive' and because the alcoholic lines visible on his face revealed 'the corpse on reprieve within each of us'.[1] Noir films are full of moments where the plot has become inconsequential (noir is famous for incomprehensible plots anyway) and the simple experience of disorientation, of ambiguity, is expressed with sublime poignancy. Such moments do not make for passive spectatorship, but engage viewers in a risky negotiation of meaning. As such, as I hope to show, they are good for the mind.

Film noir has become a concept of enormous proportions. My interest is in one of its particular core features: *ambiguity*. That is because *ambiguity* is more than a theme of noir. It is a lens through which characters struggle to make sense of the world, themselves and each other. It is an intellectual and spiritual condition, a stance of being in relation to others. Through all of the gaps and unanswered questions noir poses, viewers are engaged in an intellectually demanding process. I will argue that it is a process that resonates with some of the most provocative material of the Hebrew Bible.

Ambiguity can manifest itself many ways in noir, and these instances are intriguing attempts at frustrating clear lines of meaning for viewers to pursue. They are achieved through visual style (unusual and unexpected camera angles with unconventional frame composition), narratorial judgement (that is, a lack of it), story gaps, and linguistic play.

[. . .]

Recently some broad affinities of noir to Hebrew biblical literature have been recognized independently by three scholars. Cheryl Exum sees in Delilah the figure of the classic femme fatale. Audiences and film-makers in the 1940s and 1950s, she argues at length, generally demanded that the bad women of the cinema either be reformed or die. Neither happens to the Delilah of the Bible, but in retellings of her story she is either reformed (Milton's *Samson Agonistes*), knocked off or both (as in De Mille's 1949 film, *Samson and Delilah*). Carol Newsom recognizes in the neo-noir film, *Fatal Attraction* (1987), the 'strange woman' of Proverbs 1–9:

> The 'strange woman', Alex, is portrayed as belonging to the margin in many ways . . . She has no husband or recognized lover. She stands outside the realm of socially ordered sexuality . . . Like the strange woman of Proverbs 7 she has a brilliant power of speech, always more than a match for her male victim . . . It is 'the wife of his youth' who must rescue him. The wife has been presented, as is the wife of Proverbs 5, as herself a deeply erotic, desirable woman . . . Her symbol is the house, where, more than once we see the brightly burning kitchen hearth.[2]

The most sustained theological dialogue with noir appears in Christopher Deacy's *Screen Christologies*. Starting by recognizing film as both a bearer and locus of religious meaning and reflection, Deacy develops the idea of film noir being particularly concerned with the activity of redemption. Films provide viewers the opportunity to examine the human condition as 'privileged witnesses'.[3] The eventual focus of the study, however, is the noir-ish films of Martin Scorsese. Early in his study Deacy develops an intriguing comparison of classic noir to the book of Ecclesiastes, suggesting that for Qoheleth (i.e. 'the Preacher' of Ecclesiastes) as in noir, there is little hope under the sun except for finding a way out through a transformation of everyday existence – what Ecclesiastes would call enjoying all the days of your absurd life under the sun.

To his analysis I would add that particular existential themes have been identified in Ecclesiastes by a range of scholars (among whom I include myself), such as the experience of extreme circumstances and the judgement of the world as absurd. Perhaps most interestingly, however, Ecclesiastes presents a developed attempt at asking what the self is made of, and it does so through a disjunctive and radical use of first-person narrative – a melancholy investigation into the protagonist's past. Like Mitchum's Jeff Bailey, and other noir 'heroes', Qoheleth is brought tantalizingly close to his own redemption and finds it always beyond his reach. Finally, just as in noir, in Ecclesiastes' emphatic judgement of the absurdity of the world is implied a desire for something better.[4]

More can briefly be said regarding the shared themes of noir and the Hebrew Bible. In the same way that the noir world threatens the stability of the American dream, narratives like Judges and Samuel threaten the stability of Israel's convenantal relationship, and exposit the contingency of access to the promised land. The cycle of judges stories destabilizes the reader's ability to come to a positive assessment of Israel's relationship to the land because of the fundamental ambiguity of its stories: narrative gaps, lack of narratorial judgement and conflicting testimony all mean that we cannot know whether the judges experiment was ultimately good. Also, the judges of Israel, even Gideon and Samson, deliver at the micro-level, specifically not the macro. That is, there is a resignation in the judges cycle to Israel's reliable rebellion and the consequent transient nature of deliverance 'for a time'. This social observation is present in noir. Describing Raymond Chandler's Philip Marlowe, Spicer suggests that unlike 'Sherlock Holmes, Marlowe realizes that although he may solve an individual case, it is part of a wider corruption that is too deep to be eradicated'.[5] And right to the end of the classic noir cycle, those who represent the law fail spectacularly. These are only outlines of what I am convinced is a fruitful area for reflection.

In his absorbing study, *The Flight from Ambiguity*, Donald Levine suggests that ambiguity offers a positive model for reflection: 'it appears that to become aware of the multivocality of certain central concepts is not necessarily to identify a need to eliminate their ambiguities . . . The toleration of ambiguity can be productive if it is taken not as a warrant for sloppy thinking but as *an invitation to deal responsibly with issues of great complexity*.'[6] (Of the Hebrew Bible, Levine suggests that its 'sparse detail has been a standing invitation for evocative interpretations'.[7]) Helpfully in relation to noir, Levine identifies an 'American aversion toward ambiguity'.[8] Citing a 'Nigerian novelist' who had lived in the USA for more than 20 years, he suggests that 'Americans tend to be direct and literal rather than allusive and figurative, stark rather than subtle. They are happier dealing with statistics than with nuances.'[9] Levine further points to tendencies in governmental policy towards the openness of information and privacy: 'Americans resent esoteric knowledge of any sort as symptomatic of "undemocratic" snobbishness.'[10] Levine traces the particularly extreme forms of American aversion to ambiguity to Puritanism, which 'discouraged aesthetic pleasures, including the enjoyment of ambiguous figures in repartee . . . Puritanism stressed the moral imperative of honesty . . . that came to be cherished to a remarkable degree in American society'.[11] Univocal and unambiguous discourse are to be aligned with human 'capabilities for gaining cognitive mastery of the world'.[12] Ambiguity answers 'the need for expressivity under a regime of . . . formal rationalities, and *the need to protect privacy in a world of extended central controls*'.[13] (This latter descriptive fits perfectly the noir response to censorial controls.)

To view film noir, and to read it carefully, is to engage with ambiguity born not of 'sloppy thinking', but of rigour, tolerance of multivocality and willingness to question conventions and norms. It offers always *an invitation to deal responsibly with issues of great complexity*. Such valuable intellectual structures are produced within the ebb and flow of cultural ideas. As David Aaron comments in his recent study of the Hebrew Bible, *Biblical Ambiguities*,

> One generation's solutions to the unknown become another generation's source of uncertainty . . . The tolerance for uncertainty constantly shifts with an era's preferences. There is no progression from concrete to abstract, literal to metaphorical, plurality of meaning to singularity of meaning. All of these are natural by-products of the human struggle to make sense.[14]

'Movements' like noir, or indeed the texts of the Bible that are counter-conventional, cannot be manufactured. As is widely recognized, the makers of noir had no cognizance of a 'genre', of the term 'film noir', yet alone a series of films to be practically venerated in years to come (Robert Mitchum: 'Hell, we didn't know what film noir was in those days. Cary Grant and all the big stars got all the lights. We lit our sets with cigarette butts').[15] Yet within the discourse of film viewing and study, film noir has become a critical idea greater than the sum of its parts. It was a luminous and influential moment of cinematic defiance (and sadly for those who fell victim to McCarthyism, one coupled with resignation and personal loss), and thankfully it continues to exercise the mind.

Notes

1   As cited in James Naremore, *More Than Night: Film Noir in Its Contexts*, Berkeley: University of California Press, 1998, 25.

2   'Women and the Discourse of Patriarchal Wisdom: A Study of Proverbs 1–9', in P. L. Day (ed.), *Gender and Difference in Ancient Israel*, Minneapolis: Fortress Press, 1989, 142–60 (157–8).

3   Chris Deacy, *Screen Christologies: Redemption and the Medium of Film*, Cardiff: University of Wales Press, 2001, 18.

4   The existential themes of Qoheleth are explored in Eric S. Christianson, *A Time to Tell: Narrative Strategies in Ecclesiastes*, Sheffield: Sheffield Academic Press, 1998, 259–74.

5   Andrew Spicer, *Film Noir*, Harlow: Longman, 2002, 7.

6   Donald N. Levine, *The Flight from Ambiguity: Essays in Social and Cultural Theory*, Chicago: University of Chicago Press, 1985, 17 (my italics).

7   Levine, *Flight from Ambiguity*, 24.

8   Levine, *Flight from Ambiguity*, 31.

9   Levine, *Flight from Ambiguity*, 28.

10   Levine, *Flight from Ambiguity*, 33.

11   Levine, *Flight from Ambiguity*, 37.

12   Levine, *Flight from Ambiguity*, 39.

13   Levine, *Flight from Ambiguity*, 40, my italics.

14   David H. Aaron, *Biblical Ambiguities: Metaphor, Semantics and Divine Imagery*, Leiden: Brill, 2001, 199.

15   Cited in Arthur Lyons, *Death on the Cheap: The Lost B Movies of Film Noir*, New York: Da Capo Press, 2000, 2.

Chapter 56

Robert Jewett

SAINT PAUL AT THE MOVIES

The Apostle's Dialogue with American Culture

MY APPROACH to the relationship between films and biblical texts follows the idea of an interpretive arch, which operates by seeking analogies between ancient and modern texts and situations. I visualize an arch with one end anchored in the ancient world and the other in a contemporary cultural situation. There is a conversation at each end of the arch because the original message was in response to an original situation in the life of the early church. I therefore understand a Pauline text in the light of its bearing on a specific cultural and historical context, and I look for modern analogies not just to the words Paul wrote but also to the situations he addressed. I understand Paul's letters as rhetorically sophisticated efforts to persuade, written for specific rhetorical situations in the life of early Christian communities. An understanding of the words Paul wrote thus depends on understanding the situation and the communities they address. Pauline texts also involve conversations in that his ideas were influenced by his colleagues and were intended to be conveyed and were interpreted by trusted letter bearers; they employ shared communal resources like hymns, confessions, lists of quotations, benedictions, doctrinal traditions, and so forth, drawn from the common life of early Christian congregations. Despite the tradition of abstract, dogmatic interpretation that has tended to dominate Pauline studies, I am operating on the assumption that every word of a Pauline letter is embedded in a story of a concrete community in conversation with other faith communities.

The arch between the ancient moment and the present encompasses the history of interpretation, including some of the greatest theologians in Christendom as well as the Pauline scholars of the past who reinterpreted Paul for their own cultural and historical situations. Each current interpreter's arch contains certain patron saints that shape the contours of his or her particular interpretive tradition. Mine includes Augustine, Luther, Calvin, Wesley, Barth, Ernst Käsemann, and James Dunn among others too numerous to mention. The interpretive arch also contains the popular preachers and teachers of my own particular denominational tradition as well as those who shaped the broader cultural tradition in the United States of America. We each stand in a "community of interpreters."[1] My work with both the Pauline texts and contemporary films is influenced by communities of interpretation inside and outside of the academic realm. No interpreter works alone; we all negotiate the interpretive arch along cables woven by our traditions and our communities.

The contemporary end of the interpretive arch rests in my own denominational and cultural situation, which is why I avoid generalizations that claim to be universal in their scope. My interest is in relating Paul to my own cultural situation. I want to counter the tradition of claiming objectivity in Pauline theology while at the same time avoiding the tendency to think of Paul as an abstract thinker. Since every Pauline letter is embedded in a story, I look for parallel stories in the contemporary world that resonate with the stories behind each letter. In selecting a film to relate to a particular text, I look for thematic and narrative similarities. Once a film is selected, it deserves and requires interpretive efforts equal to those expended on the biblical text itself. Even an amateur like myself can view a film repeatedly, study its structure and dialogue, discuss it with colleagues and friends, and read reviews and articles that relate to its story and meaning. I try to devote the same energy to film exegesis as to biblical text exegesis, although of course my professional training was strictly in the latter. By allowing these stories to interact, the biblical and the cinematic, new insights emerge. I look for the spark that flies between the two arches of the biblical text and the contemporary film. It is a prophetic process in which contextual truths are disclosed that throw light on contemporary situations, both within my faith community and within my civic community and its broader ecumenical horizon. And like all prophetic insights within the Pauline traditions, they bear on particular moments and communities and they are a matter of "prophesying in part," of "seeing through a glass darkly" (1 Cor. 13:8, 12). Whether these sparks light up the present hour must be left for my readers to discern and weigh.

The discipline of the interpretive arch has led me to abandon the tradition of using modern materials as mere "illustrations" of Pauline truth. To illustrate presumes that truth is already fully understood by the speaker, whereas in reality truth is itself dialectical, revealing itself to us in particular historical contexts. Thus I have chosen to interweave Pauline texts with modern stories and issues, allowing each side to throw light on the other. When I select an important novel or film whose themes and story correlate closely with a biblical text, the modern artifact should be treated with a level of respect that allows it to become a full partner in conversation with Paul the apostle. The movie must be seen and interpreted within its cultural context, if our task is to be accomplished. So these essays offer a conversation between several partners, interwoven into what I hope is a coherent whole. But my impulse is prophetic rather than didactic; the creation of holistic vision does not constitute the claim of seeing timeless truth.

I need to make clear, therefore, that while each movie is treated with respect, the Pauline word is allowed to stand as primus inter pares. It is the first among equals because the inspired text of scripture has stood the test of time by revealing ultimate truth that has gripped past and current generations with compelling power when concretized in relation to particular historical circumstances. There are ways in which great movies are also inspired. But biblical texts have sustained the life and morals of faith communities in circumstances both adverse and happy over several thousand years; they are formative in my own denominational community of interpreters as well as in American culture, providing the narrative framework for many forms of contemporary entertainment, not to speak of their effect on the national consciousness and the civil religion. I come from a Wesleyan tradition that wanted to be a religion "of one book," and from a cultural tradition that viewed the Bible as the most decisive book in the world. But although the texts in the Bible deserve to be granted a measure of priority, we shall not find them to be overbearing partners in the dialogue with contemporary films. Like Paul in his willingness to accommodate himself to the needs of various cultural groups, I find that biblical texts when understood in the context of their original stories are flexible, adaptable, and provocative.

Notes

1   See Robert S. Corrington, *The Community of Interpreters: On the Hermeneutics of Nature and the Bible in the American Philosophical Tradition*, Macon, Ga.: Mercer University Press, 1987.

Chapter 57

J. Cheryl Exum

PLOTTED, SHOT, AND PAINTED
Cultural Representations of Biblical Women

Bathsheba plotted, shot, and painted

> You painted a naked woman because you
> enjoyed looking at her, you put a mirror in her
> hand and you called the painting *Vanity*, thus
> morally condemning the woman whose
> nakedness you had depicted for your own
> pleasure.
>> John Berger, *Ways of Seeing*

> To be given in free exchange, to be willingly
> kept in ocular circulation, to serve as object for
> readerly and visual reception, not to hold out on
> the viewer, is already surely an act of
> generosity, if not forced.
>> Mary Ann Caws, 'Ladies Shot and Painted:
>> Female Embodiment in Surrealist Art'

'**PLOTTED' IN THE** title of this chapter refers, of course, to the narrative handling of the story of David and Bathsheba in 2 Samuel 11. 'Shot' has nothing to do with Bathsheba's death, which is not recounted in the Bible, but rather invokes the camera, since I want to consider how Bathsheba is treated in movies based on the biblical story. I also want to look at some famous paintings of Bathsheba, from the fifteenth, sixteenth, and seventeenth centuries. My primary interest in the comparison between narrative, painting, and film is in the representation of the female body; specifically, I want to investigate how Bathsheba, who is a kind of paragon of sensuality, is portrayed as the object of sexual desire and aggression, and to inquire how her body is focalized, first in the text itself, and then in visual representations of it. I shall be looking, then, at women – for we are dealing with more than one Bathsheba here – as the object of the male gaze. And I shall be arguing that there is more to Bathsheba than meets the eye. Since I shall be self-consciously looking at looking, I invite the reader to join me in looking at our own gaze – at our collusion, or complicity, or resistance when faced with the exposure of female flesh for our literary or visual consumption. Surely female and male readers and viewers will react differently to the textual and visual images. The female reader or spectator, like it or not, is identified with the body observed. To the extent we view the naked woman as object, we are co-opted into objectifying our own bodies and reading the textual and visual representations against our own interests.

Bathsheba plotted

The biblical story of David and Bathsheba holds a place in popular imagination both as a tale of unbridled lust and also, curiously, as a famous 'love story'. It is, in fact, as a love story that producer Darryl F. Zanuck and director Henry King presented *David and Bathsheba* in the 1951 film by that name. What is it about David and Bathsheba as a topos and about us as consumers of this topos that makes us so eager to imbue their encounter with feeling – with mutual feeling – rather than dismissing it as an isolated incident, a gratified whim of the king with disastrous consequences for him and his kingdom? The biblical version is no love story. Bathsheba, the wife of Uriah, is 'sent for' by King David, who has sex with her in a moment of passion. That brief encounter might have been the end of it but for one complication: Bathsheba becomes pregnant. Unlike King's film version, where David and Bathsheba romp about the countryside enjoying bucolic trysts, in the biblical account David and Bathsheba do not have sex again until after she has become his wife. Nor is there any evidence in the biblical version to suggest that David *wanted* Bathsheba either for his wife (as the film is at pains to show) or his paramour. On the contrary, the text makes clear that David would prefer to have Uriah assume paternity of the child and, presumably, continue in his marriage to Bathsheba as before. David has Uriah killed and then marries Bathsheba only because his ploy to get Uriah to 'go down to his house' – that is, to have sex with his wife (11.8–13) – fails.

In the biblical account, David's erotic involvement with Bathsheba occupies only one verse of narrative time.

> David sent messengers and took her. She came to him and he lay
> with her, while she was purifying herself from her uncleanness.
> Then she returned to her house (2 Sam. 11.4).

Since Bathsheba will become pregnant, the clause, 'while she was purifying herself from her uncleanness', is necessary to establish David's paternity. Apart from this essential information, only five actions – three on David's part and two on Bathsheba's – are minimally described. He sent, he took, and he lay: the verbs signify control and acquisition. In contrast, only her movement is described: she came and she returned.

This encounter is set in a narrative context of aggression and violence. 'All Israel' (2 Sam. 11.1) – that is, all the men except the king – are away at war, besieging a city, while David is at home, taking a woman.[1] Is Bathsheba, like Rabbah of the Ammonites, taken by force? We cannot be sure, for although 'sent' and 'took' indicate aggression on David's part, 'came' and 'returned', the two verbs of which Bathsheba is the subject, are not what one would expect if resistance were involved. The king sends for a subject and she obeys. Does she know for what purpose she is summoned? For news about her husband Uriah, who is away on the battlefield (which is the pretext used in the film *David and Bathsheba*)?[2] Or for sex? An actual demand for her sexual services is not necessary to make her feel she must agree to sex. David is, after all, the king, so is she free to refuse?

Both the placement of this scene within the account of the Ammonite war and its consequences suggest force. When, as part of his punishment, David's children reenact his sins, David's adultery with Bathsheba is replayed as rape, not once but twice. First Amnon rapes his sister Tamar (2 Sam. 13) and later, to signal his takeover of his father's kingdom, Absalom rapes ten of David's wives. The ten women are raped in a tent on the roof, a location which serves both to remind us of the place where David sinned and to fulfill Nathan's prophecy that God will do to David in the sight of the sun and all Israel what David had done in secret (2 Sam. 12.11–12; 16.21–22).

Both the 1951 film *David and Bathsheba* and the 1985 *King David*[3] (for example), are unable to resist the appeal of seduction in order to make David less guilty at Bathsheba's expense. *David and Bathsheba* is sensitive to the possibility of coercion: is Bathsheba free to say no? 'You are the king', says Bathsheba. 'What other answer can I give, sire? You have sent for me and made known to me your will, what else is there for me to say?' This response represents Bathsheba as a subject who feels she cannot refuse her king, one who yields to his authority, and at this point we may think that the film is out to restore Bathsheba's honor. But pursuing this characterization of Bathsheba would cast King David in too negative a light. David therefore responds to Bathsheba's submission to his will with a long speech in which he prides himself for refusing ever to take anything by force, not even the kingdom: 'So I said nothing to you until you told me that there is no love in your marriage. Yes, you told me that, and so did Uriah . . .'[4] Only when he tells Bathsheba that she may leave, proving his respect for her right to refuse, does Bathsheba confess to having planned the whole thing! She watched him walking on his balcony every evening and knew she could count on his being there to see her. She had heard he had found no woman to please him. She wants to be the woman who will make him happy. She wants to be his wife.

In the 1985 film *King David*, drastic changes are made to make David look better. He sees Bathsheba bathing, but does not send for her. He has sex with her only after their marriage, which takes place after Uriah is dead (a death David arranges to rid Bathsheba of an abusive husband). As a result of these and other distortions of the story line, nothing that happens later in the film makes much sense. In particular, the disasters that befall David's house now appear arbitrary and random rather than as having some connection to his sin and his punishment in kind. Though Bathsheba is not clearly guilty of planning the affair, as in *David and Bathsheba*, she is nonetheless complicit in letting herself be seen bathing. When David first meets her face to face, he says, 'I've seen you once before', to which she responds, 'I know'.

What I have described is not just a contribution of Hollywood. Biblical scholars draw similar conclusions. When commentators on 2 Samuel 11 suggest that Bathsheba shares the blame, are they picking up on a latent message in the text, or are they reading their own gender stereotypes back into it? George Nicol, for example, maintains:

> It cannot be doubted that Bathsheba's action in bathing so close to the king's residence was provocative, nor can the possibility that the provocation was deliberate be discounted. Even if it was not deliberate, Bathsheba's bathing in a place so clearly open to the king's palace can hardly indicate less than a contributory negligence on her part.[5]

Similarly, Hans Wilhelm Hertzberg, in his commentary on the books of Samuel, says, 'We must, however, ask whether Bathsheba did not count on this possibility', and then quotes Alfons Schulz – 'one cannot but blame her for bathing in a place where she could be seen' – before concluding, 'not, of course, that this possible element of *feminine flirtation* is any excuse for

David's conduct'.[6] Though he holds David accountable, Hertzberg manages to blame the woman also. He goes on to propose that, although we know nothing of Bathsheba's point of view, 'her consciousness of the danger into which adultery was leading her (Deut. 22.22) must have been out-weighed by her realization of the honour of having attracted the king'.[7] I find it more than a little disquieting that what is arguably a violation and certainly an objectification has so easily, in the view of the conventional commentator, become an honor.

Why is it that (male) interpreters are so quick to blame Bathsheba for appearing on the scene in some state of undress? What about the responsibility of the narrator, who made the decision to portray her in the act of washing? It is, after all, the biblical narrator who, using David as his agent, makes Bathsheba the object of the male gaze. When biblical commentators imply that Bathsheba desired the king's attentions and when popular renditions of the story attribute such motivation to her, they let the narrator off the hook at the woman's expense.

We also are involved in the narrator's pretense. By introducing Bathsheba to us through David's eyes, the biblical narrator puts us in the position of voyeurs:

> . . . he saw from the roof a woman bathing, and the woman was very beautiful (2 Sam. 11.2).

I have discussed the voyeuristic nature of this scene in my book, *Fragmented Women*.[8] The narrator controls our gaze; we cannot look away from the bathing beauty but must consider her appearance: 'very beautiful'. We presume she is naked or only partially clad, and thinking about it requires us to invade her privacy by undressing or dressing her mentally. The intimacy of washing is intensified by the fact that this is a ritual purification after her menstrual period, and this intimacy, along with the suggestion of nakedness, accentuates the body's vulnerability to David's and our shared gaze. A woman is touching herself and a man is watching. The viewing is one-sided, giving him the advantage and the position of power: he sees her but she does not see him. Readers of this text are watching a man watching a woman touch herself. Can male and female readers possibly react in the same way to the scene? For my part, I am uncomfortable being put in the position of voyeur, watching a naked woman being watched.

Nor are we and David the only voyeurs: 'Is this not Bathsheba, the daughter of Eliam, the wife of Uriah the Hittite?' (v. 3). It is not clear who says these words, whether David or an attendant, but in any event, 'Is this not Bathsheba?' suggests that someone else is looking too.

The woman is focalized through the male gaze:

> ... and he saw a woman bathing, and the woman was very beautiful.

How does David, through whose eyes we see the woman's body, react to what he sees? The sight of Bathsheba's body arouses his desire, and he acts on it: he sends for her and has sex with her. Lustful looking is the prelude to possessing. The story thus raises the question of the relationship between looking, desiring, and acting on the basis of desire. Fortunately, not every voyeur acts on his lustful impulses. The text condemns David for doing so, but only because the woman is another man's property. The voyeuristic gaze at the female body that can lead to appropriation is permanently inscribed in the text, and we, its readers, are implicated in it. With all this looking, it is little wonder Bathsheba has become the quintessential object of the gaze in literature and art through the ages. Her 'punishment' for being desired is to be forever visualized as the sensual woman who enflames male lust.

This is how the paintings and films I want to consider treat her, dramatically reinscribing the text's voyeuristic gaze at the naked female body. As readers or spectators, we are implicated in this gaze, but as gendered subjects, we are implicated differently. The biblical story, it is fair to say, was written by men for men. To the extent that female readers assume its male perspective, we are forced to read against our own interests: to accept the concept of woman as a source of temptation that can bring about a man's downfall. Even if we do not identify with Bathsheba, we cannot escape feeling included in the indictment of woman that she represents.[9] The paintings of Bathsheba are also by men and for assumed male spectators and male owners. In commenting upon the Western artistic tradition, John Berger observes,

> In the average European oil painting of the nude the principal prot-agonist is never painted. He is the spectator in front of the picture and he is presumed to be a man. Everything is addressed to him. Everything must appear to be the result of his being there. It is for him that the figures have assumed their nudity. But he, by definition, is a stranger – with his clothes still on.[10]

Finally, the films, like most Hollywood movies, are produced and directed by men, and in spite of the fact that their audience consists of women and men, the naked female body remains focalized through the male gaze. The woman holds the look; she plays to and signifies male desire. As Laura Mulvey has argued in her classic study on 'Visual Pleasure and Narrative Cinema': 'In their traditional exhibitionist role women are simultaneously looked at and displayed, with their appearance coded for strong visual and erotic impact so that they can be said to connote *to-be-looked-at-ness*'.[11]

The male viewer of the paintings and the films, like the male reader of the biblical story, is invited to take David's symbolic position as the focalizer of the gaze: he can look through David's eyes; he can fantasize himself in David's place. The woman is naked for his pleasure. The female spectator's involvement is more complicated. Our position is that of both surveyor and surveyed, or, to use Mulvey's terms, we are both the image and the bearer of the look. The male spectator is invited to identify with the male protagonist and to desire the female image. The female spectator is also invited to look at the female image with the phallic power of the gaze, yet we are identified with that image as well. Identification and desire, which for the male spectator remain separate operations, are collapsed for us.[12] We might find the male perspective we are asked to assume uncomfortable, and therefore reject it and, with it, the pleasurable cinematic experience. Or we might enjoy the control and freedom of action that identification with the male protagonist gives us.[13] Either way, it would seem that it is not possible for our desire to be acknowledged.

[. . .]

the gaze is male in classical Hollywood cinema, and women as well as men in the theater audience are invited to adopt the male gaze at the female image on the screen. As Mulvey observes, for women 'trans-sex identification is a *habit* that very easily becomes *second* nature'.[14] The male spectator can participate in the male protagonist's power and possess the woman vicariously through him. In Samson's case, the male spectator can identify with him up to the point he is duped by the woman, and then take the superior position by thinking, 'Of course, I wouldn't fall for that'. The female spectator can resist the identification with the male point of view. Does this mean that the resisting female spectator must forgo the pleasure of narrative cinema?[15] If so, what accounts for the attraction feminist film critics admit to, and I share, to classical Hollywood cinema of the forties, fifties, and sixties?[16]

It seems to me that the female spectator, though not necessarily approving of it, might envy Delilah's power to get what she wants, her ability to use her sexuality to manipulate the men around her. There is, after all, a way that women can control men. 'Even Samson's strength must have a weakness', insists Delilah. 'There isn't a man in the world who will not share his secrets with some woman.'

Desire for the male spectator is active. For the female spectator desire is passive: the desire to be attractive like the woman, the desire to be desired. For both there is likely to be something fascinating about the possibility of being loved obsessively, at least in the safe fantasy world of film. A desire so intense that it consumes itself along with its object is a heady aphrodisiac.

Notes

1   See J.P. Fokkelman, *Narrative Art and Poetry in the Books of Samuel*. I. *King David* (Assen: van Gorcum, 1981), pp. 41–70, and Mieke Bal, *Lethal Love: Feminist Literary Readings of Biblical Love Stories* (Bloomington: Indiana University Press, 1987), pp. 10–36, for discussion of the combination of war, sexuality, and violence in 2 Sam. 11. For other explorations of the connection between women, war, and metaphors of sexual violence, see the essays in Claudia V. Camp and Carole R. Fontaine (eds.), *Women, War, and Metaphor: Language and Society in the Study of the Hebrew Bible*, Semeia, 61; Atlanta: Scholars Press, 1993.

2   In the film, David tells Abishai to invite Bathsheba to dine with him so that he can reward her for Uriah's valor in battle.

3   For interesting comments about his role as advisor to the film, see Jonathan Magonet, 'My Part in the Fall of "King David" – the Bible Goes to the Movies', in *A Rabbi's Bible*, London: SCM Press, 1991, 73–85.

4   At the beginning of the film, Uriah has already indicated to David that he prefers the soldier's life to the marriage bed.

5   George Nicol, 'Bathsheba, a Clever Woman?', *Expository Times* 99 (1988), p. 360.

6   Hans Wilhelm Hertzberg, *I & II Samuel* trans. J.S. Bowden; The Old Testament Library; Philadelphia: Westminster Press, 1964, 309, italics mine. In the German original, *Die Samuelbücher* (Das Alte Testament Deutsch, 10; Göttingen: Vandenhoeck & Ruprecht, 2nd rev. edn, 1960), 254 the term is 'Koketterie'.

7   Hertzberg, *I & II Samuel*, p. 310.

8   For the following discussion, see J. Cheryl Exum, *Fragmented Women: Feminist (Sub)versions of Biblical Narratives*, Journal for the Study of the Old Testament Supplement Series, 163; Sheffield: JSOT Press/Valley Forge, PA: Trinity Press International, 1993, 174–75, 194–95.

9   The position of the female reader is well described by Judith Fetterley, 'Palpable Designs: An American Dream: "Rip Van Winkle" ', in *Feminisms: An Anthology of Literary Theory and Criticism* ed. R.R. Warhol and D. Price Herndl; New Brunswick, NJ: Rutgers University Press, 1991, 507.

10   John Berger, *Ways of Seeing*, London: Penguin, 1972, 54.

11   Laura Mulvey, *Visual and Other Pleasures*, Houndmills: Macmillan, 1989, 19, italics hers.

12   See Mary Ann Doane, *The Desire to Desire: The Woman's Film of the 1940s*, Houndmills: Macmillan, 1987, 157, 168–69.

13   See Mulvey, *Visual and Other Pleasures*, 29–38. The nature and the possibilities of a female gaze is a subject of debate among feminist film critics; see Kaplan, *Women and*

Film, 23–35, 200–206; Doane, *The Desire to Desire*, 155–83; Doane, *Femmes Fatales: Feminism, Film Theory, Psychoanalysis* London: Routledge, 1991, 17–43; Kaja Silverman, *The Acoustic Mirror: The Female Voice in Psychoanalysis and Cinema* Bloomington: Indiana University Press, 1988, 187–234; and the essays in Lorraine Gamman and Margaret Marshment (eds.), *The Female Gaze: Women as Viewers of Popular Culture* London: The Women's Press, 1988.

14   Mulvey, *Visual and Other Pleasures*, 33; italics hers. Actors are looked at too, but in a different way: 'As the spectator identifies with the main male protagonist, he projects his look onto that of his like, his screen surrogate, so that the power of the male protagonist as he controls events coincides with the active power of the erotic look, both giving a satisfying sense of omnipotence. A male movie star's glamorous characteristics are thus not those of the erotic object of the gaze, but those of the more perfect, more complete, more powerful ideal ego conceived in the original moment of recognition in front of the mirror' (20). The comparison is with Lacan's mirror stage.

15   It seems to me that this is Mulvey's contention, at least in her earlier article on 'Visual Pleasure and Narrative Cinema', but she puts a different spin on the question in 'Afterthoughts on "Visual Pleasure and Narrative Cinema" Inspired by King Vidor's *Duel in the Sun* (1946)', reprinted in *Visual and Other Pleasures*, pp. 29–38. Kaplan and other feminist film critics have resisted this conclusion; the influence of their work, and Mulvey's, on my discussion here will be evident to those familiar with feminist film theory.

16   Mulvey, *Visual and Other Pleasures*, p. 29; Kaplan, *Women and Film*, p. 26; Doane, *The Desire to Desire*, pp. 3–13, 178–83; and especially the survey of female spectators in Jackie Stacey, *Star Gazing: Hollywood Cinema and Female Spectatorship*, London: Routledge, 1994, 126–75.

Chapter 58

Larry J. Kreitzer

THE NEW TESTAMENT IN FICTION AND FILM
ON REVERSING THE HERMENEUTICAL FLOW

Literature and film adaptation: Hermeneutics in action

A **GREAT DEAL** can be learned about the nature of the interpretative act by watching how a film director handles and treats the literary material, how he or she conforms to the underlying story-line, how and why this story-line might be left behind. Nowhere is this more evident than in some of the film versions of the life of Jesus Christ, which, arguably, have become the most important vehicle of the gospel story for the modern world. This is not to suggest that modern film presentations of the Christ-story are without their antecedents; that would be woefully inaccurate. One need only think of the Oberammergau Passion Play as a time-honoured visual presentation of the gospel story. But it goes without saying that the present age has entered into the visual world in such a grand way that such earlier attempts are left behind. In terms of modern technical progress, not to mention the difference in terms of audience impact, this quantum-leap forward is undeniable.

When we examine closely such cinematic interpretations of the life of Jesus we do well to consider what film director Franco Zeffirelli has said about his own work, generally considered to be one of the most faithful and reverential of all such films:

Jesus of Nazareth is not a story where one can throw in too much personal conjecture or bring too much fantasy and imagination. Of course, it's obvious that any author or director, whether he is mediocre, modest or a genius, ends up giving a personal point of view just through his very reaction and sensitivity to the material at hand. How he treats it and what he selects, reflects his opinions.[1]

At the same time we can occasionally gain a tremendous insight into the very nature of the biblical materials themselves by a careful examination of key cinematic techniques. Perhaps the best illustration that comes to mind involves the long-running television show M*A*S*H, acknowledged by critics as one of the best comedy series ever produced in Hollywood and recipient of no less than 14 Emmy Awards. The characters of the 4077th Army hospital are known to hundreds of millions the world over and their weekly antics have become a staple of our national TV diet. The setting for the series is South Korea during the Korean War of 1950–53 and all of the action takes this as its backdrop. Costumes, uniforms and military equipment all conform to this setting, the newsreels which appear from time to time are all actual footage from the 1950s, as are many of the social and political issues (such as McCarthyism) which are discussed within the dialogue of the episodes. In fact, however, the series of 251 episodes was actually produced in 1972–1983 during the waning years of the Vietnam War and it is really that setting which is being addressed by the film producers, not the Korean War. True, it purports to be the Korean conflict, and the original idea of M*A*S*H was the brain-child of Richard Hooker, a medical doctor who served in the Korean conflict, but it is Vietnam which broods in the background, shaping the issues and setting the tone for the show. As producer Gene Reynolds comments: 'We were literally in Korea but figuratively in Vietnam'.[2] It is the American struggle with Vietnam which is being addressed in M*A*S*H, although it is projected backwards onto an earlier generation and another (related) setting. Is this not remarkably like the situation which we have in the NT Gospels, where many of the problems and concerns of early Christian communities are being played out against the backdrop of Jesus of Nazareth's own struggles with Judaism a generation before? If we examine closely many of the Gospel stories do we not find that the authors of Matthew, Luke, John and even the foundational Gospel, Mark, are primarily addressing their own audiences by presenting Jesus in the way that they do? Is this not the heart of Mark's interpretative gloss recorded in 7.19 ('Thus he declared all foods clean'), or his warning to his readers in 13.14 ('Let the reader understand')? There is much that can be gained by approaching the gospel material in precisely this way, making sure to look beyond the superficial setting to see what is actually being said and to whom it is being addressed.

In short, watching how such processes of cinematic interpretation work may also provide us with a helpful doorway through which to enter the hermeneutical arena of New Testament (NT) studies. It enables us to begin to compare how interpreters follow similar paths as they engage their materials and seek to bring them to interpretative expression. It is remarkable how much of an overlap there is between the two fields of study, that of interpreting the NT documents and that of interpreting a literary classic by means of cinema.

Reversing the flow

Perhaps I need to say at the outset that I am by training a NT scholar and not a specialist in world literature. Nevertheless, I share with others a great love of literature and am, I must confess, addicted to cinema. Such a triumvirate of interest alone seems sufficient to justify these studies. In so doing, I hope that I have been fair to the matters raised in connection with the literary works themselves and that I have presented them fairly and engaged the necessary secondary sources to raise the discussion beyond the superficial level.

[. . .] [T]he primary object of these short studies is to examine the NT texts from another direction, to approach them in a different manner. Realization of our place within the so-called 'hermeneutical circle' has become something of a given today and we sometimes take it very much for granted. Yet it can be so easily forgotten how much of our own ideas and influences we bring to the NT when we seek to interpret it. I do not want to diminish the importance of these ideas and influences, for they can often add significantly to our understanding of an issue. On the contrary, I would wish to give them their due and proper place, especially when they may help us in grappling with a difficult biblical text. Thus, the aim is to reverse the flow of influence within the hermeneutical process and examine select NT passages or themes in the light of some of the enduring expressions of our own culture, namely great literary works and their film adaptations. It is the interface between the world of biblical scholarship and that of literature which is our focus here. These essays demonstrate a range of ways in which world literary classics serve to help illuminate both the NT texts as well as our own cultural context. In that respect they are all Janus-like in nature, facing two directions at the same time. What unites the essays is the fact that each, in its own way, encourages us to recognize and identify particular facets of our cultural heritage, and then to apply it to our understanding of the NT materials. This will in turn lead us to a greater appreciation of the biblical documents, as well as of our own contemporary setting. Thus, the on-going cycle of biblical interpretation is assumed, even if the means whereby we enter into the cycle, or the direction in which we travel in so doing, might at first appear rather unconventional. Yet the approach we adopt is novel. By interjecting study of the cinematic interpretations of the relevant literary classics, a new factor is added to the equation. It is a dimension which pays due attention to the place that cinema has in our age and one which recognizes the influence of film upon us.

Notes

1   Quotation taken from the promotional materials accompanying the boxed set of videos of the film. The filming of *Jesus of Nazareth* is also discussed by Zeffirelli in *Autobiography*, London: Arena Books, 1987, 274–87.
2   Quoted in S. Kalter, *The Complete Book of M*A*S*H*, Bromley, Kent: Columbus Books, 1984, 22.

Chapter 59

Adele Reinhartz

SCRIPTURE ON THE
SILVER SCREEN

THERE WAS A TIME in our household when Cecil B. DeMille's *The Ten Commandments* (1956) was the hands-down favorite of the under-ten set, who viewed all 220 minutes of it several times a week. Even now, they can describe each scene in detail. They were enthralled with the grand vistas, the raw emotion, and the beautiful actors, but, above all, with how the film gave life to a story that they had heard told and retold since birth.

With the passing of the epic film genre, there have been relatively few feature films that explicitly set out to retell biblical narratives. But the Bible has by no means disappeared from the cinema. In fact, every year sees growth in the inventory of mainstream commercial films in which the Bible appears, in roles great and small.

In some films, the Bible appears as a "prop" on the screen. In the 1993 comedy *Coneheads*, for example, an alien couple, newly arrived on Earth, explores the various items they find in their motel room. While the male Conehead, Beldar, samples the soup and toilet paper in the bathroom, his spouse, Prymaat, leafs through the Gideon's Bible she has found on the nightstand and laughs uproariously – not the response we might expect to a book that we commonly associate with solemn religious piety. By contrast, the main character in the 1996 drama *Sling Blade*, a so-called "retarded man" newly released from the state prison hospital, carries his Bible with him everywhere and treasures it not just for its contents but for its material presence in his life. On his release from the prison hospital, he meets a young boy named Frank. To Frank he gives his Bible, along with the rest of his small book collection, at the end of the film. In giving Frank his Bible, he gives him a part of himself, in order that Frank might continue to remember him and feel connected with him even after they must separate.

Just as explicit as the physical presence of a Bible on the screen is the use of direct biblical quotation. Spider Man's adoptive mother (*Spider Man*, 2002) recites Psalm 23 when she fears death at the hands of the Green Goblin. In *Liar, Liar*, Fletcher Reid, a smooth-talking lawyer, proclaims, "The Truth shall set you free" (John 8:32); in doing so, he pledges to stop lying for twenty-four hours in answer to his young son's fervent birthday wish.

Even more prevalent than biblical quotations are biblical allusions. Often these are verbal allusions to biblical phrases, people, and places. *The Matrix* (1999) has several prominent allusions: the holy city is called Zion, a biblical synonym for Jerusalem; the rebel space ship is the Nebuchadnezzar, the powerful Babylonian king whose armies conquered the Kingdom of Judah and destroyed Solomon's temple in 586 B.C.E. Another film rich in biblical allusion is *Deep Impact* (1998), in which the President of the United States launches Operation Noah's Ark to save the world from a deadly comet, an act accomplished by Space Mission Messiah.

Many films feature main characters who are explicitly modeled on one biblical character or another. Sister Agnes, the lead character in the 1985 film *Agnes of God*, is a Virgin Mary figure in her insistence that her baby, born in the convent, had no human father. The sexual behavior of Bess McNeill, the protagonist of the 1996 drama *Breaking the Waves*, [discussed earlier in this reader – see reading 34] initially recalls the traditional images associated with Mary Magdalene; by the end of the film, she is portrayed in Christ-like terms as she sacrifices herself to save her husband.

Biblical stories often form the basis of film narratives that on the surface are entirely unconnected to the Bible. This is true of at least some of the movies already mentioned; for example, *Deep Impact* has obvious affinities with the biblical flood story (Genesis 7), and *Agnes of God* with the Jesus' infancy narratives (Luke 1; Matthew 1). The classic horror film *Frankenstein* (1931) evokes (or subverts) the Genesis creation narratives in its focus on a scientist who hopes to usurp the divine role in the creation of human life. The animated film *The Lion King* (1994) features a Moses-like hero who flees the land of his birth, wanders in the desert, begins life anew in a foreign land, and is persuaded to return as leader after experiencing a theophany [see reading 45]. Most prevalent, however, is the use of the Jesus story in stories of salvation and redemption, such as *Cool Hand Luke* (1967), *The Green Mile* (1999), as well as most of the films we have already mentioned (*Sling Blade, The Matrix, Deep Impact, Breaking the*

Waves), all of which feature heroes who sacrifice themselves for the sake of others.

My interest in the movies is entirely amateur, in both senses of the term: I am an amateur in my pure and often uncritical enjoyment of movies, which are one of my favorite forms of entertainment (neck in neck with reading novels); and I am an amateur in the sense of professing no professional training or expertise. I am not a film critic, a professional student of film, or a scholar in film studies, nor am I a film maven who can rattle off actors, directors, and film plots by the dozen. Rather, I am a Bible scholar who has become particularly attuned to the frequent appearance of scripture on the silver screen. But only in recent years has it occurred to me to make some use of this fortuitous conjunction between my professional interests and my leisure-time pursuits. The impetus for doing so was initially circumstantial. In an effort to increase undergraduate enrollment in religious studies courses, the Department of Religious Studies in which I was teaching (at McMaster University) was encouraged to develop courses that would appeal to a broad range of students. Like many of my colleagues, I had already been using the occasional film in courses to good effect. Why not, I thought, structure an introductory Bible course systematically around film?

Beyond these pragmatic concerns, I soon saw strong pedagogical potential in a course like this. In particular, Hollywood provided obvious and welcome support for my ongoing campaign on behalf of biblical literacy. Surely the extensive and broad-ranging use of the Bible in popular films demonstrates how important it is that everyone know something about the Bible, or at least acquire some basic familiarity with its contents. As sacred canon, the Bible has an important and special role for many of us, both as individuals and as participants in Jewish and Christian communities. But for all of us, no matter our religious affiliations (or lack thereof), the Bible is a foundational document whose impact on Western history, culture, and society cannot be overestimated. Knowledge of the Bible is important not only for understanding the masterpieces of Western civilization; looking at Hollywood films through the lens of the Bible also reveals the importance of scripture for our ability to appreciate popular culture.

One of the biggest challenges in creating the course was not a dearth of films – in fact there is an embarrassment of riches – but the relative lack of secondary reading materials that focus specifically on the explicit use of the Bible in popular film. I learned much from the books that explore other, more subtle aspects of the interplay between the Bible and film, such as the work of Larry Kreitzer, who has studied the interconnections between biblical texts, selected works of Western literature, and the cinematic adaptations of those literary works; Robert Jewett, who discusses and critiques a number of popular films from the point of view of Pauline theology; and, most recently, the fascinating collection entitled *Screening Scripture: Intertextual Connections Between Scripture and Film*, edited by George Aichele and Richard Walsh. Also useful were the articles in the on-line *Journal of Religion and Film* (www.unomaha.edu/~wwwjrf/), as well as the corpus of writings in religion and film more generally. While all of these works contained discussions that were directly relevant to the material I was studying with my classes, I longed for a book that would focus specifically on the explicit role of the Bible – as distinct from biblical or religious themes – in popular film. Finally I decided to write my own.

Note

For further bibliographic references see the Bibliography in this reader.

Chapter 60

Erin Runions

HOW HYSTERICAL

Identification and Resistance in the Bible and Film

FRAMING THE GOLDEN FETISH: Three Kings and the Biblical
Exodus Tradition

SINCE ONE WAY OF understanding how things work is to look
at examples that do not, in this chapter I look at an unsuccessful attempt
to inspire resistance through film. I am interested in why excess (hysterical,
supplemental, etc.) *does not* function subversively in *Three Kings*, David O. Russell's
1999 spoof on the United States' 1991 war on Iraq, also known as Operation
Desert Storm. It is a film that attempts to be critical of American foreign policy,
yet in spite of its strong critique, it fails to generate resistance to U.S. militarism
and imperialism. The film parodies the U.S. involvement in Iraq through the
adventures of four soldiers, who, on the verge of returning home after the war
in the Persian Gulf has been declared a victory, go on an unauthorized mission
to steal Kuwaiti gold (stolen once already by Saddam Hussein from Kuwait).
After finding the gold and stealing it, they are aided in their flight by Iraqi
rebels, whom they then rescue by bequeathing them gold and enabling their
escape into Iran.

One might think that parodic as the film is, in repeating the war so as to
make some of its failures obvious, it might generate a kind of subversive excess
with respect to the United States' war in the Middle East. But the film's possibly
subversive moments are recuperated, it seems, into the general ideological work

that the film does of supporting U.S. imperialism. As reviewer J. Hoberman puts it, "The movie keeps trying to go conventional, and ultimately it does".[1] The film ends up glorifying the U.S. military and its self-prescribed role as savior. It presents and honors the ideological signifer of U.S. supremacy. One of the ways that it does this is through both overt and subtle biblical allusions and framing. The film's biblical undercurrents of messianism, exodus, and conquest highlight the way in which imperial or colonial power seems to set itself up as a salvific force that requires an endless exhibitionist staging and restaging of entry into the land. The film mirrors the biblical text's continual reinscription of rescue through exodus and conquest as it repeats, though parodically, the U.S. military's continual need to reenter the land of oil.

Three Kings in the Euphrates River Valley: The Biblical Frame

The entry point for a discussion of the biblical frame is obvious. The film's title evokes the biblical story, found in Matthew 2, of the visit of the Magi to the Christ child (modified through time to the visit of the "three kings") and the holy family's escape into Egypt. The gold that the soldiers try to steal also alludes to the gifts of gold, frankincense, and myrrh that the Magi brought to the infant Jesus (Matt. 2:11). The allusion to the biblical narrative comes at the beginning of the film as the four soldiers discuss the action scenario. The thieving party consists of Sergeant Troy Barlow (Mark Wahlberg), under whose command a map indicating the gold's whereabouts is found wedged into the ass of an Iraqi captive; Private Conrad Vig (Spike Jonze), who pulls the map out of the aforementioned ass ("man, I didn't join the Army to pull paper out of people's asses, no sir, not what I signed up for"); Staff Sergeant Chief Elgin (Ice Cube), a member of Barlow's division who has access to translation of the map; and Special Forces Major Archie Gates (George Clooney), who, alerted to the presence of a map by the investigation of reporter Adrianna Cruz (Nora Dunn), crashes the meeting of the other three and takes on the role of commando. As the four discuss the map and the location of the gold, Conrad, in an unusually astute moment, observes that it is "way north of any allied forces," to which Chief Elgin comments, "it'll just be us and the Humvee in the Euphrates River valley." Perhaps encouraged by having contributed positively to the conversation once, Conrad speaks up again, in a more typical fashion (he is unabashedly portrayed as undereducated, moronic white trash; and not surprisingly he is the dispensable member of the party, killed in action): "where they found Moses in the basket!" Exasperated, Elgin corrects him, "that was Egypt," but Conrad, undeterred, begins to hum the carol "We Three Kings of Orient Are," to which he more heartily sets his own lyrics, mixing in a little Janis Joplin, "We three kings be stealing the gold, my friends all drive Porsches, I must make amends." Annoyed by this creative intrusion at such a moment of import and decision, the others quickly shut him up. Though part of the film's parody of Army personnel, Conrad's musical interlude is also crucial for establishing the framework for the plot. Staged as the confusion of a country bumpkin, the film provides a muddled, but surely deliberate, movement from Moses, to Egypt, to the Three Kings, to American capitalist desire.

In setting up the plot this way, the film alludes not only to the biblical story of the Magi, but also to the story of Moses leading the people of Israel in the exodus from Egypt (Exodus 5–15). This is not a surprising intertextual connection, given that the text of Matthew itself interprets the events following the Magi's visits as patterned on the exodus story. As the narrator of Matthew interprets it, the holy family's sojourn in Egypt (occasioned by the Magi's visit to King Herod, whereafter he jealously orders the deaths of all Jewish baby boys in hopes of eliminating the future king of the Jews for whom the Magi search) is analogous to the ancient Israelites' sojourn in Egypt before the exodus (Matt. 2:15). Like the ancient Israelites, the Christ child is eventually called out of Egypt. For this reason commentators have often considered Moses' life – also threatened by a king who tried to kill all Jewish boys – and the exodus story as models for the Matthean story. The film seems to reflect this well-established reading tradition for Matthew 2. On the level of the film's subtext, this intertextual allusion draws an equivalence between the biblical Egypt and the contemporary Iraq (Pharaoh and Saddam), and between Moses and the filmic kings. Of significance here is the fact that the Magi in the Matthean text are merely supposed to supplement and highlight the kingship of Jesus. Indeed as scholars have pointed out, the first two chapters of Matthew are concerned with establishing the legitimacy of Jesus' messianic, Davidic kingship. But in the film's plot-setting biblical allusion, Jesus more or less falls out of the picture. So there is an absence here, in the parallel between Moses and the soldiers, that the frame establishes: a missing messianic figure. But a hint appears early on that the messianic role will come into play, when Chief Elgin confides to a somewhat surprised Conrad and Troy that he has the "fire-baptized ring of Jesus." (Elgin demonstrates this gift later, by bringing down an Iraqi helicopter with an explosive football – an image that summons up the Hollywood stereotype of the soulful, athletically gifted African American.) At the beginning of the film, then, there is the hint that the men will fill in the messianic gap, because one of them has the firepower of Jesus.

The biblical frame closes up at the end of the film, picking up on the intertextual reference to the biblical exodus tradition with a climatic scene of crisis and release. By this point in the film, the gold has been partially distributed among the fleeing Iraqi rebels, with the rest stashed for the three surviving

Americans to come back and reclaim. The party has almost reached the
Iran–Iraq border when the U.S. Army, apprised of the AWOL soldiers' whereabouts, intervenes and arrests the renegade men before they can negotiate the
passage of the refugees through the border. Barlow, Gates, and Elgin resist arrest
in order to continue helping the refugees, despite being severely berated by
their superiors (as is Adrianna Cruz, who has been reporting the scene). The
Iraqi border patrols arrest the refugees and herd them into a small pen. Amid
the chaos, Barlow nearly dies because, hand-cuffed, he cannot reach the valve
that releases air from a recently acquired chest wound. He gasps for breath until
the soldier guarding him ignores orders and cut his cuffs. In the moment of
calm after Troy's near-death experience, the three men decide to sacrifice their
gold and to reveal its whereabouts in exchange for the negotiated release of the
hostage refugees. On hearing about the gold, Colonel Horn (Mykelti Wil-
liamson) decides to negotiate with the Iraqi border guards to let the captives go
into the land of their potential freedom, Iran. As he walks back, he signals the
wrap-up of the operation (and the film): the helicopter propellers whirl, the
music begins again, and the captives are released into Iran, while the "three
kings" watch on in farewell, eyes brimming.

There is a clear exodus trope at work here. True to the film's opening, the
men are like Moses figures, negotiating the people's crossing out of enslave-
ment. And true to the biblical text, the men, like Moses, are not able to cross
with the people (Moses having been banned from the promised land for dis-
obeying Yahweh's commands [Num. 20:1–12; Deut. 3:21–29]). But the men's
"self-sacrifice" in that climactic scene (made somewhat more serious by the
presence of Conrad's shrouded body), also gives them a Christlike status, filling
out the early hint of Jesus' presence with/as them and making the parallel of
Jesus and Moses complete. As savior figures, the three men step in to fill the
lacuna opened up at the beginning of the film around the figure of Jesus. In
this way, the biblical imagery frames the men's action as both Mosaic and
messianic.

However, by making its messiah/Moses figures members of the U.S.
military, *Three Kings* cannot help but highlight what some biblical scholars
have emphasized as the inseparability of the exodus story from the conquest
narratives. With Yahweh's very first promise of deliverance from Egypt, the
Israelites are also told that the exodus will culminate with entry into the promised land, the land of Canaan. The Israelites are assured that they will expunge
the inhabitants of Canaan (Exod. 3:8, 17; 13:5; 23:23, 28; 33:2; 34:11). Thus
the Israelites' exodus is followed by a series of violent encounters with the
peoples residing in Canaan. Time and again the recently enslaved Israelites
destroy cities and peoples, leaving no survivors (e.g., Num. 21:35; Josh. 8:22,
10:36–42; 11:12–21). Versions of the exodus and conquest repeat throughout

the Hebrew Bible, in its historical narratives, in its figurative writing, and in its prophetic texts, like a repetitive hysterical symptom – compulsively repeating some original trauma. The film builds on this repetition, by repeating/citing Matthew 2, itself already a repetition of the repeating biblical tradition. Thus the film merely follows the logic of the exodus-conquest tradition to which it alludes when it restages yet another entry into new lands. The action begins after the war has ended – the soldiers should be going home, but instead they start a new foray into the land of Iraq, only to come again to exodus. The film even acknowledges that it depicts this kind of colonial restaging when Colonel Horn says angrily, in response to Gates' dissatisfaction over the accomplishments of the U.S. military in Iraq, "Your work in Iraq was over, done . . . whaddaya wanna do, occupy Iraq? Do Vietnam all over?" Apparently this is precisely what Gates wants and what the film's narrative requires.

Significantly, this affective scene is part of the biblical frame. The task of dealing with emotion is shifted from the more typical woman frame onto the biblical frame in the film. But, taking a cue from the (thick) woman frame, it may be possible to read the filmic exodus-conquest trope along the lines of the hysterical symptom. The exodus scene, with its emphasis on release of captives, does the work of a hysterical symptom. The audience is able to live emotionally through the familiar cycle of tension and release in the exodus-conquest motif. Like its prototype, the biblical story of exodus-conquest, this scene offers tension and release in the movement from oppression into victory; it occasions a surge of emotions.

As a flashpoint for viewers' emotions, the exodus scene is like a hysterical symptom that facilitates forgetting. The image of the freed Iraqis enables the viewer to forget facts like the frenzied U.S. bombing of many thousands of Iraqi troops in their retreat from Kuwait. It effaces the bombing of civilian targets and the utter destruction of water and sewage systems in the country. Combined with the film's emphasis on the "liberation of Kuwait" and its digs at the soldiers' dissatisfaction with their fighting time in Iraq, the exodus scenario intimates that it was indeed a clean war, a war that helped people rather than hurt them. (This sentiment is corroborated by the opening shots of the film – following a caption that tells that the war has just ended – in which Barlow shoots an Iraqi soldier who is signaling surrender, to which Conrad says, "Dag! Didn't think I'd get to see anybody shot in this war." Though it may be argued that this is satirical, the scene still disavows mass slaughter.) While the film does show images of the horrors of war (the internal view of Troy's bullet wound, the birds caught in the oil slick), somehow the force of these images is rendered ineffectual by the film's opening (the liberation of Kuwait) and closing (the liberation of the Iraqi refugees). Closing with an exodus scenario does away with any lasting memory of the violence that attends conquest.

Moreover, it enables the viewer to forget that still, again, in 1999, the time that this film was being produced, the United States under Bill Clinton was bombing Iraq, having started in December 1998. It enables the viewer to forget the disastrous long-term health and environmental effects of depleted uranium used in U.S. ammunition. More recently, when Three Kings aired again on NBC in the spring of 2002 – at a moment when support for George Bush's military effort against terrorism might have been flagging after the initial fervor – it no doubt facilitated forgetfulness of the violence already inflicted on Afghanistan and planned again for Iraq.

Thus the biblical frame as hysterical symptom is not subversive, not only because it valorizes the U.S. military, but also precisely because in the name of a laugh at a past event, it stands in for events past and present that are neither able nor allowed to be represented. It blocks knowledge. As hysterical symptom, this framing device deals with the traumatic affect of doing violence so as to make it bearable to a population that may not know, or remember, the violence incurred in its name by political leadership and the military. In short, it may be that the film's production of affect provides an outlet for emotions produced and left unabreacted by the violence of various U.S. neocolonial wars.

Notes

1   J. Hoberman, "Burn, Blast, Bomb, Cut." Review of Three Kings. Sight and Sound 2000: 2: 18–20.

PART 5

Recent Reflections on the Relation between Religion and Film

INTRODUCTION

WE BEGAN THIS READER BY providing a series of early reflections upon the interaction between religion and film. We conclude this collection by offering several more recent accounts of this relation. Put alongside the readings from previous sections, the readings here illustrate how there are both continuities and discontinuities with earlier conversations on religion and film (see parts 1 and 2). Some scholars have concentrated on films which focus upon explicit religious themes, artifacts, or personalities while others have sought to uncover more hidden religious undercurrents and the way in which film might even function as a form of religion.

Most of the readings in this section focus on one or two intertwined aspects of the relation between religion and film. First, authors emphasize the specificities of the formal medium of film, pointing out how montage, lighting, and cinematography can help create a religious experience for the viewer. Second, many note that the viewing experience itself is a type of religious experience. In this way, these readings are representative of a new way of understanding the religion–film intersection, moving beyond the formal, narrative analyses that have been the staple of scholarship in religion and film. Like many of the other writers examining the religion–film relation the authors here have to contend with rapidly evolving contexts, both in terms of technological advances and social transformations.

This can be seen both in countries which have produced very few films up to this point and nations that have a long history of producing movies, many of which engage implicitly or explicitly with religious themes in their films. Consider, for example, what is described by its producers as the first Saudi Arabian feature-length film, *Keif al-Hal* (*How are you?* 2006). This tale, directed by Izidore Musallam and filmed in Dubai, tells the story of a young woman's conflict with her more religiously conservative family. Compare this recent Saudi film with a controversial comic satire set in Iran: *Marmoulak* (*The Lizard*, 2004). It is one of hundreds of films that have emerged out of Iran in the last decade. This film, directed by Kamal Tabrizi, is about a small-time thief, Reza, who escapes prison dressed as a Mullah, only to find himself having to act as a cleric for far longer than he anticipated. *Marmoulak* provides an interesting case study of how a film can become both an expression of religiously resonant themes and a site of religious debate. It attracted "serpentine" queues in Tehran in the first few weeks after it was released, only to be banned by the religious authorities. In an Iranian context the film itself is a rarity in that it eschews the usual cinematic reverence towards the figure of the cleric. Instead, *Marmoulak* playfully depicts how the authority of a religious leader depends not only on the character of the leader, but also the desires of his followers. It remains respectful towards the divine and celebrates several of the pillars of Islam. Nevertheless, compared to many other Iranian films, some of which were discussed in earlier readings [e.g., 11 and 12], it is unique in its explicit depictions of piety, devotion, and everyday life around a mosque. Unlike many other examples of post-revolutionary Iranian cinema, the mosque moves from being a presence in the background to a central space in the film's foreground. It is an endearing narrative, which casts Shi'ite Islam in a humane light. Both in Iran and among the Iranian diaspora it provoked many informal debates around both the virtues and the failings of this film.

Films initially intended for the local Iranian market are increasingly finding their way to international audiences. For instance, *Marmoulak* became one of Iran's most successful films ever in terms of box office receipts outside Iran, earning well over a million dollars in the United States alone. It is somewhat surprising that a theocratic Muslim nation, which has been demonized by certain leading Western politicians, produces films that are becoming increasingly popular beyond the Middle-East. There are many reasons for their magnetic appeal, including: their distinctive cinematic style, their crafted and diverse approach to telling stories, their ability to reveal glimpses of the intriguing real worlds of Iran, their blending of realistic and idiosyncratic moments, their gentle reflections on spiritual or religious themes, and the way that they show, in the words of the Persian poet Sadi, "The rose and the thorn, and sorrow and gladness are linked together." When these are crafted cinematically together, for some viewers at least, they can become moments of epiphany or as Michael Bird describes — hierophanies. In the reading provided here Bird defines what he means by hierophany. This excerpt is taken from his essay on "Film as Hierophany," which resonates with several of the readings in the second part of this reader, discussing the relation between realist and formalist approaches to film-making. Bird draws upon the work of Mircea Eliade and Paul Tillich to describe how a film's style "might enable an exploration of the sacred" and become "a disclosure of the transcendent or sacred precisely through the material of reality" (reading 61).

Bird's essay is taken from a book entitled *Religion in Film* (1982), which makes an interesting contrast with the title of John Lyden's more recent book *Film as Religion* (2003). Working through previous approaches to the relation between religion and film (including that set out by the Joel Martin reading below), Lyden argues through analogy, suggesting that "the practice of film viewing can be understood as a religion." Thus, the relation of religion and film is set as a type of "interreligious dialogue," in which both partners have intrinsic value at the discussion table (reading 64).

The next two readings work in a similar way by highlighting some of the specificities of *how* film is able to assert itself as an analogue to religion. Francisca Cho argues for a "cultic" mode of film viewing, a mode that is resonant with Chan Buddhist engagements with the arts in general. By examining the formal structures of Yong-Kyun Bae's 1989 *Why Has the Bodhi-Dharma Left for the East?*, Cho's 1999 article implicitly suggests that the filmic medium can provide a site for religious involvement for viewers (reading 62). Experimental and documentary filmmaker Nathaniel Dorsky also connects with the formal dimensions of film, suggesting that there are ways of making films that lend themselves to devotional attitudes in the viewing experience. Dorsky's 2003 article "Devotional Cinema" (reading 63), was originally given as a lecture at the Modern Museum of Art's exhibition on "The Hidden God," an exhibition that showcased the religion-film relation. Because of his background, Dorsky especially praises avant-garde film for its abilities to rearrange space and time, providing an experience for the viewer unlike any other human experience. Film has the potential to "realign our metabolism," and in this way performs an imminent revelatory function.

Meanwhile, in "The Footprints of Film" (2006) S. Brent Plate extends the religious experience of film-viewing into the cultural spaces beyond that of the initial screening (reading 66). He views the religion–film relation through the broader lens of visual culture, noting the myriad ways in which films leave the theaters and living rooms to reinvigorate traditional religious rituals such as bat mitzvahs and pilgrimages, midnight masses and weddings.

Plate implicitly suggests that "religion and film" cannot simply be sidelined to the margins of religious studies, but that anywhere the scholar of religion looks, she or he will find cinema.

Joel W. Martin and Conrad Ostwalt's book *Sreening the Sacred: Religion, Myth, and Ideology in Popular American Film* (1995) was, at its time of publication, ground-breaking in that it provided a model of how the film–religion relation could be studied from a number of different perspectives: theological, mythological, and ideological. These three are outlined out by Martin in the introduction to that volume (reading 65). Both their framework and the essays that they assembled gestured towards new directions in the study of film and religion. More recently, in *Religion and Film: An Introduction*, Melanie Wright provides a critique of previous approaches and outlines a method that attempts to avoid the danger of either casting film or religion in a subordinate role (reading 67). She makes a case for a cultural studies approach, going on from Margaret Miles' work in *Seeing and Believing* (1998), which will "be enhanced by focusing on the verbal, visual, distributional, promotional and other dimensions of the film experience, in addition to the narrative or textual ones."

There is an inevitable incompleteness about this reader. We began listing films for a filmography but found that it was never ending, assuming that we were to include the vast diversity of ways in which religion appears in films. We soon realized that given the energetic and rapidly evolving nature of discussions around religion and film, a reader could never be comprehensive, reflecting every single approach or written piece of significance. Instead we have offered a selection of windows onto debates, theories, and specific films. These windows provide views that are emblematic of how film, whether shown in a video-shop in West Africa, a renovated old hall in Europe, a newly opened cinema in the Middle-East, an outdoor screen in Asia, or a multiplex in North America, will continue to interact on many different levels with religious themes, personalities, and artifacts.

Chapter 61

Michael Bird

RELIGION IN FILM

Film as hierophany

IN HIS CLASSIC study of the mythic and ritualistic dimension of religion, Mircea Eliade introduces a concept that serves well the purposes of theological explorations of culture and art. This is the term *hierophany*, utilized by Eliade "to designate the *act of manifestation* of the sacred."[1] This concept is particularly valuable for those explorations that begin with the everyday raw material of existence, for a hierophany is a disclosure of the transcendent or sacred precisely through the material of reality, "the manifestation of something of a wholly different order, a reality that does not belong to our world, in objects that are an integral part of our natural 'profane' world."[2]

The paradoxical nature of reality seen in this light consists in the fact that it discloses not only itself but also another dimension underlying it. "By manifesting the sacred, any object becomes *something else*, yet it continues to remain *itself*." While particular objects and places have traditionally been set aside in religious cultures as holy objects or spaces, a hierophanous manifestation can occur anywhere. "All nature is capable of revealing itself as cosmic sacrality. The cosmos in its entirety can become a hierophany."[3]

In proceeding from a general theological analysis of culture to a specific consideration of artistic expression – in our case, the film – it becomes necessary to clarify the special relation that film possesses to culture or reality. The popular reference to film as a "window" on culture does not of itself indicate the film–culture relationship, for the open window of Coventry Cathedral with its view of the surrounding urban-industrial setting is surely not attuned to culture in the same manner as the translucent apertures of Chartres or the sensual windows of the Art Nouveau Age. If film is to be considered as the locus of a hierophanous manifestation, it becomes imperative first to consider in what way culture itself can be said to point beyond itself toward the transcendental dimension, and then to specify the unique position among the arts that cinema holds in the realistic representation of the world. In any cinematic theology one is required to delineate the objects of study; in the case at hand, they are culture, art, and film.

[. . .]

The aesthetic realism of film

The aesthetic defense of cinematic realism, a dramatic rejection of the formative theory of Arnheim and others, did not surface in a noticeable manner until the 1950s. Its chief spokesmen were André Bazin, Henri Agel, Alain Bandelier, Amédée Ayfre, and others in France, and, almost simultaneously, Siegfried Kracauer in Germany.

Bazin began his reformulation of classical film theory by revising the art-reality formula that had been dominant in the 1920s. Where it is the function of "art" to transform nature (referring particularly to painting), it is the "virtue" of photography, according to Bazin, to record nature as objectively as possible. Photography and cinema possess an *inherent* realism in that their relationship to nature is chemical.

[. . .]

Film realism and spiritual realism

The foregoing discussion of film theory has emphasized the development of the gradual recognition of film's special affinity with reality. If film is understood to possess a continuity with the world it represents, then in order for cinema to have a means by which it can open us to the dimension of the sacred, this means would have to be directed to the discernment of the holy *within the real*, rather than leading away from the real as in the case of art that abolishes reality.

While many films have portrayed ostensibly religious subjects, these films have too often erred precisely in their disregard for the medium's stylistic virtues. Rather than the "biblical blockbusters" and insipid trivialities that are frequently offered under the guise of "religious films," what is required in a cinematic theology is a consideration of how the *style* of film can enable an exploration of the sacred (one recalls here the view of Tillich, in his analysis of religious art, that it is *style*, not subject matter, which is of primary significance).

One of Bazin's disciples, Amédée Ayfre, has developed what is possibly the most succinct and formidable exposition of a cinematic theology. As opposed to contrived "dramatizations" (the Hollywood religious film) on the one hand, or strict documentary records of daily reality on the other hand, Ayfre suggests that there is a cinematic approach to the sacred that discloses not only its surface appearances but also its inner strivings that point to its depth. "Genuinely" religious films, by no means restricted to explicitly religious subjects, are those in which the cinematographic recording of reality does not exhaust reality but rather evokes in the viewer the sense of its ineffable mystery. This cinematic realism confronts the spectator with a reality "in which there is more than that of which it is the image."[4] A fundamental criterion for such a cinematic realism is that it explore the real by means of the real. It should transcend the every day precisely through the every day. This phenomenon is described by one writer as "the manifestation of the evangelical paradox," according to which it is necessary to lose oneself in order to find oneself. The criterion of the authenticity of an "image of mystery" is that the image must deliver something other than itself, but by no means other than itself.[5] It is not necessary to seek to contrive mystery by re-creating it, since it is the character of reality to point toward its ground. Bandelier thus polemicizes against Simone de Beauvoir: "The preliminary question formulated by Simone de Beauvoir: 'Never have I perceived on earth any celestial sign; if there is a trace, it is terrestrial,' is to forget the nature even of a sign."[6]

The search for the holy by means of a "spiritual realism" means the recognition of both the incarnational (a rootedness in reality itself) and the transcendent element (a self-negating quality discernible in reality). It is this "spiritual realism" as a cinematic style that enables the religious film to go outside a parochial subject matter. From the standpoint of a "spiritual realism," most of these films are in fact not religious at all: "If, in effect, one places them in aesthetic structures which have not been well thought out to receive them, or if one arrives at them with an insufficient sense of their incarnation and transcendence, their normal 'load' of mystery and the supernatural dissolves, leaving only traces of moral reminiscences, a few manufactured 'miracles' or some artificial 'idealizations.' "[7]

In these realist statements, one finds something of a *creed* in which cinema's technical properties become the vehicle of meditation. This creed requires a particular spiritual sensitivity in which the sacred is sought as the depth in reality itself. This understanding of reality has been expressed by film makers who adhere to this realist manifesto. A notable spokesman is the French director Robert Bresson, who said with respect to his 1956 film *A Man Escaped*: "I was hoping to make a film about objects which would at the same time have a soul. That is to say, to reach the latter through the former."[8] This understanding of reality pointing toward its depth is determinative of Carl Dreyer's realism in his film *The Passion of Joan of Arc*, as that realism is described by Henri Agel: "Thus Dreyer remains in love with the epidermic surface of things and beings. It is because Dreyer is concerned with this 'physicality' of his characters (Joan of Arc), because 'each pore of the skin is made familiar to us,' that the transfiguration of a tormented human substance can become a Christ-substance."[9]

This assessment of Dreyer's work suggests its affinity with Dufrenne's maxim, "To feel is, in a sense, to transcend." Indeed, paralleling Dufrenne's view that "the real solicits disclosure" or that "the real expects its meaning to be spoken" is Agel's lively description of nature as the "mother of images" (borrowed from Gaston Bachelard): "Nature is poetic in some of the images it offers because it is itself a poet in its own way, because it is not the Mother Earth, the Lucretian Venus, but is rather the mother of images. . . . These images are pregnant with their own world – their unveiling goes beyond the given data."[10]

The linking of images with nature, and of beauty with meaning, both ideas that are to be found in Dufrenne's phenomenology of aesthetic experience, means that a realism which is poetic (sensitive to beauty) is simultaneously a realism which is spiritual (sensitive to meaning). Cinema can heighten our perception of things pointing beyond themselves by means of a realism which is sensitive to the paradoxical character of reality, to be aware of a "distance within the heart of things," to see a thing "present in its very absence, graspable in its ungraspability, appearing in its disappearing."[11]

The critique of "contrived religious films" expressed variously by Bazin, Ayfre, Agel, and others brings to mind in a most pointed fashion the ancient debate over the religious function of Christian icons. Those who wished to save (or later reinstate) the tradition of icon-veneration were compelled to demonstrate that popular piety could comprehend the distinction between image and ultimate reality. Is this not the theological dilemma posed by the very idea of a "religious film"? The most dreaded consequences of misguided icon-veneration (giving way to worship of the image itself) are surely not lost in Agel's criticism of Eisenstein, for example. Eisenstein's films, for all their majestic drama and technical beauty, are works that seek to create experience rather than engender it. The spectator's encounter with reality or its ground is undermined by an art that overwhelms nature, as in the case of so many of the supposedly religious films in which an arsenal of cinematic devices is called upon to "create" supernatural happenings. Like Agel, Bandelier warns, "the image is not reality, it only gives the illusion. . . . It is necessary to recognize that this is the road paved by so many good intentions, from the great biblical 'machines' to the small hagiographic 'tricks.' "[12]

Common to all of these writers in defense of the inherent realism of cinema is the recognition of a spiritual orientation necessitated by the medium itself. This is cinema's "openness" to the cosmos which it seeks to represent. According to Kracauer, the film possesses, along with the novel, a capacity for the "rendering of life in its fullness" and a "tendency toward endlessness."[13] This openness allows the film to begin with reality and advance toward its spiritual depth. "The cinema is materialistically-minded: it proceeds from 'below' to 'above.' "[14] The encounter with the sacred cannot bypass the material world to which the film medium is so closely wedded. As Kracauer puts it, "we cannot hope to embrace reality unless we penetrate to its lowest layers. . . . But how can we gain access to these lower depths? One thing is sure, the task of contacting them is greatly facilitated by photography and film, both of which not only isolate physical data but reach their climax in representing."[15]

Of the films frequently emphasized by proponents of realist cinema when drawing attention to film's sacred or hierophanous possibilities, one work particularly worthy of consideration is Robert Bresson's The Diary of a Country Priest. Bresson repeatedly intensifies moments and events so as to create a paradoxical realism, in which the humblest subjects reveal within them certain stirrings of the sacred: "Yet, without obviously changing anything in this mediocrity and apparent filthiness, without expressionistic lighting or musical effects, simply through the precision of directing and acting, everything is turned inwards and takes on a different meaning. Beyond this surface, which is still and sordid as ever, one can glimpse another dimension: that of the soul."[16]

Bresson is one of few directors who has managed in his cinematic realism to focus simultaneously upon the familiar and the mysterious. Some writers (Ayfre, for one) have called attention to both the realism and the strangeness of Bresson's films. This is especially the case with Bresson's actors, who according to his dictates concerning realist cinema refrain from acting at all. Instead they pose as transparent figures through or behind whom a spiritual significance is discerned. "They open up a literally endless perspective on themselves, on the universe, even on the whole of existence. In fact there is always something fundamental and mysterious in them which escapes us."[17] This mysterious and discomforting quality is later described by Ayfre as the surface indicator of the depth of experience that each character possesses. Indeed, the significance of the mystery of characters for Bresson's style may be precisely that his style suggests his self-understanding as an artist, who is "not a god, but a mediator"

(Agel), who lets his own experience of the awesome distance from the Absolute become that of the spectator. Concerning Bresson's characters, it is suggested that "they are people whose ultimate secret is beyond them, too."[18] The mystery of negation and affirmation, of absence and presence, is expressed by Bresson by means of a realism that is "charged" – Raymond Durgnat calls it an "intense realism."[19] Durgnat argues that the power of feeling of such a physical work is what enables The Diary of a Country Priest to express the spiritual: "This intense 'physicality' and 'materialism' explain how the film feels so intense even though, dramatically, there is so little emphasis and so many omissions."[20] This description of Bresson's style echoes Dufrenne's understanding of "the sensuous" in aesthetic experience and its power of expression through feeling.

In Bresson's films, the human boundary-situation is reached through his frequent intensification of the physical world, accompanied by a dissolution of that very world. In The Diary of a Country Priest, for example, the conclusion of the film is marked by an absence of the foregoing world of "physicality" and "materiality" in favor of a sustained photograph of a plain cross accompanied by the voice of the Curé de Torcy which describes the death of the priest. Bazin says of this conclusion, "At the point which Bresson has reached, the image can become more eloquent only by disappearing altogether."[21] In this view, the final scene gains its power from the realism of the film, by which the spectator experiences simultaneously an interrelatedness of affirmation and negation: "For the final shot of the cross acquires its meaning by its relationship to the drama, by the way in which it 'supplants' the physical world by the venerable cinematic principle of montage. Bresson's film is firmly rooted in the physical – in the reflection of cancer in the priest's face – and the cross is an image of its total sacrifice. The spiritual has devoured the flesh."[22]

Bresson's realism is manifest in the almost non-expressive acting which he imposes upon his cast, a minimization which seems to produce that transcendence of which Ayfre speaks – a translucence to another world underlying surface appearances. Speaking of a man's countenance as the "imprint of his soul," Bazin says of Bresson's portrayal of faces: "What we are asked to look for in their faces is not for some fleeting reflection of the words but for an uninterrupted condition of soul, the outward revelation of an interior destiny."[23]

[. . .]

In its intensification of those movements and spaces where reality is seen to be straining in its anguish, its void, its divisions, toward its boundary-situation, at which the dimension of depth breaks in, cinema becomes at least the witness for and frequently the agent of "the manifestation of something of a wholly different order, a reality that does not belong to our world."[24] At such points film becomes hierophany.

Notes

1   Mircea Eliade, *The Sacred and the Profane*. New York: Harper, 1961, 11.

2   Ibid.

3   Ibid., 12.

4   Amédée Ayfre, "Conversion aux Images?," in Henri Agel, *Le Cinéma et le Sacré*. Paris: Editions du Cerf, 1961, 12.

5   Alain Bandelier, "Cinéma et Mystère," as quoted in Amédée Ayfre, *Cinéma et Mystère*. Paris: Editions du Cerf, 1969, 86.

6   Ibid., 108.

7   Ibid., 16.

8   As quoted in Amédée Ayfre, "The Universe of Robert Bresson," in *The Films of Robert Bresson*, ed. Ian Cameron. New York: Praeger, 1969, 8.

9   Henri Agel, *Poétique du Cinéma*. Paris: Editions du Signe, 1960, 59.

10   Ibid., 14.

11   Ibid., 50.

12   Bandelier, "Cinéma et Mystère," in Ayfre, *Cinéma et Mystère*, 80–81.

13   Kracauer, *Theory of Film*, 233.

14   Ibid., 309.

15   Ibid., 298.

16   Ayfre, "The Universe of Robert Bresson," in Cameron, *The Films of Robert Bresson*, 11.

17   Ibid., 12.

18   Ibid.

19   Raymond Durgnat, "Le Journal d'un Curé de Campagne," in Cameron, *The Films of Robert Bresson*, 47.

20   Ibid., 48.

21   Ibid. Bazin describes this scene as the culmination of a spiritual pilgrimage: "The spectator has been led, step by step, toward that night of the senses the only expression of which is a light on a blank screen," *What is Cinema?*, 140.

22   Durgnat, "Le Journal d'un Curé de Campagne," in Cameron, *The Films of Robert Bresson*, 48. The use of montage here is certainly one of the cinema's more restrained examples of the principle.

23   Bazin, *What is Cinema?*, 133.

24   Eliade, *The Sacred and Profane*, 11.

Chapter 62

Francisca Cho

IMAGINING NOTHING AND IMAGING OTHERNESS IN BUDDHIST FILM

THE GROWING INTEREST in the relationship between religion and film provides us with an opportunity to articulate fully the way in which visual images signify meaning. As scholars of religion who are immersed in logocentric forms of communication, it is tempting to treat film as yet another text that discloses itself in the same way. It is interesting, I propose, to try to articulate and appreciate film as a "cultic" experience that participates in a broader and distinctly non-logocentric tradition of religious signification. The cultic mode of signification can be elaborated through a theory of religious meaning that dovetails with Chan Buddhist "antidiscourses" about the experience of otherness, or religious breakthrough. Hence, the theoretical portion of this essay is inextricably bound up with the religious and cultural milieu in which the analysis is situated.

The Buddhist film

Why Has Bodhi-Dharma Left for the East? is a Buddhist film. The title is derived from a Chan (Zen) Buddhist koan, which is a public record of dialogues between medieval Chinese masters and their disciples. The figure Bodhidharma (460–534) that is evoked in this koan riddle is the Indian monk who journeyed to China and whom Chan Buddhism recognizes as the first patriarch of its lineage. The film tells the story of three contemporary Buddhist monks living in a dilapidated hermitage on a remote mountaintop above the main temple complex, and high above a bustling city. Haejin is the orphan child who was discovered and adopted by Hyegok, the Chan master of the temple. Kibong is the young disciple who abandoned his impoverished mother and sister in order to seek self-transcendence through religion. Hyegok, the mature master, guides both disciples as he himself moves towards death. The Korean director, Bae Yong-kyun, was drawn to Asian philosophy as a troubled adolescent and spent some time in Buddhist study and practice. In college, Bae focused on painting and art history, eventually earned a doctorate and joined the Faculty of Fine Arts as a teacher of painting. In fulfilling a lifelong dream of making a film, Bae completely circumvented the mainstream film industry and single-handedly wrote, directed, filmed, and edited Bodhi. It was released in 1989, after ten years in the making, and garnered recognition at the Cannes Film Festival and Korea's first ever director's prize at the Locarno Film Festival.

The label of "Buddhism" or "Buddhist" can be somewhat of a burden, as Bae admits. He states, "I'm afraid to call myself a Buddhist because belief cannot be attained easily nor can it be measured."[1] Bodhi would probably disappoint the viewer in search of discursive explanations of Buddhist dogma. If this betrays the point of calling Bodhi a Buddhist film, then Bae's own self-accounting, at least, follows Buddhist tradition. "The ten years I committed to the making of Bodhi were a kind of practice for me," he states. "Even though I didn't practice conventionally, the process of creating that movie was like holding a koan in one's mind." To harness one's art as one's spiritual practice invokes centuries of Chan tradition, which was perhaps most broadly – and certainly most famously – realized in Japanese Zen. The zenga, or Zen arts of Japan, is comprised mostly of the paintings and calligraphy of Zen masters, but has also been associated with all manner of cultural practices (e.g., tea ceremony, flower arrangement, No drama), making for a broad aesthetic association. If some object to such a broad usage of the term Zen art, its very existence nevertheless exemplifies the Chan wisdom that enlightenment is "nothing special," that it inheres in the mundane things of this world and that it can be expressed through worldly activity – a wisdom that is traditionally and paradoxically contemplated in isolated hermitages.

The theological, mythological, and ideological modes of film analysis can all be equally contrasted to what I call the cultic mode of signification. I interpret Bodhi as cultic art in which ideological content is subservient to its significance as ritual function. Although rituals usually have ideological content, their "meaning" is defined more relevantly as an event. The religious significance of these events, since we must attempt to verbalize it in some way, is that they create or manifest a momentous form of "presence." In our discourse, of course, we want to know how this "presence" may be understood, both by the practitioners and by us, the theorists. Very extensive definitions of this presence demonstrate how easily the ideological reading can overtake the cultic form of appreciation. One example is offered by Mircea Eliade's understanding of the sacrality of all art, by which he means that art functions as hierophany. Eliade uses a theophantic model that imitates the Christian mystery of the Incarnation. Art is sacred because it reveals the divine by means of "something other" than itself. Crucial to this model is the doctrine that the divine is formless and limitless – completely "Other" (God), which through art can paradoxically take on limited material form (the Incarnation). Although Eliade's approach to art participates in a cultic reading, it is overshadowed by the ideological interpretation supplied by his use of explicitly Christian categories. A critical question that is raised by this example is whether or not, in our limited academic discourse, it is ever possible to avoid the hegemony of ideological readings. Before attending to this issue, I will first account for my own version of cultic reading.

The model that I employ borrows from David Freedberg's theory of response based on his art historical study of images. According to Freedberg's cross-cultural theory, the power of images is that they make real what is represented, and hence present what is otherwise absent. The absent/present object can be understood as historical or spiritual, depending on the image and the viewer's culturally conditioned response to it. There is an inherent religious signification in this process, however, in that the painter's status as magician or seer in pre-modern cultures puts the artist on a par with divine creators. In Buddhist East Asia, this status is attested to by the numerous miracle tales of images that come alive, often in response to the behests and needs of the pious. The tales invest Buddhist icons with the power of movement and speech, and their lifelike quality is emphasized by details such as their ability to grow hair. These tales arise from an active cult of icons in which images are enlivened by the worshipper. Thus if artists have the ability to breathe life into icons, then this power is also dependent on a cultic imagination and a context of cultic practice. Such a cultural environment mandates the perspicacity of the image maker, sometimes even in spite of himself, as the following tale recounts. An old book from the Silla dynasty (seventh to tenth century Korea) tells of how a court artist was ordered to paint a portrait of the Chinese Emperor's favorite beauty. While completing the finishing touches, the artist is so moved by his lifelike creation that he trembles and his brush slips, marking a mole below the portrait's navel. The Emperor is infuriated by this evidence of the painter's intimacy with the lady, but the artist is liberated from a death sentence after he successfully paints the lovely woman that the Emperor dreamt of the previous night. This lady turns out to be an image of the Bodhisattva Guanyin.

The appearance of the Bodhisattva in the Emperor's dream proves to be the artist's saving grace, but as a vehicle, it also reiterates the painter's status as an almost unwitting conduit of reality. Eliade invokes this status for modern secular artists as well – although most have little use for overt religious symbols, their creative activity nevertheless "camouflages" a cosmic religiosity. One might accuse Eliade of having it backwards – it is not the ideological symbols that are so interesting but rather the power behind them that elicits our response. The slide from artistic representation to cultic presence that is at the center of Freedberg's theory of response, in any case, is a psychological and behavioral construct that is separate from the many and varied ideological interpretations that can be put upon it. To be sure, the constructs of psychology are no less declamatory than the dogmas of Christianity, but in Freedberg's hands, they have a broad application that makes for much theoretical usefulness. The cultic power of art is the universal ability of art to provoke responses by virtue of the human tendency to move from the gaze, to arousal, to the enlivening of the image. Quite importantly, Freedberg's theory of response does not require ideological self-awareness in order to be activated and appreciated. Indeed, Freedberg emphatically proposes that cognitive understanding and rationalization – he is concerned primarily with the discourse of art criticism – functions to mask and repress cultic responses to art. The broad applicability of Freedberg's theory of response is also evident in its indifference to distinctions between "high" and "low" art, and ultimately to the distinction between religious and secular art. In refusing to be bound by these ideology-based distinctions, Freedberg's insights into the power of images offer a clarity and simplicity that avoid the awkwardness of premises such as the "camouflaging of the sacred."

A cultic reading of the religious, or more specifically, the Buddhist significance of Bodhi is consistent with how most Buddhists have read and responded to Buddhist icons in the popular ritual context. This is, to some degree, an observation about cultural differences. The ideological bias in how religion is defined and studied – that is, the privileging of belief systems over ritual praxis – is often traced to the doorstep of Protestant Christianity. It has been charged that the study of religion as a discipline has been overly infected by this denominational bias. Buddhist studies has been informed by the Protestant ethic since its beginnings, with its emphasis on doctrine and canonical texts, and only of late has followed its colleagues in "primitive" religions in employing alternative definitions of religion. David Freedberg's own study of art history also posits the exceptional nature of the Protestant attitude and urges the fruitfulness of a cultic understanding of Christian images and practices. The ideological-cultic polarity, then, is indicative of an academic cleavage in the understanding of religion.

There is a particular difficulty, however, in advocating a cultic understanding of religious significance. If I am serious about this notion of meaning, then I can do no better than to halt my own discourse and simply commend the reader to a viewing of the film. But this too presents a problem. Westerners who survive the pace and subverted narrative conventions of Bodhi will invariably want to know what it "means." The obstacle lies in the broader cultural prevalence of the ideological notion of meaning. My task, then, is to describe the nature of cultic response rather than to provoke one. My rational discourse cannot metamorphose into the cultic experience that it describes, but it can hopefully aid the reader to recognize it. This descriptive task is historical in that it appeals to the evidence of specific cultures, and normative in that it advocates the reality and importance of the cultic mode of religious signification. Both the historical and normative endeavors are nevertheless themselves ideological in how they signify. Just as a theory of the novel must always speak in an idiom that is separate from that of fiction itself, I cannot avoid discursive language in arguing for the theoretical construct of cultic power.

The Buddhist metaphysics of presence that I utilized in the narrative interpretation of Bodhi also provides an intellectual basis for the reading/viewing of film as a form of cultic power. With this new application of Buddhist thought, I turn to Buddhism as the source of my theory making rather than as the object of ideological clarification. In other words, Buddhism is the instrument of my analysis rather than its target. My use of Buddhist theory to ground an understanding of cultic power is related to the historical dimension of my descriptive task. To reiterate, Buddhist icons and the Buddhist practices surrounding them have traditionally been experienced as cultic rather than as ideological forms of meaning. This Buddhist experience instantiates a more pervasive phenomenon in East Asia, where even pre-Buddhist icons – the ghost money and funerary tablets used in the native practice of ancestor worship, for example – serve as signs that trap within themselves the power of ultimate reality. What I add to these observations is the claim that Buddhist ideological discourse provides the most effective framework for appreciating this phenomenon – within Buddhism and potentially beyond. Thus my use of Buddhist sources is more than an effort to interpret Buddhist practices through the lens of its own theories. It is a claim about the efficacy of the Buddhist theory qua theory, whatever the context of practice. Conversely, because the purpose of the Buddhist theory is to clarify the nature and operations of cultic power generally, its effect is to slight Buddhism's denominational distinctness. Against the strategy of using film in the service of religious ideological disclosure, one can reduce the Buddhism of Bodhi to nothing more than the cultic power of art itself.

Let us return to another look at Bodhi, then, and describe a portion of it in specifically cultic rather than ideological perspective. I will do so by concentrating on one aspect of the film *qua* film – specifically, its quality of montage, or sequence and juxtapositioning of scenes. One of the challenging aspects of watching *Bodhi* is its tendency to violate the convention of narrative continuity. It jumps back and forth, for example, between the present identity of Kibong as a Buddhist monk and his past life as a householder without any warning or any indication that the two are even the same person. Pointing to other crosscut scenes, one reviewer of the film remarks, "Temporal and spatial leaps like these cause us to wonder which part of the film is reality, which part dream."[2] Bae's nonlinear deployment of montage is evident from the very beginning of the film, and underscored by the fact that the first fifteen minutes is devoid of any story establishing dialogue or narration. I will focus on this portion of the film and explore how its montage shapes the viewing experience.

The opening shot dwells on a young man at a railroad crossing, his figure dominated by the flashing red light that looms in the foreground. The next scene jumps to a closely cropped shot of a window, beautifully dilapidated and traditional in its paper and wood construction. The soundtrack switches from clanging city noises to the sound of idyllic insects, impinged by the gentle voice of an old man calling the name "Haejin." The window opens to reveal a serene courtyard. The scene cuts to a cluster of ripe berries hanging from a tree, which is picked and eaten by a young child whose face is mostly obscured by the tight camera frame. Back in the hermitage courtyard, an old monk picks up a piece of a fallen window frame and fits it back in place. At this point the viewer has been "introduced" to the three characters of the film – Kibong, Hyegok, and Haejin, but these opening scenes hardly do the work of conventional establishing shots. Instead of story, the emphasis is on images, as made evident in the subsequent sequence of tightly framed shapes and textures: Water is scooped from a pear-shaped gourd into a round cup. The roundness of the cup is echoed in a shot of Haejin's bald head reflected in rippling pond water. Boiling water is poured into the cup, and the scene cuts to a back shot of Hyegok seated on a veranda drinking tea. Another cut to a looming shot of a golden Buddha statue, centered on its imperturbable face.

Bodhi has been observed to "[teach] not through its narrative but through its overpowering visual offerings."[3] That these visual scrutinies are meant to "teach" anything at all is perhaps conveyed by the next shot. The old master Hyegok reads from a sutra, offering the only spoken lines in the film's opening, and appears to preach to a retreating and indifferent frog (in a cut-away shot) about the interchangeability of beginnings and endings, and of life and death. The didactic Buddhist content of this verbal intrusion binds the montage of opening shots into a visual koan that signifies meaning through the very process of upsetting the expectations of narrative and logical coherence. If koans are accounts of the non sequitur verbal and physical exchanges between

Chan masters and their disciples, then the visual entry into *Bodhi* – as well as much of its unfolding – is similar in its non-narrative aspects. *Bodhi's* montage does not convey an obvious storyline and, as a result, it "demands that the viewer bring a lot to the interpretation."[4] Like the koan, however, standard forms of interpretation yield little fruit and the point seems to lie in the confusion itself, which can be experienced as either frustrating or enlightening. The end result is determined by the individual viewer, but it is provoked by strategies that parallel the perlocutionary tactics of the koan.

I have been referring to *Bodhi's* narrative (or lack thereof) simply in terms of characters, plot and sequential time. It will be useful, however, to move to an exact definition of narrative that distinguishes it from other literary genres such as the lyric and drama (both of which also utilize character, plot, and sequence). In addition to a story (events or persons that are narrated), the most telling quality of narrative has been defined as its "magisterial voice."[5] In literary form, this entails a storyteller or narrator "who possesses (and implicitly promises) magisterial overview, the ability to see persons and events comprehensively, cohesively, intelligibly, and with minimal instability. . . ."[6] In the literary medium, the third person voice offers the most unalloyed of narrative perspectives. Its omniscient and distancing posture contrasts sharply with the first person, subjective and intimate voice of the lyric; and the multiple, limited, and competing voices of the drama.

I delineate these genre distinctions in order to draw a limited comparison to film – to suggest that the *experience* of viewing film (as opposed to actual film genres) is often akin to the narrative voice of literature. This is so because film is a visual medium. The power of images – which is more immediate than the abstract code of language – creates the experience of presence, and therefore the presumption of reality. As film theorists have noted, the cinematic image seduces with its directness and hides the fact that visual apprehension can also be a form of manipulation. The ideological mode of film criticism is concerned to point out that the verisimilitude of cinema is an illusion that communicates something more than its images, and that these images are lyrical manufactures of a specific creator. The insight of this criticism is predicated on the ability of film to reinforce the spectator's sense of omniscience by allowing her to occupy the controlling consciousness of the film.

Film can resort to actual voice-over narration, but montage is the more effective aspect of film grammar that allows the spectator this experience of mastery. When conventional montage is deployed, the spectator's ability to follow the story and the characters produces the experience of an "infallible perceptual fullness."[7] In other words, watching film reinforces our unconscious sense of intelligibility, which in turn keeps our sense of coherent and unified selfhood intact. But words and images can also be utilized to opposite purpose.

"Ch'an discourse," for example, "is disruptive, first of itself and then of its reader, by overturning and undercutting any effort to hold on to it as correct vision or true belief."[8] If koans are speech acts specifically designed to violate and therefore call attention to the illusion of mastery, then Bodhi is a film that accomplishes the same objective in the context of its own language. The specific result of both perlocutionary texts is to throw one into confusion because the violation of normal grammar confounds one's sense of reality. While it is easy to dismiss such ungrammatical representations as bad speech or art, Chan Buddhism utilizes this very strategy as a form of soteriology that destroys illusory constructs of reality and self.

Bodhi can be described as non-narrative in two distinct but related ways. First, its opening montage fails to establish the expected elements of story – the delineation of character, plot, and time sequence. Second, this failure impugns the viewer's expectation of mastery and demands a very different version of perceptual fullness. If the power of images can be bent to reinforcing standard constructions of intelligibility, it can also be utilized to break that construct down and scrutinize it. Bodhi's montage does not respect the conventional barriers between individual selves and between the human and natural worlds, following traditional Buddhist teachings that emphasize the egalitarian emptiness of all things and the unifying dominance of movement and process. This message is the essence of Hyegok's sutra reading, and the subsequent scenes reinforce it. We see Kibong in his monk's habit chopping wood high atop the hermitage mountain range. The breathtaking landscape that Kibong pauses to contemplate is only one of many such cinematic inquiries. Here the contemplation is bracketed by Kibong's human activity, which is brought to a halt when he cuts his own hand and the blood mingles with the elements of earth and wood. The next scene features another natural setting – a stream from which Haejin emerges to stone the bird whose death and whose mate will haunt him throughout the film. The water interlude transitions back to Kibong bearing his load of chopped wood through the mountain trails, but this fragment of narrative continuity is quickly lost as the scene cuts from his deep contemplation of trees and rocks to his former, secular self in depressive contemplation in the family slum dwelling. This prolonged and jarring juxtapositioning finally cuts back to the mountain valley, this time devoid of all human presence and dominated only by the wind. The inventory of nature comes to one full circle as the scene switches to the roaring fire in the hermitage hearth, and the first dialogue of the film commences as Haejin, who is tending the fire, engages an unseen Kibong in a conversation about the world below the mountain and the mother he has never known.

Bodhi's opening images allows for "no controlling consciousness – no human point from which the narrative is constructed which the viewer can occupy as her own."[9] The alternative, then, is the metaphysics of presence in which perceptual fullness is derived from attentiveness to what simply is, minus the usual conceits of intelligibility. Bae's use of montage in a way that destroys the expected delineations of narrative has didactic – and therefore ideological – content, but the film communicates only by virtue of the ability of the viewer to tolerate and profit by its cinematic transgressions.

> Delusion and enlightenment
> two sides of a coin
> Universal and particular
> just parts of one whole
> All day long I read the wordless scriptures
> All night I practice no-practice meditation
> On the riverbank, a bush warbler
> sings in the weeping willow
> In the sleeping village
> a dog bays at the moon
> Nothing troubles the free flow of my feelings
> But how can this mind be passed on?[10]

Notes

1   "A Conversation with Bae Yong-Kyun," in *Tricycle: The Buddhist Review*, Summer 1994: 104.

2   Linda Ehrlich's review in *Film Quarterly*, 48.1, Fall 1994, 27.

3   Ibid., 31.

4   See Michael Gillespie's "Picturing the Way in Bae Yong-Kyun's *Why Has the Bodhi-Dharma Left for the East?*", in *Journal of Religion and Film*, 1.1, April 1997: http://www.unomaha.edu/jrf/gillespi.htm.

5   I take this point from Frederick Ruf's *Entangled Voices*, New York: Oxford University Press, 1997.

6   Ibid., 62.

7   I borrow the phrase "infallible perceptual fullness" from David James. This phrase arose in the context of our conversation of September 1, 1998, about montage and the French New Wave school of film theory, represented by figures such as Jean-Luc Godard.

8   Dale Wright, "Discourse of Awakening," *Journal of the American Academy of Religion* 61.1, Spring 1993, 33.

9   David James, in specific reference to *Bodhi*, from the same conversation referenced in note 7.

10 Quoted in Ryuichi Abe, "A Poetics of Mendicancy," in *Great Fool Zen Master Ryokan*. Honolulu: University of Hawaii Press, 1996, 42.

Chapter 63

Nathaniel Dorsky

DEVOTIONAL CINEMA

WHEN I FIRST ENCOUNTERED avant-garde films in the early 1960s, the works I found most interesting were those that were discovering a language unique to film, a language that enabled the viewer to have the experience of film itself and, at the same time, allowed film be an evocation of something meaningfully human. I began to notice that moments of revelation or aliveness came to me from the way a filmmaker used film itself. Shifts of light from shot to shot, for instance, could be very visceral and affective. I observed that there was a concordance between film and our human metabolism, and that this concordance was a fertile ground for expression, a basis for exploring a language intrinsic to film. In fact, film's physical properties seemed *so* attuned to our metabolism that I began to experience film as a direct and intimate metaphor or model for our being, a model which had the potential to be transformative, to be an evocation of spirit, and to become a form of devotion.

The word "devotion," as I am using it, need not refer to the embodiment of a specific religious form. Rather, it is the opening or the interruption that allows us to experience what is hidden, and to accept with our hearts our given situation. When film does this, when it subverts our absorption in the temporal and reveals the depths of our own reality, it opens us to a fuller sense of ourselves and our world. It is alive as a devotional form.

[. . .]

The post-film experience

I think the first time I began to suspect that film was powerful, even something to be feared, was when I was nine years old. This was in the early 1950s, before television had become all-pervasive. I used to go to the movies on Saturday afternoons, and on one particular day there was a special kiddie matinee that included three features, ten cartoons, and a good dose of previews, all in one sitting. We entered into darkness at twelve noon and came out hours later at 6:30. As the last film ended, the green metal side doors opened into the late-afternoon light, and we walked up the alley onto the street. I remember having the oddest sensation. The texture of the sunlight seemed strange, and people's voices sounded distant. In front of the theater cars were whooshing by the storefronts. Quite suddenly, the normal things that were my usual reference points, everything that had been familiar to me in my hometown, all its arche-types and icons, became eerie and questionable. I felt alien and estranged. I remember walking home alone through the park and passing the duck pond and the baseball diamonds, and then down a small path, a dirt shortcut worn through the lawn that eventually disappeared into the grass. All those little details were presenting themselves to me in a way I was unused to. It was truly disturbing. Eventually I got home, and it even seemed odd that I was in my house. I was feeling this quite strongly and was trying my best to recover from the giant hole that had opened up in the middle of my head. I remember having to get some things out of the refrigerator to reorient myself and make it all right again.

[. . .]

I began to wonder about what this post-film experience is. How do we feel when a film is over? There are films, for instance, that are intellectually rigorous, or "adult," but when the lights come up at the end of them we feel unhealthy in some way. We're embarrassed to be with one another. We've all had the experience of walking out of a theater and not really wanting to see anyone – of looking down at the bizarre design on the rug, the soda stains, and so forth, and averting our eyes from our fellow filmgoers. I realized from these experiences that there was something in cinema beyond its intellectual or narrative content. There was something in the actual nature of the cinema, its view, that could produce health or illness in an audience. There might be a film that had a very meaningful subject but was so inelegantly handled that it actually left one feeling unhealthy or alienated.

I began to become more sensitive to these post-film experiences and the qualities in a film that might produce either health or ill health. I knew from my experience that this possibility extended into other media. I remember once being quite sick when my friend Jerome and I went to a student production of *Così fan tutte* at a local college. I didn't want to go but I went anyway. And when I came out of the opera, I was completely cured. The youthful performance was endearing and sometimes painful, but because the genius of the music is so uncompromised, so transforming to the metabolism, the experience of going to the opera healed me. This has happened to me quite a few times from going to a Mozart opera.

Similarly, attending the ballets of George Balanchine can realign one's energy in a way that is deeply, alchemically healthy. I believe this occurs when there is something metaphysically true about a work's energy. In Greek theories of medicine it was taught that illness came from a dreamlike absorption, a state of imbalance. The sanctuary of Epidaurus was created in order to let citizens realign themselves and awaken to the full energy of the present. Long periods of relaxation and sleep, called "temple sleep," were followed by theater pieces, chanting, and poetry. All this took place in a setting of sublimely proportioned architecture. So art has had a long history of being used as a healthy model.

What is it about the nature of film that can produce health or ill health? It is film's ability to mirror and realign our metabolism.

[. . .]

The illuminated room

We view films in the context of darkness. We sit in darkness and watch an illuminated world, the world of the screen. This situation is a metaphor for the nature of our own vision. In the very process of seeing, our own skull is like a dark theater, and the world we see in front of us is in a sense a screen. We watch the world from the dark theater of our skull. The darker the room, the more luminous the screen.

It is important to understand what we're participating in, to realize that we rest in darkness and experience vision. Many people take vision as a given and don't realize that they are actually seeing.

[. . .]

Film, insofar as it replicates our experience of vision, presents us with the tools to touch on and elucidate that experience. Viewing a film has tremendous mystical implications; it can be, at its best, a way of approaching and manifesting the ineffable. This respect for the ineffable is an essential aspect of devotion.

When cinema can make the internalized medieval and externalized Renaissance ways of seeing unite and transcend themselves, it can achieve a transcendental balance. This balance point unveils the transparency of our earthly experience. We are afloat. It is a balance that is neither our vision nor the belief in exterior objectivity; it belongs to no one and, strangely enough, exists nowhere. It is within this balance that the potential for profound cinema takes place.

Less visionary cinema is imbalanced toward one or the other of these two ways of seeing. One imbalance assumes that the world is out there and you are going to photograph it. In this case there is no view whatsoever; the subject matter seems somehow just to exist. That the film is even a film is somewhat arbitrary. We see these movies every time we get on an airplane, or wander desperately into our local multiplex. This form of film ignores the very substance it is made of. There is certainly no awareness of the formal dignity of existence that we have been speaking about.

Intermittence

The quality of light, as experienced in film, is intermittent. At sound speed there are twenty-four images a second, each about a fiftieth of a second in duration, alternating with an equivalent period of black. So the film we are watching is not actually a solid thing. It only appears to be solid.

On a visceral level, the intermittent quality of film is close to the way we experience the world. We don't experience a solid continuum of existence. Sometimes we are here and sometimes not, suspended in some kind of rapid-fire illusion. After all, do any of us know *who* we actually are? Although we assume that we are something solid, in truth we only experience and maneuver through our existence. After all, can anything really be solid?

On close examination, even our vision appears to be intermittent, which explains why, in film, pans often feel artificial or forced. This stems from the fact that one never pans in real life. In truth, when we turn our heads we don't actually see a graceful continuum but a series of tiny jump-cuts, little stills joined, perhaps, by infinitesimal dissolves. Thus our visual experience in daily life is akin to the intermittence of cinema.

[. . .]

Allowing intermittence into a film activates the viewer's mind. There is an opportunity to make connections, to feel alive and stimulated. Making these connections, activating these synapses, brings the viewer into the present moment.

Time

Time is one of the essential elements in film's alchemy. It is one of the most potent tools film has, yet few films connect profoundly with the plasticity of time and use the nature of time in their structure. It is the substance that, when handled properly, opens the door to the possibility of devotion.

There are two basic types of time in filmmaking. The first could be called relative time, which is how any film progresses from the first shot to the last. How a river flows from a mountain to the ocean, or how we progress from crawling infants to old people with walkers. The qualities of relative time are both subtle and dramatic: every river has white water followed by deep, translucent pools, then swirling currents, stagnant backwaters with mosquitoes, places where foam and sludge pile up. There are spectacular, frothy waterfalls and flat little rippling areas glistening in sunlight. A complete emotional range exists in our experience of relative time, and a film must respect these qualities. They are part of our lives.

At the same time, inspired filmmaking includes the presence of the other type of time: what might be called absolute time, or nowness. Nowness is always . . . nowness. Every moment of time exists in the context of nowness, the eternal now. Experiencing the relationship of nowness to relative time is akin to walking on a treadmill: the nowness is your presence while relative time passes under your feet. Nowness in cinema deeply respects the nowness in an audience.

[. . .]

For film to have a devotional quality both absolute and relative time must be active and present – not only present but functioning simultaneously and invigorating one another. Transformative film rests in the present and respects the delicate details of its own unfolding. How is this small miracle achieved? How do we manifest nowness in the ongoing context of the relative? It is not unlike having a heartfelt discussion with a friend. You hear what your friend says, and you respond from a place you may never have responded from before. You hear your friend again, you wait a second, and there's an actual moment of connection, a moment of genuine exploration that touches upon things never quite touched on before. That's when heart, intelligence, instinct, and awareness all come together. Reality opens and responds to itself.

[. . .]

Integrating these two qualities of time is a difficult and delicate task. Carl Theodor Dreyer accomplishes this in *The Passion of Joan of Arc* (1928) and *Ordet*

(1955), films made in different periods of his career. *The Passion of Joan of Arc*, which is silent and full of dramatically confrontational cuts and bold camera movements, is at the same time compassionately connected to its subject. Each shot, while part of the progression of the narrative's temporality, is nevertheless absolutely present as deep, vertical nowness. The photography doesn't *observe*, it *is*. The cuts, often propelled by the characters' head movements and facial gestures, spark with urgency and snap in declaration of the renewed presence of the narrative. The film is a complete unity of expression, a piece of light sculpture in time. All is present.

Ordet, made some thirty years later, has sound and a bare minimum of close-ups and character-motivated intercuts, which are reserved for the concluding scene. The strange altered light in this film, both interior and exterior, sets us in a suspended time. We are privileged to participate in a rare and purified world, a world of transformation. Time and space are never collapsed by temporal necessity. We find ourselves immersed in the long, flowing, earthbound takes. The ongoingness of the shots allows us to deepen our experience of nowness. Gaps in the narrative open up within the continuum of the shots. As the camera follows a character from one section of the room to another, the dialogue and character placement intensify and decompress, along with the energy of the drama. Between these moments of intensity we are lulled into relaxation, and thus when the shot intensifies again we feel our presence all the more strongly. This intensification sometimes happens through the unexpected entrance of a character into the frame, sometimes by a cut to the next unfolding event. This continual renewal gives the mystical intensity of the climactic scene a living presence, a grounded reality.

[...]

When the absolute and temporal are unified, film becomes a narrative of nowness and reveals things for what they are rather than as surrogates for some predetermined concept. It is the fear of direct contact with the uncontrollable present that motivates the flight into concept. The filmmaker seeks the safety net of an idea, or something to accomplish that is already known.

If we do relinquish control, we suddenly see a hidden world, one that has existed all along right in front of us. In a flash, the uncanny presence of this poetic and vibrant world, ripe with mystery, stands before us. Everything is expressing itself as what it is. Everything is alive and talking to us.

[...]

Shots and cuts

Shots and cuts are the two elemental opposites that enable film to transform itself. Shots are the accommodation, the connection, the empathy,
the view of the subject matter we see on the screen. The cuts are the clarity that continually reawakens the view. When there is a balance of these
essential elements, a film blossoms as light in the present tense and gives
devotion the space to manifest. Shots and cuts must each participate in this
clarity.

If the filmmaker is not cognizant of the fact that a shot must express both
the seer and what is seen, then the film's view isn't totally conscious. The
view is make-believe; it does not admit that vision is a meeting ground of
ourselves and the world. The filmmaker and what is seen are not in union.
The basic ingredients for alchemy are not present. So the question becomes:
how does a filmmaker selflessly unite the viewer with what is seen? If there is
too much self, then there is too much view. This imbalance often manifests as
the empty vanity of composition that overwhelms a less-felt subject matter.
On the other hand, if there is too much subject matter, then there is no view.
This imbalance ignores or sacrifices the visual fabric of film, which is its
strongest aspect, and the image becomes too illustrative. In either case the
film's vision is one-dimensional. Light in union with subject is no longer an
active element.

The camera must give itself completely and wholly to its subject, yet it
cannot give itself away to its subject. When a filmmaker is fully and selflessly
present, the audience becomes fully and selflessly present. The filmmaker's
physical relationship to the world manifests as the camera's relationship to the
image and becomes the audience's relationship to the screen. To the degree that
a filmmaker can relate directly to the heart of an object, the viewer will also
connect directly to the heart of the object. The audience will see the screen as
the camera sees the objects, and a great unity of heart will take place between
filmmaker and audience.

Shots and cuts need each other. They are cinema's primal handmaidens.
The shots, as moments of luminous accommodation, ripen and expand and are
popped like soap bubbles by the cut. The cuts redeclare the clarity of the shots,
restating the primal clarity of the view. Otherwise the shots become too solid.
For cinema to be transformative, there must be a balance between these two
basic elements. If a film is cut in a manner that forces the progression of the
shots, not allowing the shots to come into fullness, then no connection with
presence can take place. In such a film, the aggressive cutting might mask the
emptiness of the view. On the other hand, if the poignancy of what a cut has to
offer is ignored, or if the shots are so excessively proud and varnished with

visual egoism that cutting from them would be a disruption to the visual surface itself, then the delicacy of this essential counterbalance cannot develop. In the former case the film is too armored and evasive, in the latter too self-serious and solid.

Cuts seem to work in a hierarchy. First, a cut has to work on a visual level, in terms of shape, texture, color, movement, and weight. Somehow the shift from one shot to the next has to create a visual freshness for the psyche. Something happens to the nature of the cinematic space that is right. This quality is so intrinsic to film that it is difficult to describe. In a film that we love, each progressing moment enlivens and deepens the subject and our experience of the screen simultaneously.

When the cut works visually, two aftershocks may occur. The first is in the area of dream connectives, or poetry – the way our mind uses images in its own nighttime arena. The sudden shift in space caused by the cut enlivens the unnameable. This stimulation is beyond the subject on either side of the cut. It is poignancy itself. A great cut brings forth the eerie, poetic order of things.

The second aftershock is based on the literal implications of the sequence of images. It activates the logic and thought processes that are our daytime mind. Sometimes we call it meaning. It is the simple narrative sense we have for survival.

The three elements of the hierarchy have to be well-proportioned and in the proper order for a film to echo accurately the fullness of our being. First, the cut has to work spatially, then the poetic connectives must resonate, and finally there must be some sense of logic or inevitability. The climactic scene of The Passion of Joan of Arc is a perfect example of this hierarchy. We see a flock of birds circling high in the sky intercut with burning logs and close-ups of Joan at the stake, inhaling the rising smoke. The cuts between the birds and Joan have a visual vitality but also the poetic resonance of soaring and release in contrast with her suffering. A moment later, our mind turns to the thought of heaven, to the logic of the story.

[. . .]

Devotion is not an idea or a sentiment. It is born out of the vastness and depth of our view. Out of darkness, behind all light, this vastness abides in nowness. It reveals our world. It is accurate and humbling and yet, for all its pervasiveness, it is not solid.

That the ineffable quality of vision can be expressed by projected light within darkness gives film great power. When a film is fully manifest it may serve as a corrective mirror that realigns our psyches and opens us to appreciation and humility. The more we are open to ourselves and are willing to touch the depths of our own being, the more we are participating in devotion. Similarly, the more film expresses itself in a manner intrinsic to its own true nature, the more it can reveal for us.

Chapter 64

John C. Lyden

FILM AS RELIGION
Myths, Morals and Rituals

Interreligious dialogue and film

IF **THE PRACTICE** of film viewing can be understood as a religion, as I have argued, then the dialogue between "religion" and "film" is really just another form of interreligious dialogue – and perhaps the insights gained by historians of religion and theologians in regard to how religions should understand one another may be applied fruitfully to this dialogue as well. Rather than assume that religion and culture are entirely different entities, or that religion can assume a hegemonic position in relation to culture, perhaps traditional religions might benefit from learning to listen to the religions of popular culture just as they are learning to listen to one another.

To adopt such a view is to follow the broader approaches of Heim, Cobb, and Panikkar rather than those of traditional exclusivism, Rahner's inclusivism, or Hick's pluralism. It is to suggest that we not assume that we are right and the other is wrong, or that there is only one possible valid view. It is to allow for genuine differences in approach and perspective so that our judgments do not condemn others simply for disagreeing with us but rather seek to hear and allow for different goals and purposes as potentially valid. It is not to accept all points of view as valid, but it is to consider the reasons why people view them as valid and to consider that they might be valid for them in their particular context and from their particular vantage point.

There must be an alternative to the exclusivism of left-wing and right-wing ideological critics as well as to the inclusivism of theological interpretations that read film only through Christian categories or those of other traditional religions. I have suggested that this alternative can be found in viewing film as itself a religion. Interestingly, however, traditional religion has always reacted to film as if it were a religion, even when this was not explicitly admitted. By relating to it either as a demonic threat to their own religion, or a mirror image of it, religious film critics were essentially already viewing film through the categories of religion. If film did not supply an alternative value system and way of viewing the world, expressed through the ritual of filmgoing, it would not have been perceived as such a threat to traditional religion. The fact that it was perceived in this way indicates that it was perceived as addressing the same set of issues, albeit in a very different way. If it was denied the status of "religion," this may reflect an attempt to discredit the alternative it presented, in the same way that early Christian explorers of the Americas were reluctant to call the practices of the "Indians" by the name of religion. Not only was it so different that it did not seem to fit the category of religion as they knew it, but it was also successfully demonized and marginalized by refusing to grant it this title. Today it is much more the case than it was then that we feel we should tolerate that which we call "religion," and therefore we are reluctant to bestow this title on phenomena we would rather reject as "ideologies," "cults," and "sects"– thereby dismissing them from being serious dialogue partners. If it cannot be made to resemble our own religion, with an inclusivist interpretation, we reject it as other and therefore as bad.

Jonathan Z. Smith has reflected on the ways in which we marginalize others with whom we would rather not have dialogue, and nowhere more pointedly than in "The Devil in Mr. Jones," a short article written two years after the 1978 mass suicide of the followers of Jim Jones in Guyana. Here he suggested that scholars of religion cannot simply dismiss such a phenomenon as "demonic," as Billy Graham had done in that case, for it is our commission to seek to understand even that which we would rather not. If we choose to demonize that which is too shocking or offensive to us, falling into the sort of emotional judgments that characterized the media treatment of the situation, we are surrendering the scholarly value that seeks to understand all human behavior through the light of reason rather than through cultural prejudice. We are also essentially choosing to view such people as nonhuman if we decide that they are beyond reason or understanding, and in the process we make them totally other to ourselves and to our way of thinking. While Smith agrees that mass suicide is repellent to us and requires moral judgment, he holds that such judgment cannot occur without first seeking to gain some understanding of the motives of the participants. If instead we choose to dehumanize them, we give up the value of a common humanity, and relinquish the very value we hope to uphold.

Since Smith wrote the article over two decades ago, research on "cults" like Jonestown has progressed beyond demonization toward the sort of understanding of motives and worldview that Smith was encouraging. He came up with two theories about Jonestown himself in the original article. One idea is to understand what happened as a sort of "Dionysiac praxis" that sought to overcome social and racial distinctions by a retreat to a created utopia. When this utopia was threatened by outsiders, the community saw no choice other than to leave this world for a better one. There are parallels here to the events at the Branch Dravidian compound in Waco, Texas, in 1993, which saw the followers of David Koresh seeking escape from this world before capture. Second, Smith believes that the mass suicide could be understood as an act of revolutionary protest against those who sought to destroy their utopia, and the audiotapes the community left behind seem to confirm that they understood their action in this way.

Smith suggests that if we seek to understand their motives, we may have more sympathy for them and not simply view them as misguided or brainwashed followers of a psychotic leader. People do have reasons for their behaviors, and it behooves us to uncover those reasons even when we do not agree with them. Smith recognizes that we can no longer appeal naively to our own cultural version of "reason" as if this were identical with some universal reason, but he insists that our awareness of this cultural relativity should not lead us to the total relativism that says there is no basis for judging any culture but our own. We must continue to attempt to formulate "rules of reason" by which we can make judgments, even though we know we cannot come to a definitive formulation of them.

Smith's approach also seems helpful in regard to judgments about popular culture. To admit that we ought to take popular culture seriously is to admit that we should seek to understand its worldview and values, and its appeal, rather than simply dismiss it as a mindless and nihilistic glorification of sex and violence. But to attempt to understand why people are drawn to movies, and what they get out of them, is not to celebrate all the values they present or to be totally uncritical of them. Ideological critics feel that they must guard against the uncritical acceptance of popular culture as "harmless fun," and indeed we should not preemptively decide it is harmless any more than we should preemptively decide that it is harmful. Any judgments that are made must be made on the basis of study and an attempt to understand how film functions for people as a worldview, a system of values, and a ritual practice for joining the two – in other words, as a "religion" in the sense in which I have defined the term.

Ideological criticism of popular culture, by religion scholars and those in other fields, will and should continue as a necessary method for uncovering the ways in which films function ideologically in support of hegemonic systems. But ideological critique cannot be the only method used for the analysis of popular culture, or we will find ourselves seeing culture only through the small aperture afforded by such a critique. Film should not be reduced to its ideological function any more than religion should be. If we analyze films utilizing such a method, we must remember that ideology is only one aspect of film and its appropriation by viewers. Within the field of film criticism proper, there has already begun the critique of ideological interpretations that decide what films "mean" for their audiences based not on what audiences say but rather on what the theorists believe; as a result, studies of audience reception of films have increased in number and quality. Scholars of religion who interpret films would also do well to learn to listen to film viewers and seek to understand why they go to the movies and what they get out of them. Only then can we hope to understand the "religious" power of films, just as we can only understand Jonestown by studying what its members said and believed rather than imposing on them our own view of what they believed.

In the chapters that follow, we will begin to apply this method to the study of various films and genres. This is only intended to be a beginning, and the interpretations I suggest are necessarily tentative. I have based some of my ideas on audience response data when it is available, either from my own personal observations and conversations or from published studies of others, but the lack of extensive work in this area has made some speculation about audience reaction unavoidable. Of course, even with extensive data, the scholar necessarily imposes some categories on the data in the process of interpreting it. In trying to hear how films are understood by their audiences and what effect films have on them, one will never understand the viewers as they understand themselves – just as the best anthropologist never comes to understand her subjects as they do themselves, even if she "goes native." The unavoidability of the scholar's personal subjectivity, however, is not (as Geertz observed) license to do "surgery in a sewer." We can attempt to avoid the "contamination" of our own views, even though they will be present even in the "cleanest" of interpretations, first by being aware of them, and second by realizing that there are other ways of viewing things that we can seek to understand. This attitude will make us more open to seeing the films as their viewers may, instead of seeing them as scholars are wont to do.

There is another rather obvious point to be made here; scholars are viewers, too, and as such may participate in the filmic religion as well. Once we give up narrower definitions of "religion" that only identify it with formal institutions that go by that label, we can recognize that multiple religious influences affect each one of us. It is not the case that there are some who follow the religion of film and others who follow Christianity or Judaism; unless we completely distance ourselves from the power and pleasure of the movies (as some ideological critics have sought to do), we are already implicated in our subject matter. This does not mean that one is worshiping false gods every time one goes to the cinema, any more than a Christian who studies Buddhism has deserted his or her religion. We can learn from a number of religious influences, and if "religion" is not the monolithic entity it was once thought to be, then we may find ourselves drawing from a variety of sources in the construction of our religious beliefs. All the major religions of history have done the same thing, as, for example, Christianity developed out of Judaism and its encounter with Hellenistic religion, incorporating ideas from other religious communities and transforming them in the process. No religion appears in the world without a heritage of religious influences, and no religion remains alive unless it deals with the continuing encounters it has with other religions. When one realizes this, one sees another reason why the attempt to guard against all cultural influences is doomed unless one can completely isolate one's religious community.

Chapter 65

Joel W. Martin

SCREENING THE SACRED

Religion, Myth, and Ideology in Popular American Film

Three approaches to religion

DURING THE PERIOD in which the field of religious studies has been recognized as an academic discipline, it has had time to develop considerable internal diversity. We cannot pretend to introduce the many ways in which scholars approach the study of religion; we refer curious readers to more detailed surveys. For the purposes of this text, however, we can describe three basic approaches to religion current in the field: the theological, the mythological, and the ideological. Their conception of what constitutes religion varies greatly.

[. . .]

These are suggestive, not exhaustive, characterizations, but they point to basic paradigms that prevail in our nation's divinity schools and universities. By making explicit the existence of these paradigms, and by showing how each engenders a distinct type of criticism of film (theological criticism, mythological criticism, ideological criticism), we hope to contribute to the current debates concerning the definition of religion and the interpretation of religious texts and actions. More than that, by putting these paradigms into motion, by fleshing them out through the study of film, we hope to bring to the debates an unprecedented degree of concreteness and color. Films are fascinating and popular visual texts. By focusing on films, we think we have found a graphic way to explicate the major intellectual divisions in the study of religion. Finally, we argue that each of the three major types of criticism has commendable strengths but also inevitable weaknesses. All are valuable; none is perfect. This suggests that a new, fourth type of criticism is needed. Perhaps it will be a blend of theological, mythological, and ideological criticism. This book raises the question of what this type will look like; only future study and discussion will provide the answer.

[. . .]

Three types of criticism

Theological criticism draws upon an incredibly rich tradition of ethical reflection and exegetical commentary. When Larry Grimes considers the meaning of resurrection in relation to *Psycho*; when Ted Estess explores how *Ironweed*'s humble characters experience a redemptive mystery; when Avent Beck shows how the Christian narrative informs the plot of *Platoon*; when Conrad Ostwalt examines how the apocalypse is imagined in current films, they are not writing in a void but are engaging questions that have been asked by many generations of Christian scholars. It is little wonder that in this section of the book we encounter elegant, soul-searching writing. Among other things, these authors' criticism reveals that many contemporary films engage traditional religious themes. Their criticism helps us to realize that our popular culture, even though it may present itself as thoroughly secular, continues to wrestle with Christian claims, symbols, and expectations.

For this and other insights, we need theological criticism. As Larry Grimes argues, some things in films simply make much more sense if interpreted through traditional Christian theology. However, if the theological approach makes an irreplaceable contribution, it is also true that we need additional approaches to religion and film. Theological critics are most at home in talking about religion in its Christian or Jewish forms. Their first impulse is to link modern cultural expressions to scriptural antecedents. When they examine films, theological critics inevitably focus on films that feature Christ figures and that deal with classic theological themes such as the existence of evil and the nature of God. Such specificity characterizes the chapters in a book such as *Religion in Film* and *Image and Likeness*. Concerning the latter a reviewer wrote, "The reader is left uneasy with the way in which the stories of the films – including *Citizen Kane*, *2001: A Space Odyssey*, *The Wizard of Oz*, *Casablanca*, and *One Flew Over the Cuckoo's Nest* – are meshed with the stories of the Jewish and Christian scriptures." Theological criticism is important, even essential in cultures strongly shaped by Christianity and Judaism, but it is not sufficient. It defines religion too narrowly and tends toward ethnocentrism. If we want to understand the relation of religion and film, we will need to employ nontheological approaches as well.

A more inclusive, cross-cultural understanding of religion is exemplified in the works of scholars of comparative mythology. As Mircea Eliade, Joseph Campbell, and others have argued, religion can be defined in a nontheological manner as the quest of humanity for contact with the sacred. Such a definition leads myth critics to search for religion in all cultures, in art and architecture, in dreams, in all symbolic activities, and especially in mythic narratives – stories that reveal the foundational values of a culture. Employing an expansive definition of religion, myth critics find much to analyze in popular film. Eliade recognized the fertile relationship between myth and film: "A whole volume could well be written on the myths of modern man, on the mythologies camouflaged in the plays he enjoys, in the books that he reads. The cinema, that 'dream factory,' takes over and employs countless mythical motifs – the fight between hero and monster, initiatory combats and ordeals, paradigmatic figures and images (the maiden, the hero, the paradisal landscape, hell, and so on)."

Eliade's contemporary Joseph Campbell not only observed the connection between myth and film; his work on myth informed the making of Hollywood films. Campbell summarized what he felt was the basic plot of all hero stories: "The standard path of the mythological adventure of the hero is a magnification of the formula represented in the rites of passage: separation-initiation-return. . . . A hero ventures forth from the world of common day into a region of supernatural wonder: fabulous forces are there encountered and a decisive victory is won: the hero comes back from a mysterious adventure with the power to bestow boons on his fellow man." This plot was appropriated by director George Lucas, who credited Campbell as the inspiration for Lucas's *Star Wars* trilogy [see reading 40].

Part 2 focuses on films that reinterpret myths to make them vital for contemporary viewers. Andrew Gordon employs Joseph Campbell's description of the monomyth to show that Luke Skywalker in *Star Wars* follows the classic pattern of the mythic hero. Caron Ellis, influenced by Eliade's willingness to see the sacred beyond Christianity, finds beneficent power in the sky. Specifically, Ellis argues that the friendly aliens that come to earth in science-fiction films serve to alleviate our anxieties regarding nuclear proliferation and global pollution. Meanwhile, in the films *Alien* and *Aliens* Janice Rushing identifies the reemergence of the earth goddess as a vital cultural power. Drawing on Jung's theory of the collective unconscious, Rushing identifies the earth goddess as a transcultural archetype, a primordial image of profound importance to humanity. It does not matter if such a figure has a biblical prototype. The earth goddess is older and more primordial than the Bible, than Christianity, than all organized religions. She symbolizes a kind of spiritual power with which we must come to terms if we are to live fully human lives. If she is appearing now in our cultural myths and on the screens of our movie theaters as a monstrous fury, it means we need to change the way we relate to both feminine power and nature.

Myth criticism employs a much broader definition of religion than does theological criticism. This enables myth critics to perceive religion when a theological critic might miss it or deny its presence altogether. For all of its breadth and vitality, however, myth criticism has some limits. If it is adept at identifying the presence of non-Christian, mythic powers in film, myth criticism does a much less satisfactory job of showing how these powers relate to the kinds of mundane power social scientists and historians analyze. In short, sky gods and earth goddesses tend to be treated as ahistorical archetypes the human unconscious throws up in response to existential challenges. Myth critics focus on our psychological quest for meaning but tend to ignore the way meaning is always politicized and historicized. Not surprisingly, Campbell, Eliade, and Jung have been attacked on political grounds.

To appreciate how myths affect society, we need another type of criticism. Ideological criticism, in contrast to myth criticism, focuses primarily upon the political effects of cultural expressions; the quest for meaning is secondary, and the relationship to a traditional religious figure or theme is even less relevant. Ideological critics tend to be historicists. This means they think culture and art do not transcend politics but shape and are shaped by politics, and they consider claims that symbols and archetypes are transcultural or timeless to be naive and incorrect. Ideological critics want to know how a specific cultural expression reinforces or undermines the structure of power relations in a given society at a particular time, not how such an expression fulfills a universal human need for meaning. Ideological critics study the relationship of religion and society. Thus, when Joel W. Martin examines the film Rocky, he is not primarily concerned about seeing if the film's hero acts like a Christ figure (which Rocky does) or understanding how the film provides mythic meaning for its audience (which it does). Rather than treating the film primarily as a theological or mythic text, he interprets it as a political and social text that employs religion for ideological ends. The film, in this reading, blames African Americans for real social problems experienced by working-class people who are not African American. It turns religious symbols and mythic meanings toward concrete political and social ends. In a different vein, Elizabeth McLemore, in her treatment of Blue Velvet, shows how this postmodern film subverts interpretative schemes that presuppose fixed, archetypal meanings. Whereas some critics would like to see Blue Velvet as an allegorical battle of good and evil, McLemore thinks the film does not allow such a simple interpretation. Finally, when Irena Makarushka views Nine and a Half Weeks, she is not concerned first with showing how the film mediates theological or mythic meaning to viewers but, rather, with tracing how the film reveals the political and social effects of religious images on young women. She argues that gender relations have been defined in relation to female archetypes (Eve, Mary) created by male desire. She is concerned with the effects these archetypes have on women and asks if women's experience can be reclaimed and named by women. She finds some intriguing answers in the film.

Race, class, gender, and the postmodern are a few of the central interpretative categories for ideological critics. Without question, they can be used to shed considerable light on most Hollywood films and on the form of film itself. However, if critics rely too exclusively on these categories, they may overemphasize only one dimension of religion and ignore or distort others. Some ideological critics focus so tightly on politics that they end up treating religion simplistically. Because they have forgotten the complexity of religion and its relative autonomy as a domain of culture, these critics cannot properly be said to be practicing religious studies. Such is the case with ideological critics such as Michael Ryan and Douglas Kellner.

In their recent book, *Camera Politica: The Politics and Ideology of Contemporary Hollywood Film* (1988), Ryan and Kellner do not even define religion, although they refer to it many times. Influenced by Marxist criticism but lacking Marx's rich vision regarding the contradictory impact of religion on society, they assume that religion can only be the opiate of the people, a mystifying set of symbols and ideas that always promotes individualism and conservatism. In their view, religion is always regressive.

Even with such a limited perspective, Ryan and Kellner produce some valuable insights regarding religion and popular films. For instance, *Saturday Night Fever* (1977), in their view, provided the white working class with visions of transcendence from their historical and economic situation. In the movie, temporary escape from working-class drudgery is as easy as immersing oneself in the world of disco. Permanent escape can be obtained by crossing the bridge into Manhattan. Such a vision captivated viewers and seduced them into believing again in the American Dream. Ryan and Kellner would much prefer that Americans perceive the ways in which gross social inequities and differential income levels are integral parts of a capitalist, sexist, racist system. They want viewers to be skeptical of visions of transcendence.

All this is well and good, except it sounds the only note Ryan and Kellner know how to play regarding religion. Although they are willing to grant that films can be politically self-contradictory, they do not explore the complexity of religion, its ability to reinforce the worst injustices, and its prophetic ability to move people into the street to resist injustices (e.g., the U.S. civil rights movement, the anti-shah marches in Iran, the People Power movement in the Philippines). In their view, religion is a fixed, known, stable force not requiring interpretation or deconstruction. In fact, it is a much more complex phenomenon. Not only can it serve contradictory ideological purposes, it can also affect human beings on multiple levels and in manifold ways. To do justice to this multidimensional phenomenon, we need to rely not just on ideological criticism – which focuses exclusively on the political dimension – but also on theological and mythological perspectives. Although not as sensitive to the political effects of religion, these approaches are at least "bold enough to take the things of the spirit spiritually."

As we study the relation of religion and film, we need to learn how to tap the strengths of theological criticism, mythological criticism, and ideological criticism while recognizing their respective weaknesses. Each type of criticism is necessary; none alone is sufficient. This book makes these points clearly in the way it is structured. Each type is given its due in a tripartite structure. Whereas such a structure is the best one possible at the present moment – a kind of federal system involving three branches that check and balance each other – we can imagine a future synthesis of these types of criticism. Such a synthesis will be a criticism deeply grounded in generations of thought about the sacred, broadly open to the diverse ways in which the sacred manifests itself, and acutely sensitive to the political and social effects of religious and mythological texts.

Such criticism, as yet unnamed, may emerge. Indeed, we can catch glimpses of it in this book when our critics show an awareness of the limits of the various approaches they employ. So although it is true that our theological critics focus on classic Christian themes, it is also true that they know religion encompasses mythological traditions beyond Christianity and that religious stories can serve ideological ends. Our mythological critics may emphasize the archetypal qualities of the gods and goddesses they examine, but they also suggest that these sacred beings tell us something about our political situation, the fear of nuclear weapons, and our desire for a new relationship with nature. Finally, whereas our ideological critics are very concerned with the way race, class, and gender are represented, they are also sensitive to the ways in which sacred traditions – Christian and otherwise – shape these representations. This book, then, can serve as a model both of types of criticism as they are practiced today and for criticism as it may be practiced tomorrow.

Chapter 66

S. Brent Plate

THE FOOTPRINTS OF FILM:

After Images of Religion in American Space and Time

IN **FRONT OF** Philadelphia's stately Museum of Art—with its extensive, well-respected collections of Asian and American Art—one can find the
footprints of Rocky at the top of the great steps. Tourists from all over the world
have made mini-pilgrimages here as they climb the enormous stairway leading
to the museum and the footprints, and many stop to take their picture alongside
this little hunk of cement with its indented footprints of Rocky's Converse high
tops. Jumping up and down with arms raised, these tourist-pilgrims have their
picture taken, then they will go home and put that image in their scrapbooks
and web pages to say, "Look, I stood where Rocky stood!" "Rocky," as many
will remember, refers here to "Rocky Balboa," the character played by Sylvester
Stallone in the *Rocky* films. While Grauman's Chinese Theater in Hollywood is
well known for its footprints and handprints of famous movie stars in the
walkway outside, the impressions there are accompanied by the actors' real
names, people who have actual hands that can make an imprint in setting
cement. But in the case of Rocky's footprints, we realize there is no "Rocky," he
was only a fictional character in a movie.

The religious landscape of the United States is littered with just such footprints of film. Far from being immaterial – nothing but light projected on a
two-dimensional surface – filmic images have leapt off the screen and entered
physical, three-dimensional spaces, leaving their marks in American cement,
religious consciousness, and ritual practices. Like the character Tom Baxter (Jeff

Daniels) in Woody Allen's *Purple Rose of Cairo*, film has stepped down from the screen to infiltrate political, social, and religious lives. My argument here is that religion and film leave the temples and theaters, synagogues and living rooms, and meet in the streets, stairways, parking lots, weddings, funerals, cities, and deserts of the United States.

Ritualizing films

Recently, as part of a weekly response to class readings, one of my students discussed how her brother had chosen *Matrix*-style clothing – leather trench-coats, sunglasses, etc. – for his wedding. I have seen the *Matrix* trilogy on many occasions, have shown *The Matrix* to my classes every year for the past 5 years, and read a lot about the films. I know there are a lot of aficion-ados (or cult followers depending on how you phrase it) of these films, but until I read my student's paper I had not thought about the ways it leaves its own formal confines and infiltrates the lives and ritual structures of average U.S. citizens. This provoked me to think further about how films have impacted rituals and I did some research on film and ritual in the United States.

According to a September 2001 article in *Brides* magazine, "theme wed-dings," including those based on films, are a hot trend in the wedding industry. Many wedding planning guides offer a variety of focal themes, from Renais-sance themes to underwater weddings, from Hawaiian to Scottish to fairy tale lands, and the ever-popular Elvis impersonator presiding. Online sites offer a plethora of theme wedding packages including Roaring 20s themes, Disney themes, Star Trek themes, and the "Hollywood theme" which one online wed-ding planner describes this way:

> As your white limo whispers to a halt before the expectant crowd, the handsome man at your side smiles lovingly into your eyes. You step gracefully from the car, your diamonds sparkling with every movement. ("Diamonds" are a state of mind!) You pause as a mass of avid fans and photographers surround you, begging a moment of your precious time. Magnanimously, you scrawl your autograph and casually tilt your head for the snapshot of the century. (First making sure your good side is towards the camera, of course!) Finally, clinging possessively to your leading man, you reluctantly tear yourself away from your adoring fans and head for the elaborate reception that is being held in your honor.
> Is this all just a dream? No, this could be your wedding![1]

The site "Wedding Shops Online" offers suggestions of wedding themes like "country/western," "ethnic," "nautical," and "Movie or Television." For the latter they give the idea: "Have all in attendance dress up as characters from your favorite movie or television program (i.e. Star Trek). Carry the theme throughout the reception – serve food that was served during the movie, play theme music, etc. Send invitation and program designed as a 'Play Bill.' "[2] Other Internet searches reveal couples having theme weddings based on films such as *Gone with the Wind*, *Casablanca*, and *Braveheart*. And lovetripper.com, a resource for Honeymoon planning, offers a list of "romantic movie quotes" to "spice up your love letters," including one-liners from *Bridges of Madison County* ("This kind of certainty comes but once in a lifetime"), *West Side Story* ("Goodnight, goodnight, sleep well and when you dream, dream of me . . ."), and *Crouching Tiger, Hidden Dragon* ("A faithful heart makes wishes come true").

Similar film themes can be created for b'nai mitzvahs (mitzvoth). Indeed, Woody Allen's 1997 film, *Deconstructing Harry*, depicts a *Star Wars*-themed bar mitzvah, complete with child cutting the cake with a light saber. Yet, the scene did not stem from the imaginative mind of Allen, but from life itself. The online partypop.com offers suggestions and planning for bar mitzvahs with themes like "Back to the Future," "The Terminator," and "Lost in Space." The online sales pitch tells us the story of "Marcus" who recently had a Terminator-theme for his coming of age party/ritual:

> Everything in the hall looked like metal. . . . There were even jungle gyms and slides painted in camouflage colors for them to play on.
>
> Once everyone had arrived, the Aliea La Tora [sic] was performed on the hall stage. Then, since everyone was already in the hall, Marcus' grand entrance was a ride around the hall in an electric scooter decorated to look like the Terminator's motorcycle in T2. It was his bar mitzvah gift from his parents. Marcus got on and made a victory lap while the DJ played the "Terminator" theme music.

Or note Lisa Niren's *Titanic* theme bat mitzvah, reported by the Associated Press:

> Thirteen-year-old Lisa Niren, described by her sister as obsessed with "Titanic," got the bat mitzvah of her dreams over the weekend.
>
> A hotel ballroom was transformed into the luxury liner, with 12-foot steaming smokestacks at the buffet table, phosphorescent artificial icebergs and a "steerage" section for the children. [. . .]
>
> The piece de resistance was a gigantic photo, 10 feet above the floor, featuring Lisa's face superimposed over actress Kate Winslet's

body in a famous "Titanic" scene on the prow of the ocean liner. Lisa appeared to have teen heartthrob Leonardo DiCaprio smiling over her shoulder. [. . .]

Reflective aqua-tinted lighting along the walls and the phosphorescent blue and green icebergs made it appear as if the ballroom was under water.

Tables featured roses, crystal candelabras and replicas of the heart-shaped blue diamond necklace from the movie.

"This is incredible," said Heather Levy, a friend of Lisa's mother. "A lot of people do things for their children because they love them, but this goes beyond all that. I'm just standing here smiling."[3]

Granted, such b'nai mitzvahs and weddings make up a small but growing percentage of all ceremonies conducted in the United States, yet their existence indicates some of the ways young people and couples are searching for ways to "personalize" their rituals.

Plenty of other religious services realize this need for the updating of media and are happily incorporating film into their liturgies. This seems to be particularly true among evangelical Christian churches. In fact, it seems that the more conservative a church is theologically the less problem it has pulling down a screen in the middle of a Sunday morning sermon and playing a clip from a film. Meanwhile the mainline Protestant and Roman Catholic churches tend to relegate film to the Adult Education courses on Sunday mornings or Wednesday nights.[4]

[. . .]

My student whose Matrix-inspired brother re-outfitted his matrimonial wardrobe had been reading Ronald Grimes's thoughtful work, Deeply into the Bone: Re-Inventing Rites of Passage. Grimes plays with the possibilities of having renewed rituals to keep us contemporary humans inspired, to give us meaning in the patterns of our lives, and to connect within a society that too often produces alienation. Throughout his book, Grimes is concerned with what seems to be a growing absence of rites of passage in the modern age, and offers an interesting, if not extreme, quote from the Encyclopedia of World Problems and Human Potential: "The absence of rites of passage leads to a serious breakdown in the process of maturing as a person. Young people are unable to participate in society in a creative manner because societal structures no longer consider it their responsibility to intentionally establish the necessary marks of passing from one age-related social role to another[.]"[5] Humans have an ongoing need for ritual, as many have suggested, but Grimes also raises the concern that "traditional rites themselves can become so ethereal that they fail to connect with the bodily realities and spiritual needs of those who undergo them."[6] And this is where the need for re-invented rites becomes so important. The *Matrix* marriage had an air of novelty to it, but perhaps was a way to lighten what some felt was an overly solemn occasion (marriage should be fun, right? so why not relax a little). Perhaps it is the assumed solemnity of the occasions that produce alienation and disconnection and new media create a sense of lightness and approachability.

Since a Jewish boy is automatically a bar mitzvah at age 13 and a girl at age 12 is automatically a bat mitzvah, with or without the ritual, perhaps the theme of the festivities is not important. But others *do* see it all as intertwined. Concerned with the stodgy old ways of creating bar/bat mitzvah rituals and parties, Gail Greenberg recently wrote a popular book and created a company called "MitzvahChic." She says: "Since the 1950s b'nai mitzvah have followed the same formula and *nothing* has changed except which trendy themes are in vogue. But now, we recognize that there's *got* to be more, that we've exhausted the thrills and satisfaction we can get through decorating and the old routines alone." Greenberg, and it seems many others who have heeded her advice, realizes there is still power in ritual, and without much scholarly knowledge of ritual studies, she seems to implicitly know that a re-invention of rituals is vital to religious tradition. Not wholly advocating the throwing out of tradition, nor simply suggesting anything goes, the "mitzvahChic" approach attempts to bring the deep significance of the older traditions together with personal meaning in a contemporary age: "Today's bar mitzvah/bat mitzvah has a new level of spirituality; new ways of adding tzedakah, having fun and making it beautiful."[7] The Terminator theme noted earlier may have questionable meaning-making abilities (a victory lap in an electric scooter?!) but the need for personal connection in ritual is very real.

As quantified evidence for the role of popular media in the shaping of contemporary religiosity, Lynn Schofield Clark has offered a number of intriguing studies on media and adolescent religious identity in the United States. Her book *From Angels to Aliens: Teenagers, The Media and the Supernatural*, based on hundreds of interviews with teenagers and their families, demonstrates how many youth today express their own understanding of "religion," "spirituality," and the "supernatural" through media symbols. Television shows and films such as *Buffy the Vampire Slayer*, *X-Files*, *The Sixth Sense*, and *Harry Potter* provide articulations for the ways U.S. teens understand themselves to be "religious." Clark suggests "A great deal of evidence suggests that the media play an important role in how young people form and articulate their identities. Young people learn from and identify with characters they watch and with celebrities they admire. Their choices for media consumption have a lot to do with the identifications they hold according to their participation in different racial, class, gender, and friendship groups. . . . Given the significance of the entertainment media in the lives of teens, it's worth exploring what teens mean when they identify themselves as religious, and what such identifications might have to do with what they see, hear, and consume in the media."[8] Among other interesting findings, Clark's work, along with that of her colleagues at the University of Colorado, demonstrates how the secularization thesis has not taken account of the role of media in actively shaping what can only be called religious views of U.S. culture. While non-traditional religious movements are replacing "traditional" religious institutions, media such as film, television, comic books, and video games are replacing traditional institutional worldviews with new articulations, new descriptions and depictions, of very old religious categories like good and evil, sin, angels, demons, and god.

Ritualizing and world building are necessary to religion, but the same old ritual in the same old way, the same old message in the same old medium, leaves people feeling disconnected. Central to re-ritualizing processes is the necessity of attention to the media of transmission. From orality to literacy, printing presses to the Internet, "tradition" becomes abstract and stale if everyone repeats the same things in rote manner through the same medium. To invent new and meaningful rites many people now turn to film (and other forms of media such as television, comic books, and games) to help them through stages of life. These media have become familiar, comfortable. In many instances it may be just good clean fun, but in other very real ways films offer linguistic and symbolic registers and ways of understanding the world from vital, new perspectives, touching on sensual aspects that words alone are too limited to deal with.

Creating new rituals: from *Rocky* to *Rocky Horror*

New media alter old rituals, but they also produce brand new rituals, in places and times the traditionally-minded religious person would not think to look. As I write this, thousands of people are camping on the streets – a few, notably, have been camping for months – waiting for the tickets to go on sale for the final installment of the *Star Wars* series. These fans are dressed in Star Wars-specific costumes, spending time with friends along the way, just to be able to participate in that special, set apart time and place where they can watch *Star Wars: Episode III*. The religion of *Star Wars* has often been noted in popular and scholarly literature alike, and a Romanian-based fan club has just opened the first known "Jedi Academy."[9] Indeed, in the 2001 Australian national census, over 70,000 people marked "Jedi" as their religion, hoping to get it listed as an official religion recognized by the nation. Responding to this religious/political movement, Chris Brennan, director of the Star Wars Appreciation Society of Australia, stated, "This was a way for people to say, 'I want to be part of a movie universe I love so much.' "[10] Brennan's words are telling, especially when compared to Jonathan Z. Smith's definition of ritual: "Ritual is a means of performing the way things *ought to be* in conscious tension to the way things are in such a way that this ritualized perfection is recollected in the ordinary, uncontrolled, course of things."[11] *Star Wars* fans reenact and recollect an alternate reality – standing in line for days and weeks, dressing the part, being with like-costumed and like-minded people, *participating* in a world (both on the streets outside the theater and as part of the filmed world on screen) that expresses "the way things ought to be" – a reality in contradistinction to the hum-drum existence of office spaces, mortgage installments, and traffic commutes.

Perhaps no other film, blockbuster or otherwise, has created a greater ritualized following than the 1975 *Rocky Horror Picture Show* (dir. Jim Sharman). While many religious studies scholars might write-off *Rocky Horror* as a campy production with little ethical or religious value, it has nonetheless elicited a mass, cult following since its debut. The plot line is a retelling of the bourgeoisie (represented by Brad and Janet – played by Barry Bostwick and Susan Sarandon) encountering another, alternate social reality (here at the underworldly castle-home of Dr. Frank N. Furter – Tim Curry) and being transformed by the experience. "Normal" social behavior is mocked throughout the film; polymorphous perversions and various acts of violence (the reason it is a "horror show"), including cannibalism, are demonstrated on screen, turning Brad and Janet's "traditional" values upside down. They are transformed through their experiences. The plot itself relates to Victor Turner's (following Van Gennep's) tri-partite schema of religious ritual entailing: separation, liminality, reincorporation. But it is in the watching of the film where the true religious dimensions surface, as it *functions* religiously by way of audience interaction, who also go through the three-part ritual process argued by Van Gennep. Now, thirty years after its creation, in almost any major city across the United States and elsewhere, at the liminal hour of Saturday Midnight, one can find a screening of the film and a devoted crowd of people still gathering, donning costumes related to the film, along with their special "props." A fair number of people have now seen the film over 1,000 times. Those who have never attended a screening are termed "virgins" (and often are made to wear a lipsticked "V" on their foreheads). Indeed, an entire vocabulary has been developed in relation to the screenplay.

In their article, "Toward a Sociology of Cult Films: Reading *Rocky Horror*," Patrick Kinkade and Michael Katovich explore the phenomenon of secular filmic cult audiences. Drawing on previous work in the field, they define "cult film audiences" as "a type of secular cult organization, and cultish attachments to these films replace a charismatic actor with a document granted charismatic appeal."[12] Such a definition is intriguing for the ways in which it redefines traditional central sacred texts and figures, implicitly noting the ways in which media affect what can only be called "piety." As Kinkade and Katovich continue, cult film audiences, "construct ritual and belief systems through their viewing experience. Cult film attachments, therefore, become obsessions and enduring shared foci for habitues."[13]

Such behavioral systems are readily apparent at screenings of Rocky Horror, as audience members enact ritual activities in tandem with other audience members and in conjunction with the film scenes. In the film theater, audience members perform events that mimic the events on screen. At several points viewers will get up and re-enact key scenes as they are taking place on screen: the audience throws rice at the point when Brad and Janet get married at the beginning of the film; and people bring actual toast with them so at the point when Frank N. Furter proposes a "toast," the audience throws their toast at the screen. These responses have been repeated and codified over the years, so that now one can attend a Rocky Horror screening across the world and encounter the same performative actions. Cult audiences, including those often seen at Rocky Horror screenings, are often comprised of disenfranchised members of a society who find connection, meaning, and solace within such liminal activities as a type of "spontaneous communitas" is formed.

[. . .]

In Clifford Geertz's well-known definition, religion offers: symbols, powerful and pervasive moods and motivations, as it formulates "conceptions of a general order of existence," arranging all of this to seem "uniquely realistic."[14] Through special effects, editing, cinematography, and finely honed acting, films and their reception offer much of the same. The trailers at the cinema even tell us as much. As we sit down with our popcorn – perhaps dressed as a stormtrooper or a Wookie – waiting for the feature presentation, we hear the voiceover for the coming attractions: "In a world where you have to fight to be free . . ." "In a world where love is within reach . . ." "In a world . . ." We the viewers are invited into other worlds, alternate renditions of reality that through seamless editing, precise special effects, carefully placed cameras, and elaborate props offer views of the world that seem "uniquely realistic." Film, like religion, tells of another reality, of a world that could be, of a world that viewers want to live in – or in the case of apocalyptic films a world viewers want to avoid. Regardless, films present other realities that stimulate moods and motivations. One way or other, film viewers have their eyes and ears opened to differing ways of imagining the world outside the film theater, but also outside our own social status in the world "out there." In the audio-visual experience of viewing film, human bodies and minds have an experience that becomes internalized, ultimately affecting behaviors, attitudes, practices, and beliefs. And we often find the experience of film somehow transformed, translated, and transposed into the granite structures, the cement surfaces, and Saturday night haunts that constitute contemporary religious life.

Conclusion

To conclude, I leave one final footprint. In Austin, Texas, between the state's capitol and judicial buildings, there is a 6ft x 3ft granite sculpture of the Ten Commandments, chiseled in a quasi-Gothic script (in King James English of course), with decorative flourishes – the Christic Greek chi-ro characters, stars of David, and an American flag – surrounding the words. This "monument" was erected in 1961 and my research reveals little interest in it since that time. But in the 2000s, the Austin sculpture has become one of many contested sites in the United States in which church–state relations have been put to the test. The case has gone all the way to the U.S. Supreme Court on the grounds that such a presentation entails the government endorsing religion, while conservative lawmakers argue for the ways in which these commandments pay tribute to the religious and legal history of the United States.

What neither side rarely admits – or simply remains ignorant of the history of these sculptures – is that the plethora of Ten Commandment sculptures outside courthouses, capitols, and urban squares in the United States today actually came into being through the publicity stunts of the great filmmaker, Cecil B. DeMille. In the mid-1950s, DeMille was finishing his second version of The Ten Commandments, famously starring Charlton Heston as Moses. As promotion for the film, DeMille got in touch with the Fraternal Order of Eagles, a nationwide association of civic-minded clubs (founded in 1898, interestingly enough, by a group of theater owners), who had been distributing copies of the Ten Commandments to courtrooms across the country as "guidance" for juvenile delinquents. DeMille and the FOE upped the symbolic stability of the Decalogue by commissioning hundreds of granite sculptures of Moses' tablets to be placed outside courthouses across the United States, including Austin, Texas. DeMille died in 1959, but the FOE continued the task of planting the sculptures through the 1960s, and they are now the focal point of Supreme Court decisions that impinge directly on church–state issues in the United States.

Film has left its footprints in United States culture, society, political discourse, and religious consciousness. These footprints are not those of abstract thought, but of material structures in physical time and space. Film progresses from its two-dimensional, light-projected status, to incarnated, three-dimensional aspects. And the point at which it becomes so interesting is when it is realized that film has so permeated cultural consciousness that people forget how material "reality" can have its origins in ethereal light projected onto a screen. There is no "Rocky," and granite Ten Commandments are as much vestigial publicity stunts as they are making a statement about God-given law as the origin of the modern legal system. The image is confused for the real, and we realize therein that the real is always already imagined, and oftentimes primarily imaged.

In the contemporary United States, film is no longer existent only in celluloid, or even in digital code. Film has left the theater house, infiltrated old rituals and fashioned new rituals. It has made its marks in cement, and these concrete places become, in turn, an alluring topography that attracts people to them. Film merges into the public spaces of civic life as it engenders court cases promoting deep political dialogue that harkens back to the founding of the nation, long before the moving, refracted-light image was a twinkle in the eye of the Lumìere brothers or Thomas Edison.

Notes

1   http://www.take2weddings.com.

2   http://www.advol.com/wedshops/ceremony.htm. Accessed 3 February, 2005.

3   "Girl Gets Titanic Bat Mitzvah," Associated Press, Thursday, October 29, 1998; 1:43 a.m. EST., online at: http://www.vho.org/News/GB/SRN29-30_98.html3. Accessed 7 June, 2005.

4   What is interesting in the liberal-conservative divide, as an independent study with my student Tiffany Austin revealed this year, is that there is a correspondence between the length of film clips shown (and related biblical passages referred to) and theo-political divide. In a survey of curriculum resources for various Christian groups, it is clear that the more conservative the church and their corresponding curricula, the shorter the film clips and biblical passages. Conservative churches place more emphasis on shorter biblical passages (usually 1–2 verses) and shorter film clips (usually 1–2 minutes), while the mainline churches offer advice for lengthier quotes and clips (often up to 10 minutes). However, the theologically conservative churches unabashedly offer the film clips in the main Sunday service while the more liberal churches relegate such cultural interactivity to the "Adult Education" courses. Cf. conservative publications such as Bryan Belknap, *Group's BlockBuster Movie Illustrations* (Loveland, CO: Group, 2001) and the slightly more left-leaning *Videos that Teach* by Doug Fields and Eddie James, Grand Rapids, MI:

Zondervan, 1999 with Abingdon Presses periodical *Reel to Real: Making the Most of the Movies with Youth*, Issue 1.1, 1997.

5   From the *Encyclopedia of World Problems and Human Potential*, produced by the Union of International Associations in Brussels and available online at: www.uia.org/ uiapubs/pubency.htm. Quoted in Ronald Grimes, *Deeply Into the Bone*, Berkeley: University of California Press, 2000, 91.

6   Grimes, *Deeply Into the Bone*, 100.

7   http://www.mitzvahchic.com/index.php. Accessed 25 May, 2005. See also the recent *Thirteen and a Day: The Bar and Bat Mitzvah Across America* by Mark Oppenheimer. New York: Farrar, Straus and Giroux, 2005.

8   Lynn Schofield Clark, *From Angels to Aliens: Teenagers, the Media, and the Supernatural*. Oxford; New York: Oxford University Press, 2003, 15–16, 17.

9   For   a   brief   news   story,   see: http://www.ananova.com/news/story/ sm_1086432.html. Accessed 2 June 2005. The website of the Romanian fan club is: http://www.jedi.ro/index.htm (in Romanian).

10   See Stewart Taggart, "Bad Movie Hurts Jedi Down Under," *Wired News*, August 31, 2001;   http://www.wired.com/news/culture/0,1284,54851,00.html.   Accessed 6 June 2005.

11   Jonathan Z. Smith, *Imagining Religion*. Chicago: University of Chicago Press, 1982, 63; emphasis added.

12   Patrick T. Kinkade and Michael A. Katovich, "Toward a Sociology of Cult Films: Reading *Rocky Horror*," *The Sociological Quarterly* 33.2 (1992), 192.

13   Kinkade and Katovich, "Toward a Sociology," 194. Other cult films include such diverse offerings as *Wizard of Oz*, *Eraserhead*, *Harold and Maude*, and *The Texas Chainsaw Massacre*.

14   Clifford Geertz, "Religion as a Cultural System," in *The Interpretation of Cultures: Selected Essays* (New York: Basic Books, 1973), 87–125.

Chapter 67

Melanie J. Wright

RELIGION AND FILM

A proposal

WHICH WAY NOW? Work in religion and film and theology and film has some way to travel before it can be regarded as a credible field of enquiry. Fundamentals need to be reviewed and perhaps overhauled; it is important to think seriously about what is involved in doing interdisciplinary work. Without firmer foundations, particularly an ability to engage film *qua* film, the survival of religion (and theology) and film cannot be assumed. Film work has, for example, failed to secure its place as a topic for routine coverage in many of the longer-established periodicals in theology and religious studies. It is more often the subject of a 'special issue' – positioned as something urgent, but ultimately marginal to mainstream scholarly discourse. Without sounder underpinnings this will not change, and worse still, the work itself will continue to offer sometimes interesting but frequently irrelevant and inadequate readings of arbitrarily selected films.

Addressing the limitations of current work in religion and theology and film requires a willingness to listen to and debate with others engaged in serious writing on the cinema. As the tendency to elide film meaning into narrative illustrates, few writers on religion (or theology) and film address theoretical questions. Some ignore mainstream writing on film; others address it inconsistently. Amongst some scholars there is open resistance to film studies.

In confessionally grounded writing this is occasionally born of a desire to see theology re-throned as the 'queen of sciences'. Alternatively, it can stem from the recognition that contemporary film studies, with its roots in Marxism and psychoanalysis, often dismisses or devalues the place of religion in contemporary society: 'It is almost as if the discourse of cutting-edge film criticism is designed to exclude attention to religion', complains Martin.[1] However, this perception does not provide a warrant for those in religious studies or theology to reciprocate poor practice.

A decent course on film within a theology and/or religious-studies programme should regard familiarising students with key areas of film-studies practice as one of its aims. After all, students who want to progress in other areas are expected to develop a challenging range of competencies. Drury lists as follows the demands placed on Bible students: 'knowledge of at least two ancient and two modern languages, of textual criticism and of testingly obscure episodes in history, of religion in its popular and philosophical manifestations, of a vast and sometimes barely readable secondary literature'.[2] Not teaching the skills needed to address film texts and their audiences implicitly devalues the medium of film, and adds credibility to the position of those who regard the study of mass cultural forms as simply the hors d'oeuvre before the 'real work' of theology and religious studies begins.

There is of course a potential danger hidden in the suggestion that religion (and theology) and film must attend to film studies. Such a move could see one 'tyranny' simply replaced with another (that of film or cinema studies). I am not advocating a wholesale or uncritical adoption of film theory, although achieving the goals of dialogue and interdisciplinarity will impact on the subject, processes and products of research.

Noting that both individual scholars and the institutions with which they engage (including employing universities, and political and funding bodies) are often unsure about how to judge interdisciplinarity, Thompson Klein suggests that the focus should be on two dimensions. The first of these is 'depth', which she defines as competence in pertinent knowledges and approaches to the subject matter; and the second is 'rigor', in the form of an ability to develop processes that integrate theory and knowledge from the disciplines being brought together. According to this model, creating a truly interdisciplinary approach to religion (or theology) and film requires much more than either a simple extension of the subject matter of religious studies, or ad hoc borrowings of tools and concepts from a neighbouring discipline. It mandates a high degree of self-reflexivity, since it is necessary to learn and reflect on how the disciplines involved characteristically look at the world. And it requires the cultivation of a spirit of enquiry, coupled with a willingness to check repeatedly the accuracy and validity of 'borrowed' material and ideas.[3]

I am not advocating that scholars and students of religion and theology start mimicking their peers in film studies. There is already a body of people who do 'straight' film criticism well; it is more sensible to develop approaches to film that will play to the distinctive strengths of religion specialists. Moreover, although ambitious, religion (and theology) and film's oft-stated goals of dialogue and interdisciplinarity are laudable, and cannot be achieved if the insights of religious studies (or theology) are simply cast aside. Film studies, too, is beset with its own debates and difficulties. According to some, it faces a crisis of relevance.

In a piece of 'shameless polemic', Miller castigates contemporary film studies, arguing that for the most part, it 'doesn't matter': it has little influence over discourse on film, public policy, or commercial or not-for-profit film-making practice.[4] Interestingly, similar charges could be levied against religion and film. There are many films handling religious or spiritual themes and topics. The turn of the century saw a number of films dealing with supernatural themes and spiritual questions, like *Dogma* (Kevin Smith, 1999), *End of Days* (Peter Hyams, 1999) and *Stigmata* (Rupert Wainwright, 1999); the past few years have seen the appearance of further popular features, as diverse as *Bruce Almighty* (Tom Shadyac, 2003), *Kingdom of Heaven* (Ridley Scott, 2005), *The Man Who Sued God* (Mark Joffe, 2001) and *Millions* (Danny Boyle, 2005). Moreover, some of the most controversial recent features have handled religious subject matter. Mel Gibson's *The Passion of The Christ* (2004) is one obvious example, and Martin Scorsese's 1988 *The Last Temptation of Christ* another. Describing the former's significance as a marker of (certain kinds of) contemporary Christian identity, *The Economist* went as far as to suggest that, 'The 2004 [US Presidential] election could well turn into a choice between Michael Moore's *Fahrenheit 9/11* and Mel Gibson's *The Passion of The Christ*'.[5]

However, few religion and film (or theology and film) specialists are party to public debates about film. The most prominent participants in the controversies surrounding the production of *The Passion*, for example, were those who wrote or spoke as interfaith activists and New Testament scholars. They judged the film to be in violation of academic consensus about the origins and purpose of the Gospel accounts of Jesus' death and resurrection, and of post-Vatican II guidelines governing Catholic presentation of Jews and Judaism in preaching, teaching and dramatisation [see reading 53 in this book]. These interventions proved largely ineffectual in persuading Gibson away from elements of the film that some feared might inflame antisemitism – in part because they demonstrated little insight into the specific challenges facing those who try to film the life and death of Jesus. In a telling illustration of this gap in understanding, the most vociferous scholars based their initial arguments on their *reading* of the screenplay, whilst Gibson's canny and successful response was to organise screenings that allowed people to *see* a rough version of the film.[6]

Miller's proposal for film criticism is that it achieves relevance through a more extensive integration with cultural studies. He is not alone in making this suggestion: cultural studies has transformed film studies in the past decade. A cultural-studies approach to film does not imply a rejection of previous film theories, but rather a building on older agendas and methods. Traditional film studies emphasises the analysis of individual film texts, their methods of production and associated technologies. Cultural studies looks additionally at film distribution, exhibition and reception. It involves a widening from an interest in the production and interpretation of a film 'text' to an interest in the inter-relation of 'texts, spectators, institutions and the ambient culture'.[7] In other words, it is a means of avoiding the twin poles of auteurism and reader response (of regarding either the film-maker or the film viewer as an exclusive, determinative influence). It traces the ways in which films acquire meanings by triangulating between film 'texts', contexts and audiences.

Like traditional film studies, cultural studies approaches are interested in gender, 'race', and queer theory, and in ideas about post-colonialism, post-structuralism and materialism. What is particularly relevant for conversations about the future of religion (and theology) and film as a subject area is that proponents of this approach (or family of approaches) to film acknowledge that their practices are multi- or anti-disciplinary, that they are subject to ongoing contest and debate, and that they draw inspiration from anthropology and the study of religion as much as from literary analysis and cinema studies.[8] That is, cultural studies provides a way of examining film that on occasion professes a link to the academic study of religions.

Unsurprisingly, the relation of cultural studies to film studies is itself a subject of debate. As Stam notes, the name 'film studies' implies attention to a single medium, and 'cultural studies' points to wide interests.[9] Culture may be defined in extremely broad terms as referring to all human production, including concepts and social structures as much as objects or artefacts. And as a cultural form that is produced by mass industrial techniques and is ultimately marketed for profit to consumers, film may be likened to a host of other things including television, music CDs, clothing, the microwave or the bicycle. In this way, cultural studies may be perceived as a threat to film studies' founding principle: the distinctiveness of film. But others see cultural studies as an organic, necessary development of film studies, pointing out that much traditional film theory, with its positing of ahistorical, decontextualised film viewers and concern with the production of signifying systems, was becoming alienated from its object of study.

Further objections are raised by those sceptical of the willingness of cultural-studies proponents to look at not only high art but also popular films, and the surrounding culture of fandom. For Willemen, known for his work on Third Cinema, this risks the de-skilling of the profession: film studies may slide into popularism, losing its critical edge and traditional concern for aesthetic value.[10] In response to this, the limits of the art/popular distinction have already been discussed. It is also a mistake to hold that cultural studies does not analyse film 'texts', or that a study of the popular necessarily implies popularism.[11] Nevertheless, these cautions about cultural-studies approaches to film are pertinent.

I suggest, then, that the territory of cultural studies, into which much of film studies has been shifting, offers a discursive space in which the oft-touted dialogue between religious (or theological) studies and film studies is perhaps newly possible. For religion specialists, there is an opportunity to engage with film criticism in a way that does not imply a subordinate relationship, in which the exchange of insight is not a one-way process from film studies to religion (and theology). Crucially, cultural studies too rejects the kinds of totalising (and atheistic) explanations that earlier ways of theorising film, such as Marxism, structuralism and psychoanalysis tended to espouse.[12] It is inherently dialogical and does not automatically assume secularism as a given, nor does it exclude the possibility that those with an expertise in religious studies (or theology) may bring to film competencies and insights that are both distinctive and worthwhile.

The movement towards establishing some kind of common ground is not confined to developments within film and cinema studies. Ever-omnivorous, religious studies shows increasing interest in cultural studies. One of the leading British advocates of this approach, Nye, has argued that the study of religions should in fact be reconceptualised and renamed as 'religion and culture', observing that 'what we think of as "religious studies" is, in many ways, a form of cultural studies, or at least there is much in cultural studies that those in the study of religions need to be aware.'[13] Why is this? On the other side of the Atlantic, Ochs notes that 'more scholars of religions are now acknowledging what religious or spiritual people worldwide . . . have long known, from observation, lived experience and intuition: that material objects – things made by people – are vessels that create, express, embody and reflect sacredness'.[14]

This approach argues that religion is embedded and enacted in material culture and artefacts. It contends that the material (including books, films, or art) has no intrinsic meaning of its own, and that it cannot be 'read' without attention to historical context:

> Meaning . . . is not given in some independently available set of
> code, which we can consult at our own convenience. A text does

not carry its own meaning or politics already inside of itself; no text is able to guarantee what its effects will be. People are constantly struggling, not merely to figure out what a text means, but to make it mean something that connects to their own lives, experiences, needs and desires.[15]

In short, it brings to the study of religion(s) a heightened focus on the material dimension and on occasionality – the details of the conditions in which religious meanings are re-created and expressed. In the growth of cultural studies' approaches to film, and concern on the part of proponents of religious studies for the enacting of relilgous ideas and beliefs in the material world, we can begin to see how a way of doing religion and film might develop that strikes a balance between respect for film and film studies, and a regard for religious traditions and their adherents. There is potential here for the fields to grow towards each other, creating an interface of theories and subject matter – the kind of genuinely interdisciplinary work that has rarely happened to date.

Notes

1   Joel W. Martin, "Introduction: seeing the sacred on screen", in Martin and Ostwalt: *Screening the Sacred*, 2.

2   John Drury (ed.), *Critics of the Bible 1724–1873*, Cambridge: Cambridge University Press, 1989, 1.

3   Julie Thompson Klein; *Crossing Boundaries: Knowledge, Disciplinarities, and Interdisciplinarities.* Charlottesville University Press of Virginia, 1996.

4   Toby Miller, 'Cinema studies doesn't matter, or I know what you did last semester", in Matthew Tinkcomm and Amy Villarejo (eds), *Keyframes: Popular Cinema and Cultural Studies*, London: Routledge, 2001, 303, 309. Miller also discusses the need for film to escape the thrall of literary criticism in his earlier "(How) Does film theory work?", *Continuum (Journal of Media and Cultural Studies)*, 6/1, 1992, 186–212. From a quite different perspective, Nöel Carroll depicts a crisis in film studies in "Prospects for film theory: a personal assessment," in David Bordwell and Noël Carroll (eds), *Post-Theory: Reconstructing Film Studies*, Madison: University of Wisconsin Press, 1996, 37–70.

5   Unattributed, "The passion of the Christians", *The Economist*, 2 October 2004, 50.

6   Peter J. Boyer, "The Jesus war", *The New Yorker*, 15 September 2003, 58–71.

7   Robert Stam, *Film Theory: An Introduction*, Oxford: Blackwell, 2000, 225. See also Graeme Turner, "Cultural studies and film", in John Hill and Pamela Church Gibson (eds), *Film Studies: Critical Approaches*, Oxford: Oxford University Press, 2000, 193–9.

8   Tinkcomm and Villarejo (eds): *Keyframes*, 13.

9   Stam: *Film Theory*, 226.

10   Meaghan Morris, "Brasschaat-Bombay: a way of inhabiting a culture", in Paul
     Willemen, *Looks and Frictions: Essays in Cultural Studies and Film Theory*, London: BFI, 1994,
     20–1.

11   See further Dominic Strinati, *An Introduction to Theories of Popular Culture*, London:
     Routledge, 1995, 255–60.

12   See Richard Johnson, "What is cultural studies anyway?", *Social Text*, No. 16, 1986,
     74, on open, multi-layered readings. In its crucial 1970s phase, psychoanalytic
     criticism analysed films for repressed contents, and evidence of the workings of
     unconscious desires. More recent developments have taken on board feminist and
     post-colonialist critiques of the cultural specificity of Freud's work, but use psycho-
     analytic theories of the uncanny and bodily horror to interpret film. Structuralist
     film criticism, associated primarily with the influential film journal *Screen* and the
     work of Christian Metz, and drawing on Claude Levi-Strauss's writings on myth,
     which are also influential in religious studies, understands film as a language – a
     mode of communication that encodes or imposes a narrative logic upon its raw
     material in accordance with a set of identifiable conventions.

13   Malory Nye, *Religion: The Basics*, London: Routledge, 2003, 21.

14   Vanessa Ochs, "What makes a Jewish home Jewish?", *CrossCurrents*, 49/4, 2000, at
     www.crosscurrents.org/ochsv.htm (current on 1 November 2001). For a classic articula-
     tion see also Colleen McDannell, *Material Christianity: Religion and Popular Culture in
     America*, New Haven: Yale University Press, 1995.

15   Lawrence Grossberg, "Is there a fan in the house? The affective sensibility of
     fandom", in Lisa Lewis (ed.), *The Adoring Audience: Fan Culture and Popular Media*, London:
     Routledge, 1992, 52–3. See also James Procter, *Stuart Hall*, London: Routledge, 2004,
     57–72 (discussion of Hall's seminal essay on "encoding" and "decoding").

Bibliography

Aichele, George, ed. *Culture, Entertainment and the Bible*. JSOT Supplement Series 309. Sheffield: Sheffield Academic Press, 2000.

Aichele, George and Richard Walsh, eds. *Screening Scripture: Intertextual Connections Between Scripture and Film*. Harrisburg, PA: Trinity Press International, 2002.

Alsford, Mike. *What If? Religious Themes in Science Fiction*. London: Longman & Todd, 2000.

Amin, Shahid. "On representing the Musulman." In *Sarai reader 2004: crisis/media*. Delhi: Sarai: 92–7 (1984).

Anderson, Digby, and Peter Mullen, eds. *Faking it: the sentimentalism of modern society*. London: Penguin, 1998.

Anker, Roy M. *Catching Light: Looking for God in the Movies*. Grand Rapids: Eerdmans, 2004.

Aylmer, Kevin J. "Towering Babble and Glimpses of Zion: Recent Depictions of Rastafari in Cinema." In: *Chanting Down Babylon: The Rastafari Reader*, eds. Nathaniel Samuel Murrell, William David Spencer, and Adrian Anthony McFarlane. Philadelphia: Temple University Press, 1998.

Asad, Talal. *Genealogies of religion: discipline and reasons of power in Christianity and Islam*. Baltimore: Johns Hopkins University Press, 1993.

——— . *Formations of the secular: Christianity, Islam, modernity*. Stanford: Stanford University Press, 2003.

Babington, B. and P. W. Evans. *Biblical Epics: Sacred Narrative in Hollywood Cinema*. Manchester: Manchester University Press, 1993.

Bach, Alice, ed. *Biblical Glamour and Hollywood Glitz. Semeia* 74 (1996).

Bandy, Mary Lea and Antonio Monda, eds. *The Hidden God: Film and Faith*. New York: The Museum of Modern Art, 2003.

Barsotti, Catherine M and Robert K. Johnston. *Finding God in the Movies: 33 Films of Reel Faith*. Grand Rapids: Baker, 2004.

Baugh, Lloyd *Imaging the Divine: Jesus and Christ Figures in Film*. Kansas City, MO: Sheed & Ward, 1997.

Beal, Timothy K. and Tod Linafelt, eds. *Mel Gibson's Bible: Religion, Popular Culture, and The Passion of the Christ*. Chicago: University of Chicago Press, 2006.

Berkey-Gerard, Mark. "Woody Allen and the Sacred Conversation," *The Other Side* 33/1 (Jan/Feb 1997): 60–62.

Bergesen, Albert and Andrew M. Greeley. *God in the Movies: A Sociological Investigation*. With a preface by Roger Ebert. New Brunswick, N.J.: Transaction Publishers, 2000.

Bharucha, Rustom. *In the name of the secular: cultural practice and activism in India today*. Delhi: Oxford University Press, 1998.

The Bible According to Hollywood. Produced by Passport International Productions. Westlake Village, CA: Brentwood Home Video, 1994. Videorecording.

Billingsley, K.L. *The Seductive Image: A Christian Critique of the World of Film*. Westchester, IL: Crossway Books, 1989.

Black, Gregory D. *Hollywood Censored: Morality Codes, Catholics, and the Movies*. Cambridge: Cambridge University Press, 1994.

——. *The Catholic Crusade against the Movies, 1940–1975*. Cambridge: Cambridge University Press, 1998.

Blake, Richard A. *Screening America: Reflections on Five Classic Films*. New York: Paulist, 1991.

——. *Woody Allen: Profane and Sacred*. Lanham, MD: Scarecrow Press, 1995.

——. *Afterimage: The Indelible Catholic Imagination of Six American Filmmakers*. Chicago: Loyola, 2000.

——. "Uncovering the Sacred: Substance and Style in the American Film." Lilly Fellows Program in Humanities and the Arts: Network Activities. http://www.lillyfellows.org/conference-uncovering.html.

Blessing, Kimberly A. and Paul J. Tudico, eds. *Movies and the Meaning of Life: Philosophers Take on Hollywood*. Chicago and Lasalle, IL: Open Court, 2005.

Bliss, Michael. *The Word Made Flesh: Catholicism and Conflict in the Films of Martin Scorsese*. Lanham, MD: Scarecrow Press, 1995.

Blizek, William, ed. "Special issue on *The Passion of the Christ*." *The Journal of Religion and Film*. www.unomaha.edu/jrf/previous.htmPassion, 8/1 (Nebraska, April 2004).

Boer, Roland. *Knockin' on Heaven's Door: The Hebrew Bible and Cultural Criticism*. New York: Routledge, 1999.

Buchanan, Judith. "Gospel Narratives on Film." In *Cambridge Companion to Literature on Screen*, eds. D. Cartmell and I. Whelehan. Cambridge: Cambridge University Press, 2006.

Burch Brown, Frank. *Good taste, bad taste, and Christian taste: aesthetics in religious life*. New York: Oxford University Press, 2000.

Burnett, Richard George, and E. D. Martell. *The Devil's Camera. Menace of a Film-Ridden World*. London: 1932.

Burnham, Jonathan, ed. *Perspectives on the Passion of the Christ: Religious Thinkers and Writers Explore the Issues Raised by the Controversial Movie*. Bolton, ON: H. B. Fenn & Co., 2004.

Butler, Ivan. *Religion in the Cinema*. New York, A. S. Barnes, 1969.

Carroll, Noël. *The Philosophy of Horror, or, Paradoxes of the Heart*. London: Routledge, 1990.

Cawkwell, Tim. *The Filmgoer's Guide to God*. London: Darton, Longman and Todd, 2004.

Chattaway, Peter. "Jesus in the Movies." *Bible Review* (February 1998): 29–35, 45–46.

Chatterjee, Partha. *Nationalist thought and the colonial world: a derivative discourse?* London: Zed Books for the United Nations University, 1986.

——. *The nation and its fragments: colonial and postcolonial histories*. Delhi: Oxford University Press, 1993.

Christian Century, May, 1996. Includes essays on Christian interpretation of film.

Christianity and Literature 42/3 (1993). Special issue.

Christianson, Eric S., Peter Francis, and William R. Telford, eds. *Cinéma Divinité: Religion, Theology and the Bible in Film*. London: SCM Press, 2005.

Clark, Lynn Schofield. *From Angels to Aliens: Teenagers, the Media, and the Supernatural*. Oxford: Oxford University Press, 2003.

Clarke, Anthony J. and Paul S. Fiddes, eds. *Flickering Images: Theology and Film in Dialogue*. Oxford: Smyth & Helwys, 2005.

Coates, Paul. *Cinema, Religion, and the Romantic Legacy*. Aldershot, UK: Ashgate, 2003.

Cooper, John C. and Carl Skrade. *Celluloid and Symbols*. Philadelphia: Fortress, 1970.

Corley, Kathleen E. and Robert L. Webb, eds. *Jesus and Mel Gibson's The Passion of the Christ: The Film, the Gospels and the Claims of History*. London: Continuum International Publishing, 2004.

Cosandey, R., A. Gaudreault, and T. Gunning, eds. *An Invention of the Devil? Religion and the Early Cinema. Une Invention du Diable? Cinéma des Premiers Temps et Religion*. Sainte Foy, Canada: Les Presses de l'Université Laval, 1992.

Couch, Steve, ed. *Matrix Revelations: A Thinking Fan's Guide to the Matrix Trilogy*. Southampton, UK: Damaris, 2003.

Cross Currents (Spring, 2004). Theme issue, "The Passion of Cinema: Religion, Film, and Visual Ethics." Online at: http://www.crosscurrents.org/Spring2004.htm

Cunneen, Joseph. *Robert Bresson: A Spiritual Style in Film*. London & New York: Continuum, 2003.

Cunningham, David S. *Reading is Believing: The Christian Faith through Literature and Film*. Grand Rapids, MI: Brazos, 2002.

Cunningham, Philip A., ed., *Pondering the Passion: What's at Stake for Christians and Jews?* Lanham, MD: Sheed and Ward, 2004.

Das, Veena. "The mythological film and its framework of meaning: an analysis of *Jai Santoshi Ma.*" *International Centre Quarterly* 8/1 (1980): 43–56.

Deacy, Christopher. *Screen Christologies: Redemption and the Medium of Film.* Cardiff: University of Wales Press, 2001.

——. *Faith in Film: Religious Themes in Contemporary Cinema.* Burlington, VT: Ashgate, 2005.

Devji, Faisal. *Landscapes of the jihad: militancy, morality, modernity.* London: C. Hurst & Co., 2005.

Dhondy, Farrukh. "Keeping Faith: Indian Film and its World." Special edition of *Daedalus* on *The Moving Image* 114/4 (Fall 1985): 125–140.

Dönmez-Colin, Gönül. *Women, Islam and Cinema.* London: Reaktion Books, 2004.

Drew, Donald J. *Images of Man: A Critique of Contemporary Cinema.* Downers Grove, IL: InterVarsity, 1974.

Dwyer, Rachel. *All you want is money, all you need is love: sex and romance in modern India.* London: Cassell, 2000.

——. *Filming the Gods: Religion and Indian Cinema.* Abingdon: Routledge, 2006.

Egan, Joe. *Brave Heart of Jesus: Mel Gibson's Postmodern Way of the Cross.* Blackrock: Columba Press, 2004.

Eilers, Franz-Josef. *Church and Social Communication: Basic Documents.* 2nd ed. Manila: Logos Publications, 1997.

Elley, D. *The Epic Film: Myth and History.* London: Routledge and Kegan Paul, 1984.

Exum, J. Cheryl. *Plotted, Shot, and Painted: Cultural Representations of Biblical Women* Journal for the Study of the Old Testament Supplement Series, 215. Sheffield: Sheffield Academic Press, 1996.

——, ed. *The Bible and Film: The Bible in Film.* Originally published in *Biblical Interpretation* 14/1–2 (2006). Reprint, Brill, 2006.

Faller, Stephen. *Beyond the Matrix: Revolutions and Revelations.* St. Louis, MO: Chalice Press, 2004.

Ferlita, Ernest and John R. May. *Film Odyssey: The Art of Film as a Search for Meaning.* New York: Paulist, 1976.

Flesher, Paul V.M. and Robert Torrey. *Film and Religion: An Introduction.* Nashville, TN: Abingdon Press, 2007.

Forest, Ben, with Mary Kay Mueller. *God Goes to Hollywood: A Movie Guide for the Modern Mystic.* Lincoln, NE: Writers Club Press (iUniverse.com), 2000.

Forshey, Gerald Eugene. *American Religious and Biblical Spectaculars.* Westport, CT: Praeger, 1992.

Fraser, Peter. *Images of the Passion: The Sacramental Mode in Film.* Westport, CT: Praeger Publishers, 1998.

Fraser, Peter and Vernon Edwin Neal. *Reviewing the Movies: A Christian Response to Contemporary Film.* Focal Point Series. Wheaton, IL: Crossway Books, 2000.

Fredrickson, Paula. *On The Passion of the Christ: Exploring the Issues Raised by the Controversial Movie.* Berkeley: University of California Press, 2006.

Friedman, Lawrence S. *The Cinema of Martin Scorsese.* New York: Continuum, 1997.

Garbowski, Christopher. *Krzysztof Kieslowski's Decalogue Series: The Problem of the Protagonists* and their Self-Transcendence. Eastern European Monographs, 452: New York: Columbia University Press, 1996.

Gervais, Marc. Ingmar Bergman: Magician and Prophet. Montreal and Kingston: McGill-Queens University Press, 1999.

Getlein, Frank and Harold C. Gardiner, S.J., eds. Movies, Morals, and Art. New York: Sheed and Ward, 1961.

Gibson, A. The Silence of God: Creative Response to the Films of Ingmar Bergman. New York: 1969.

Gire, Ken. Reflections on the Movies: Hearing God in the Unlikeliest of Places. Reflective Living Series. Colorado Springs, CO: Chariot Victor Publishing, 2000.

Godawa, Brian. Hollywood Worldviews: Watching Films With Wisdom & Discernment. Downers Grove, IL: InterVarsity, 2002.

Goodacre, Mark. "The Synoptic Jesus and the Celluloid Christ: Solving the Synoptic Problem Through Film." Journal for the Study of the New Testament 80 (2000): 31–43.

Grace, Pamela. "Gospel Truth? From Cecil B. DeMille to Nicholas Ray." In: A Companion to Literature and Film. eds. Robert Stam and Alessandra Raengo. Malden, MA: Oxford: Blackwell, 2004.

Graham, Elaine L. Representations of the Post/Human: Monsters, Aliens and Others in Popular Culture. Manchester: Manchester University Press, 2002.

Greeley, Andrew M. God in Popular Culture. Chicago, IL: The Thomas More Press, 1988.

Guneratne, Anthony and Wimal Dissanayake. Rethinking Third Cinema. London: Routledge, 2003.

Guptara, Prabhu. "Religion Has Shaped Indian Film." Action (January 1980): 19–22.

Gurney, Robin (ed.). The European John Templeton Film Prize 1997–2006: Film Sermons by Hans Werner Dannowski. Bern, Switzerland and West Conshohocken, PA: Interfilm and John Templeton Foundation, 2007.

Haynes, Jonathan (ed.). Nigerian Video Films, Revised Edition. Athens: Ohio University Press, 2000.

Hertenstein, Mike. "Star Trek's Undiscovered Country," Cornerstone 25/109 (n.d.): 15–20.

Herx, Henry. "Religion and film." In: Encyclopedia of the American Religious Experience: Studies of Traditions and Movements. eds. Charles H. Lippy and Peter W. Williams. New York: Scribner, 1988.

Higgins, Gareth. How Movies Helped Save My Soul: Finding Spiritual Fingerprints in Culturally Significant Films. Lake Mary, FL: Relevant Books, 2003.

Holloway, Richard. Beyond the Image: Approaches to the Religious Dimension in the Cinema. Geneva: WCC, 1977.

Hoover, Stewart M. Religion in the Media Age. London: Routledge, 2006.

Hughes, Stephen and Birgit Meyer, eds. Postscripts 1.2–3 (2006). Special issue.

Hurley, N. P. Theology through Film. New York: Harper & Row, 1970.

—— . The Reel Revolution: A Film Primer on Liberation. Maryknoll, NY: Orbis, 1978.

———— . *Soul in Suspense : Hitchcock's Fright and Delight.* Metuchen, NJ: Scarecrow Press, 1993.

Irwin, William. *The Matrix and Philosophy: Welcome to the Desert of the Real.* Chicago, IL: Open Court, 2002.

Jaffrelot, Christophe. *India's silent revolution: the rise of the lower castes.* London: C. Hurst & Co., 2003.

Jasper, David. *The Sacred Desert: Religion, Literature, Art, and Culture.* Oxford: Blackwell, 2004.

Jesus Christ, Movie Star. Videorecording, London: CTVC Production for Channel 4, 1992.

Jewett, Robert. *Saint Paul at the Movies: The Apostle's Dialogue with American Culture.* Louisville, KY: Westminster John Knox Press, 1993.

———— . *Saint Paul Returns to the Movies: Triumph Over Shame.* Grand Rapids: Eerdmans, 1998.

Johnston, Robert K. *Reel Spirituality: Theology and Film in Dialogue.* Grand Rapids, MI: Baker, 2000. Second edition, 2006.

———— . *Useless Beauty: Ecclesiastes Through the Lens of Contemporary Film.* Grand Rapids, MI: Baker, 2004.

———— . (ed.). Reframing Theology and Film: New Focus for an Emerging Discipline. Grand Rapids: Baker Academic, 2007.

Journal of Religion & Film. http://www.unomaha.edu/jrf/.

Jump, Herbert A. "The Religious Possibilities of the Motion Picture." Film History 14/2 (2002): 216–228.

Kahle, Roger and Robert E. A. Lee. *Popcorn and Parable: A New Look at the Movies.* Minneapolis, MN: Augsburg, 1971.

Kapell, Matthew and William G. Doty, eds. *Jacking into the Matrix: Cultural Reception and Interpretation.* New York: Continuum, 2006.

Kapur, Anuradha. *Actors, pilgrims, kings and gods: the Ramlila at Ramnagar.* Calcutta: Seagull Books, 1990.

———— . "The representation of gods and heroes: Parsi mythological drama of the early twentieth century." *Journal of Arts and Ideas,* 23–4: 85–107 (1993a).

———— . "Deity to crusader: the changing iconography of Ram." In Gyanendra Pandey (ed.) *Hindus and others: the question of identity in India today.* New Delhi: Penguin: 74–109, 1993b.

Ketcham, Charles B. *The Influence of Existentialism on Ingmar Bergman: An Analysis of the Theological Ideas Shaping a Filmmakers's Art.* Lewiston, NY: E. Mellen Press, 1986.

Keyser, Lester J., and Barbara Keyser. *Hollywood and the Catholic Church: The Image of Roman Catholicism in American Movies.* Chicago: Loyola University Press, 1984.

Kickasola, Joe. *The Films of Krzysztof Kieslowski: The Liminal Image.* New York: Continuum, 2004.

Kinnard, Roy and Tim Davis. *Divine Images: A History of Jesus on the Screen.* New York: Citadel Press, 1992.

Kreitzer, Larry J. *The New Testament in Fiction and Film: On Reversing the Hermeneutical Flow.* Biblical Seminar 17. Sheffield: Sheffield Academic Press, 1993.

——— . *The Old Testament in Fiction and Film: On Reversing the Hermeneutical Flow*. The Biblical Seminar 24. Sheffield: Sheffield Academic Press, 1995.

——— . *Pauline Images in Fiction & Film: On Reversing the Hermeneutical Flow*. Biblical Seminar 61. Sheffield: Sheffield Academic Press, 1999.

——— . *Gospel Images in Fiction and Film: On Reversing the Hermeneutical Flow*. The Biblical Seminar 84. Sheffield: Sheffield Academic Press, 2002.

Kristeva, Julia. *Powers of Horror: An Essay on Abjection*. New York: Columbia University Press, 1982.

Krzysztof Kieslowski: I'm So So. . . . Directed by Krzysztof Wierzbicki. 56 min. Poland, 1995. Videorecording.

Kupfer, Joseph H. *Visions of Virtue in Popular Film*. Boulder, CO: Westview, 1999.

Landres, J. Shawn and Michael Berenbaum, eds. *After the Passion is Gone: American Religious Consequences*. Walnut Creek, CA: AltaMira Press, 2004.

Lane, T. *What's Wrong with the Movies?* Los Angeles, CA: 1923.

Larkin, Brian. "Hausa Dramas and the Rise of Video Culture in Nigeria." In: *Nigerian Video Film*, ed. Jonathan Haynes. Athens, OH: Ohio University Press, 2002.

——— . "The Materiality of Cinema Theaters in Northern Nigeria." In: *Media Worlds: Anthropology on New Terrain*, eds. Faye Ginsburg, Lila Abu-Lughod, and Brian Larkin, 319–336. Berkeley, CA: University of California Press, 2002.

Lawrence, John Shelton and Robert Jewett. *The Myth of the American Superhero*. Grand Rapids, MI: Eerdmans, 2002.

Leab, D.J., ed. "Film and Religion" issue of *Film History: An International Journal* 14/2 (2002).

Leonard, Richard, S.J. *The Cinematic Mystical Gaze: The Films of Peter Weir*. University of Melbourne, PhD thesis, 2003. http://eprints.unimelb.edu.au/archive/00000471/

——— . *Movies that Matter: Reading Film through the Lens of Faith*. Chicago, IL: Loyola Press, 2006.

Lindvall, Terry. *The Silents of God: Selected Issues and Documents in Silent American Film and Religion, 1903–1925*. Lanham, MD: Scarecrow Press, 2001.

——— . "Religion and Film, Part 1: History and Criticism." *Communication Research Trends* 23, no. 4 (2004): 1–44.

——— . "Religion and Film, Part 2: Theology and Pedagogy." *Communication Research Trends* 24, no. 1 (2005): 1–40.

——— . *Sanctuary Cinema: Origins of the Christian Film Industry*. New York: New York University Press, 2007.

Literature and Theology 12/2 (1998). Special issue on religion and film.

Loughlin, Gerald. "Seeing in the Dark: Plato's Cinema and Christ's Cave," *Studies in Christian Ethics* 13/1 (2000): 33–48.

——— . *Alien Sex : The Body and Desire in Cinema & Theology*. Challenges in Contemporary Theology. Oxford: Blackwell, 2002.

Lyden, John C. *Film as Religion: Myths, Morals, and Rituals*. New York and London: New York University Press, 2003.

Lynch, William F. *The Image Industries.* London: Sheed & Ward, 1960.

MacDonald, Alan. *Movies in Close-Up: Getting the Most from Film and Video.* Downers Grove, IL: InterVarsity, 1992.

Madan, T.N. *Non-renunciation: themes and interpretations of Hindu culture.* Delhi: Oxford University Press, 1997.

McDowell, John C. *The Gospel According to Star Wars.* Louisville, KY: Westminster John Knox Press, 2007.

McNulty, Edward. *Films and Faith.* Viaticum Press, 1999.

McNulty, Edward N. *Praying the Movies: Daily Meditations from Classic Films.* Louisville, KY: Geneva Press, 2001.

——— . *Praying the Movies II: More Daily Meditations from Classic Films.* Louisville, KY: Westminster John Knox Press, 2003.

Malone, Peter. *Movie Christs and Anti-Christs.* New York: Crossroad, 1990.

——— . *Can Movies be a Moral Compass?* London: St Pauls, 2005.

——— . *Through a Catholic Lens: Religious Perspectives of 19 Film Directors from Around the World.* Rowan & Littlefield, 2007.

Malone, Peter, with Rose Pacatte. *Lights, Camera . . . Faith: A Movie Lover's Guide to Scripture.* 3 Vols. Pauline Books and Media, 2001, 2002, and 2003.

Marsden, Michael T., John G. Nachbar, and Sam L. Grogg, Jr., eds. "Western Films: America's Secularized Religion." In: *Movies as Artifacts: Cultural Criticism of Popular Film,* 105–114. Chicago: Nelson-Hall, 1982.

Marsh, Clive. *Cinema and Sentiment: Film's Challenge to Theology.* Milton Keynes, UK and Wanyesboro, GA: Paternoster, 2004.

——— . *Theology Goes to the Movies: An Introduction to Critical Christian Thinking.* London: Routledge, 2007.

Marsh, Clive and Gaye W. Ortiz, eds. *Explorations in Theology and Film: Movies and Meaning.* Oxford: Blackwell, 1997.

Martens, John W. *The End of The World: The Apocalyptic Imagination in Film and Television.* Winnipeg, MB: J. Gordon Shillingford Publishing, 2003.

Martin, Joel W. and Conrad E. Ostwalt, Jr., eds. *Screening the Sacred: Religion, Myth, and Ideology in Popular Film.* Boulder, San Francisco, Oxford: Westview Press, 1995.

Martin, Thomas M. *Images and the Imageless: A Study in Religious Consciousness and Film.* Lewisburg, PA: Bucknell University Press, 1981.

Matties, Gordon. "On Movies as a Spiritual Discipline," *Direction* 34/2 (2005): 270–286.

May, John R. *Nourishing Faith Through Fiction: Reflections of the Apostles' Creed in Literature and Film.* Kansas City, MO: Sheed & Ward, 2001.

May, John R., ed. *Image and Likeness: Religious Visions in American Film Classics.* Isaac Hecker Studies in Religion and American Culture. New York: Paulist Press, 1991.

——— . *New Image of Religious Film.* Kansas City, MO: Sheed & Ward, 1997.

May, John R. and Michael Bird, eds. *Religion in Film.* Knoxville, TN: The University of Tennessee Press, 1982.

Medved, Michael. *Hollywood vs. America: Popular Culture and the War on Traditional Values.* London: HarperCollins, 1992.

Meyer, Birgit. "Money, Power and Morality: Popular Ghanaian Cinema in the Fourth Republic." *Ghana Studies* 4 (2001): 65–84.

——— . "Prayers, Guns and Ritual Murder: Popular Cinema and Its New Figures of Power and Success." English translation of the French published text from *Politique Africaine* 82 (2002): 45–62. See http://www2.fmg.uva.nl/media-religion/publications/prayers.htm

——— . "Occult Forces on Screen: Representation and the Danger of Mimesis in Popular Ghanaian Films." *Etnofoor* 15 (1/2) (2002): 212–221.

——— . "Pentecostalism, Prosperity and Popular Cinema in Ghana." *Culture and Religion* 3 (1) (2003): 67–87.

Meyer, Birgit, ed. Special Issue. Religion and the Media. *Journal of Religion in Africa* 33 (2) (2003): 125–128.

Meyer, Birgit and Peter Pels. *Magic and Modernity: Interfaces of Revelation and Concealment.* Stanford, CA: Stanford University Press, 2003.

Meyer, Birgit and Annelies Moors. *Religion, Media, and the Public Sphere.* Bloomington, IN: Indiana University Press, 2006.

Middleton, Darren J.N. *Scandalizing Jesus: Kazantzakis's* The Last Temptation of Christ *Fifty Years On.* New York: Continuum, 2005.

Miles, Margaret R. *Seeing and Believing: Religion and Values in the Movies.* Boston, MA: Beacon Press, 1996.

Miller, Monica Migliorino. *The Theology of the Passion of the Christ.* Staten Island, NY: St. Pauls, 2005.

Mitchell, Jolyon. "West African Popular Video Film." *Omnibus*, radio documentary, BBC World Service, 28 May 2002.

——— . "From Morality Tales to Horror Movies: Towards an Understanding of the Popularity of West African Video Film." In: *Belief in Media: Cultural Perspectives on Media and Christianity*, eds. Peter Horsfield, Mary E. Hess, and Adán M. Medrano, 107–121. Aldershot: Ashgate, 2004.

——— . "Theology and Film" in *The Modern Theologians*, ed. David Ford, 736–759. Oxford: Blackwell, 2005.

——— . "Sacred Film". In: *Implications of The Sacred in (Post)Modern Media*, eds. Johanna Sumiala-Seppänen, Knut Lundby, and Raimo Salokangas, 197–215. Göteborg, Sweden: Nordicum, 2006.

——— . *Media Violence and Christian Ethics.* Cambridge: Cambridge University Press, 2007.

Mitchell, Jolyon and Sophia Marriage, eds. *Mediating Religion: Conversation in Media, Religion and Culture.* London: T & T Clark, 2003.

Morgan, David. *The Sacred Gaze: Religious Visual Culture in Theory and Practice.* University of California Press, 2005.

——— . *The Lure of Images: A History of Religion and Visual Media in the United States.* London: Routledge, 2007.

Musser, Charles. "Passions and the Passion Play: Theatre, Film, and Religion in

America, 1800–1900." *Film History* 5 (1993): 419–456.

Naficy, Hamid. *An Accented Cinema: Exilic and Diasporic Filmmaking*. Princeton: Princeton University Press, 2001.

Nathanson, Paul. *Over the Rainbow: The Wizard of Oz as Secular Myth of America*. Albany: State University of New York Press, 1992.

Neely, Alan. "Images: Mission and Missionaries in Contemporary Fiction and Cinema," *Missiology* 24/4 (1996): 451–478.

Nolan, Steve. "Film and Religion Bibliography." In: *Mediating Religion: Conversations in Media, Religion and Culture*, eds. Jolyon Mitchell and Sophia Marriage, London: Continuum, 2003.

Nowell-Smith, Geoffrey. *The Oxford History of World Cinema*. Oxford: Oxford University Press, 1997.

O'Brien, Tom. *The Screening of America: Movies and Values from "Rocky" to "Rainman"*. New York: Continuum, 1990.

Oropeza, B. J., ed. *The Gospel According to Superheroes*. New York: Peter Lang, 2005.

Ostwalt, Conrad E. "Religion and Popular Movies." *Spotlight on Teaching* (American Academy of Religion), 6/1 (1998): 8.

Overstreet, Jeffrey. *Through a Screen Darkly: Looking Closer at Beauty, Truth and Evil in the Movies*. Regal Books, 2007.

Pacatte, Rose and Peter Malone. *Lights, Camera . . . Faith! The Ten Commandments*. Boston: MA, 2006.

Paffenroth, Kim. *Gospel of the Living Dead: George Romero's Visions of Hell on Earth*. Waco: Baylor University Press, 2006.

The Passion: Films, Faith and Fury. Produced by Zig Zag Productions. 101 min. London, 2006. Videorecording.

Patterson, Thomas. *At a Theatre Near You: Screen Entertainment from a Christian Perspective*. Wheaton, IL: Harold Shaw, 1994.

Pinney, Christopher. *"Photos of the gods": the printed image and political struggle in India*. London: Reaktion Books, 2004.

Plate, S. Brent. "Religion and Film." In *Encyclopedia of Religion*, 2d ed., Lyndsey Jones, Ed. 3097–3103. Macmillan, 2005.

Plate, S. Brent, ed. *Representing Religion in World Cinema: Filmmaking, Mythmaking, Culture Making*. New York: Palgrave Macmillan, 2003.

—— *Re-Viewing the Passion: Mel Gibson's Film and its Critics*. New York: Palgrave, 2004.

Plate, S. Brent and David Jasper, eds. *Imagining Otherness: Filmic Visions of Living Together*. Oxford: Oxford University Press, 1999.

Porter, Jennifer E. and Darcee L. McLaren, eds. *Star Trek and Sacred Ground: Explorations of Star Trek, Religion, and American Culture*. New York: State University of New York, 1999.

Presler, Titus Leonard. "At Play in the Fields of Missiology: Quincentennial Faces of Mission in the Films of Popular Culture." *Missiology* 24/4 (1996): 479–491.

Pungente, John J., and Monty Williams. *Finding God in the Dark: Taking the Spiritual Exercises of St. Ignatius to the Movies*. Boston: Pauline Books & Media, 2004.

Radix Magazine 23/1 (1994). The issue is devoted to "Faith in Film."

Reinhartz, Adele. *Scripture on the Silver Screen*. Louisville: Westminster, 2003.

—— . *Jesus of Hollywood*. Oxford: Oxford University Press, 2006.

Rice, John R. *What Is Wrong with the Movies?* Grand Rapids, MI: Zondervan, 1938.

Richards, Thomas. *The Meaning of Star Trek*. New York: Doubleday, 1997.

Riley, Robin. *Film, Faith, and Cultural Conflict: The Case of Martin Scorsese's The Last Temptation of Christ*. Westport, CT: Praeger, 2003.

Romanowski, William D. "John Calvin Meets the Creature from the Black Lagoon: The Christian Reformed Church at the Movies 1928–1966." *Christian Scholar's Review* 25/1 (1995): 47–62.

—— . *Eyes Wide Open*. Rev. and expanded edn. Grand Rapids, MI: Brazos Press, 2007.

Rosenberg, Joel. "What the Bible and Old Movies Have in Common." *Biblical Interpretation* 6 (1998): 266–291.

Roy, Olivier. *Globalised Islam*. London: C. Hurst & Co., 2004.

Runions, Erin. *How Hysterical: Identification and Resistance in the Bible and Film*. New York: Palgrave Macmillan, 2003.

Ryan, Judylyn S. *Spirituality as Ideology in Black Women's Film and Literature*. Charlottesville: University of Virginia Press, 2005.

Sanders, Teresa. *Celluloid Saints: Images of Sanctity in Film*. Macon, GA: Mercer University Press, 2002.

Schillaci, Anthony. *Movies and Morals*. Notre Dame, IN: Fides, 1968.

Schrader, Paul. *Transcendental Style in Film*. New York: Da Capo Press, 1972.

Scott, Bernard Brandon. *Hollywood Dreams and Biblical Stories*. Minneapolis, MN: Fortress, 1994.

Seay, Chris and Greg Garrett. *The Gospel Reloaded: Exploring Spirituality Faith in the Matrix*. Boulder, CO: NavPress, 2003.

Sheen, Erica. " 'The Light of God's Law': Violence and Metaphysics in the '50s Widescreen Biblical Epic." *Biblical Interpretation* 6 (1998): 292–312.

Sison, Antonio. *Screening Schillebeeckx: Theology and Third Cinema in Dialogue*. New York: Palgrave, 2006.

Sinetar, Marsha. *Reel Power: Spiritual Growth Through Film*. Liguori, MS: Triumph Books, 1993.

Sitney, P. Adams. *Visionary Film: The American Avant-Garde, 1943–2000*. 3rd edn. Oxford: Oxford University Press, 2002.

Solomon, Jon. *The Ancient World in the Cinema*. Revised and Expanded edn. New Haven: Yale University Press, 2001.

Spencer, Lewerenz and Barbara Nicolosi, eds. *Behind the Screen: Hollywood Insiders on Faith, Film, and Culture*. Grand Rapids: Baker, 2005.

Staub, Dick. *Christian Wisdom of the Jedi Masters*. Indianapolis, IN: Wiley, 2005.

Steimatsky, Noa. "Pasolini on Terra Sancta: Towards a Theology of Film." *The Yale Journal of Criticism* 11 (1998): 239–258.

Stern, Richard C., Clayton N. Jefford, Guerric DeBonna. *Savior on the Silver Screen*. New York: Paulist, 1999.

Sterritt, David. *The Films of Jean-Luc Godard: Seeing the Invisible.* Cambridge: Cambridge University Press, 1999.

Stibbe, Mark. *Passion for the Movies: Spiritual Insights from Contemporary Films.* CITY: Authentic/OM Literature, 2006.

Stone, Bryan P. *Faith and Film: Theological Themes at the Cinema.* St. Louis, MO: Chalice Press, 2000.

Tatum, W. Barnes. *Jesus at the Movies: A Guide to the First Hundred Years.* Santa Rosa, CA: Polebridge Press, 1997.

Telford, William R. "The New Testament in Fiction and Film: A Biblical Scholar's Perspective." In: *Words Remembered, Texts Renewed: Essays in Honour of John F. A. Sawyer.* JSNT Supplement 195. Sheffield: Sheffield Academic Press, 1995.

Vaux, Sara Anson. *Finding Meaning at the Movies.* Nashville, TN: Abingdon, 1999.

Vollmer, Ulrike. "I Will Not Let You Go Unless You Teach Me the Tango: Sally Potter's The Tango Lesson." *Biblical Interpretation* 11/1 (2003): 98–112.

Voytilla, Stuart. *Myth and the Movies.* Studio City, CA: Michael Wise Productions, 1999.

Wall, James M. *Church and Cinema: A Way of Viewing Film.* Grand Rapids: Eerdmans, 1971.

Walsh, Frank. *Sin and Censorship: The Catholic Church and the Motion Picture Industry.* Yale: Yale University Press, 1996.

Walsh, Richard. *Reading the Gospels in the Dark.* Harrisburg, PA: Trinity Press International, 2003.

——. *Finding St. Paul in Film.* Toronto: University of Toronto Press, 2005.

Wells, P. *The Horror Genre: From Beelzebub to Blair Witch.* London: Wallflower, 2000.

Weisenfeld, Judith. *Hollywood Be Thy Name: African American Religion in American Film, 1929–1949.* Berkeley: University of California Press, 2007.

Wilkinson, David. *The Power of the Force: The Spirituality of the Star Wars Films.* Herts, Engand: Lion, 2000.

Williams, Peter W. "Review Essay: Religion Goes to the Movies." *Religion and American Culture* 10/2 (Summer 2000): 225–239.

Wilson, Eric G. *Secret Cinema: Gnostic Vision in Film.* London: Continuum, 2006.

Worthing, Mark W. *The Matrix Revealed: The Theology of the Matrix Trilogy.* CITY: Hindmarsh, Australia: ATF Press, 2005.

Wright, Melanie J. *Religion and Film.* London: I.B. Tauris, 2007.

There are numerous Web sites providing Religion and Film resources, including:

- *American Film Institute* offers recent industry news, events, educational seminars (mostly North American), and reviews http:// www.afionline.org/ CineMedia/welcomes/you.html
- *Bible Films.* For a fairly extensive review of Bible in film, see Matt Page's Bible Films Blog: http://biblefilms.blogspot.com/

- Film.com features reviews, movie clips, recent news, articles and a calendar of upcoming events http://www.film.com/film.html
- *Reading Room.* History both on and in film, containing conference papers and scholarly essays on a range of film history topics http:// wwwmc-c.murdoch.edu.au/ReadingRoom/hfilm/contenth.html
- "The Influence and Portrayals of the Gospel of John in Film, Television, and Multi-Media" http://catholic-resources.org/John/Films.html
- *Internet Movie Data Base* http://www.imdb.com
- *Journal of Religion and Film* http://avalon.unomaha.edu/jrf/
- *Journal of Religion and Popular Culture* (which contains a number of useful discussions of film and religion): http://www.usask.ca/relst/jrpc/index.html
- *Movie Theology: Movie Review and Resource Page*, compiled by Gordon Matties: http://www.cmu.ca/library/faithfilm.html
- *Screensite* provides data on films, film conferences, archives and useful links to other academic cinema sites http://www.tcf.ua.edu/screensite/contents.htm
- *Senses of Cinema – Great Directors:* http://www.sensesofcinema.com/contents/directors/index.html
- Other sites are simply devoted to one director, see, for example: http://www.patoche.org/kieslowski/biblio.htm
- *The British Film Institute* provides a good general database of film, video, and books: http://www.bfi.org.uk/
- *The Media and Communications Study Site* lists resources and links to a variety of topics and bibliographies in film studies http:// www.aber.ac.uk/~dgc/mcs.html
- *The Media Resource Center* run by the Moffitt Library at the University of California Berkeley contains many useful links and bibliographies, including AV resources: http://www.lib.berkeley.edu/MRC/level2.html
- *Simply Scripts.* There are several sites that provide film scripts, but these may not be the final draft, see for example: http:// www.simplyscripts.com/movie.html

Index